365 SHORT STORIES FROM THE BIBLE

Jesse Lyman Hurlbut

A Barbour Book

ISBN 1-55748-413-9

Also published under the title *Bedtime Bible Story Book*
ISBN 1-55748-264-0

DAY 1

THE STORY OF CREATION

Genesis 1:1-2:3

THIS great world of ours is very old; so old that no one knows when it was made. But long before there was any earth, or sun, or stars, God was living, for God always was. And long, long ago, God spoke, and the earth and the heavens were formed. But the earth was not beautiful as it is now, with mountains and valleys, rivers and seas, trees and flowers. It was a great smoking ball, with land and water mixed up together. And all the earth was blacker than midnight, because there was no light on it. No man could breathe its air, no animals could walk on it, and no fish could swim in its black waters. There was no life on the earth at all.

While all was dark on earth, God said, "Let there be light," and then light began to come upon the world. Part of the time it was light, and part of the time it was dark, just as it is now. God called the dark time *night* and the light time *day*, and that was the first day on this earth after a long night.

Then at God's word, the dark clouds all around the earth began to break, and the sky came in sight, and the water that was in the clouds began to be separate from the water that was on the earth. And the arch of the sky over the earth God called *Heaven*. The night and the morning made a second day.

Then God said, "Let the water on the earth come together in one place, and let the dry land rise up." And so it was. The water that had been all over the world came together and formed a great ocean, and the dry land rose up from it. And the great water God called *sea*, and the dry land he named *earth*. And God saw that the earth and the sea were both good. Then God said, "Let grass, trees, flowers, and fruits grow on the earth." All at once, the earth began to be green and bright with grass, flowers, and trees bearing fruit. This made the third day on the earth.

Then God said, "Let the sun, moon, and stars come into sight from the earth." So the sun began to shine by day, and the moon and the stars began to shine in the night. This was done on the fourth day.

God said, "Let there be fishes in the sea, and let there be birds to fly in the air." So the fishes — great ones and small — began to swim in the sea; and the birds began to fly in the air over the earth, just as they do now. This was the fifth day.

Then God said, "Let animals come to the earth, great animals and small ones, those that walk and those that creep and crawl on the earth." And the woods and fields came alive with animals of all kinds. Now the earth began to be more beautiful, with green fields and bright flowers and singing birds in the trees and animals of every kind walking in the forests.

But there were no people in the world — no cities or houses, and no children playing under the trees. The world was all ready for men and women to enjoy, and so God said, "I will make man different from all other animals. He shall stand up and have a soul, and shall be like God. He shall be the master of the earth and all that is on it."

So God took some of the dust that was on the ground, and out of it he made man. God breathed the breath of life into him, and man became alive, and stood up on the earth.

So the man God had made might have a home, God planted a beautiful garden on the earth, at a place where four rivers met. We might call it a park, for it was much larger than any garden you have ever seen — miles and miles in every direction. In this garden God planted trees, caused grass to grow, and made flowers bloom. This was called The Garden of Eden. In one of the languages of the Bible, the word that means "garden," or "park," is quite like the word "Paradise," so this Garden of Eden has often been called Paradise. This garden God gave to the man he had made. He told him to care for it, to gather the fruits on the trees and the plants, and to live on them. And God gave the first man the name of Adam. Then God brought all the animals he had made to Adam and let Adam give each one its name.

Adam was all alone in the beautiful garden God had made for him, and God said, "It is not good for man to be alone. I will make someone to be with Adam and to help him." When Adam was asleep, God took a rib from Adam's side and made a woman. Then he brought her to Adam, and Adam called her Eve. Adam and Eve loved each other, and they were happy in the beautiful garden God had given them for a home.

Thus in six days the Lord God made the heavens and the earth and the sea, and all that is in them. And on the seventh day God rested from his work.

Discussion Questions: *1. What was there before God made the earth, sun or stars? 2. Name some of the things God created after he made the earth, moon, and stars. 3. Why did God make man? 4. What was the name of the first man? 5. What was the name of the first woman?*

DAY 2

ADAM AND EVE
DISOBEY GOD

Genesis 2:15-3:24

FOR a time — we don't know how long — Adam and Eve were at peace in their beautiful garden. They did just as God told them to do, and they talked with God as a man would talk with his friend, and they did not know of anything evil or wicked. It was important for Adam and Eve to understand that they must always obey God's commands, so God said to Adam and Eve, "You may eat the fruit of all the trees in the garden except one. In the middle of the garden is a tree with fruit on it that you must not eat and must not touch. If you eat the fruit of that tree, you will die."

ADAM AND EVE IN THE GARDEN OF EDEN - GENESIS 2:7-25

Now among the animals in the garden there was a snake, and this snake said to Eve, "Has God told you that there is any fruit in the garden you are forbidden to eat?"

Eve answered the snake, "We can eat the fruit of all the trees except the one that stands in the middle of the garden. If we eat the fruit of that tree, God says we must die."

3

Then the snake said, "No, you will not die. God knows that if you eat the fruit of that tree, you will become as wise as he is, for you will know what is good and what is evil."

Eve listened to the snake, and then she looked at the tree and its fruit. As she saw it, she thought it would taste good, and if it would really make her wise, she would like to eat it, even though God had told her not to. She took the fruit and ate it, and then she gave some to Adam, and he ate it.

Adam and Eve knew they had done wrong by not obeying God's words, and now for the first time they were afraid to meet God. They tried to hide themselves from God's sight among the trees of the garden. The Lord God called and said, "Adam, where are you?"

Adam said, "Lord, I heard your voice in the garden, and I was afraid, and I hid myself."

God said, "Why were you afraid to meet me? Have you eaten the fruit of the tree I told you not to touch?"

Adam said, "The woman you gave to be with me gave me some of the fruit, and I ate it."

Then God said to the woman, "What have you done?"

Eve said, "The snake told me it would do me no harm, and so I took some of it and ate it."

Then the Lord God said to the snake, "Because you have led Adam and Eve to do wrong, you shall no more walk like other animals. You shall crawl in the dust and the dirt forever. You will hate the woman, and the woman will hate you. You will try to kill her and her children, and they shall try to kill you."

Then the Lord God said to the woman, "Because you led your husband to disobey me, you shall suffer and have pain and trouble all the days of your life."

And God said to Adam, "Because you listened to your wife when she told you to do what was wrong, you must suffer. You must work for everything that you get from the ground. You will find thorns and thistles and weeds growing on the earth. If you want food, you must dig and plant and reap and work, as long as you live. You came from the ground, for you were made of dust, and your body shall go back into the dust when you die."

Because Adam and Eve had disobeyed the word of the Lord, they were driven out of the beautiful Garden of Eden that God had made as their home. They were sent out into the world, and to keep them from going back into the garden, God placed his angels before its gate, with swords that flashed like fire.

So Adam and his wife lost their garden, and no man has ever been able to go back to it since then.

DAY 3

CAIN AND ABEL

Genesis 4:1-17

SO Adam and his wife went out into the world to live and work. For a time they were all alone, but after a while, God gave them a little child of their own, the first baby born into the world. Eve named him Cain. After a time, another baby came, whom she named Abel.

When the two boys grew up, they worked, just as their father worked before them. Cain chose to work in the fields, raising grain and fruits. Abel had a flock of sheep and became a shepherd.

While Adam and Eve were living in the Garden of Eden, they could talk with God and hear God speaking to them. But now that they were out in the world, they could no longer talk with God freely. So when they came to God, they built an altar of heaped-up stones. Upon it, they laid something as a gift to God, and burned it, to show that it was not their own, but was given to God, whom they could not see. Then they made their prayers to God, asking him to forgive their sins, all they had done that was wrong, and to bless them and do good to them.

Each of these brothers, Cain and Abel, offered God his own gift. Cain brought the fruits and the grain he had grown. Abel brought a sheep from his flock, killed it, and burned it on the altar. For some reason, God was pleased with Abel and his offering but was not pleased with Cain and his offering. Perhaps God wished Cain to offer something that had life, as Abel did, or perhaps Cain's heart was not right when he came before God.

Anyway, God showed that he was not pleased with Cain. Cain, instead of being sorry for his sin and asking God to forgive him, was very angry with God and Abel. When they were out in the field together, Cain struck his brother Abel and killed him. So the first baby in the world grew up to be the murderer of his own brother.

The Lord said to Cain, "Where is Abel, your brother?"

Cain answered, "I don't know. Why should I take care of my brother?"

Then the Lord said to Cain, "What have you done? Your brother's blood is like a voice crying to me from the ground. Do you see how the ground has opened, like a mouth, to drink your brother's blood? As long as you live, you will be under God's curse for the murder of your brother. You will wander over the earth and never find a home because you have done this wicked deed."

Cain said to the Lord, "My punishment is greater than I can bear. You have driven me out from men and hidden your face from me. If any man finds me, he will kill me, because I will be alone, and no one will be my friend."

God said to Cain, "If anyone harms you, he shall be punished for it." And the Lord God placed a mark on Cain, so whoever met him would know him and would also know that God had forbidden any man to harm him. Then Cain and his wife went away from Adam's home, to live by themselves. There they had children, and Cain's family built a city in that land, and Cain named the city after his first child, Enoch.

Discussion Questions: *1. How was talking to God different after Adam and Eve left the garden? 2. Who was Cain? Abel? 3. Why was Cain angry? 4. What did Cain do to Abel? 5. How did God punish Cain?*

DAY 4

ENOCH AND NOAH

Genesis 4:25-6:22

FTER Abel was killed and his brother Cain had gone into another land, God gave another child to Adam and Eve. This child they named Seth. Other sons and daughters were given to them, for Adam and Eve lived many years. But at last they died, as God had said they must because they had eaten of the tree he had forbidden them to eat from.

By the time Adam died, there were many people on the earth, for the children of Adam and Eve had many children, and when these grew up, they also had children.

In those early times, people lived much longer than they do now. Very few people now live to be 100 years old, but in those days, men often lived to be 800 or even 900 years old. So after a time, that part of the earth began to be full of people.

As time went on, more and more of these people became wicked, and fewer and fewer of them grew up to become good men and women. All the people lived near one another and few went away to other lands, so even the children of good men and women learned to be bad like the people around them.

When God looked down on the world he had made, he saw how wicked the men in it had become.

While most of the people in the world were very wicked, there were some good people, though they were very few. The best of all the men who lived at that time was a man named Enoch. (He was not the son of Cain, but another Enoch.) While so many around Enoch were doing evil, he only did what was right. He walked with God, and God walked and talked with him. At last, when Enoch was 365 years old, God took him away from earth to heaven. He did not die, as all the people since Adam have died, but "he was not, for God took him." This means that Enoch was taken up from earth without dying.

Enoch left a son whose name was Methuselah. We don't know anything about Methuselah, except that he lived to be 969 years old, which was longer than any other man who ever lived. But at last Methuselah died, and by then the world was very wicked.

God looked down on the earth and said, "I will take away all men from the earth because they are always evil."

But even in those bad times, God saw one good man. His name was Noah. Noah tried to do right in the sight of God. As Enoch had walked with God, so Noah walked with God, and talked with him. Noah had three sons named Shem, Ham, and Japheth.

God said to Noah, "The time has come when all the men and women on the earth are to be destroyed. Everyone must die, because they are all wicked. But you and your family shall be saved, because you alone are trying to do right."

Then God told Noah how he could save his life and the lives of his sons. He was to build a very large boat, as large as the largest ships that are made in our time. It was to be very long and very wide and very deep, with a roof over it, like a long, wide house of three stories. God told Noah to build this ark and to have it ready for when he would need it.

"For," said God to Noah, "I am going to bring a great flood of water on the earth, to cover all the land and drown all the people on the earth. Since the animals on the earth will be drowned with the people, you must make the ark large enough to hold a pair of each kind of animal, so there will be animals as well as men to live on the earth after the flood has passed away. You must take food for yourself and your family, and for all the animals with you — enough food to last for a year, while the flood is on the earth."

Discussion Questions: *1. What happened after Adam and Eve died? 2. What were the people like? 3. How did that make God feel? 4. Who was Noah?*

DAY 5

NOAH'S ARK

Genesis 7:1-9:17

NOAH did what God told him to do, although he must have seemed very strange to all the other people, building a great ark when there was no water around at all. Noah and his sons were at work building the ark for 120 years while the wicked people around wondered and no doubt laughed at Noah.

At last the ark was finished, standing like a great house on the land. There was a door on one side and a window on the roof, to let in the light. Then God said to Noah, "Go into the ark, you and your wife, your three sons and their wives, for the flood of waters will come very soon. And take with you animals of all kinds, and birds, and things that creep. Take seven pairs of those that will be needed by men, and one pair of all the rest, so that all kinds of animals will be kept alive on the earth."

So Noah and his wife and his three sons, Shem, Ham, and Japheth, with their wives, went into the ark. And God brought to the door of the ark the animals, the birds, and the creeping things of all kinds, and they went into the ark. Noah and his sons put them in their places and brought in food for them all. Then the door of the ark was shut, so no more people and no more animals could come in.

In a few days the rain began to fall as it had never fallen before. It seemed as though the heavens were pouring great floods upon the earth. The streams filled, the rivers rose higher and higher, and the ark began to float on the water. The other people left their houses and ran up to the hills, but soon the hills were covered, and all the people on them were drowned.

Some had climbed up to the tops of higher mountains, but the water rose higher and higher, until even the mountains were covered and all the people, wicked as they were, were drowned in the great sea that now rolled over all the earth. And all the animals — cattle, sheep, oxen, lions, tigers, and all the rest — were also drowned. Even the birds were drowned, because their nests in the trees were swept away and there was no place they could escape the terrible storm. For forty days and nights the rain kept on, until there was no life remaining outside of the ark.

After forty days the rain stopped, but the water stayed on the earth for more than six months. The ark, with everyone in it, floated over the great sea that covered the land. Then God sent a wind to blow over the water and dry it

8

up, so gradually the water grew less and less. First the mountains rose above the water, then the hills rose up, and finally the ark ceased to float, and lay aground on Mount Ararat.

But Noah could not see what had happened on the earth, because the door was shut and the window may have been in the roof. He felt that the ark was no longer moving, and he knew that the water must have gone down. So, after waiting for a time, Noah opened a window and let out a raven. Now the raven has strong wings, and this raven flew round and round until the water had gone down and it could find a place to rest, and it did not come back to the ark.

After Noah waited for it for a while, he sent out a dove. But the dove could not find any place to rest, so it flew back to the ark and Noah took it in again. Then Noah waited a week more and sent out the dove again. In the evening, the dove came back to the ark, which was its home, and in its bill was a fresh leaf it had picked off an olive tree.

THE DOVE RETURNED TO THE ARK - GENESIS 8:9

So Noah knew the water had gone down enough to let the trees grow once more. He waited another week and sent out the dove again. This time the dove flew away and never came back, so Noah knew the earth was becoming dry again. He took off a part of the roof and looked out, and saw that there was dry land all around the ark. Noah had now lived in the ark a little more than a year, and he was glad to see the green land and the trees once more.

God said to Noah, "Come out of the ark with your wife and your sons and their wives and all the living things that are with you in the ark."

So Noah opened the door of the ark, came out, and stood on the ground. All the animals and birds and creeping things in the ark came out also, and began to bring life back to the earth.

The first thing that Noah did when he came out of the ark was give thanks to God for saving all his family. He built an altar, laid on it an offering to the Lord, and gave himself and his family to God, promising to do God's will.

NOAH BUILT AN ALTAR TO THE LORD - GENESIS 8:20

God was pleased with Noah's offering, and said, "I will not destroy the earth again on account of men, no matter how bad they may be. From this time, no flood shall ever cover the earth. The seasons of spring and summer and fall and winter shall remain without change. I give you the earth; you shall be the rulers of the ground and of every living thing on it."

Then God caused a rainbow to appear in the sky, and he told Noah and his sons that whenever they or the people after them saw the rainbow, they should remember God had placed it in the sky as a sign of his promise that he would always remember the earth and the people on it, and would never again send a flood to destroy men.

So, whenever we see a beautiful rainbow, we should remember it is the sign of God's promise to the world.

Discussion Questions: *1. What did God tell Noah to do? 2. How do you think Noah felt? What did he do? 3. What happened to all the other people? Why did God do that? 4. After the flood was over, what did Noah do? 5. What did God promise Noah?*

10

DAY 6

The Tower of Babel

Genesis 11:1-9

AFTER the great flood, Noah's family and those who came after him grew in number until, as the years went on, the earth began to be full of people again. But there was one great difference between the people who had lived before the flood and those who lived after it. Before the flood, all the people stayed close together, so very many lived in one land and no one lived in other lands. As far as we know, all the people on the earth before the great flood lived in the lands where the Tigris and Euphrates flowed. This part of the world was very full of people, but few or none crossed the mountains on the east or the desert on the west, and the great world beyond was without people. After the flood, families began to move from one place to another, seeking new homes. Some went one way, and some another.

This moving about was part of God's plan to have the whole earth used as the home of men, and not merely a small part of it. Then, too, a family who wished to serve God and do right could go away to another land if the people around them became evil. In a place by themselves, they could bring up their children the right way.

From Mount Ararat, where the ark rested, many of the people moved southward into the country between the rivers Tigris and Euphrates. There they built houses for themselves and undertook to build a great city, which would rule all the people around them. They found that the soil in that country could be made into bricks and the bricks could be heated and made hard, so it was easy to build houses and walls around their city.

And the people said to one another, "Let us build a great tower that will reach up to the sky, so we may be kept together and not scattered abroad on the earth."

So they began to build their great tower out of bricks, one story above another. But God did not wish all the people on the earth to live close together, as they had lived before the great flood. God knew that if they all kept together, those that were wicked would lead away from God those that were good, and all the world would become evil again, as it had been before the flood.

While they were building this great city and tower to rule the world, God caused their speech to change. At that time, all men were speaking one language, so everybody could understand what every other person said.

11

God caused men to change their language, perhaps not all at once, but by degrees, little by little. After a time, the people that belonged to one family found they could not understand what the people of another family were saying, just as now it's hard to understand people from other countries.

As people began to grow apart in their speech, they moved away into other places, where the families speaking one language could understand each other. The men building the city and the great tower could no longer understand one another; they left the building without finishing it, and many of them went away to other lands, so the building stayed forever unfinished.

This city was named Babel, a word that means "confusion." It was afterward known as Babylon, and for a long time was one of the greatest cities of that part of the world, even after many of its people had left it to live elsewhere.

Part of the people who left Babylon went up to the north and built a city called Nineveh, which became the ruling city of a great land called Assyria, whose people were called Assyrians.

Another company went to the west, settled by the great river Nile, and founded the land of Egypt.

Another company wandered northwest until they came to the shore of what we call the Mediterranean Sea. There they founded the cities of Sidon and Tyre. These people were sailors, sailing to countries far away and bringing home many things from other lands to sell to the people of Babylon, Assyria, Egypt, and other countries.

So after the flood, the earth again became covered with people living in many lands and speaking many languages.

Discussion Questions: *1. What did people do after the flood? 2. What did the people want to build? 3. Why didn't God want the people to live together? 4. What did he do to keep them in different places?*

DAY 7

ABRAM'S JOURNEY

Genesis 12:1-13:4

NOT far from the city of Babylon was another city, called Ur of the Chaldees. The Chaldees were the people who lived in the country of Chaldea, where the Euphrates and Tigris rivers come together. Among these people at Ur was a man named Abram. Abram was a good man, for he prayed to the Lord God and always tried to do God's will.

But the other people who lived in Ur did not pray to God. They prayed to idols, images made of wood and stone. They thought these images were gods that could hear their prayers and help them. Since these people who worshiped idols did not call on God, they did not know his will, and they did many wicked things.

The Lord God saw that Abram was good and faithful, even though wicked people were living all around him. God did not wish to have Abram's family grow up in such a place, for then they too might become wicked.

So the Lord spoke to Abram, and said, "Abram, gather together all your family and go out from this place, to a land far away that I will show you. And in that land I will make your family a great people, and I will bless you and make your name great, so all the world will give honor to your name. If you do as I command you, you will be blessed, and all the families of the earth shall obtain a blessing through you."

Abram did not know just what this blessing would be, but we know that Abram's family grew, after many years, into the Israelite people. Jesus, the Saviour of the world, was a descendant of Abram. That is, a long time afterward, Jesus was born into the family begun by Abram. Thus Abram's family became a blessing to all the world by giving it a Saviour.

Although Abram did not know just what the blessing was to be or where the land lay, he obeyed God's word. He took all his family: his father, Terah (who was very old), his wife, Sarai, his brother Nahor and his wife, and another brother's son, whose name was Lot. And Abram took all he had — his tents, his flocks of sheep and herds of cattle, and went forth on a long journey to a land he did not even know the name of.

He journeyed far up the great Euphrates River to the mountain region, until he came to a place called Haran, in a country called Mesopotamia between the Tigris and Euphrates. They all stayed for a time at Haran. Perhaps they stopped there because Terah, the father of Abram, was too old to travel further, for they stayed there until he died.

After the death of his father, Terah, Abram again went on his journey, and Lot, his brother's son, went with him. But Nahor, Abram's brother, stayed in Haran, and his family and his descendants lived at Haran for many years.

From Haran, Abram and Lot turned toward the southwest and journeyed for a long time, having the mountains on their right hand and the great desert on their left. They crossed over rivers and climbed the hills, and at last they came to the land of Canaan, which was the land God had spoken to Abram about.

This land was called Canaan because the people who were living in it were the descendants of a man who had lived long before, whose name was Canaan. A long time after this, it was called the Land of Israel, from the people who lived in it, and because the Lord Jesus lived there many years afterward, we now call it The Holy Land.

When Abram came into the land of Canaan, he found a few cities and villages of the Canaanites. But Abram and his people did not go into the towns to live. They lived in tents, out in the open fields, where they could find grass for their sheep and cattle. Not far from a city called Shechem, Abram set up his tent under an oak tree.

There the Lord came to Abram, and said, "I will give this land to your children, and to their children, and this shall be their land forever."

Abram built an altar there, made an offering, and worshiped the Lord. Wherever Abram set up his tent, there he built his altar and prayed to God, because Abram loved God, served God, and believed God's promises.

Abram and Lot moved their tents and their flocks to many places to find grass for their flocks and water to drink. At one time they went down to the land of Egypt, where they saw the great river Nile. Perhaps they saw also the pyramids, the Sphinx, and the wonderful temples in that land, for many of them were built before Abram lived.

Abram did not stay long in Egypt. God did not wish him to live in a land where the people worshiped idols, so he sent Abram back to the land of Canaan, where he could live apart from cities and bring up his servants and his people to worship the Lord. He came to a place where later the city of Bethel would stand, and there he built an altar and prayed to the Lord.

Discussion Questions: *1. What was Abram like? 2. Why did God tell him to move? 3. Where did Abram finally go? 4. What did God promise Abram?*

DAY 8

ABRAM'S NEW HOME

Genesis 13:5-18

LOT, the son of Abram's dead younger brother, was with Abram. Like Abram, he had flocks of sheep and herds of cattle, and many tents for his people. Abram's shepherds and Lot's shepherds quarreled because there was not enough grass in one place for both of them to feed their flocks. Besides Abram and Lot, the Canaanites were also in the land, so there was not enough room for them all.

When Abram heard of the quarrel between his men and the men under Lot, he said to Lot, "Let there be no quarrel between you and me, or between your men and my men. You and I are like brothers to each other. The whole land is before us; let us go apart. You shall have the first choice, too. If you take the land on the right, then I will take the land on the left. If you choose the left, then I will take the right."

This was noble and generous in Abram, for he was the older, and might claim the first choice. Then, too, God had promised all the land to Abram, so he might have said to Lot, "Go away. This land is all mine!" But Abram showed a kind, good heart by giving Lot his choice of the land.

Lot looked over the land from the mountain where they were standing, and saw the river Jordan flowing between green fields, where the soil was rich. He saw the cities of Sodom and Gomorrah on the plain near the Dead Sea, into which the Jordan flows, and Lot said, "I will go down there, to the plain."

And he went down the mountain to the plain, with his tents and his men, and his flocks of sheep and his cattle, leaving the land on the mountains, which was not so good, to his uncle Abram. Perhaps Lot did not know that the people in Sodom were the most wicked of all the people in the land, but he went to live near them, and gradually moved his tent closer to Sodom, until after a time he was living in that wicked city.

After Lot had separated from Abram, God said to Abram, "Lift up your eyes from this place, and look east and west, north and south. All the land that you can see, mountains and valleys and plains, I will give to you, your children, their children, and those who come after them. Your descendants shall have all this land, and they shall be as many as the dust of the earth. Rise up and walk through the land wherever you please, for it is all yours."

Then Abram moved his tent from Bethel and went to live under an oak tree near the city of Hebron in the south, and there he again built an altar to the Lord. _____

Discussion Questions: *1. Why did the shepherds quarrel? 2. Why do you think Abram let Lot choose first? 3. What happened when Lot chose his land? 4. What happened to Abram?*

DAY 9
_____

ABRAM SAVES LOT

Genesis 14:1-24

 O Lot lived in Sodom and Abram lived in his tent on the mountains of Canaan. At that time in the plain of Jordan, near the head of the

15

Dead Sea, there were five cities, of which Sodom and Gomorrah were two, and each of the five cities was ruled by its own king. But over all these little kings and their little kingdoms was a greater king, who lived far away, near the land of Chaldea, from which Abram had come. He ruled all the lands, far and near.

After a time these little kings in the plain would not obey the greater king, so he and his army made war on them. A battle was fought on the plain near Sodom, and the kings of Sodom and Gomorrah were beaten in the battle, and their soldiers were killed. Then the king who had won the victory over his enemies came to Sodom, took everything he could find in the city, and carried away all the people in the city, intending to keep them as slaves. After a battle, in those times, the army that won the victory took away all the goods and made slaves of all the people who had been beaten.

Lot, with all he owned, was carried away by the victors, who went up the valley from Sodom and did not stop to rest until they came to the headwaters of the river Jordan, at a place afterward called Dan. So, all that Lot's selfish choice gained for him was to lose all he had and to be made a slave.

Someone ran away from the battle and came to Abram, who was living in his tent under the oak tree near Hebron. As soon as Abram heard what had happened, he called together all his men — his servants, his shepherds, his people, and his friends — and led them after the enemy that had taken away Lot. He followed as fast as his men could march and found the enemy, with all the goods they had taken and all their prisoners, at Dan, one of the places where the Jordan River begins.

Abram rushed on the enemies at night, while they were asleep, fought them, and drove them away so suddenly that they left everything behind and ran far off into the mountains. In their camp Abram found his nephew Lot, safe, with his wife and daughters, all his goods, and also all the goods and the other people who had been carried away from Sodom.

Then the king of Sodom came to meet Abram at a place near the city of Jerusalem that was afterward called The King's Valley. With him came the king of Jerusalem (which at that time was called Salem). The name of this king was Melchizedek, and unlike most other kings in the land at that time, he was a worshiper of the Lord God, as Abram was. King Melchizedek blessed Abram, and said, "May the Lord God Most High, who made heaven and earth, bless Abram; and blessed be the Lord God Most High, who has given your enemies into your hand."

Abram made a present to King Melchizedek because he worshiped the Lord, giving him all the people and all the goods that had been taken away. He would not take any pay for having saved them.

You would have thought that after this, Lot would have seen it was wrong for him to live in Sodom, but he went back to that city and made his home there once more, even though his heart was made sad by the wickedness he saw around him.

Discussion Questions: *1. How did Lot become a slave? 2. What did Abram do when he heard about it? 3. Why do you think Abram won? 4. Why had God let Lot become a slave? Did he listen?*

DAY 10

GOD'S COVENANT WITH ABRAM

Genesis 15:1-18

AFTER Abram had gone back to his tent under the oak trees at Hebron, one day the Lord God spoke to him, and said, "Fear not, Abram. I will be a shield to keep you safe from enemies, and I will give you a very great reward for serving me."

Abram said, "O Lord God, what good can anything do to me, since I have no child to whom I can give it? After I die, the man who will own everything I have is not my son, but a servant." For although Abram had a large family of

GOD PROMISED A SON FOR ABRAM- GENESIS 15:5

17

people around him and many servants, he had no son, and he was now an old man, and his wife Sarai was also old.

God said to Abram, "The one to receive what you own shall not be a stranger, but shall be your own son."

That night God brought Abram out of his tent, under the heavens, and said to him, "Look now up to the sky, and count the stars, if you can. The people who shall spring from you, your descendants in the years to come, shall be many more than all the stars you can see."

Abram did not see how this promise of God could be kept, but he believed God's word, and did not doubt it, and God loved Abram because he believed the promise. Although Abram could not see how God's promise could be kept, we know that it was kept, for the Israelite people in the Bible story and the Jews everywhere in the world now all came from Abram.

Another day, just as the sun was going down, God came to Abram again and told him many things that would happen in the future. God said to Abram, "After your life is ended, those who are to come from you, your descendants, shall go into a strange land. The people of that land will make slaves of them and be cruel to them. They will stay in that strange land four hundred years, and afterward they shall come out of that land, not as slaves, but very rich. After the four hundred years they will come back to this land, and this shall be their home. All this shall come to pass after your life, for you shall die in peace and be buried at a good old age. And all this land where you are living shall belong to your people."

So that Abram might remember this promise of God, God told him to prepare an offering of a lamb, a goat, and a pair of pigeons, to divide them in pieces, and place them opposite to each other. That night Abram saw smoke and fire, like a flaming torch, passing between the pieces of the offering.

So a promise was made between God and Abram: God promised to give Abram a son, a people, and a land, and Abram promised to serve God faithfully.

A promise like this, made between two people, was called a covenant. This was God's covenant with Abram.

Discussion Questions: *1. What didn't Abram have? 2. What did God promise him? 3. How did Abram know what God promised would happen?*

DAY 11

THE ANGEL BY THE WELL

Genesis 16:1-17:21

YOU remember that Abram's wife, who had journeyed with him from Ur of the Chaldees and lived in his tent all those years was named Sarai. Now Sarai had a maid, a servant who waited on her, whose name was Hagar. She came from the land of Egypt. But Sarai and her maid Hagar had some trouble; they could not agree, and Sarai was so sharp and severe with Hagar, that at last Hagar ran away from Sarai's tent.

She went out into the desert and took the road that led down to Egypt, her own country, the land from which she had come. On the way she stopped beside a spring of water. There an angel from the Lord met her, and said to her, "Hagar, are you not the servant of Sarai, Abram's wife? What are you doing here? Where are you going?"

Hagar said to the angel, "I am going away from my mistress Sarai because I do not wish to stay with her and serve her any longer."

Then the angel said to Hagar, "Go back to your mistress Sarai and submit to her, for that is better for you than going away. God knows all your troubles. He sees you and hears you, and he will help you. By and by you will have a son, and you shall call his name Ishmael, because God has heard you." The word *Ishmael* means "God hears," so whenever Hagar spoke her boy's name, she would think, "God has heard me."

Then the angel told Hagar her son Ishmael should be strong and fierce, and that no one would be able to overcome him or those who came after him.

So Hagar was comforted, and went back again to serve Sarai.

After this, the well where she saw the angel was called by a name which means, "The well of the Living One who sees me." After this, Hagar had a son, and as the angel told her, she called his name Ishmael; that is, "God hears."

While Abram was living near Hebron, the Lord came to him again and spoke to him while Abram bowed his face to the ground. God said, "I am the Almighty God. Walk before me, and be perfect, and I will make you a father of many nations. And your name shall be changed. You shall no more be called Abram, but Abraham, a word that means 'Father of a multitude,' because you will be the father of many nations of people. And your wife's name shall also be changed. She shall no more be called Sarai, but Sarah, 'princess.' And you and Sarah shall have a son you shall call Isaac. He shall have sons when he becomes a man, and his descendants shall be very many people." So from this time, he was no longer Abram, but Abraham, and his wife was called Sarah.

_____

Discussion Questions: *1. Why did Hagar run away? 2. What did God give her? 3. What does* Ishmael *mean? Do you think Hagar thought that was a good name? 4. Why did God change Abram's name? Did he like his new name?*

DAY 12

_____

ABRAHAM TALKS TO GOD AGAIN
Genesis 18:1-33

NE day Abraham was sitting in the door of his tent when he **saw** three men coming toward him. He knew from their looks that **they** were not common men. They were angels, and one of them seems to **have** been the Lord God himself, coming in the form of a man.

When Abraham saw these men coming, he went out to meet them, bowed to them, and said to the one who was the leader, "My Lord, do not pass by. Come and rest a little under the tree. Let me send for water to wash your feet, then eat some food and stay with us a little while."

So this person, who was God in the form of a man, sat with his two

ABRAHAM ENTERTAINED THE ANGELS - GENESIS 18:8

followers in Abraham's tent under the oak trees at Hebron. They took some food that Sarah, Abraham's wife, made for them, and the Lord talked with Abraham. He told Abraham again that very soon God would send him and Sarah a little boy, whose name should be Isaac. In the language that Abraham spoke, the name *Isaac* means "laughing," because Abraham and Sarah both laughed aloud when they heard it. They were so happy that they could scarcely believe the news.

Then the three persons rose up to go, and two of them went on the road that led toward Sodom, down on the plain of Jordan, below the mountains. But the one whom Abraham called "My Lord" stopped after the others had gone away, and said, "Shall I hide from Abraham what I am going to do? For Abraham is to be the father of a great people, and all the world shall receive a blessing through him. And I know that Abraham will teach his children and all those that live with him to obey the will of the Lord, and to do right. I will tell Abraham what I am going to do. I am going down to the city of Sodom and the other cities that are near it, and I am going to see if the city is as bad as it seems to be, for the wickedness of the city is like a cry coming up before the Lord."

Abraham knew that Sodom was very wicked, and he feared that God was about to destroy it. Abraham said, "Will you destroy the righteous with the wicked, the good with the bad, in Sodom? Perhaps there may be fifty good people in the city. Won't you spare the city for the sake of fifty good men who may be in it? Shall not the Judge and Ruler of all the earth do right?"

The Lord said, "If I find in Sodom fifty good people, then I will not destroy the city, but will spare it for their sake."

Then Abraham said again, "Perhaps I ought not to ask anything more, for I am only a common man, talking with the Lord God. But suppose that there should be forty-five good people in Sodom. Will you destroy the city because it needs only five good men to make up the fifty?"

The Lord said, "I will not destroy it if there are forty-five good men in it." And Abraham said, "Suppose there are forty good people in it. What then?" And the Lord answered, "I will spare the city, if I find in it forty good men." And Abraham said, "O Lord, do not be angry if I ask that if there are thirty good men in the city, it may be spared." The Lord said, "I will not do it, if I find thirty good men there." Abraham said, "Let me venture to ask you to spare it if twenty are there." The Lord said, "I will not destroy it for the sake of twenty good men, if they are there." Then Abraham said, "O, let not the Lord be angry, and I will speak only this once more. Perhaps there may be ten good men found in the city." The Lord said, "If I find ten good men in Sodom, I will spare the city."

Abraham had no more to say. The Lord went on his way toward Sodom, and Abraham turned back and went to his tent.

_____

Discussion Questions: *1. Who came to talk to Abraham? 2. What was he going to do? Why did he decide to tell Abraham? 3. Why did Abraham ask God not to destroy Sodom? (Who did he know there?)*

DAY 13

_____

THE RAIN OF FIRE

Genesis 19:1-30

YOU remember that Lot, the nephew of Abraham, chose the land of Sodom for his home, even though the people were so wicked. You remember, too, how Lot was carried away captive when Sodom was taken by its enemies, and how he was rescued by Abram. But after all that had happened, Lot went to live in Sodom again, and he was there when the angels came to Abraham's tent.

Two of the angels who had visited Abraham went down to Sodom and walked through the city, trying to find some good men, for if they could find only ten, the city would be saved. But the only good man they could find was Lot. He took the angels, who looked like men, into his house, treated them kindly, and made a supper for them.

The men of Sodom, when they found that strangers were in Lot's house, came before the house in the street and tried to take the two men out and do them harm.

But the men of Sodom could do nothing against them, for when they tried to break open the door, and Lot was greatly frightened, the two angels struck all those wicked men blind in a moment, so they could not see, and felt around in the dark for the door.

Then the angels said to Lot, "Have you here any others besides yourself. Any sons or sons-in-law or daughters? If so, get them out of this city quickly, for we are here to destroy this place because it is very wicked."

Lot went to the houses where the young men lived who had married some of his daughters, and said to them, "Hurry, and get out of this place, for the Lord will destroy it."

But his sons-in-law would not believe his words. They only laughed at him. What a mistake it was for Lot to live in a wicked city, where his daughters were married to young men living there!

And when the morning was coming, the two angels tried to make poor Lot hasten away. They said, "Rise up quickly, and take your wife and your two daughters that are here. If you do not hurry, you will be destroyed with the city."

But Lot was slow to leave his house, his married daughters, and all that he had, so the two angels took hold of him, his wife, and his two daughters, and dragged them out of the city. God was good to Lot, to take him out of the city before it was destroyed.

And when they had brought Lot and his wife and his daughters out of the city, one of the angels said to him, "Escape for your life. Do not look behind you. Do not stop anywhere in the plain. Climb up the mountain, or you may be destroyed!"

Lot begged the angels not to send him so far away. He said, "O my Lord, I cannot climb the mountain. Have mercy upon me, and let me go to that little city over there. It is only a little city, and you can spare it. Please let me be safe there."

So the angel said, "We will spare that city for your sake, and we will wait until you are safe before we destroy these other cities."

So Lot ran to the little city, and there he found safety. In the language of that time, the word *Zoar* means "little," so that city was afterward called Zoar. Lot arrived at Zoar at sunrise.

Then, as soon as Lot and his family were safely out of Sodom, the Lord caused a rain of fire to fall upon Sodom and the other cities on the plain. With

LOT AND HIS DAUGHTERS ESCAPED FROM THE CITY - GENESIS 19:15-26

23

the fire came great clouds of sulphur smoke, covering all the plain. So the cities were destroyed, and all the people in them. Not one man, woman, or child was left.

While Lot and his daughters were flying from the city, Lot's wife stopped and looked back, and she became a pillar of salt, standing there on the plain. Lot and his two daughters escaped, but they were afraid to stay in the little city of Zoar. They climbed up the mountain, away from the plain, and found a cave, and there they lived. So Lot lost his wife and all he had because he had made his home among the wicked people of Sodom.

When Abraham, from his tent door on the mountain, looked down toward the plain, the smoke was rising from it like the smoke of a great furnace.

And that was the end of the cities of the plain: Sodom, Gomorrah, and the other cities with them. Zoar alone was saved, because Lot, a good man, prayed for it.

_____

Discussion Questions: *1. Why did the angels want Lot and his family to leave Sodom? 2. Why did they tell him not to look back at the city? 3. Who looked back? What happened? 4. Why was the city of Zoar saved?*

DAY 14
_____

ISHMAEL

Genesis 21:1-13

AFTER Sodom and Gomorrah were destroyed, Abraham moved his camp and went to live near a place called Gerar, not far from the sea. And there the child God had promised Abraham and Sarah was born when Abraham was 100 years old.

They named this child Isaac, as the angel had told them he should be named. Abraham and Sarah were so happy to have a little boy that they gave a great feast in honor of little Isaac.

So now there were two boys in Abraham's tent: the older boy, Ishmael, the son of Hagar, and the younger boy, Isaac, the son of Abraham and Sarah.

Ishmael did not like little Isaac and did not treat him kindly. This made his mother Sarah very angry, so she said to her husband, "I do not wish to have this Ishmael growing up with my son, Isaac. Send away Hagar and her boy, because they trouble me."

Abraham felt very sorry to have trouble come between Sarah and Hagar and between Isaac and Ishmael, for Abraham was a kind and good man, friendly with them all.

But the Lord said to Abraham, "Do not be troubled about Ishmael and his mother. Do as Sarah has asked you to do, and send them away. It is best that Isaac should be left alone in your tent, for he is to receive everything that is yours. I, the Lord, will take care of Ishmael and will make a great people of his descendants."

Discussion Questions: *1. How did Abraham and Sarah feel when Isaac was born? 2. Why didn't Ishmael like Isaac? 3. Who wanted to send Hagar and Ishmael away? Why? 4. Why do you think God told Abraham to send them away?*

DAY 15

ISHMAEL IN THE DESERT

Genesis 21:14-20

THE next morning, Abraham sent Hagar and her boy away, expecting them to go back to the land of Egypt, from which Hagar had come. He gave them some food for the journey and a bottle of water to drink on the way. The bottles in that country were not made of glass, like ours. They were made from the skin of a goat, sewed tightly together. Abraham filled one of

HAGAR AND HER SON WANDERED IN THE WILDERNESS – GENESIS 21:14

these skin bottles with water and gave it to Hagar.

Hagar went away from Abraham's tent, leading her little boy. But somehow she lost the road and wandered over the desert, not knowing where she was, until all the water in the bottle was used up and her poor boy, in the hot sun and the burning sand, had nothing to drink. She thought he would die of his terrible thirst, and she laid him down under a little bush and then went away, saying to herself, "I cannot bear to look at my poor boy suffering and dying for want of water."

Just at that moment while Hagar was crying and her boy was moaning with thirst, she heard a voice saying to her, "Hagar, what is your trouble? Do not be afraid. God has heard your cry and the cry of your child. God will take care of you both and will make your boy into a great nation of people."

It was the voice of an angel from heaven. Hagar looked, and there close at hand was a spring of water in the desert. How glad Hagar was, as she filled the bottle with water and took it to her suffering boy under the bush!

After this, Hagar did not go down to Egypt. She found a place near this spring, where she lived and brought up her son in the wilderness, far from other people. God was with Ishmael and cared for him, and Ishmael grew up in the desert and learned to shoot with the bow and arrow. He became a wilderness man, and his children after him grew up to be wilderness men, also. They were the Arabians of the desert, who even to this day wander through the desert and live as they please. So Ishmael came to be the father of many people, and his descendants, the Arabians of the desert, are living to this day in that land, just as the Jews, who are the descendants of Isaac, are living all over the world.

Discussion Questions: *1. What happened to Hagar and Ishmael when they went away? 2. Who took care of them? 3. What did God promise Hagar? 4. Why do you think Hagar did not go down to Egypt?*

DAY 16

ABRAHAM'S SACRIFICE

Genesis 22:1-13

OON, God gave Abraham a command he did not mean to have obeyed, though he did not tell this to Abraham. He said, "Take your son, your only son Isaac, whom you love so greatly, and go to the land of

Moriah. There, on a mountain that I will show you, offer him for a burnt offering to me."

Though this command filled Abraham's heart with pain, yet he was not as surprised to receive it as a father would be in our day, for such offerings were very common among all the people where Abraham lived. Abraham never for one moment doubted or disobeyed God's word. He knew that Isaac was the child whom God had promised, and God had promised that Isaac would have children, and those coming from Isaac should be a great nation. He did not see how God could keep his promise with regard to Isaac, if Isaac was killed as an offering, unless God raised him from the dead afterward. But Abraham undertook at once to obey God's command. He took two young men with him and an ass laden with wood for the fire, and he went toward the mountain in the north, Isaac walking by his side. For two days they walked, sleeping under the trees at night in the open country. On the third day, Abraham saw the mountain far away. As they drew near to the mountain, Abraham said to the young men, "Stay here with the ass, while I go up the mountain with Isaac to worship. When we have worshiped, we will come back to you."

Abraham believed that in some way God would bring Isaac back to life. He took the wood from the ass, placed it on Isaac, and the two walked up the mountain together. As they were walking, Isaac said, "Father, here is the wood, but where is the lamb for the offering?"

Abraham said, "My son, God will provide himself the lamb."

And they came to the place on the top of the mountain. There Abraham built an altar of stones and earth and placed on it the wood. Then he tied the hands and feet of Isaac, and laid him on the wood on the altar.

THE OFFERING OF ISAAC - GENESIS 22:10

Abraham lifted up his hand, holding a knife to kill his son. A moment longer, and Isaac would be killed by his own father. But just at that moment, the angel of the Lord called to Abraham, and said, "Abraham! Abraham!" And Abraham answered, "Here I am, Lord." Then the angel of the Lord said, "Do not lay your hand on your son. Do no harm to him. Now I know that you love God more than you love your only son, and that you are obedient to God, since you are ready to give up your only son to God."

What relief and joy these words from heaven brought to the heart of Abraham! How glad he was to know it was not God's will for him to kill his son! Then Abraham looked around, and there in the thicket was a ram caught by his horns. Abraham took the ram and offered him up for a burnt offering in place of his son. So Abraham's words came true, when he said that God would provide a lamb. The place where this altar was built Abraham named Jehovah-jireh, meaning, in the language that Abraham spoke, "The Lord will provide."

This offering, which seems so strange, did much good. It showed Abraham and Isaac that Isaac belonged to God, for he had been offered to God. In Isaac, all his descendants had been given to God. Then it showed Abraham and all the people after him that God did not wish children or men killed as offerings for worship. While all the people around offered such sacrifices, the Israelites, who came from Abraham and Isaac, never offered them, but offered oxen and sheep and goats instead. And it looked onward to a time when, just as Abraham gave his son as an offering, God would give his Son Jesus Christ to die for the sins of the world. All this was taught in this act of worship on Mount Moriah.

Discussion Questions: *1. What did God ask Abraham to do? Was Abraham ready to do it? 2. What did Abraham believe? Do you think that was hard? 3. What did God do to stop Abraham? 4. What did the sheep stand for?*

DAY 17

A WIFE FOR ISAAC

Genesis 24:1-27

AFTER the death of his mother, Sarah, Isaac was lonely, and as he was now old enough to marry, Abraham sought a wife for him. In those countries, the parents always chose the wives for their sons and husbands for their daughters. Abraham did not wish Isaac to marry any of the people in the land where he was living, for they were all worshipers of idols and would not teach their children the ways of the Lord. For the same reason, Abraham did not settle in one place and build himself a city. By moving from place to place, Abraham kept his people apart from the natives of the area.

You remember that when Abraham made his long journey to the land of Canaan, he stayed for a time at a place called Haran, in Mesopotamia, between the two rivers Tigris and Euphrates. When Abraham left Haran to go to Canaan, his brother Nahor and his family stayed in Haran. They worshiped the Lord, as Abraham and his family did, and Abraham thought it would be good to find a wife for Isaac there.

Since Abraham could not leave his own land and go to Haran to find a wife for Isaac, he called his chief servant, Eliezer, a man he trusted, who cared for all his flocks and cattle and ruled over his other servants, and sent him to Haran to find a wife for Isaac.

The servant took ten camels and many presents, went on a long journey, and at last came to the city of Haran, where the family of Nahor, the brother of Abraham, was living. At the well just outside the city, he made his camels kneel down. Then the servant asked the Lord to send him the right young woman for Isaac.

As the servant was praying, a beautiful young woman came to the well with her pitcher on her shoulder. As she drew the water and filled her pitcher, the servant came up, bowed to her, and said, "Will you kindly give me a drink of water from your pitcher?"

She said, "Drink, my lord," and held her pitcher for him to drink. Then she said, "I will draw some water for your camels, too." She emptied her pitcher into the trough by the well and drew more water, until she had given a drink to all the camels.

The servant of Abraham looked at her and wondered if she might be the right woman for Isaac to marry. He said to her, "Will you tell me your name, young lady, and whose daughter you are? And do you suppose that I could find a place to stay at your father's house?" Then he gave her a gold ring and gold bracelets for her wrists.

The beautiful young woman said, "My name is Rebekah, and my father is Bethuel, the son of Nahor. You can come right to our house. We have room for you, and a place and food for your camels."

The man bowed his head and thanked God, for he saw that his prayer was answered, since this kind and lovely young woman was a cousin to Isaac, his master's son. He told Rebekah that he was the servant of Abraham, a close relative of her own family.

———————

Discussion Questions: *1. Why didn't Abraham want his son to marry anyone in the land where he was living? 2. Who did he send to find Isaac a wife? 3. Why did the servant pray? Did God answer his prayer? How did he know?*

DAY 18

REBEKAH

Genesis 24:28-67

REBEKAH ran home, told her parents of the stranger, and showed them the presents he had given to her. Her brother Laban went out to the man, brought him into the house, and found a place for his camels. Then they washed his feet, for that was the custom of the land, where people did not wear shoes, but sandals. They set the table for a supper, and asked him to sit down and eat with them. But the man said, "I will not eat until I have told my errand."

After this he told them all about Abraham's riches and how Abraham had sent him to Haran to find a wife for Isaac, his son. He said he felt sure Rebekah was the one the Lord would choose for Isaac's wife, and then he asked that they allow Rebekah to be married to Isaac.

When he had told his errand, Laban, Rebekah's brother, and Bethuel, her father, said, "This comes from the Lord. It is his will, and it is not for us to oppose it. Here is Rebekah; take her, and let her be the wife of your master's son, for the Lord has shown it to be his will."

Then Abraham's servant gave rich presents to Rebekah, her mother, and her brother Laban, and that night they had a feast, with great joy.

The next morning, Abraham's servant said, "Now I must go home to my master." But they said, "Oh, not so soon! Let Rebekah stay with us for a few days, ten days at least, before she goes away from her home."

And he said to them, "Do not hinder me. Since God has given me what I came for, I must go back to my master."

So they called Rebekah, and asked her, "Will you go with this man?" And she said, "I will go."

So the servant of Abraham went away, and took with him Rebekah, with good wishes and blessings, and prayers from all in her father's house. After a long journey, they came to the place where Abraham and Isaac were living. When Isaac saw Rebekah, he loved her. She became his wife, and they were faithful to each other as long as they both lived.

Afterward Abraham, great and good man that he was, died when he was almost 180. Isaac and Ishmael buried Abraham in the cave at Hebron, where Abraham had buried Sarah.

Then Isaac became the owner of all the riches of Abraham: his tents, his flocks of sheep, herds of cattle and camels, and servants. Isaac was a peaceful, quiet man. He did not move his tents often, as his father had done, but stayed in one place nearly all his life.

Discussion Questions: 1. Who was Rebekah? 2. What did Rebekah's brother and father say when Abraham's servant told them what he wanted? 3. Why do you think Rebekah wanted to go with him?

DAY 19

JACOB BUYS HIS BROTHER'S BIRTHRIGHT
Genesis 25:21-34

AFTER Abraham died, his son Isaac lived in the land of Canaan. Like his father, Isaac's home was a tent. Around him were the tents of his people, and many flocks of sheep and herds of cattle feeding wherever they could find grass to eat and water to drink.

Isaac and his wife, Rebekah, had two children. The older was named Esau and the younger Jacob. Esau was a man of the woods, very fond of hunting. He was rough, and covered with hair. Even as a boy he was fond of hunting with his bow and arrow. Jacob was quiet and thoughtful, staying at home and caring for the flocks of his father. Isaac loved Esau more than Jacob, because Esau brought his father what he killed in his hunting. But Rebekah liked Jacob best, because she saw he was wise and careful in his work.

Among the people in those lands, when a man dies, his older son receives twice as much as the younger.

This was called his birthright, for it was his right as the oldest. So Esau, as the older, had a birthright to more of Isaac's possessions than Jacob. Besides this, there was the privilege of the promise of God that the family of Isaac should receive great blessings.

Now Esau, when he grew up, did not care for his birthright or the blessing God had promised. But Jacob, who was a wise man, wished greatly to have the birthright that would come to Esau when his father died. Once, when Esau came home hungry and tired from hunting in the fields, he saw that Jacob had a bowl of something he had just cooked for dinner. And Esau said,

"Give me some of that red stuff in the dish. Will you not give me some? I am hungry."

Jacob answered, "I will give it to you, if you will sell me your birthright."

ESAU SOLD HIS BIRTHRIGHT TO JACOB — GENESIS 25:33

Esau said, "What is the use of the birthright to me now, when I am almost starving to death? You can have my birthright if you will give me something to eat."

Then Esau made Jacob a solemn promise to give Jacob his birthright, all for a bowl of food. It was not right for Jacob to deal so selfishly with his brother, but it was very wrong of Esau to care so little for his birthright and God's blessing.

Some time after this, when Esau was forty years old, he married two wives. Though this would be very wicked in our times, it was not supposed to be wrong then, for even good men then had more than one wife. But Esau's two wives were women from the people of Canaan, who worshiped idols, and not the true God. And they taught their children to pray to idols, so those who came from Esau, the people who were his descendants, lost all knowledge of God and became very wicked. But this was long after that time.

Isaac and Rebekah were very sorry to have their son Esau marry women who prayed to idols and not to God, but still Isaac loved his active son Esau more than his quiet son Jacob.

Discussion Questions: *1. How were Esau and Jacob different? 2. Why was a birthright important? 3. Why do you think Esau didn't care about the birthright? 4. What did Esau do later? How do you think God felt about that?*

DAY 20

JACOB STEALS
HIS BROTHER'S BLESSING (PART 1)

Genesis 27:1-17

IN time, Isaac became very old and feeble, and so blind that he could see scarcely anything. One day he said to Esau, "My son, I am very old, and do not know how much time I have. But before I die, I wish to give to you, as my older son, God's blessing on you, your children, and your descendants. Go out into the fields and shoot some animal that is good for food, and make me a dish of cooked meat, which you know I love. After I have eaten it, I will give you the blessing."

Esau ought to have told his father that the blessing did not belong to him, for he had sold it to his brother Jacob. But he did not tell his father. He went out into the fields, hunting for the kind of meat his father liked the most.

Now Rebekah was listening, and heard all that Isaac said to Esau. She knew it would be better for Jacob to have the blessing than for Esau, and she loved Jacob more than Esau. So she called to Jacob, told him what Isaac had said to Esau, and said, "Now, my son, do what I tell you and you will get the blessing instead of your brother. Go to the flocks and bring to me two little kids from the goats. I will cook them just like the meat Esau cooks for your father. You will bring it to your father, and he will think you are Esau and give you the blessing. It really belongs to you."

But Jacob said, "You know that Esau and I are not alike. His neck and arms are covered with hair, while mine are smooth. My father will feel me and find I am not Esau. Then, instead of giving me a blessing, I am afraid he will curse me."

But Rebekah answered her son, "Never mind. You do as I have told you, and I will take care of you. If any harm comes, it will come to me, so do not be afraid. Go and bring the meat."

Then Jacob went and brought a pair of little kids from the flock, and his mother made a dish of food that tasted just as Isaac liked it. Then Rebekah found some of Esau's clothes and dressed Jacob in them. She placed on his neck and his hands some of the skins of the kids, so that his neck and hands would feel rough and hairy to the touch.

———————

Discussion Questions: *1. Why did Rebekah want Jacob to have the birthright? 2. What did she do to make sure he got it? 3. Do you think Rebekah and Jacob were right to do what they did?*

DAY 21

———————

JACOB STEALS
HIS BROTHER'S BLESSING (PART 2)

Genesis 27:18-40

THEN Jacob came into his father's tent, bringing the dinner and speaking as much like Esau as he could. He said, "Here I am, my father."

Isaac said, "Who are you, my son?"

Jacob answered, "I am Esau, your oldest son. I have done as you told me. Now sit up, and eat the dinner I have made, and then give me your blessing, as you promised me."

Isaac said, "How is it that you found it so quickly?"

Jacob answered, "Because the Lord your God showed me where to go, and gave me good success."

Isaac did not feel certain this was Esau, so he said, "Come nearer and let me feel you, so that I may know you are really my son Esau."

Jacob went up close to Isaac's bed, and Isaac felt his face, his neck, and his hands, and he said, "The voice sounds like Jacob, but the hands are the hands of Esau. Are you really my son Esau?"

Jacob again told a lie to his father, and said, "I am."

Then the old man ate the food Jacob had brought him, and he kissed Jacob, believing him to be Esau, and gave him the blessing, saying to him, "May God give you the dew of heaven, and the richness of the earth, and plenty of grain and wine. May nations bow down to you and people become your servants. May you be the master over your brother, and may your family and descendants that shall come from you rule over his family and his descendants. Blessed be those that bless you, and cursed be those that curse you."

Just as soon as Jacob had received the blessing, he rose up and hastened away. He had scarcely gone out, when Esau came in from his hunting with the dish of food he had cooked, and said, "Let my father sit up, and eat the food I have brought, and give me the blessing."

Isaac said, "Why, who are you?"

Esau answered, "I am your son, your oldest son Esau."

And Isaac trembled and said, "Who then is the one that came in, and brought me food? And I have eaten his food, and have blessed him; yes, and he shall be blessed."

When Esau heard this, he knew he had been cheated. He cried aloud, with a bitter cry, "O my father, my brother has taken away my blessing, just as he took away my birthright! But can't you give me another blessing, too? Have you given everything to my brother?" And Isaac told him all that he had said to Jacob.

He said, "I have told him that he shall be the ruler, and that all his brothers and their children will be under him. I have promised him the richest ground for his crops, and rains from heaven to make them grow. All these things have been spoken, and they must come to pass. What is left for me to promise you, my son?"

But Esau begged for another blessing, and Isaac said, "My son, your dwelling shall be of the riches of the earth, and of the dew of heaven. You shall live by your sword, and your descendants shall serve his descendants. But in time to come, they shall break loose, and shall shake off the yoke of your brother's rule, and shall be free."

All this came to pass many years afterward. The people who came from Esau lived in a land called Edom, in the south of Israel, where Jacob's descendants lived. And after a time the Israelites became rulers over the Edomites. Later still, the Edomites made themselves free from the Israelites. But all this took place hundreds of years after both Esau and Jacob had passed away. The blessing of God's covenant came to Israel, and not to the people from Esau.

It was better that Jacob's descendants should have the blessing, for Jacob's people worshiped God, and Esau's people walked in the way of the idols, and became wicked. But it was very wrong of Jacob to obtain the blessing the way he obtained it.

————————

Discussion Questions: *1. At first, who did Isaac think Jacob was? 2. Why did he decide he must be Esau? 3. How do you think Isaac felt when he knew he had made a mistake? What did he give to Esau in the end?*

DAY 22

Jacob's Wonderful Dream

Genesis 27:41-28:22

AFTER Esau found he had lost his birthright and his blessing, he was very angry with his brother Jacob. He said to himself, and told others, "My father Isaac is very old, and cannot live long. As soon as he is dead, I shall kill Jacob for having robbed me of my right."

When Rebekah heard this, she said to Jacob, "Before it is too late, go away from home, and get out of Esau's sight. Perhaps when Esau sees you no longer, he will forget his anger, and then you can come home again. Go and visit my brother Laban, your uncle in Haran, and stay with him for a little while, until Esau's anger is past."

So Jacob went out of Beersheba, on the border of the desert, and walked alone toward a land far to the north, carrying his staff in his hand. One evening, just about sunset, he came to a place in the mountains more than sixty miles from his home.

As he had no bed to lie down on, he took a stone and rested his head upon it for a pillow, and lay down to sleep. We would think that's a hard pillow, but Jacob was tired and soon fell asleep.

JACOB'S DREAM - GENESIS 28:12

On that night, Jacob had a wonderful dream. In his dream he saw stairs leading up to heaven from the earth, with angels coming down and going up the stairs. And above the stairs, he saw the Lord God standing. And God said to Jacob, "I am the Lord, the God of Abraham and the God of Isaac your father. And I will be your God, too. The land where you are lying shall belong to you and to your children after you, and your children shall spread over the lands — east, and west, and north, and south — like the dust of the earth. In your family all the world shall receive a blessing. And I am with you in your journey. I will keep you where you are going, and will bring you back to this land. I will never leave you, and I will surely keep my promise to you."

In the morning, Jacob awaked from his sleep and said, "Surely the Lord is in this place and I did not know it! I thought I was all alone, but God has been with me. This place is the house of God; it is the gate of heaven!"

And Jacob took the stone on which his head had rested, and he set it up as a pillar, and poured oil on it as an offering to God. And Jacob named that place Bethel, which in the language that Jacob spoke means The House of God.

Jacob made a promise to God at that time, and said, "If God really will go with me, and will keep me in the way that I go, and will give me bread to eat, and will bring me to my father's house in peace, then the Lord shall be my God, and this stone shall be the house of God. Of all that God gives me, I will give back one-tenth as an offering."

_____

Discussion Questions: *1. Why did Esau hate Jacob? 2. Do you think Jacob was afraid of his brother? Why? 3. Was God faithful to Jacob, even though he had deceived his father? How do you know?*

DAY 23

_____

JACOB'S WIVES

Genesis 29:1-29

HEN Jacob went onward in his long journey. He waded across the river Jordan in a shallow place, feeling the way with his staff; he climbed mountains, and journeyed beside the great desert on the east, and at last he came to the city of Haran. Beside the city was the well where Abraham's servant had met Jacob's mother Rebekah. There, after Jacob had waited for a time he saw a young woman coming with her sheep, to give them water.

Jacob took off the flat stone that was over the mouth of the well, and drew water, and gave it to the sheep. And when he found that this young woman was his own cousin Rachel, the daughter of Laban, he was so glad that he wept for joy. At that moment, he began to love Rachel, and longed to have her for his wife.

Rachel's father, Laban, who was Jacob's uncle, welcomed Jacob and took him into his home.

And Jacob asked Laban if he would give his daughter Rachel to him as his wife, and Jacob said, "If you will give me Rachel, I will work for you seven years." Laban said, "It is better that you should have her than that a stranger should marry her."

So Jacob lived seven years in Laban's house, caring for his sheep and oxen and camels, and such was his love for Rachel that the seven years seemed like a few days.

At last the day came for the marriage, and they brought in the bride, who after the manner of that land was covered with a thick veil, so her face could not be seen. And she was married to Jacob. And when Jacob lifted up her veil, he found that he had not married Rachel, whom he loved, but her older sister Leah, who was not beautiful, and whom Jacob did not love at all.

Jacob was very angry that he had been deceived, though that was just the way Jacob himself had deceived his father and cheated his brother Esau. But his uncle Laban said, "In our land we never allow the younger daughter to be married before the older daughter. Keep Leah for your wife, and work for me seven years longer, and you shall have Rachel also."

For in those times, as we have seen, men often had two wives, or even more than two. No one thought it was wrong then to have more than one wife, although now it is considered very wicked. So Jacob stayed seven years more — fourteen years in all — before he received Rachel as his wife.

While Jacob was living at Haran, eleven sons were born to him, but only one of these was the child of Rachel, whom Jacob loved. This son was Joseph, who was dearer to Jacob than any of his other children, partly because he was the youngest, and also because he was the child of his beloved Rachel.

Discussion Questions: *1. How much did Jacob love Rachel? 2. How did he show his love? 3. How did he feel when he saw he had been cheated? 4. Why had Laban cheated him? Do you think he was right?*

DAY 24

Jacob Leaves for Home

Genesis 31:17-32:22

JACOB stayed a long time in the land of Haran, much longer than he had expected to stay. And in that land, Jacob became rich. As wages for his work with Laban, Jacob took a share of the sheep, oxen, and camels. And since Jacob was very wise and careful in his work, his share grew larger, until Jacob owned a great flock. At last, after twenty years, Jacob decided to go back to the land of Canaan to his father Isaac, who was still living, though now very old and feeble.

Jacob did not tell his uncle Laban that he was going away. While Laban was absent from home, Jacob gathered together his wives and children, all his sheep, cattle, and camels, and stole away quietly. When Laban found Jacob had left him, he was not at all pleased. He wished Jacob to care for the things he owned, for Jacob managed them better than Laban and God blessed everything that Jacob undertook. Then, too, Laban did not like to have his two daughters, the wives of Jacob, taken so far away from him.

So Laban and the men who were with him followed after Jacob, but that night God spoke to Laban in a dream, and said, "Do no harm to Jacob, when you meet him."

Therefore, when Laban came to where Jacob was on Mount Gilead, he spoke kindly to Jacob. Jacob and Laban made a covenant, a promise between them. They piled up a heap of stones, and on it they set up a large rock like a pillar. Beside the heap of stones they ate a meal together, and Jacob said to Laban, "I promise not to go past this heap of stones and this pillar and do you harm. The God of your grandfather, Nahor, and the God of my grandfather, Abraham, be the judge between us."

Laban made the same promise to Jacob, then he kissed his daughters and all of Jacob's children, and bade them good-by. Laban went back to Haran, and Jacob went on to Canaan.

And Jacob gave two names to the heap of stones where they made the covenant. One name was Galeed, a word that means, "The heap of Witness." The other was Mizpah, which means "Watchtower." For Jacob said, "The Lord watch between you and me, when we are absent from each other."

While Jacob was going back to Canaan, he heard news that filled him with fear. He heard that Esau, his brother, was coming to meet him, leading an army of 400 men. He knew how angry Esau had been long before, and how he had threatened to kill him. Jacob feared that Esau would now come upon him and kill not only himself, but his wives and children. If Jacob had acted rightly toward his brother, he need not have feared Esau's coming, but he knew he had wronged Esau, and he was terribly afraid to meet him.

That night Jacob divided his company into two parts, so that if one part were taken, the other part might escape. And he sent before him, as a present to his brother, a great number of oxen, cows, sheep, goats, camels and asses, hoping that his brother might be kind toward him. Then Jacob prayed earnestly to the Lord God to help him. After that he sent all his family across a brook that was in his path, called the brook Jabbok, while he stayed alone on the other side of the brook to pray again.

Discussion Questions: *1. Why did Jacob decide to go home? 2. Many years had gone by. Had Jacob changed? 3. Do you think Jacob and Laban trusted each other? Why or why not? 4. Why was Jacob still afraid of his brother?*

DAY 25

A Wrestling Match

Genesis 32:24-33:18

WHILE Jacob was alone, he felt that a man had taken hold of him, and Jacob wrestled with this strange man all the night. And the man was an angel from God. They wrestled so hard, that Jacob's thigh was strained in the struggle.

The angel said, "Let me go, for the day is breaking."

And Jacob said, "I will not let you go until you bless me."

And the angel said, "What is your name?"

Jacob answered, "Jacob is my name."

Then the angel said, "Your name shall no more be called Jacob, but Israel, that is 'He who wrestles with God.' For you have wrestled with God and have won the victory."

And the angel blessed him there. The sun rose as the angel left him, and Jacob gave a name to that place. He called it Peniel, or Penuel, words that in his language mean The Face of God. "For," said Jacob, "I have met God face-to-face." After this, Jacob was lame, for in the wrestling he had strained his thigh.

As Jacob went across the brook Jabbok early in the morning, he looked up, and there was Esau right before him. He bowed his face to the ground, over

JACOB WRESTLED WITH THE ANGEL – GENESIS 32:24-31

and over again, as people do in those lands when they meet someone of higher rank than their own. But Esau ran to meet him, and placed his arms around his neck, and kissed him, and the two brothers wept together. Esau was kind and generous to forgive his brother all the wrong he had done, and at first he would not receive Jacob's present, for he said, "I have enough, my brother." But Jacob urged him, until at last he took the present. And so the quarrel was ended, and the two brothers were at peace.

Jacob came to Shechem, in the middle of the land of Canaan, and there he set up his tents. At the foot of the mountain — although there were streams of water all around — he dug his own well, great and deep, the well where Jesus sat and talked with a woman many ages after that. Even now the traveller who visits that place may drink water from Jacob's well.

After this, Jacob had a new name, Israel, which means "The one who wrestles with God." Sometimes he was called Jacob, and sometimes Israel. And all those who come from Israel — his descendants — were called Israelites.

After this Isaac died and was buried by his sons Jacob and Esau in the cave at Hebron where Abraham and Sarah were already buried. Esau went away to a land on the southeast of Canaan, which was called Edom. And Jacob, or Israel, lived in the land of Canaan, dwelling in tents and moving from place to place, where they could find good pasture or grass upon which to feed their flocks.

41

DAY 26

JOSEPH GOES ON AN ERRAND
Genesis 35:16-37:14

AFTER Jacob came back to the land of Canaan with his eleven sons, another son was born to him, the second child of his wife Rachel, whom Jacob loved so well. But now a great sorrow came to Jacob, for soon after the baby came, Rachel died. Even to this day you can see the place where Rachel was buried on the road between Jerusalem and Bethlehem. Jacob named the child that Rachel left Benjamin. Now Jacob had twelve sons. Most of them were grown up men, but Joseph was a boy of seventeen, and his brother Benjamin was almost a baby.

Of all his children, Jacob loved Joseph the best because he was Rachel's child, was so much younger than most of his brothers, and because he was good, faithful, and thoughtful. Jacob gave Joseph a robe or coat of bright colors, made like a long cloak with wide sleeves. This was a special mark of Jacob's favor to Joseph, and it made his older brothers very envious of him.

Then, too, Joseph did what was right, while his older brothers often did wrong acts, which Joseph sometimes told their father, and this made them very angry at Joseph. But they hated him still more because of two strange dreams he had and told them about.

"Listen to this dream I had. I dreamed that we were out in the field binding sheaves, when suddenly my sheaf stood up, and all your sheaves came around it, and bowed down to my sheaf."

And they said, scornfully, "Do you suppose the dream means you will someday rule over us, and we will bow down to you?"

Then, a few days later, Joseph said, "I have dreamed again. This time I saw in my dream the sun and the moon and eleven stars all come and bow down to me."

His father said to him, "I do not like you to dream such dreams. Shall I and your mother and your brothers come and bow down before you, as if you are a king?"

His brothers hated Joseph, and would not speak kindly to him, but his

42

JOSEPH TOLD HIS BROTHERS ABOUT HIS DREAMS - GENESIS 37:5

father thought about what Joseph had said.

Once, Joseph's ten older brothers were taking care of the flock in the fields near Shechem, which was nearly fifty miles from Hebron, where Jacob's tents were spread. Jacob wished to send a message to his sons, so he called Joseph and said to him, "Your brothers are near Shechem with the flock. I wish you would go to them, take a message, see if they and the flocks are doing well, and bring me word from them."

That was quite an errand for a boy, but Joseph could take care of himself and could be trusted, so he went forth on his journey.

Discussion Questions: *1. Why did Jacob love Joseph best? How did he show it? 2. How did Joseph's brothers feel? Would you have felt that way? 3. Why didn't his brothers like the dream? 4. Do you think Joseph's father trusted him? How do you know?*

DAY 27

JOSEPH SOLD AS A SLAVE

Genesis 37:15-35

WHEN Joseph reached Shechem, he could not find his brothers, for they had taken their flocks to another place. A man met Joseph wandering in the field, and asked him, "Whom are you seeking?"

Joseph said, "I am looking for my brothers, the sons of Jacob. Can you tell me where I will find them?"

The man replied, "They are at Dothan. I heard them say they were going there."

Joseph walked over the hills to Dothan, which was fifteen miles further, and his brothers saw him coming toward them. They knew him by his bright garment, and one said to another, "Look, that dreamer is coming! Come, let us kill him, and throw his body into a pit, and tell his father that some wild beast has eaten him. Then we will see what becomes of his dreams."

One of his brothers, whose name was Reuben, felt more kindly toward Joseph than the others, but he did not dare oppose the others openly. Reuben said, "Let's not kill him. Let's throw him into this pit and leave him to die."

Reuben intended to come back later, take Joseph out of the pit, and take him home to his father. The brothers did as Reuben told them; they threw Joseph into the pit, which was empty. He cried and begged them to save him, but they would not. They calmly sat down to eat their dinner on the grass, while their brother called up to them from the pit.

After dinner, Reuben went to another part of the field, so he was not at hand when a company of men passed by with their camels, going from Gilead — on the east of the river Jordan — to Egypt, to sell spices and fragrant gum from trees to the Egyptians. Judah, another of Joseph's brothers, said, "What good will it do us to kill our brother? Would it not be better for us to sell him to these men, and let them carry him away? After all, he is our brother, and we should not kill him."

His brothers agreed with him. They stopped the men who were passing and drew Joseph up from the pit, and for twenty pieces of silver, they sold Joseph to these men, who took him away with them to Egypt.

After a while, Reuben came to the pit and looked into it, but Joseph was not there. Then Reuben was in great trouble, and he came back to his brothers saying, "The boy is not there! What shall I do?"

His brothers told Reuben what they had done, and they all agreed to deceive their father. They killed one of the goats and dipped Joseph's coat in its blood. Then they brought it to their father and said to him, "We found this coat out in the wilderness. Look at it, and see if you think it was your son's." Jacob knew it at once. He said, "It is my son's coat. Some wild beast has eaten him. There is no doubt that Joseph has been torn in pieces!"

Jacob's heart was broken over the loss of Joseph, all the more because he had sent Joseph alone on the journey through the wilderness. They tried to comfort him, but he would not be comforted. He said, "I will go to my grave mourning for my poor lost son."

So the old man sorrowed for his son Joseph, and all the time his wicked brothers knew Joseph was not dead, but they would not tell their father the dreadful deed they had done.

Discussion Questions: *1. What did Reuben tell the brothers to do with Joseph? Why? 2. Why didn't the brothers kill Joseph? 3. How do you think Reuben felt when he saw his brother was gone? 4. Why did they dip Joseph's coat in blood?*

DAY 28

JOSEPH IN PRISON
Genesis 39:1-40:19

THE men who bought Joseph from his brothers were called Ishmaelites, because they belonged to the family of Ishmael, who, you remember, was the son of Hagar, the servant of Sarah. These men carried Joseph southward over the plain that lies beside the great sea on the west of Canaan. After many days they brought Joseph to Egypt.

The Ishmaelites sold Joseph as a slave to a man named Potiphar, who was an officer in the army of Pharaoh, the king of Egypt. Joseph was a beautiful boy, cheerful and willing and good at anything he undertook. His master, Potiphar, became friendly to him, and after a time he placed Joseph in charge of his house and everything in it. For some years Joseph continued in the house of Potiphar, a slave in name, but in reality the master of all his affairs and ruler over his fellowservants.

Potiphar's wife, who at first was very friendly to Joseph, afterward became his enemy, because Joseph would not do wrong to please her. She told her husband falsely that Joseph had done a wicked deed. Her husband believed her, was very angry at Joseph, and put him in prison with those who had been sent there for breaking the law. How hard it was for Joseph to be charged with a crime when he had done no wrong and to be thrust into a dark prison among wicked people!

But Joseph had faith in God, knowing it would all come out right, and in the prison he was cheerful, kind, and helpful, as he had always been. The keeper of the prison saw Joseph was not like the other men around him, and he was kind to Joseph. In a little while, Joseph was placed in charge of all his fellowprisoners, and took care of them, just as he had taken care of everything in Potiphar's house. The keeper of the prison scarcely looked into the prison at all, for he had confidence in Joseph, knowing he would be faithful and wise in doing the work given to him. Joseph did right and served God, and God blessed Joseph in everything.

While Joseph was in prison, two men were sent there by the king of Egypt because he was displeased with them. One was the king's chief butler, who served the king his wine; the other was the chief baker, who served him his bread. These two men were under Joseph's care, and Joseph waited on them, for they were men of rank.

One morning, when Joseph came into the room in the prison where the butler and the baker were kept, he found them looking quite sad. Joseph said to them, "Why do you look so sad today?" Joseph was cheerful and happy, and he wanted others to be happy, even in prison.

One of the men said, "Each one of us dreamed a very strange dream, and there is no one to tell us what our dreams mean."

In those times, before God gave the Bible to men, he often spoke to men in dreams, and there were wise men who could sometimes tell what the dreams meant.

"Tell me," said Joseph, "what your dreams were. Perhaps my God will help me understand them."

Then the chief butler told his dream. He said, "In my dream I saw a grape vine with three branches. As I looked, the branches shot out buds, and the buds became blossoms, and the blossoms turned into clusters of ripe grapes. And I picked the grapes, and squeezed their juice into King Pharaoh's cup, and it became wine.

I gave it to King Pharaoh to drink, just as I used to do when I was beside his table."

Then Joseph said, "This is what your dream means. The three branches mean three days. In three days, King Pharaoh will call you out of prison and will put you back in your place, and you shall stand at his table and give him his wine, as you have given it before. But when you go out of prison, please remember me, and try to find some way to get me out of this prison. I was stolen out of the land of Canaan and sold as a slave, and I have done nothing to deserve being put in this prison. Speak to the king for me, so I may be set free."

Of course the chief butler felt very happy to hear his dream had so pleasant a meaning. Then the chief baker spoke, hoping to have an answer just as good. "In my dream," said the baker, "there were three baskets of white bread on my head, one above the other, and on the topmost basket were all kinds of roasted meat and food for Pharaoh. Then birds came, and ate the food from the baskets on my head."

Joseph said to the baker: "This is the meaning of your dream, and I am sorry to tell it to you. The three baskets are three days. In three days, by order of the king, you shall be lifted up and hanged upon a tree, and the birds shall eat your flesh from your bones as you are hanging in the air."

_____

Discussion Questions: *1. Why did Potiphar put Joseph in charge of his house? 2. Why wouldn't Joseph do wrong to please Potiphar's wife? 3. Why was Joseph cheerful in prison? 4. How did Joseph know what the other prisoners' dreams meant?*

DAY 29

_____

PHARAOH'S DREAM

Genesis 40:20-41:43

AND it came to pass just as Joseph had said. Three days later, King Pharaoh sent his officers to the prison. They came and took out both the chief butler and the chief baker. The baker they hung up by his neck to die, and left his body for the birds to pick. The chief butler they brought back to his old place, where he waited at the king's table and handed him his wine to drink. In his gladness, he forgot all about Joseph.

Two full years passed by, and Joseph was in prison until he was thirty years old.

But one night, King Pharaoh dreamed a dream — in fact, two dreams in one. In the morning, he sent for all the wise men of Egypt and told them his dreams, but no one could tell what they meant. The king was troubled, for he felt the dreams had some meaning that was important for him to know.

Then suddenly the chief butler, who was by the king's table, remembered his own dream in prison two years before, and remembered the young man who had told its meaning so exactly. And he said, "Two years ago King Pharaoh was angry with his servants, with me and the chief baker, and he sent us to the prison. While we were in the prison, one night each of us dreamed a dream, and the next day a young man in the prison, a Hebrew from the land of Canaan, told us what our dreams meant, and in three days they came true, just as the Hebrew had said. I think that if this young man is still in prison, he could tell the king the meaning of his dreams."

Then King Pharaoh sent to the prison for Joseph. Joseph was taken out, dressed in new garments, and led to Pharaoh in the palace. Pharaoh said to Joseph, "I have dreamed a dream, and there is no one who can tell what it means. I have been told that you have power to understand dreams and what they mean."

JOSEPH BEFORE PHARAOH — GENESIS 41:14

Joseph answered Pharaoh, "The power is not in me. But God will give Pharaoh a good answer. What is the dream the king has dreamed?"

"In my first dream," said Pharaoh, "I was standing by the river, and I saw seven fat and handsome cows come up from the river to feed in the grass. And while they were feeding, seven other cows followed them up from the river, very thin, poor, and lean — miserable creatures. The seven lean cows ate up the seven fat cows, and after they had eaten them, they were as lean and miserable as before. Then I awoke.

"And I fell asleep again, and dreamed again. In my second dream, I saw seven heads of grain growing on one stalk, large, strong, and good. And then seven heads came up after them that were thin, poor, and withered. And the seven thin heads swallowed up the seven good heads, and afterward were as poor and withered as before."

Joseph said to the king, "The two dreams have the same meaning. God has been showing King Pharaoh what he will do in this land. The seven good cows mean seven years, and the seven good heads of grain mean the same seven years. The seven lean cows and the seven thin heads of grain also mean seven years. The good cows and the good grain mean seven years of plenty, and the seven thin cows and thin heads of grain mean seven poor years. Egypt will have seven years of plenty, when the fields shall bring greater crops than ever before. And after those years shall come seven years when the fields shall bring no crops at all. Then for seven years there shall be such need that the years of plenty will be forgotten, for the people will have nothing to eat.

"Now, let King Pharaoh find some man who is able and wise, and let him set this man over the land. And during the seven years of plenty, let a part of the crops be put away for the years of need. If this is done, then when the years of need come, there will be plenty of food for all the people, and no one will suffer, for all will have enough."

King Pharaoh said to Joseph, "Since God has shown you all this, there is no man as wise as you. I will appoint you to do this work and to rule over the land of Egypt. All the people shall be under you. Only I will be above you."

PHARAOH HONORED JOSEPH - GENESIS 41:38-45

And Pharaoh took from his own hand the ring that held his seal, and put it on Joseph's hand, so he could sign for the king. He dressed Joseph in robes of fine linen and put a gold chain around his neck. And he made Joseph ride in a chariot that was next in rank to his own. And they cried out before Joseph, "Bow the knee." Thus Joseph was ruler over all the land of Egypt.

So the slave boy who was sent to prison without deserving it came out of prison to be a prince and a master over all the land. You see, God had not forgotten Joseph, even when he seemed to have left him to suffer.

Discussion Questions: *1. Why did King Pharaoh send for Joseph? 2. How did Joseph know what the dreams meant? 3. Did God forget Joseph while he was in prison? How do you know?*

49

DAY 30

JOSEPH'S BROTHERS COME TO EGYPT

Genesis 41:46-42:3

WHEN Joseph was made ruler over the land of Egypt, he did just as he had always done. He found his work at once and began to do it faithfully and thoroughly. He went out over all the land of Egypt, and saw how rich and abundant the fields of grain were. He told the people not to waste it, but to save it for the coming time of need.

He told the people to give the king one bushel of grain out of every five, to be stored. The people brought their grain, after taking out what they needed, and Joseph stored it in great storehouses in the cities. There was so much that no one could keep account of it.

The king of Egypt gave Joseph a wife named Asenath, and she gave Joseph two sons. The oldest son he named Manasseh, a word that means "making to forget."

"For," said Joseph, "God has made me forget all my troubles and my toil as a slave."

The second son he named Ephraim, a word that means "fruitful."

"Because," said Joseph, "God has not only made the land fruitful, but he has made me fruitful in the land of my troubles."

The seven years of plenty soon passed by, and then came the years of need. In all the lands around, people were hungry, and there was no food for them to eat, but in Egypt, everybody had enough. Most of the people soon used up the grain they had saved. Many had saved none at all, and they all cried to the king to help them.

"Go to Joseph," said King Pharaoh, "and do whatever he tells you to do."

Then the people came to Joseph, and Joseph opened the storehouses, and sold the people all the grain they wished to buy. Not only the people of Egypt came to buy grain, but people of all the lands around, as well, for there was great need and famine everywhere.

The need was as great in the land of Canaan, where Jacob lived, as in other lands. Jacob was rich in flocks and cattle, gold and silver, but his fields gave no grain, and there was danger that his family and people would starve. And Jacob — who was now called Israel — heard there was food in Egypt. He said to his sons, "Why do you look at each other, asking what to do to find food? I have been told that there is grain in Egypt. Go down to that land with money and buy grain, so we may have bread and live."

DAY 31

JOSEPH SEES HIS BROTHERS

Genesis 42:3-38

SO the ten older brothers of Joseph went down to Egypt. They rode upon asses, for horses were not much used in those times, and they brought money with them. But Jacob would not let Benjamin, Joseph's younger brother, go with them, for he was all the more dear to his father, now that Joseph was no longer with him, and Jacob feared harm might come to him.

Joseph's brothers came to Joseph to buy food. They did not know him, grown up, dressed as a prince, and seated on a throne. Joseph was now nearly forty, and it had been almost twenty-three years since they had sold him. But Joseph knew them as soon as he saw them. He decided to be sharp and stern with them, not because he hated them, but because he wished to see if they were as selfish, cruel, and wicked as they had been in other days.

They came before him and bowed, with their faces to the ground. Then, no doubt, Joseph thought of the dream that had come to him while he was a boy, of his brothers' sheaves bending down around his sheaf. He spoke to them as a stranger, as if he did not understand their language, and he had their words translated into the language of Egypt.

"Who are you? And from what place do you come?" said Joseph, in a harsh, stern manner.

They answered him, very meekly, "We have come from the land of Canaan to buy food."

"No," said Joseph, "I know what you have come for. You have come as spies, to see how helpless the land is, so you can bring an army against us and make war on us."

"No, no," said Joseph's ten brothers, "we are no spies. We are the sons of one man, who lives in the land of Canaan, and we have come for food, because we have none at home."

"You say you are the sons of one man. Who is your father? Is he living?

51

Have you any more brothers? Tell me all about yourselves."

They said, "Our father is an old man in Canaan. We did have a younger brother, but he was lost, and we have one more brother, who is the youngest of us all, but his father could not spare him to come with us."

"No," said Joseph, "you are not good, honest men. You are spies. I shall put you all in prison, except one of you. He shall go and bring that youngest brother of yours. When I see him, then I will believe that you tell the truth."

So Joseph put all ten men in prison and kept them under guard for three days. Then he sent for them again. They did not know he could understand their language, and they said to each other, "This has come upon us because of the wrong we did to our brother Joseph more than twenty years ago. We heard him cry and plead with us when we threw him into the pit, and we would not have mercy on him. God is giving us only what we deserve."

Reuben, who had tried to save Joseph, said, "Did I not tell you not to harm the boy? And you would not listen to me. God is bringing our brother's blood upon us all."

When Joseph heard this, his heart was touched, for he saw his brothers were really sorry for the wrong they had done him. He turned away from them, so they could not see his face, and he wept. Then he turned back to them and spoke roughly, as before. "This I will do, for I serve God. I will let you all go home except one man. One of you I will shut up in prison, but the rest of you can go home and take food for your people. But you must come back, and bring your youngest brother with you. Then I shall know that you have spoken the truth."

Then Joseph gave orders, and his servants seized one of his brothers, whose name was Simeon, and bound him, and took him away to prison. He ordered his servants to fill the men's sacks with grain, and to put every man's money back into the sack before it was tied up, so they would find the money as soon as they opened the sack. Then the men loaded their asses with the sacks of grain and started home, leaving their brother Simeon a prisoner.

When they stopped on the way to feed their asses, one of the brothers opened his sack and found his money lying on the top of the grain. He called out to his brothers, "Look, my money's here!" They were frightened, but they did not dare go back to Egypt and meet the stern ruler of the land. They went home and told their old father all that had happened to them, how their brother Simeon was in prison until they returned with Benjamin. They spoke of going back to Egypt with Benjamin, but Jacob said to them, "You are taking my sons away from me. Joseph is gone, and Simeon is gone, and now you would take Benjamin away. All these things are against me!"

Reuben said, "Here are my own two boys. You may kill them, if you wish, in case I do not bring Benjamin back to you."

But Jacob said, "My youngest son shall not go with you. His brother is dead, and he alone is left to me. If harm should come to him, it would bring down my gray hairs with sorrow to the grave."

Discussion Questions: *1. Why was Joseph hard on his brothers, when they came to Egypt? 2. How do you think his brothers felt? 3. Why did the brothers think they were in prison? Were they right? 4. Why do you think Joseph wanted them to bring Benjamin to him?*

DAY 32

A Lost Brother Found

Genesis 43:1-44:2

THE food Jacob's sons brought from Egypt did not last long, for Jacob's family was large. Most of his sons were married and had children of their own. Jacob's children and grandchildren totaled sixty-six, plus the servants who waited on them and the men who cared for the flocks. So around Jacob's tent was quite a camp of tents and an army of people.

When the food from Egypt was nearly eaten up, Jacob said to his sons, "Go down to Egypt again and buy some more food for us."

Judah, Jacob's son who had urged his brothers to sell Joseph to the Ishmaelites, said to his father, "It is no use for us to go to Egypt, unless we take Benjamin with us. The man who rules that land said to us, 'You shall not see my face unless your youngest brother is with you.' "

Israel said, "Why did you tell the man you had a brother? You did me great harm when you told him."

"Why," said Jacob's sons, "we could not help telling him. The man asked us all about our family. Is your father living? Have you any more brothers? And we had to tell him, his questions were so sharp. How could we know he would say, 'Bring your brother here for me to see him'?"

Judah said, "Send Benjamin with me, and I will take care of him. I promise you I will bring him safely home. If he does not come back, let me bear the blame forever. He must go, or we will die for want of food."

Jacob said, "If he must go, then he must. But take a present to the man, some of the choicest fruits of the land, spices, perfumes, nuts, and almonds. And take twice as much money, besides the money that was in your sacks. Perhaps that was a mistake, when the money was given back to you. Take your brother Benjamin, and may the Lord God make the man kind to you, so he will set Simeon free and let you bring Benjamin back. But if it is God's will that I lose my children, I cannot help it."

So ten brothers of Joseph went down a second time to Egypt, Benjamin going in place of Simeon. They came to Joseph's office, the place where he sold grain to the people, and they stood before their brother and bowed as before. Joseph saw that Benjamin was with them, and he said to his steward, the man who was over his house: "Make ready a dinner, for all these men shall dine with me today."

When Joseph's brothers found themselves being taken into Joseph's house, they were filled with fear. They said to one another, "We have been taken here on account of the money in our sacks. They will say we have stolen it and will sell us all for slaves."

But Joseph's steward treated the men kindly, and when they spoke of the money in their sacks, he would not take it again. The steward received the men into Joseph's house and washed their feet, according to the custom of the land. At noon, Joseph came in to meet them. They brought him the presents from their father, and again they bowed before him, with their faces on the ground.

Joseph asked them if they were well, and said, "Is your father still living, the old man of whom you spoke? Is he well?"

They answered, "Our father is well, and he is living."

Joseph looked at his younger brother, Benjamin, the child of his own mother, Rachel, and he said, "Is this your youngest brother? God be gracious to you, my son."

Joseph's heart was so full that he could not keep back his tears. He went quickly to his own room and wept there. Then he washed his face, came out again, and ordered the table to be set for dinner. They set Joseph's table for himself, as the ruler, another table for his Egyptian officers, and another for the eleven men from Canaan, for Joseph had brought Simeon out of the prison and had given him a place with his brothers.

Joseph himself arranged the order of the seats for his brothers, with the oldest at the head, and all in order of age down to the youngest. The men wondered at this, and could not see how the ruler of Egypt should know the order of their ages. And Joseph sent dishes from his table to his brothers, giving Benjamin five times as much as the others. Perhaps he wished to see whether they were as jealous of Benjamin as they had been toward him.

After dinner, Joseph said to his steward, "Fill the men's sacks with grain, as much as they can carry, and put each man's money in his sack. Put my silver cup in the sack of the youngest, along with his money."

Discussion Questions: *1. Why didn't Jacob want to send Benjamin to Egypt? 2. Why did Jacob send gifts to the Egyptian ruler? 3. How do you think Joseph's brothers felt when they found out they had to go back to his house? 4. Why did Joseph give Benjamin more than the others?*

DAY 33

JOSEPH REVEALS HIMSELF

Genesis 44:3-45:24

THE steward did as Joseph had said, and early in the morning the brothers started to go home. A little while afterward, Joseph said to his steward, "Hasten after the men from Canaan, and say, 'Why have you wronged me, after I treated you kindly? You have stolen my master's silver cup, out of which he drinks.' " The steward followed the men, overtook them, and charged them with stealing.

They said to him, "Why should you talk to us in this manner? We have stolen nothing. Why, we brought back to you the money we found in our sacks, and is it likely we would steal your lord's silver or gold? Search us, and if you find your master's cup on any of us, let him die, and the rest of us be sold as slaves."

Then they took down the sacks from the asses and opened them, and in each man's sack was his money, returned again. And when they came to Benjamin's sack, there was the ruler's silver cup! In the greatest sorrow, they tied up their bags again, laid them on the asses, and came back to Joseph's palace.

Joseph said to them, "What have you done? Didn't you know I would find out your deeds?"

Then Judah said, "O my lord, what can we say? God has punished us for our sins, and now we must all be slaves, both us that are older and the youngest, in whose sack the cup was found."

"No," said Joseph, "only one of you is guilty, the one who has taken away my cup. I will hold him as a slave, and the rest of you can go home to your father."

Joseph wanted to see whether his brothers were still selfish and would let Benjamin suffer, if they could escape.

Judah, the brother who had urged his brothers to sell Joseph as a slave, came forward, fell at Joseph's feet, and pleaded with him to let Benjamin go. He told again how Benjamin was the one his father loved the most, now that his brother was lost. He said, "I promised to bear the blame if this boy was not brought home safely. If he does not go back, it will kill our poor old father, who has seen much trouble. Let my youngest brother go home to his father, and I will stay here as a slave in his place!"

Joseph knew now what he had longed to know, that his brothers were no longer cruel and selfish, but one of them was willing to suffer so his brother might be spared. And Joseph could not keep his secret any longer, for his heart longed after his brothers, and he was ready to weep again, with tears of love and joy. He sent all his Egyptian servants out of the room, so he might be alone with his brothers, and then said, "Come near to me. I wish to speak with you." They came closer, wondering. Then Joseph said, "I am Joseph. Is my father really alive?"

How frightened his brothers were, as they heard these words spoken in their own language by the ruler of Egypt, and for the first time, knew that this stern man who had their lives in his hand was their own brother they had wronged!

Then Joseph said again, "I am Joseph, your brother, who you sold into Egypt. But do not feel troubled because of what you did. God sent me here to save your lives. There have been already two years of need and famine, and there are to be five years more, when there shall neither be plowing of the fields nor harvest. It was not you who sent me here, but God, and he sent me to save your lives. God has made me like a father to Pharaoh and ruler over all the land of Egypt. Now go home, and bring down my father and all his family, for that is the only way to save their lives."

JOSEPH WELCOMED HIS BROTHERS - GENESIS 45:15

Then Joseph placed his arms around Benjamin's neck, kissed him, and wept upon him. And Joseph kissed all his brothers, to show them he had fully forgiven them. After that, his brothers began to lose their fear of Joseph and talked with him more freely.

Afterward Joseph sent his brothers home with good news, rich gifts, and abundant food. He also sent wagons in which Jacob and his wives and the little ones of his family might ride from Canaan down to Egypt. And Joseph's brothers went home happier than they had been for many years.

Discussion Questions: *1. Do you think the brothers really wanted to go back to Joseph's palace? 2. Why do you think they did go back? 3. What had the brothers learned since they had sold Joseph as a slave? 4. Why did Joseph tell his brothers who he was? 5. How did the brothers feel at first? At the end of the story?*

DAY 34

JACOB GOES TO EGYPT

Genesis 45:25-49:33

SO Joseph's eleven brothers went home to their old father with the glad news that Joseph was alive and was ruler over the land. It was such a joyful surprise to Jacob that he fainted. But after a time, he revived, and when they showed him the wagons Joseph had sent to bring him and his family to Egypt, old Jacob said, "It is enough. Joseph my son is alive. I will go and see him before I die."

Then they went on their journey, with all their wives, children, servants, sheep, and cattle. They stopped to rest at Beersheba, which had been the home of Isaac and Abraham, made offerings to the Lord, and worshiped. That night the Lord appeared to Jacob, and said to him, "Jacob, I am the Lord, the God of your father. Fear not to go down to Egypt, for I will go down with you. There you shall see your son Joseph, and in Egypt I will make of your descendants a great people. And I will surely bring them back again to this land."

They came down to Egypt, sixty-six of Jacob's children and grandchildren. Joseph rode out in his chariot to meet his father, fell on his neck, and wept. And Jacob said, "Now I am ready to die, since I know you are still alive and I have seen your face." Joseph brought his father in to see King Pharaoh, and Jacob, as an old man, gave his blessing to the king.

The part of the land of Egypt that Joseph gave to his family as a home was called Goshen. It was on the east, between Egypt and the desert, and it was a very rich land, where the soil gave large harvests. But at that time, and for five years after, there were no crops because of the famine. During those years, Joseph's family was fed, as were all the people of Egypt, with grain from the storehouses.

Jacob lived to be almost 150. Before he died, he blessed Joseph and all his sons, and said to them, "When I die, do not bury me in the land of Egypt. Take my body to the land of Canaan, and bury me in the cave at Hebron, with Abraham and my father Isaac."

Joseph brought his two sons, Manasseh and Ephraim, to his father's bed. Jacob's eyes were dim with age, as his father Isaac's had been, and he could not see the two young men, so he said, "Who are these?"

Joseph said, "They are my two sons, whom God has given me in this land."

"Bring them to me," said Jacob, "so I may bless them before I die." Jacob kissed them, put his arms around them, and said, "I had not thought I would ever see your face, my son, but God has let me see both you and your children."

Jacob placed his right hand on Ephraim's head (the younger) and his left hand on Manasseh (the older). Joseph tried to change his father's hands, so his right hand would be on the older son's head, but Jacob would not allow him, saying, "I know what I am doing. God will bless the older son, but the greater blessing shall be with the younger, for his descendants shall be greater and stronger than the descendants of his brother."

And so it came to pass, many years after this, for the tribe of Ephraim, the younger son, became greater and more powerful than the tribe of Manasseh, the older son.

When Jacob died, a great funeral was held. They carried his body up out of Egypt to the land of Canaan, and buried it in the cave of Machpelah, where Abraham and Isaac were buried.

Discussion Questions: *1. How did Jacob feel about going to Egypt? 2. How did he know he should go? 3. How had God been good to Joseph and his family? Can you name more than one way he blessed them?*

DAY 35

Joseph Dies

Genesis 50:15-26

HEN the sons of Jacob came back to Egypt after the burial of their father, they said to one another, "Maybe Joseph will punish us, now that his father is dead, for the wrong we did to him many years ago."

So they sent a message, asking Joseph to forgive them for his father's sake. And again they came and bowed down before him, with their faces to the ground, saying, "We are your servants. Be merciful to us."

Joseph wept when his brothers spoke to him, and he said, "Fear not. Am I God, to punish and reward? It is true that you meant evil to me, but God turned it to good, so all your families might be kept alive. Do not be afraid. I will care for you, and for your children."

Joseph lived to a good old age of 110. Before he died, he said to his children and to all the children of Israel, who had now increased to very many people, "I am going to die, but God will come to you and bring you up out of this land, into your own land, which he promised to your fathers, to Abraham, Isaac, and Jacob. When I die, do not bury me in Egypt, but keep my body until you go out of this land, and take it with you."

So when Joseph died they embalmed his body, as the Egyptians embalmed the dead, so the body would not decay. They placed his body in a stone coffin and kept it in the land of Goshen with the people of Israel. Thus Joseph not only showed his faith in God's promise that he would bring his people back to the land of Canaan, but he also encouraged the faith of those who came after him. Anytime the Israelites looked at the stone coffin that held the body of Joseph, they said to one another, "There is the token, the sign that this land is not our home. This coffin will not be buried until we bury it in our own land, the land of Canaan, where God will lead us in his own time."

Discussion Questions: *1. Why were Joseph's brothers afraid when their father died? 2. What had Joseph learned in his years in Egypt? 3. What did Joseph say to his children? How did his coffin remind them of this?*

DAY 36

A BABY SAVED

Exodus 1:6-2:9

A S long as Joseph lived, and for some time after, the people of Israel were treated kindly by the Egyptians out of their love for Joseph, who had saved Egypt from the famine. But eventually a king began to rule over Egypt who cared nothing for Joseph or Joseph's people. He saw the Israelites were very many, and he feared they would soon become greater in number and power than the Egyptians.

He said to his people, "Let's rule these Israelites more strictly. They are growing too strong."

Then they set harsh rulers over the Israelites, who laid heavy burdens on them. They made the Israelites work hard for the Egyptians, build cities for

The Egyptians Made Life Bitter for The Israelites – Exodus 1:11-14

them, and give to the Egyptians a large part of the crops from their fields. They set them at work making bricks and building storehouses. They were so afraid the Israelites would grow in number, that they gave orders to kill all the little boys that were born to the Israelites, though their little girls might be allowed to live.

But in the face of all this hate, wrong, and cruelty, the people of Israel were growing in number and becoming greater and greater.

At this time, when the wrongs done to the Israelites were the greatest and their little children were being killed, a little boy was born. He was such a lovely child that his mother kept him hidden from the Egyptians. When she could no longer hide him, she made a plan to save his life, believing God would help her and save her beautiful little boy. She made a little box like a boat and covered it with something that would not let the water into it. She knew that at certain times the daughter of Pharaoh — all the kings of Egypt were called Pharaoh — would come down to the river for a bath. She placed her baby boy in the ark and let it float down the river where the princess would see it. Then she sent her daughter, a little girl named Miriam, twelve years old, to watch. How anxious the mother and sister were as they saw the little ark floating away from them on the river.

Pharaoh's daughter, with her maids, came down to the river and saw the ark floating on the water, among the reeds. She sent one of her maids to bring it to her, so she might see what was in the little boat. They opened it, and there was a beautiful little baby, who began to cry to be picked up.

PHARAOH'S DAUGHTER FOUND THE BABY MOSES - EXODUS 2:1-10

The princess felt tenderness for the baby and loved it at once. She said, "This is one of the Hebrews' children."

Pharaoh's daughter thought it would be cruel to let such a lovely baby die out on the water. Just then, a little girl came running up to her, as if by accident. She looked at the baby also, and asked, "Shall I go and find some Hebrew woman to be a nurse for you, and take care of the baby?"

"Yes," said the princess, "Go and find a nurse for me."

The little girl — who was Miriam, the baby's sister — ran as quickly as she could and brought the baby's own mother to the princess.

The princess said to the little baby's mother, "Take this child to your home and nurse it for me, and I will pay you wages for it."

How glad the Hebrew mother was to take her child home! No one could harm her boy now, for he was protected by the princess of Egypt, the daughter of the king.

———————

Discussion Questions: *1. Why did the new Egyptian king fear the Israelites? 2. What did he do to them? 3. Why did the mother hide her son? Who found him?*

DAY 37

MOSES GROWS UP

Exodus 2:10-25

WHEN the child was large enough to leave his mother, Pharaoh's daughter took him into her own home in the palace. She named him Moses, a word that means "drawn out," because he was drawn out of the water.

So Moses, the Hebrew boy, lived in the palace among the nobles of the land as the son of the princess. There he learned much more than he could have learned among his own people, for there were very wise teachers among the Egyptians. Moses gained all the knowledge the Egyptians had to give. There in the court of the cruel king who had made slaves of the Israelites, God's people, an Israelite boy who would later set his people free grew up.

Although Moses grew up among the Egyptians and gained their learning, he loved his own people. They were poor, hated slaves, but he loved them because they served the Lord God, while the Egyptians worshiped idols and animals. It was strange that wise people such as these should bow down and pray to an ox, or to a cat, or to a snake!

When Moses became a man, he joined his own people, leaving the riches and ease he might have enjoyed with the Egyptians. He felt a call from God to lift up the Israelites and set them free, but at that time, he found he could do nothing to help them. They would not let him lead them, and since the king of Egypt had become his enemy, Moses went away from Egypt, into a country in Arabia called Midian.

He was sitting by a well in that land, tired from his long journey, when he saw some young women come to draw water for their flocks of sheep. But some rough men came, drove the women away, and took the water for their own flocks. Moses saw it and helped the women, drawing water for them.

These young women were sisters, the daughters of a man named Jethro, who was a priest in the land of Midian. He asked Moses to live with him and help him care for his flocks. Moses stayed with Jethro and married one of his daughters. So from being a prince in the king's palace in Egypt, Moses became a shepherd in the wilderness of Midian.

It must have been a great change for Moses, after he spent forty years in the palace as a prince, to go out into the wilderness of Midian and live as a shepherd. He left behind the crowded cities, the pyramids, the temples of Egypt, and the great Nile River. For forty years, Moses wandered around

Midian with his flocks, living alone, often sleeping on the ground, and looking up by day to the great mountains.

He wore the rough skin mantle of a shepherd, and in his hand was a long shepherd's staff. On his feet he wore sandals instead of shoes. But when he stood before an altar to worship God, he took off his sandals, because the people of those lands take off their shoes as a sign of reverence in a sacred place.

Moses was a great man, one of the greatest men that ever lived. But he did not think himself great or wise. He was content with the work he was doing and was not ambitious. But God had work for Moses to do, and all through those years in the wilderness, God was preparing him for that work.

Discussion Questions: *1. Why did Moses love the Hebrews? 2. Why did he go to Midian? 3. Do you think Moses found it hard to become a shepherd? 4. Why did God make Moses a shepherd?*

DAY 38

THE BURNING BUSH

Exodus 3:1-4:31

ONE day, Moses was feeding his flock on a mountain called Mount Horeb. This mountain was also called Mount Sinai, and is called both names in the Bible. On the mountain, Moses saw a bush that seemed to be on fire. He watched, to see it burn up, but it was not destroyed, though it kept burning on and on.

Moses said to himself, "I will go and look at this strange thing — a bush on fire that doesn't burn up."

As Moses was going toward the bush, he heard a voice coming out of the bush, calling him by name, "Moses, Moses!" He listened, and said, "Here I am."

The voice said, "Moses, do not come near, but take off your shoes, for you are standing on holy ground."

So Moses took off his shoes and came near to the burning bush. And the voice came from the bush, saying, "I am the God of your father, the God of Abraham, Isaac, and Jacob. I have seen the wrongs and the cruelty that my people have suffered in Egypt, and I have heard their cry. I am coming to set them free from the land of the Egyptians, and to bring them up to their own land, the land of Canaan — a good land, and large. Come, now, and I will send you to Pharaoh, and you shall lead out my people from Egypt."

GOD CALLED TO MOSES FROM THE BURNING BUSH · EXODUS 3:4

Moses knew how hard it would be to lead the Israelites out of Egypt with the power of its king. He dreaded such a task, and he said to the Lord, "O Lord, who am I, a shepherd here in the wilderness, to do this great work, to go to Pharaoh and bring the people out of Egypt? It is too much for me."

And God said to Moses, "Surely I will be with you and will help you do this great work. I will give you a sign of my presence with you. When you have led my people out of Egypt, you shall bring them to this mountain, and they shall worship me here. And then you will know I have been with you."

Moses said to God, "When I go to the children of Israel in Egypt and tell them the God of their fathers has sent me, they will say to me, 'Who is this God? What is his name?' For they have suffered so much, and have sunk so low, that I fear they have forgotten their God."

God said to Moses, "My name is 'I AM,' the One who is always living. Go to your people and say to them, 'I AM hath sent me to you.' Do not be afraid. Go to your people and say what I have said to you, and they will listen to you and believe. You shall take the elders of your tribes, the leading men among them, and shall go to Pharaoh, and shall say to him, 'Let my people go, that they may worship me in the wilderness.' At first he will not let you go, but afterward, I will show my power in Egypt, and then he will let you go out of the land."

But Moses wished some sign to give to his people and to the Egyptians, to show them that God had sent him. He asked God to give him some sign. So

64

God said to him, "What is that in your hand?" Moses said, "It is a rod. My shepherd's staff, which I use to guide the sheep."

God said, "Throw it on the ground." When Moses threw it down, it was instantly turned into a snake. Moses was afraid of it, and began to run from it.

God said, "Do not fear it. Take hold of it by the tail." Moses did so, and at once it became again a rod in his hand.

God said again to Moses, "Put your hand on your chest, under your garment, and take it out again."

Then Moses put his hand under his garment, and when he took it out, it had changed, and was now as white as snow, and covered with a scaly crust, like the hand of a leper. He looked at it with fear and horror.

But God said to him, "Put your hand on your chest again." Moses did, and when he took it out, his hand was like the other, perfectly normal.

God said to Moses, "When you go to speak my words, if they will not believe you, show them the first sign, and let your rod become a snake, and then a rod again. And if they still refuse to believe your words, show them the second sign. Turn your hand into a leper's hand and then bring it back as it was before. And if they still will not believe, then take some water from the river, and it will turn to blood. Fear not. Go and speak my words to your own people and the Egyptians."

But Moses was still unwilling to go, not because he was afraid, but because he did not feel himself fit for such a great task.

He said to the Lord, "Oh, Lord, you know I am not a good speaker. I am slow of speech, and cannot talk before men."

And God said, "Am not I the Lord, who made man's mouth? Go, and I will be with your lips, and will teach you what to say."

But Moses still hesitated, and he said, "O Lord, choose some other man for this great work. I am not able to do it."

Then God said, "You have a brother named Aaron. He can speak well. Even now he is coming to see you in the wilderness. Let him help you and speak for you. Let him do the speaking, and you show the signs I have given you."

At last Moses yielded to God's call. He went from Mount Sinai with his flocks and took them home to Jethro, his father-in-law. Then he went toward Egypt, and on the way he met his brother coming to see him. The two brothers, Moses and Aaron, came to the elders of Israel in the land of Goshen. They told the people what God had said, and they showed them the signs God had given them.

And the people said, "God has seen all our troubles, and at last he is coming to set us free." And they were glad, and gave thanks to God who had not forgotten them; for God never forgets those who call upon him.

Discussion Questions: *1. What was strange about the bush Moses saw?
2. What did God want Moses to do? 3. Do you think God gave Moses a hard
job? Could Moses have done it on his own? 4. How did God convince Moses to do
the job?*

DAY 39

THE RIVER THAT RAN BLOOD

Exodus 7:10-25

AFTER Moses and Aaron had spoken to the people of Israel, they
went to see Pharaoh. At first, Moses and Aaron did not ask Pharaoh
to let the people go out of Egypt. They said, "Our God, the Lord God of Israel, has bidden us to go out, with all our people, three days into the
wilderness, and worship him there. And God speaks to you through us, saying, 'Let my people go, that they may serve me.' "

Pharaoh was very angry. He said, "What are you doing, taking your people
away from their work? Go back to your tasks and leave your people alone. I
know why the Israelites are talking about going out into the wilderness. They
don't have enough work to keep them busy. I will give them more work to
do."

The work of the Israelites was mostly making bricks and putting up the
walls of buildings for the rulers of Egypt. In mixing the clay for the brick, they
used straw, chopped up fine, to hold the clay together. Pharaoh said, "Let
them make as many bricks as before, but don't give them straw. Let the Israelites find their own straw for the brickmaking."

Of course this made their task all the harder, for it took a lot of time to find
the straw. The Israelites were scattered all through the land, finding straw and
stubble for use in making the brick, and yet they were expected to bring as
many bricks as before. When they could not do all their tasks, they were
cruelly beaten by the Egyptians. Many of the Israelites now became angry
with Moses and Aaron, who, they thought, had brought more burden and
trouble on them. They said, "May the Lord God judge you and punish you!
You promised to lead us out and set us free, but you only made our suffering
worse!"

Then Moses cried to the Lord, and the Lord said to him, "Take Aaron,
your brother, and go again to Pharaoh. Show him the signs I gave you."

So they went in to Pharaoh, and again asked him in the Lord's name to let the people go. And Pharaoh said, "Who is the Lord? Why should I obey his commands?" What sign can you show that God has sent you?"

Aaron threw down his rod, and it was turned into a snake. But there were wise men in Egypt who had heard of this, and they made a trick ready. They threw down their rods, and their rods became snakes (or seemed to). They may have been tame snakes they had hidden under their long garments and then brought out.

But Aaron's rod, in the form of a snake, ran after them and swallowed them all. Then it became a rod again in Aaron's hand. But Pharaoh refused to obey God's voice.

MOSES AND AARON BEFORE PHARAOH - EXODUS 7:8-13

Then Moses spoke to Aaron, by God's command: "Take your rod and wave it over the waters of Egypt, over the river Nile, and the canals, and the lakes."

Aaron did so. He lifted up the rod and struck the water while Pharaoh watched. In a moment, all the water turned to blood and the fish in the river all died. A terrible stench, a foul smell, rose over the land, and the people were in danger of dying. But in the land of Goshen, where the Israelites were, the water was not turned to blood. So God showed a difference between Israel and Egypt.

The people of Egypt dug wells to find water, and the wise men of Egypt brought some water to Pharaoh and made it look as though they had turned it to blood. And Pharaoh would not listen, or let the people go.

DAY 40

THE PLAGUES

Exodus 8:6-11:1

AFTER seven days, Moses took away the plague of blood, but he warned Pharaoh that another plague was coming, if he refused to obey. As Pharaoh still would not obey, Aaron stretched forth his rod again, and all the land was covered with frogs. Like a great army, they ran over all the fields, and they even filled the houses. Pharaoh said, "Pray to your God for me. Ask him to take the frogs away, and I will let the people go."

Then Moses prayed, and God took away the frogs. They died everywhere, and the Egyptians heaped them up and buried them. But Pharaoh broke his promise, and would not let the people go.

Then Aaron lifted his rod again, and struck the dust, and the dust became alive with lice and fleas. But still Pharaoh would not hear, so God sent great clouds of flies all over the land, so that their houses were filled with them, and the sky was covered. But where the Israelites lived, there were no lice, fleas, or flies.

Then Pharaoh began to yield a little. He said, "Why must you go out of the land to worship God? Worship him here in this land."

But Moses said, "When we worship the Lord, we must make an offering, and our offerings are animals the people of Egypt worship — oxen and sheep. It would make the Egyptians angry to see us offering a sacrifice of animals they call gods."

"Well," said Pharaoh, "you may go. But do not go far away, and come back." But when Moses and Aaron had taken away the plague, Pharaoh broke his promise again, and still held the people as slaves.

Then another plague came. A terrible disease struck all the animals in Egypt — the horses, asses, camels, sheep, and oxen — and they died by the thousand in one day, all over the land. But no plague came to the flocks and herds of the Israelites.

But Pharaoh was still stubborn. He would not obey God's voice. Then Moses and Aaron gathered up ashes from the furnace and threw it up, like a cloud, into the air. Instantly, boils began to break out on men and beasts all through the land.

Still Pharaoh refused to obey. Moses stretched out his rod toward the sky. At once a terrible storm burst forth upon the land, all the more terrible because in that land, rain scarcely ever falls. Sometimes there will not even be a shower of rain for years at a time. But now the black clouds rolled, thunder sounded, lightning flashed, and rain poured down. With the rain came hail, something that the Egyptians had never seen before. It struck all the crops growing in the field, and the fruits on the trees, and destroyed them.

Once again Pharaoh was frightened and promised to let the people go, but when God took away the hail, he broke his word, and would not let the Israelites leave the land.

After the hail came great clouds of locusts, which ate up every green thing the hail had spared. And after the locusts came the plague of darkness. For three days there was thick darkness, no sun shining, nor moon, nor stars. But still Pharaoh would not let the people go. Pharaoh said to Moses, "Get out of my sight. Never let me see your face again. If you come into my presence, you shall be killed."

Moses said, "It shall be as you say. I will see your face no more."

Now God said to Moses, "There shall be one plague more, and then Pharaoh will be glad to let the people go. He will drive you out of the land. Make your people ready to go out of Egypt. Your time here will soon be ended."

Discussion Questions: *1. What did Pharaoh do that was wrong? 2. Why wouldn't Moses let the Israelites stay in Egypt to worship God? 3. What happened to the animals belonging to the Egyptians? What happened to the Israelites' animals? 4. Who protected the Israelites?*

DAY 41

A NATION IS BORN

Exodus 12:1-13:22

HILE all these terrible plagues were falling on the people of Egypt, the Israelites in the land of Goshen were living safely under God's care. The waters there were not turned into blood, nor did the flies or the locusts trouble them. While all was dark in the rest of Egypt, in the land of Goshen, the sun was shining.

This made the Egyptians feel the Lord God of the Israelites was watching over his own people. They brought gifts to the Israelites — gold and silver, jewels and precious things of every kind — to win their favor and the favor of their God. So the Israelites, once very poor, suddenly began to be very rich.

Now Moses said to the people, "In a few days you are to go out of Egypt, so gather together, get yourselves in order by families and tribes, and be ready to march out of Egypt."

The people of Israel did as Moses told them. Then Moses said, "God will bring one plague more on the Egyptians, and then they will let you go. And you must take care, and obey God's command exactly, or the last terrible plague will come on your houses, too. At midnight, the angel of the Lord will go through the land, and the oldest child in every house shall die. Pharaoh's son shall die, and every rich man's son, and every poor man's son, even the son of the beggar that has no home. But your families shall be safe if you do exactly as I command you."

Then Moses told them what to do. Every family was told to find a lamb and kill it. They were to take some of the blood of the lamb and sprinkle it at the entrance of the house, on the door frame overhead, and on each side. Then they were to roast the lamb, cook some vegetables, and eat standing around the table with all their garments on, ready to march away as soon as the meal was ended. No one was to go out of his house that night, for God's angel would be out, and you might be killed if the angel should meet you.

The children of Israel did as Moses commanded them. They killed the lamb, sprinkled the blood, and ate the supper in the night as God had told them. This supper was called "the Passover Supper," because when the angel saw the doors sprinkled with blood, he *passed over* those houses and did not enter them. In memory of this great night when God kept his people from death, the Israelites were commanded to eat such a supper on that same night every year. This became a great feast of the Israelites called Passover.

Doesn't that slain lamb and his blood sprinkled to save the people from death make you think of Jesus Christ, who was the Lamb of God, slain to save us all?

That night, a great cry went up all over Egypt. In every house, the oldest son died.

Pharaoh, the king of Egypt, saw his own son lie dead and knew it was the hand of God. And all the people of Egypt were filled with terror as they saw their children lying dead in their houses.

The king now sent a messenger to Moses and Aaron, saying, "Make haste. Get out of the land. Take everything you have. And pray to your God to have mercy on us and do us no more harm."

Early in the morning, the Israelites, after 400 years in Egypt, went out of the land. They went out in order, like a great army, family by family and tribe by tribe. They went out in such haste that they had no time to bake bread for the journey. They left the dough in the pans, all ready for baking, but not yet risen, as bread is before it is baked. They set the bread pans on their heads, as people do in that land when they carry loads. And as a reminder of that day, one week in every year, all the people of Israel eat bread that is unleavened — that is, bread made without yeast, and unrisen. This rule is kept to this day by the Jews, who belong to the Israelite family.

And the Lord God went before the people of Israel as they marched out of Egypt. In the daytime, there was a great cloud, like a pillar, in front. At night, it became a pillar of fire. So both by day and night, as they saw the cloudy and fiery pillar going before, they could say, "Our Lord, the God of heaven and earth, goes before us."

When the pillar of cloud stopped, they knew that was a sign they were to pause in their journey and rest. So they set up their tents and waited until the cloud rose up and went forward. When they looked and saw the pillar of cloud was higher up in the air, as though moving forward, they took down their tents and formed in order for the march. Thus the pillar was like a guide by day and a guard by night.

You remember that when Joseph died, he commanded the Israelites not to bury his body in Egypt, but to keep it in a stone coffin as long as they stayed in Egypt. When they were going out of Egypt, the tribes of Ephraim and Manasseh, who had come from Joseph's two sons, took with them the stone coffin that held the body of Joseph. And thus the Israelites went out of Egypt 400 years after they had gone down to Egypt to live.

Discussion Questions: *1. Why did the Egyptians bring gifts to the Israelites? 2. Do you think they really believed in God? 3. How did the Israelites know they would be safe from the last plague? 4. What does the slain lamb remind us of today? 5. How do you think the Israelites felt when they left Egypt?*

DAY 42

THE RED SEA

Exodus 14:1-22

WHEN the children of Israel came out of Egypt, it was their aim to go at once to the land of Canaan, from which their fathers had come. The shortest road there followed the shore of the Great Sea and entered Canaan on the southwest. But the Philistines, a strong and warlike people, lived there, and the Israelites, after ages of slavery, were not fit to carry on war. The other way was by the southeast, through the desert of Mount Sinai, where Moses knew the land from being a shepherd there for years.

So the Israelites, led by the pillar of cloud and fire, turned to the southeast, directly toward the Red Sea, which rolled between them and the desert. In a very few days, they came to the shore of the sea, with the water before them and high mountains on each side.

As soon as the Israelites had left their homes and were on the march, Pharaoh was sorry he had let them go. Who would do all the work they had done for him? Word came to Pharaoh that the Israelites were lost in the mountains and trapped by the sea in front of them. Pharaoh called out his army, his chariots, and his horsemen, and followed the Israelites, intending either to kill them or to bring them back. Very soon the army of Egypt was close behind the host of Israel, and the hearts of the people were filled with fear. They cried to Moses, saying, "Why did you bring us out into this terrible place, shut in by the mountains and the sea, and with our enemies close behind us? It would be better to serve the Egyptians than to die here in the wilderness!"

"Fear not," answered Moses. "Stand still, and see how God will save you. As for the Egyptians, you will see them no more. The Lord will fight for you, and you will stand still and see your enemies slain." That night the pillar of fire in front of the Israelites went behind them and stood between the camp of the Egyptians and the camp of the Israelites. To Israel, it was bright and dazzling with the glory of the Lord, but to the Egyptians, it was dark and terrible, and they dared not enter it.

All that night, a mighty east wind blew, so the water was blown away. When the morning came, there was a ridge of dry land between water on one side and water on the other, making a road across the sea to the land beyond. On each side of the road, the water lay in great lakes, as if to keep their enemies away from them.

Then Moses told the people to go forward, and the pillar of cloud again went before them, and the people followed, a great army. They walked across the Red Sea as if on dry land, and passed safely over into the wilderness on the other side. So God brought his people out of Egypt, into a land they had never seen.

Discussion Questions: *1. Where were the Israelites going? 2. How did they know where to go? 3. Why did Pharaoh want the Israelites to come back? 4. How did God protect the Israelites from the Egyptians?*

DAY 43

PHARAOH'S ARMY

Exodus 14:23-15:27

WHEN the Egyptians saw them marching into the sea, they followed, with their chariots and horses. But the sand was no longer hard. It had become soft, and their chariot wheels were fastened in it, and many of them broke off of the chariots. The horses became mired, and fell down, so that the army was in confusion, and all were frightened. The soldiers cried out, "Let us fly from the face of the Israelites! The Lord is fighting for them, and against us!"

By this time, all the Israelites had passed through the Red Sea and were standing on the high ground beyond it, looking at their enemies slowly struggling through the sand, all in one heaped-up mass of men, horses, and chariots. Then Moses lifted up his hand, and at once a great tide of water swept up from the sea on the south. The road over which the Israelites had walked in safety was covered with water, and Pharaoh's army, with all his chariots, horses, and riders were drowned in the sea as the Israelites watched.

THE WATERS RETURNED AND COVERED PHARAOH'S ARMY—Exodus 14:28

Moses wrote a great song about this victory God had given them. It began like this:

I will sing unto the Lord, for he hath triumphed gloriously,
The horse and his rider hath he thrown into the sea,
The Lord is my strength and song,
And he is become my salvation.

MIRIAM LED THE WOMEN IN SINGING THE SONG OF MOSES—EXODUS 15:20

The people of Israel were no longer in a level land, with fields of grain, abundance of food, and streams of water. They were in the great desert, with a rocky path under them and mountains of rock rising all around, with only a few springs of water, and these were far apart. Such a lot of men, women, and children, with their flocks, would need much water, and they found very little.

They saw in the distance some springs of water, and ran to drink of it, for they were very thirsty. But when they tasted, they found it bitter, so they could not drink it. Then the people cried to Moses, and Moses cried to the Lord. The Lord showed Moses a tree and told him to cut it down and throw it into the water. Moses did so, and the water became fresh, pure, and good, so the people could drink it. This place they named Marah, a word which means "bitterness," because of the water they found there.

Discussion Questions: *1. What happened when the Egyptians tried to follow the Israelites? 2. Who made this happen? 3. How else did God provide for his people?*

DAY 44

MANNA FROM HEAVEN

Exodus 16:1-5

AFTER passing Marah, they came to another pleasant place, where they saw twelve springs of fresh water and a grove of seventy palm trees around them. And there they rested under the cool shade.

But soon they were in a hot desert of sand that lies between the waters of Elim and Mount Sinai, and again they were in great trouble, for there was no food for such a large number of people.

Then Moses called to God, and the Lord said, "I will rain bread from heaven upon you, and you shall go out and gather it every day."

The next morning, when the people looked out of their tents, they saw little white flakes all around the camp on the sand. It looked like snow or frost. They had never seen anything like it before, and they said, just as anybody would say, "What is it?" In the language of the Israelites, "What is it?" is the word *Manhu*. So the people said to one another, "Manhu? Manhu?" And this gave a name to what they saw — *manna*.

Moses said to them, "This is the bread the Lord has given you to eat. Go out and gather it, as much as you need. But take only as much as you need for today, for it will not keep. God will give you more tomorrow."

So the people went out and gathered the manna. They cooked it in various ways, baking it and boiling it, and the taste was like wafers flavored with honey. Some took more than they needed, not trusting God's word that there would be more on the next day, but the leftovers spoiled and smelled badly. This was to teach the people that they should trust God for their daily bread every day.

The manna left on the ground did not spoil, though. When the sun came up, it melted away, just like frost or snow flakes. Before the sixth day of the week came, Moses said to the people, "Tomorrow, on the sixth day of the week, take twice as much manna as usual. The next day is the Lord's Sabbath, the day of rest, and the manna will not come on that day."

So the next morning, all the people went out as before to gather the manna. On that day, they found the manna that was not used did not spoil, but kept fresh until the next morning.

On the Sabbath, some of the people who had failed to hear Moses and had not gathered the manna in advance for the Sabbath, went out, but they could find none. So that day, these people had nothing to eat, and all Israel learned the lesson (which we also should remember) that one day in each week belongs to God and is to be kept holy to the Lord.

All the time the Israelites lived in the wilderness — which was forty years — they ate the manna God gave them day by day. Not until they entered the land of Canaan did the manna cease to fall.

Do you remember who it was, long after this, that said "I am the bread of life. He that cometh to me shall never hunger, and he that believeth on me, shall never thirst" (*see* John 6:35).

Discussion Questions: *1. What problem did the Israelites have in the desert? 2. What did Moses do about it? 3. How did God answer him? 4. Why did they have to collect manna every day? 5. What lessons did God teach his people?*

DAY 45

God Helps Win a Battle

Exodus 17:1-16

WHILE the Israelites were journeying through the desert, they had great problems finding water. Between the wells of Elim and Mount Sinai, they found no streams or springs. Their sheep and men suffered from thirst; their little children cried for water. The people came to Moses in great anger, saying "Give us water, or we shall die. Why have you brought us up from Egypt to kill us here in the desert?"

So Moses called on God, and said, "Lord, what shall I do to this people? They are almost ready to stone me in their anger. How can I give them water?"

God told Moses what to do, and he did it. He brought the people together before a great rock, and hit the rock with his rod. Out of the rock came forth a stream of water, which ran like a little river through the camp and gave them plenty of water for themselves and their flocks.

While they were in camp around this rock at Rephidim, the wild people who had their homes in the desert — the Amalekites — made sudden war on the Israelites. They came down on them from the mountains while they were weary with marching, and killed some of the Israelites. Moses called out his people who were fit for war and made a young man named Joshua their leader, and they fought a battle with the Amalekites.

While they were fighting, Moses stood on a rock where everyone could see

WATER CAME FORTH FROM THE ROCK
EXODUS 17:1-7

him and asked God to help his people, his hands stretched out toward heaven. While Moses' hands were reaching upward, the Israelites were strong, and drove back the enemy. But when Moses' arms fell down, then the enemy drove back the men of Israel.

So Aaron, Moses' brother, and Hur (who is thought to have been Moses' brother-in-law, the husband of his sister Miriam), stood beside Moses and held up his hands until the Israelites won the victory and overcame the men of Amalek.

Discussion Questions: *1. Why did the people become angry with Moses? 2. Do you think Moses felt afraid? How do you know? 3. How did God solve Moses' problem? 4. Who was Joshua? 5. What did Moses do during the battle?*

DAY 46

THE TEN COMMANDMENTS

Exodus 19:1-24:18

IN the third month after the Israelites left Egypt, they came to a great mountain that rose straight up from the plain. This was Mount Sinai;

and it was one of a group of mountains called Horeb, where Moses earlier saw the burning bush and heard God's voice.

The Israelites made their camp in front of Mount Sinai and stayed there for many days. And God said to Moses, "Let none of the people go up on the mount or come near to touch it. If even one of your cattle or sheep touch the mountain, it must be killed. This is a holy place, where God will show his glory."

A few days after this, the people heard the sound of many trumpets coming from the top of the mountain. They looked and saw that the mountain was covered with clouds, smoke, and lightning, while thunder rolled and crashed. The mountain shook and trembled, as though an earthquake were tearing it to pieces.

The people were filled with fear. They came out of their tents, ran away from the foot of the mountain, and stood far off, trembling. Then God spoke with a voice of thunder, and said, "I am the Lord, your God, who brought you out of the land of Egypt, out of the house of bondage."

And then God spoke the words of the Ten Commandments, which you have heard many times.

All the people who heard these words, and saw the mountain smoking and the lightning flashing, were frightened. They said to Moses, "Don't let God speak to us anymore. The sound of his voice will kill us. Let God speak to you, Moses, and you can tell us God's words."

"Fear not," said Moses. "God has come to speak with you so you will fear him, and do his will."

And Moses drew near the mountain where the clouds and darkness and lightning were. Then God called Moses up to the top of the mountain, so Moses went up with his helper, Joshua. Joshua stayed on the side of the mountain, but Moses went right up to the top, into the clouds.

Moses stayed on the mountain with God for forty days, talking with God and listening to the words God spoke to him — the laws for the people of Israel to obey. Then God gave Moses two flat tablets of stone, on which God had written, with his own hand, the Ten Commandments.

Discussion Questions: *1. Why couldn't the people touch the mountain? 2. Why were the people afraid? 3. Did God still love his people, even though they were afraid? 4. What did God give Moses?*

DAY 47

The Golden Calf

Exodus 32:1-20

WHILE Moses was on the mountain alone with God for forty days, a strange and wicked thing happened in the camp on the plain. At first the people were alarmed when they saw the mountain smoking and heard the thunder. But soon they grew used to it, and when day after day passed and Moses did not come down, they said to Aaron, "Make us a god that we may worship and have to lead us. As for Moses, who brought us out of Egypt, we do not know what has become of him."

Aaron was not a strong man, like Moses was. When his brother Moses was not by his side, Aaron was weak and ready to yield to the wishes of the people. Aaron said, "If you must have a god to look at, then break off the gold earrings in your ears and in the ears of your wives and children, and bring them to me."

The people brought their gold to Aaron, and Aaron melted the gold rings into one mass, and shaped it with a tool into the form of a calf, which he brought out and stood up before the people.

Then they all cried out, "This is your god, O Israel, that brought you out of the land of Egypt." And Aaron built an altar before the image, and he said to all the people, "Tomorrow shall be a feast to the Lord."

Perhaps Aaron thought that if the people had an image they could see, they might still worship the Lord God. But in this, he was greatly mistaken. The people came to the feast, offered sacrifices, and then began to dance around the altar and do wicked deeds together, as they had seen the people of Egypt doing before their idols. And all this time, the mountain was smoking and flashing with fire, almost over their heads!

And the Lord, up on the mountain, spoke to Moses, and said, "Hasten, and get down to the camp, for your people have been very wicked. They have made an idol, and they are worshiping it now. I am angry with them, and am ready to destroy them all."

Moses pleaded with the Lord for Israel, and God did not destroy the people; but he sent Moses down to them, holding in his hands the two stone tables on which God had written the Ten Commandments. As he went down the mountain, Joshua joined him, and said to him, "I can hear the noise of war in the camp. It's not the sound of men shouting for victory, nor is it the cry of those who are beaten in battle. It is singing I hear."

As they stood where they could look down on the camp, there stood the golden calf, and around it were the people, making offerings, feasting, dancing, and singing. Moses was so angry when he saw all the wickedness and shame of his people, that he threw down the two tables and broke them in pieces on the rocks. What was the use of keeping the tables of stone when the people were breaking the laws written on them?

MOSES SAW THE GOLDEN CALF AND THE DANCING - EXODUS 32:19

Moses came straight into the midst of the throng, and suddenly all the dancing and merrymaking stopped. He tore down the golden calf, broke it in pieces, burned it in the fire, ground it to powder, and threw it into the water. Then he made the people drink the dirty water. He meant to teach the people that they would suffer punishment for their wicked deeds.

Discussion Questions: *1. Were the people faithful to God when Moses was gone? What did they do? 2. What did Moses do when he saw what they had done? 3. What lesson did he want to teach them?*

DAY 48

THE PEOPLE ARE PUNISHED

Exodus 32:21-34:35

FTER he made the people drink the water with the ground-up statue in it, Moses turned to his brother, Aaron. "What led you to an act like this?" he said. "Why did you let the people persuade you to make them an image for worship?"

Aaron said, "Don't be angry with me. You know how the hearts of this people are set to do evil. They came to me and said, 'make us a god,' and I said to them, 'give me whatever gold you have.' So they gave it to me, and I threw the gold into the fire, and this calf came out!"

Moses stood at the entrance to the camp and called out, "Whoever is on the Lord's side, come and stand by me!" One whole tribe of the twelve tribes of Israel — the tribe of Levi, all descended from one of Jacob's sons — came and stood beside Moses. And Moses said to them, "Draw your swords, and go through the camp, and kill everyone you find bowing down to the idol. Spare no one. Slay your friends and your neighbors, if they are worshiping the image." On that day, 3,000 worshipers of the idol were slain by the sons of Levi.

Then Moses said to the people, "You have sinned a great sin. But I will go to the Lord, and I will make an offering to him, and will ask him to forgive your sin."

Moses went before the Lord, prayed for the people, and said, "Oh Lord, these people have sinned a great sin. But please, forgive their sin, if you are willing. If you will not forgive their sin, then let me suffer with them, for they are my people."

The Lord forgave the sin of the people and took them once again for his

MOSES SPOKE TO THE PEOPLE ABOUT GOD'S COMMANDMENTS - EXODUS 34:32

own, and promised to go with them, and to lead them into the land he had promised to their fathers.

And God said to Moses, "Cut out two tables of stone, like those I gave you, that you broke. Bring them up to me on the mountain, and I will write the words of the law again."

So Moses went up a second time onto the mountain, and there God talked with him again. Moses stayed forty days on this second meeting with God, as he had stayed forty days before. And all this time, while God was talking with Moses, the people waited in the camp, but this time, they didn't set up any idols for worship.

Once more Moses came down the mountain, bringing the two stone tables on which God had written the words of his law, the Ten Commandments. Moses had been so close to God's glory, and had been so long in God's light, that when he came into the camp, his face was shining (though he didn't know it). The people could not look on Moses' face, it was so dazzling. When he talked with the people, he had to wear a veil over his face. When Moses went to talk with God, he took off the veil, but while he spoke to the people, he kept his face covered, for it shined like the sun and was too bright for them to look at.

———————

Discussion Questions: *1. Who did Aaron blame? 2. What did Moses do to the people? Why did he do it? 3. What did Moses say to God? How was his response different from Aaron's? Who do you think pleased God more?*

DAY 49

———

The Tabernacle (Part 1)

Exodus 35-40

GOD was very good to the Israelites, after they had forsaken him, to take them again as his own people, and he gave them a plan that would allow them to have something they could see, to remind them of their God.

At the same time, his plan would not lead them to worship an image, but would teach them a higher truth — that the true God cannot be seen by the eyes of men.

The plan was this: To have in the middle of the camp a house called The House of God, which the people could see, and to which they could come for worship. Every time an Israelite looked at this house, he might say to himself, and teach his children, "That is the house where God lives among his people," even though no image stood in the house.

Since the Israelites were living in tents and often moved from place to place, this House of God would need to be something like a tent, so it could be taken down and moved as often as the camp was changed. This tent was called a Tabernacle. The Tabernacle was the tent where God lived among his people and where the people could meet God.

We know God is a Spirit and has no body like ours, and that he is everywhere. Yet it was right to say God lived in the Tabernacle of the Israelites, because God showed his presence there in a special way, by putting a pillar of cloud over it all day and a pillar of fire all night. The Israelites believed that in one room of this Tabernacle, the glory and brightness of God's presence could be seen.

This Tabernacle stood exactly in the middle of the camp in the wilderness. In front of it and a little distance from it, stood the tent where Moses lived.

Around the Tabernacle there was what we might call an open square, though it was not exactly square, for it was about 150 feet long by 75 feet wide.

Around it was a curtain of fine linen, in bright colors, hanging on posts of brass. The posts were held in place by cords fastened to the ground with tent pins or spikes. This open square was called the Court of the Tabernacle. The curtain around it was between seven and eight feet high, a little higher than a man's head. In the middle, it could be opened for the priests to enter into the court, but no one except the priests and their helpers was ever allowed to enter it.

Inside this court, near the entrance, stood the great altar. Since a stone or earth altar could not be carried from place to place, God told the Israelites to make an altar out of wood and brass (or copper). It was like a box without a bottom or top, made of thin boards so it would not be too heavy, and then covered on the inside and outside with plates of brass or copper, so it would not catch fire and burn. Inside, a few inches below the top, was a metal grating on which the fire was built. The ashes would fall through the grating to the ground inside.

This altar had four rings on the corners, through which long poles were placed, so the priests could carry it on their shoulders when the camp was moved. The altar was a little less than five feet high and a little more than seven feet wide on each side. This was the great altar, sometimes called The Altar of Burnt-Offering, because a sacrifice was burned on it every morning and evening. Near the altar in the court of the Tabernacle stood the Laver. This was a large tank, or basin, holding water that was used in washing the offerings.

Discussion Questions: *1. Why did God want the Israelites to have a place to worship? 2. What did they call this place of worship? 3. How did God show he was there? 4. What did the tabernacle look like?*

DAY 50

THE TABERNACLE (PART 2)

Exodus 35-40

THE Tabernacle stood in the court. It was a large tent, like the tents in which the people lived, but bigger. Its walls, however, were not made from skins or woven cloth, as most tents, but of boards standing upright on silver bases and fastened together. The boards were covered with gold. The roof of the Tabernacle was made of four curtains, one above another. The inner curtain was beautifully decorated, and the outer curtain was made of rams' skins to keep out the rain. The board walls of the Tabernacle were on the two sides and the rear end; the front was open, except when a curtain was hung over it. The Tabernacle, half-tent and half-house, was about 45 feet long, 15 feet wide, and 15 feet high. Its only floor was the sand of the desert.

This Tabernacle was divided into two rooms by a curtain that hung down from the roof. The larger room — the one of the eastern end — was twice as large as the other room. It was 30 feet long, 15 feet wide, and 15 feet high, and was called the Holy Place. In the Holy Place were three things: a gold table with twelve loaves of bread, one for each of the twelve tribes; the Golden Lampstand, with seven branches, each holding a light. At the end of the Holy Place, close to the curtain, was the Golden Altar of Incense: a small altar on which fragrant gum was burned, and from which a silvery cloud floated up. The fire on this altar was always lighted from the great altar of brass that was standing outside the Tabernacle in the court. Everything in this room was made of gold or covered with gold, even the walls.

The inner room of the Tabernacle was called the Holy of Holies. It was so sacred that no one except the high-priest ever entered it, and he did only on one day a year. It was 15 feet wide, 15 feet long, and 15 feet high. All it held was a box made of wood and covered with plates of gold on both the outside and the inside. Its cover was solid gold, decorated with two strange figures called cherubim, also made of gold. This chest was called the Ark of the Covenant, and in it were the two stone tables on which God wrote the Ten Commandments. It was in this room, the Holy of Holies, that God was supposed to dwell and show his glory. But there was no image in it, to tempt the Israelites to the worship of idols.

The High Priest, Holy Ark and Table for Bread - EXODUS 39-40

Whenever the camp in the desert was to be changed, the priests first carefully covered all the furniture in the Tabernacle, then passed rods through the rings on the corners of all these articles. They took down the Tabernacle and tied its gold-covered boards, great curtains, posts, and pillars, in packages to be carried.

Then the men of the tribe of Levi, who were the helpers of the priests, took up their burdens and carried them out in front of the camp. The twelve tribes were arranged in marching order behind them. The Ark of the Covenant, unseen under its wrappings, led the way, with the pillar of cloud over it. And thus the children of Israel removed their camp from place to place for forty years in the wilderness.

When they set up camp after each journey, the Tabernacle was first set up, with the court around it and the altar in front of it. Then the tribes placed their tents in order around it, three tribes to each of its four sides.

And whenever an Israelite saw the altar with the smoke rising from it and the Tabernacle with the silver-white cloud above it, he said to himself, "Our God, the Lord of all the earth, lives in that tent. I need no image made by men's hands to remind me of God."

Discussion Questions: *1. Why do you think God had a bigger tent than the*

85

people? 2. What was the ark of the covenant? What was inside it? 3. Why wasn't there an idol in the Holy of Holies? 4. How did the ark of the covenant move?

DAY 51

How God Was Worshiped
in the Tabernacle

Leviticus 1:1-13; 8:1-13
Exodus 27:20, 21

EVERY morning at sunrise, the priests came to the great altar that was before the Tabernacle, raked the fire, and placed fresh wood on it, so it would burn brightly. This fire was never allowed to go out. God had kindled it himself, so the priests watched it closely and kept wood nearby, so it always burned.

Even while the altar was being carried from one place to another, the embers and live coals of the fire were kept in a covered pan and moved without being allowed to die out. Then the embers of the old fire were used to start the new fire on the altar.

From this altar outside the Tabernacle, every morning and afternoon a priest took a shovel full of burning coals and placed them in a bowl hanging on chains, so the fire could be carried by hand.

On these burning coals the priest placed some fragrant gum called incense, which made a bright, silvery cloud and sent forth a strong, pleasant odor. This the priest carried into the Holy Place, to teach the Israelites that, like the cloud of incense, their prayers should go up to God.

About nine o'clock in the morning, the priest brought a young ox or lamb, killed it, and caught its blood in a basin. Then he laid the offering on the burning wood. This was the offering, or sacrifice, for all the people of Israel, given twice a day. It meant that as the lamb or the ox gave up his life, so all the people were to give themselves to God — to be his, and only his. As they gave themselves to God, God would forgive and take away their sins.

There was another meaning in all this service. It pointed to the time when, just as the lamb died as an offering for the people, Jesus, the Son of God, would give his life on the cross, the Lamb of God, dying to take away the sins of the world. But this meaning, of course, the Israelites did not understand, because they lived long before Christ's time.

Sometimes a man came to the priest with a lamb or an ox as a personal offering. It had to be a perfect animal, without any defects, for God only accepts man's best. The man who wished to worship God led his lamb to the entrance of the court and laid his hands on its head, as if to say, "This animal stands in my place. When I give it to God, I give myself." Then the priest killed it and laid it on the burning wood on the altar, while the man stood at the entrance of the court of the Tabernacle and watched it burn away, offering his thanks to God and his prayer for the forgiveness of his sins.

Discussion Questions: *1. Who started the fire in the altar? 2. What did the incense stand for? 3. How did the priests use the fire? 4. What did the sacrifice stand for?*

DAY 52

THE PRIESTS

Exodus 27:20, 21

EVERY day the priest went into the Holy Place and filled the seven lamps on the lampstand with fresh oil. These lamps were never allowed to go out; some of them always had to be kept burning. While the lamps on one side were put out to be refilled, those on the other side were kept burning, so the lamps in the house of God never went out. Doesn't this make you think of One who later said, "I am the light of the world" (*see* John 8:12).

On the gold-covered table in the Holy Place always stood twelve loaves of unleavened bread — bread made without yeast. One loaf stood for each tribe of Israel. Every Sabbath morning, the priests came in with twelve fresh loaves, which they sprinkled with incense and laid on the table in place of the stale loaves. Then, standing around the table, they ate the twelve old loaves. Thus the bread on the table was kept fresh at all times.

God chose Aaron and his sons to be the priests for all of Israel. Their children, and the descendants who came after them, were to be priests as long as the worship of the Tabernacle (and the Temple that followed it) was continued. Aaron, as the high-priest, wore a splendid robe. A breastplate of precious stones was over his chest, and a peculiar hat, called a mitre, was on his head. It may seem strange to us, but when Aaron and his sons were in the Tabernacle, they wore no shoes or stockings, but stood barefooted. This was because it was a holy place, and as we have seen before, in those lands people take off their shoes when they enter places sacred to God and his worship.

AARON AND HIS SONS WERE CHOSEN AS PRIESTS - EXODUS 27:21

Aaron and his sons (Moses, too) belonged to the tribe of Levi, the one tribe that stayed faithful to God when the other tribes bowed down to the golden calf. This tribe was chosen to help the priests in the services of the Tabernacle, though only Aaron and his sons could enter the Holy Place, and only the high-priest could go into the Holy of Holies, where the Ark of the Covenant was.

Discussion Questions: *1. What did the lamps stand for? 2. What did the priests do with the bread? 3. Who were the priests of Israel? 4. Why did they go into the Tabernacle barefoot?*

DAY 53

AARON'S TWO SONS ARE PUNISHED

Leviticus 10:1-11

SOON after the Tabernacle was set up in the middle of the camp of Israel and the priests began the daily service of worship, a sad event took place that gave great sorrow to Aaron the priest, his family, and all the people. The two older sons of Aaron, whose names were Nadab and Abihu, were in the Holy Place one day. It was a part of their work to take some burning coals from the great altar in front of the Tabernacle and light the fire in the small golden altar of incense, that stood inside the Holy Place.

These young men had been drinking wine, and their heads were not clear. They didn't think what they were doing, and instead of taking the fire from the altar, they took some other fire and went into the Holy Place to burn the incense on the golden altar. God was angry with these young men for coming into his holy house drunk and for doing what he had forbidden them to do, for no fire except that from the great altar was allowed in the Holy Place.

While they were standing by the golden altar, fire came out from it, and they both fell down dead in the Holy Place. When Moses heard of it, he said, "This is the sign that God's house is holy, and that God's worship is holy. And God will make people fear him, because he is holy." Moses would not allow Aaron, the father of these two men, to touch their dead bodies. He said, "You have on the robes of the high-priest, and you are leading the service of worship. God's work must go on, and must not stop for your trouble, great as it is."

Then Aaron stood by the altar and offered the sacrifice, though his heart was breaking. And the cousins of Aaron went into the Holy Place and carried out the dead bodies of the two young men, dressed in their priests' robes. They buried these men outside the camp, in the desert.

And Moses said, "After this, let no priest drink wine or strong drink before he enters the Tabernacle. Be sober when you are leading the worship of the people, so you will know the difference between things that are holy and those that are common, and so you may teach the people all the laws the Lord has given them."

The rule that Moses gave to the priests is a good rule for everyone to keep, not only when worshiping God, but at all times.

Besides the two sons of Aaron who died, there were two other sons, named Eleazar and Ithamar. These young men took their older brothers' places in the services of the Tabernacle, and they were very careful to do exactly as the Lord had told them.

Discussion Questions: *1. Why did God become angry with Nadab and Abihu? 2. What did God do? 3. What lesson was God trying to teach the priests?*

DAY 54

The Scapegoat

Leviticus 16:1-34

YOU have read that only the high-priest could enter the inner room of the Tabernacle, called the Holy of Holies, and even the high-priest could go into this room only on one day of the year. This day was called the Great Day of Atonement.

The service on that day was meant to show the people that all are sinners and everyone must ask God to take their sins away. God teaches us these things in the Bible, but in those times there was no Bible, and very few could have read a written book, so God taught the people then by acts they could see.

As a beginning of the service on the day of atonement, everybody was required to fast from sunset on the day before until three o'clock that afternoon, the hour the offering was placed on the altar. No person could eat anything in all that time. Even children (except tiny babies) were not allowed to have any food. They were to show sorrow for their sins, and were to appear before God seeking mercy.

Early in the morning of that day, the high-priest offered what was called a sin offering for himself and his family. This was a young ox, burned on the altar. He took some of the blood of this ox, carried it through the Holy Place, lifted the veil, entered the Holy of Holies, and sprinkled the blood on the golden lid of the ark of the covenant. This was to show the priest himself was a sinner seeking mercy and forgiveness from God. The priest must have his own sins forgiven, before asking forgiveness for others.

Then the priest came back to the great altar before the Tabernacle, where two goats were brought to him.

On the forehead of one goat was written, "For the Lord," and on the other, words that meant, "To be sent away." These two goats were looked on as bearing the sins of the people. One was killed and burned on the altar. The priest, with some of the blood of the slain goat, again entered the Holy of Holies and sprinkled the blood on the ark of the covenant, thus asking God to receive the offering and forgive the sins of the people.

Then the high-priest came out of the Tabernacle again and laid his hands on the head of the living goat, the one whose forehead was marked "To be sent away," as if to place on him the sin of all the people. This goat, which was called the Scapegoat, was led away into the wilderness, so far away that he

THE SCAPEGOAT SENT OUT INTO THE WILDERNESS - LEVITICUS 16:21

would never find his way back to the camp, and was set free there. This was to show the sins of the people were taken away, never to come back to them.

When the service was over, the people believed their sins were forgiven and forgotten by the Lord. Then the regular afternoon offering was given on the altar, and after that, the people could go home happy and end their long fast with all the food they wanted.

God ordered all this to make the people feel that sin is terrible. It separates from God; it brings death; it must be taken away by blood. Long before Christ came to take away our sins by his death, God showed men the way of forgiveness and peace.

Discussion Questions: *1. What did the Great Day of Atonement show the Israelites? 2. Why didn't the people eat on that day? 3. What was a scapegoat? 4. What did it show the people? 5. How did the people feel after the service?*

DAY 55

THE SPIES

Numbers 13:1-33

THE Israelites stayed in their camp by Mount Sinai for almost a year, while they built the Tabernacle and learned God's laws from Moses. At last the cloud over the Tabernacle rose up, and the people knew this was the sign for them to move. They took down the Tabernacle and their own tents and journeyed northward toward the land of Canaan for many days, led by the pillar of cloud by day and the pillar of fire by night.

At last they came to a place just on the border between the desert and Canaan, called Kadesh. Here they stopped to rest, for there were many springs of water and some grass for their cattle. While they were waiting at Kadesh, expecting to soon march into the land that was to be their home, God told Moses to send out some men to walk through the land, look at it, and then come back and tell what they found: what kind of land it was, what fruits and crops grew in it, and what people were living in it. They needed wise, bold men for this, for it was dangerous work.

So Moses chose some men of high rank — one ruler from each tribe, twelve men in all. One of these was Joshua, Moses' helper, and another was Caleb, who belonged to the tribe of Judah. These twelve men went out and walked over the mountains of Canaan, looking at the cities and fields. Just before they came back to the camp, they cut down a cluster of ripe grapes that was so large two men had to carry it between them, hanging from a stick. These twelve men were called "spies," because they went to spy out the land.

After forty days, they came back to the camp, and this is what they said: "We walked all over the land, and found it a rich land. There is grass for all our flocks, and fields where we can raise grain, and trees bearing fruits, and streams running down the sides of the hills. But we found that the people who live there are very strong men of war. They have cities with walls that reach almost up to the sky. Some of the men are giants, so tall we felt like grasshoppers beside them."

Caleb said, "All this is true, yet we need not be afraid to go up and take the land. It is a good land, well worth fighting for. God is on our side, and he will help us overcome these people."

But all the other spies, except Joshua, said, "No. There is no use in trying to make war on such strong people. We can never take those walled cities, and we dare not fight those tall giants."

The people, who had journeyed all the way through the wilderness to find this land, were so frightened by the words of the ten spies that now, on the very border of Canaan, they dared not enter it. They forgot that God had led them out of Egypt, that he had helped them in the desert, that he had given them water out of the rock and bread from the sky and his law from the mountain.

_____

Discussion Questions: *1. How did the people know to move? 2. Where did they go? 3. When Moses sent men into Canaan, what did they do? 4. When they came back, what did most of them say? 5. What did Joshua and Caleb say?*

DAY 56

Back to the Desert

Numbers 14:1-45

ALL that night, after the spies brought back their report, the people were so filled with fear that they could not sleep. They cried out against Moses, blaming him for bringing them out of Egypt. They forgot all their troubles in Egypt, their toil and their slavery, and they resolved to go back to that land. They said, "Let us choose a ruler in place of Moses, who has brought us into all these evils, and let us turn back to the land of Egypt!"

But Caleb and Joshua said, "Why should we fear? The land of Canaan is a good land; it is rich with milk and honey. If God is our friend and is with us, we can easily conquer the people who live there. Above all, let's not rebel against the Lord or disobey him and make him our enemy."

But the people were so angry with Caleb and Joshua that they were ready to stone them and kill them. Then suddenly the people saw a strange sight. The glory of the Lord, which stayed in the Holy of Holies (the inner room of the Tabernacle), now flashed out and shone from the door of the Tabernacle into the faces of the people.

Out of this glory, the Lord spoke to Moses, and said, "How long will this people disobey me and despise me? They shall not go into the good land I have promised them. Not one of them shall enter in, except Caleb and Joshua, who have been faithful to me. All of the people who are twenty years old and over shall die in the desert. Their little children shall grow up in the wilderness, and when they become men, they shall enter in and own the land I promised to their fathers. You people are not worthy of the land I have been keeping for you. Now turn back into the desert, and stay there until you die. After you are dead, Joshua shall lead your children into the land of Canaan. And because Caleb was true to me and followed my will fully, Caleb shall live to go into the land, and shall have his choice of a home there. Tomorrow, turn back into the desert by the way of the Red Sea."

God told Moses that for every day the spies had spent in Canaan, looking at the land, the people would spend a year in the wilderness, so they would live in the desert forty years, instead of going at once into the promised land.

When Moses told all God's words to the people, they felt worse than before. They changed their minds as suddenly as they had made up their minds. "No," they all said, "we will not go back to the wilderness. We will go straight into the land, and see if we are able to take it, as Joshua and Caleb have said."

"You must not go into the land," said Moses, "for you are not fit to go, and God will not go with you. You must turn back into the desert, as the Lord has commanded."

But the people would not obey. They rushed up the mountain and tried to march into the land. But they were without leaders and order, a mob of untrained men. The people in that part of the land, the Canaanites and the Amorites, attacked and killed many of them, and drove them away. Then, discouraged and beaten, they obeyed the Lord and Moses and went back into the desert.

The children of Israel stayed nearly forty years in the desert of Paran, on the south of the land of Canaan, all because they would not trust in the Lord.

It was not strange that the Israelites should act like children, eager to go back one day and forward the next. For 400 years they had been living in the hot land of Egypt, and their hard lot as slaves had made them unfit to care for themselves. They were still lazy and weak. Moses saw they needed the free life of the wilderness and that their children, growing up as free men and trained for war, would be more able to win the land of promise than they had shown themselves to be. So they went back into the wilderness, to wait and be trained for the work of winning their land.

Discussion Questions: *1. What did the people want to do? 2. What did God do? 3. Were Joshua and Caleb right? 4. Where did God send the people? 5. Why did God do that?*

DAY 57

ANOTHER LONG JOURNEY

Numbers 20:1-29

SO the Israelites, after coming to the border of the promised land, went back into the wilderness. They stayed for nearly forty years in the wilderness of Paran, south of Canaan. Very few things happened during those years. The young men grew up to be soldiers, and one by one, the old men died, until very few of them were left.

When the forty years were almost over, the people came again to Kadesh. For some reason, they found no water there. Perhaps the wells had since dried up. The people complained to Moses, as they always complained when trouble came to them, and blamed him for bringing them into such a desert land, where there was neither fruit to eat nor water to drink, only great rocks all around.

Then the Lord said to Moses, "Take the rod, and bring the people together, and stand before the rock, and speak to the rock before them. Then the water will come out of the rock, and the people and their flocks shall drink."

Moses and Aaron brought all the people together before a great rock that stood beside the camp. Moses stood in front of the rock with the rod in his hand, but he did not do exactly what God had told him to do — speak to the rock. He spoke to the people instead, in an angry manner.

"Hear now, ye rebels," said Moses. "Shall we bring you water out of this rock?"

Moses lifted up the rod, and struck the rock. Then he struck it again, and at the second blow, the water came pouring out of the rock, just as it had come many years before, from the rock near Mount Sinai. Again, there was a plenty of water for the people and their flocks.

But God was not pleased with Moses, because Moses had shown anger and had not obeyed his command just as God had given it. God said to Moses and Aaron, "Because you did not show honor to me by doing as I commanded you, neither of you shall enter into the land I have promised the children of Israel." One act of disobedience cost Moses and Aaron the privilege of leading the people into their own land!

About this time, Miriam, the sister of Moses and Aaron, died at Kadesh. You remember that when she was a little girl, she helped save the baby Moses, her brother, from the river. She also led the women in singing the song of Moses after the crossing of the Red Sea. Soon after her death, Moses, Aaron, and Eleazar (Aaron's son) walked together up Mount Hor. On the top of the mountain, Moses took the priest's robes off Aaron and placed them on his son, Eleazar. There on the top of Mount Hor, Aaron died, and Moses and Eleazar buried him. Then they came down to the camp and Eleazar took his father's place as the priest.

While they were at Kadesh, on the south of Canaan, they again tried to enter the land. But they found that the Canaanites and Amorites who lived there were too strong for them, so they turned back to the wilderness and sought another road to Canaan. On the south of the Dead Sea, the Edomites lived. These people were descendants of Esau, Jacob's brother. Since the Israelites came from Jacob, the Edomites were closely related to them.

Moses sent to the king of Edom and said to him, "We men of Israel are your brothers. We have come out of the land of Egypt, where the people of Egypt dealt harshly with us, and now we are going to our own land, which our God has promised to us — the land of Canaan. We ask you to let us pass through your land on our way. We will do no harm to your land or your people. We will walk on the road to Canaan, not turning to the right hand or the left. And we will not rob your vineyards or even drink from your wells, unless we pay for the water we use."

But the king of Edom was afraid to have such a great crowd of people, with all their flocks and cattle, go through his land. He called out his army and attacked the Israelites. Moses was not willing to make war on a people who were so closely related to the Israelites, so instead of leading the Israelites through Edom, he went around it, making a long journey to the south, and then to the east, and then to the north again.

It was a long, hard journey through a deep valley that was very hot. For most of the journey, they were going away from Canaan, and not toward it, but it was the only way, since Moses would not let them fight the men of Edom.

_____

Discussion Questions: *1. Where did the Israelites go when they left the promised land? 2. How long did they stay there? 3. When they came back near the promised land, what did Moses do that was wrong? 4. Who wanted to fight the Israelites? Why? 5. What did Moses and his people do instead?*

DAY 58

_____

THE JOURNEY ENDS

Numbers 21

WHILE they were on this long journey, the people again found fault with Moses. They said, "Why have you brought us into this hot, sandy country? There is no water, and there is no bread — except this vile manna, which we're sick of! We wish we were all back in Egypt again!"

God was angry with the people, and he let the fierce snakes that lived in the desert crawl among them and bite them. These snakes were called fiery serpents, perhaps because of their bright color, or perhaps because of their eyes and tongues, which seemed to flash out fire. Their bite was poisonous, and many of the people died because of these snakes.

Then the people saw they had acted wickedly in speaking against Moses, for when they spoke against Moses, they were speaking against God, who was leading them. They said, "We have sinned against the Lord, and we are sorry. Now pray to the Lord for us, and ask him to take away the serpents."

So Moses prayed for the people, as he had prayed so many times before. God heard Moses' prayer, and said to him, "Make a serpent of brass, like the fiery serpents, and set it up on a pole, where the people can see it. Then everyone who is bitten may look at the serpent on the pole and live."

So Moses did as God commanded him. He made a serpent of brass, which looked like the fiery snakes, and he lifted it up on a pole, where all could see it.

Moses made a brass serpent and put it on a pole — Numbers 21:9

Then whoever was bitten by a snake looked up at the brazen snake, and the bite did him no harm.

This brazen snake was a teaching about Christ, though it was given long before Christ came. You remember the text which says, "As Moses lifted up the serpent in the wilderness, even so must the Son of man be lifted up; that whosoever believeth in him may have eternal life" (John 3:14, 15).

Northeast of the Dead Sea, above a brook called the brook Arnon, lived a people who were called the Amorites. Moses sent to their king, whose name was Sihon, and asked his permission to go through his land. But he would not allow the Israelites to pass through. He led his army against Israel, and crossed the brook Arnon, and fought against Israel at a place called Jahaz. Here the Israelites won their first great victory. In the battle they killed many of the Amorites, and with them their king, Sihon, and they took all the land as far north as the brook Jabbok. Do you remember how Jacob had once prayed by the brook Jabbok?

After this, they marched on toward the land of Canaan, coming from the east, and at last they encamped on the east bank of the river Jordan, at the foot of the mountains of Moab. Their long journey of forty years was now ended, the desert was behind them. Before them rolled the Jordan River, and beyond the Jordan they could see the hills of the land God had promised them as their own.

_____

Discussion Questions: *1. Do you think Moses got tired of the people's complaining? 2. What did God do because they complained? 3. Did Moses hold their complaining against them for long? How do you know? 4. What did God tell Moses to do to save them from the snakes? What did this stand for?*

DAY 59

_____

BALAAM

Numbers 22:1-20

WHEN the Israelites camped beside the river Jordan, a little north of the Dead Sea, they did not sit down to rest, for Moses knew that taking Canaan would be hard work. Instead, he sent out an army to the north into a region called Bashan. There they fought with King Og, who was one of the giants, killed him, and took his country. This made the Israelites masters of all the land east of the Jordan and north of the Arnon.

South of the Arnon and east of the Dead Sea lived the Moabites. This people had sprung from Lot, the nephew of Abraham. In the 500 years since Lot's time, his descendants had become the Moabites, just as Jacob's descendants were the Israelites. The Moabites were filled with alarm and fear as they saw Israel marching around their land, conquering the country, and camping on their border. The Moabites were ruled by a king whose name was Balak, and he tried to form some plan for driving the people of Israel from that region.

At that time, a man lived in the east, near the Euphrates, whose name was Balaam. This man was known far and wide as a prophet, a man who talked with God, heard God's voice, and spoke for God, as Moses did. People believed that whatever Balaam said was sure to happen, but they did not know Balaam could only say what God told him to say.

Balak, the king of the Moabites, sent men to Balaam with presents. He said to Balaam, "There is a people here who have come from Egypt, and they cover the whole land. I am afraid of them, for they have made war and beaten all the nations around. Come and curse them for me in the name of your God, for I believe that those you bless are blessed and prosper, and those you curse are cursed and fail."

The men from Moab brought this message and promised Balaam a great reward if he would go with them. Balaam answered them, "Stay here tonight, and I will ask my God what to do."

That night, God came to Balaam and said to him, "Who are these men at your house, and what do they want from you?" The Lord knew who they were and what they wanted, for God knows all things, but he wanted Balaam to tell him.

Balaam said, "They have come from Balak, the king of Moab, and they ask me to go with them and to curse a people that have come out of Egypt."

God said to Balaam, "You must not go with these men. You shall not curse this people, for this people is to be blessed."

So the next morning Balaam said to the men of Moab, "Go back to your land. The Lord will not let me go with you."

When these men brought the message back, the king thought Balaam would come for more money. So he sent other messengers, the princes of Moab, with larger gifts. They came to Balaam, and said, "Our King Balak says you must come. He will give you great honors, and all the money you want. Come and curse this people for King Balak."

Balaam said, "If Balak gave me his house full of silver and gold I still could not speak anything but what God gives me to speak. Stay here tonight, and I will ask my God what to say to you."

Now Balaam knew very well what God wished him to say, but even though he was a prophet of the Lord, he wished to be rich. He wanted to go with the men and get Balak's money, but he did not dare go against God's command. That night, God said to Balaam, "If these men ask you to go with them, you may go. But when you go to Balak's country, you shall speak only the words I give you to speak."

Discussion Questions: *1. Why was taking Canaan hard work? 2. Who was Balaam? 3. What did the king want Balaam to do? 4. Why couldn't Balaam do that?*

DAY 60

THE ANGEL AND THE DONKEY

Numbers 22:21-35

BEING allowed to go made Balaam happy, and the next day he went with the princes of Moab.

God was not pleased with Balaam, for Balaam knew very well that God had forbidden him to curse Israel, but he hoped in some way to get King Balak's money.

God sent his angel to meet Balaam on the way. In order to teach Balaam a lesson, the angel appeared first to the ass Balaam was riding. The ass could see the angel with his fiery sword standing in the way, but Balaam could not see him. The ass turned to one side, off the road, into an open field. Balaam struck the ass and drove it back onto the road, for he could not see the angel that the ass saw.

Then the angel appeared again, in a place where the road was narrow, with a stone wall on each side. And when the ass saw the angel, it turned to one side and crushed Balaam's foot against the wall. Balaam struck the ass again.

Again the angel of the Lord appeared to the ass in a place where there was no way to turn aside. The ass was frightened and fell down, while Balaam struck it again and again with his staff.

Then the Lord allowed the ass to speak, and the ass said to Balaam, "What have I done to make you strike me three times?"

Balaam was so angry that he never thought how strange it was for an animal to talk. He said, "I struck you because you will not walk as you should. I wish I had a sword in my hand, then I would kill you."

And the ass spoke again to Balaam, "Am I not your ass, the one that has always carried you? Did I ever disobey you before? Why do you treat me so cruelly?"

Then God opened Balaam's eyes and let him see the angel standing with a drawn sword in front of him. Balaam leaped off the ass and fell on his face before the angel. The angel said to Balaam, "Balaam, you know you are going the wrong way. But for the ass that saw me, I would have killed you. The road you are taking will lead you to death."

Balaam said, "I have sinned against the Lord. Let the Lord forgive me, and I will go home again."

But the angel knew that in his heart, Balaam wanted to go on to meet King Balak, so the angel said, "You may go with these men of Moab, but be sure to say only what God gives you to say."

Discussion Questions: *1. Why did God feel unhappy about what Balaam wanted to do? 2. Why do you think Balaam couldn't see the angel at first? 3. Why had God sent an angel to warn Balaam?*

DAY 61

BALAAM'S PROPHECY

Numbers 22:36-24:25

SO Balaam went on and came to the land of Moab, where King Balak said to him, "So you have come at last! Why did you wait until I sent the second time? Don't you know I will pay you all you want, if you do what I wish?"

Balaam said, "I have come to you as you asked, but I have no power to speak anything except what God gives me."

King Balak thought Balaam was only trying to get more money. He did not understand that a true prophet never says anything except what is in the will of God. He took Balaam up to the top of a mountain, to where they could look down on the camp of the Israelites.

Balaam said, "Build seven altars, and bring me seven young oxen and seven rams."

They did so, and while the offering was on the altar, God told Balaam what to say. "The king of Moab has brought me from the east, saying, 'Come, curse Jacob for me. Come, speak against Israel.' How shall I curse those whom God has not cursed? How shall I speak against those who are God's own people? From the mountaintop I see this people dwelling alone, not like other nations. Who can count the men of Israel, like the dust of the earth? Let me die the death of the righteous, and let my last end be like his!"

King Balak was surprised by Balaam's words. He said, "What have you done? I brought you to curse my enemies, and instead you have blessed them!"

Balaam answered. "Did I not tell you that I could only say the words God put into my mouth?"

King Balak decided to try again. He brought him to another place where they could look down on the Israelites, and again offered sacrifices. Again God gave a message to Balaam, who said, "Rise up, King Balak, and hear. God is not a man who lies or changes his mind. What God has said, that he will do. He has commanded me to bless this people, and they shall be blessed. The Lord God is their king, and he shall lead them, and give them victory."

Then King Balak said to Balaam, "If you cannot curse this people, do not bless them! Leave them alone!"

Balaam replied, "Did I not tell you that what God tells me to speak, I must speak?"

King Balak still was not satisfied. He brought Balaam to another place and offered more sacrifices. And again the Spirit of God came on Balaam. Looking down on the camp of Israel, he said, "How goodly are your tents, O Israel! and your tabernacles, O Jacob! God has brought him out of Egypt, and God shall give him the land of promise. He shall destroy his enemies. Israel shall be like a lion when he rises up. Blessed be everyone who blesses him, and cursed be everyone that curses him!"

Balak, the king of Moab, was very angry with Balaam the prophet. "I called you," said Balak, "to curse my enemies, and you have blessed them over and over again. Go back to your own home. I meant to give you great honor and riches, but your God has kept you from your reward!"

Balaam said to Balak, "Did I not say to your messengers, 'If Balak should give me his house full of silver and gold, I cannot go beyond God's command, to say good or evil? What God speaks, that I must speak.' Now let me tell you what this people shall do to your people in the years to come. A star shall come out of Jacob, and a scepter shall be stretched forth from Israel that shall rule over Moab. All these lands — Edom, and Mount Seir, and Moab, and Ammon — shall sometime be under the rule of Israel."

And all this came to pass, though it was 400 years afterward, when David, the king of Israel, made all those countries subject to his rule.

Balaam soon showed that he was no true servant of God. Although he could not speak a curse against the Israelites, he still longed for the money King Balak was ready to give him if he would help Balak weaken Israel. So he thought of another way to harm Israel.

Balaam told King Balak that the best plan for him and his people would be to make the Israelites their friends, to marry among them, and not to make war on them. And this the Moabites did. Many of the Israelites married the daughters of Moab and began to worship the idols of Moab.

This was worse for the Israelites than going to war. For if the people of Israel were friendly with the idol-worshiping people around them — the Moabites east of the Dead Sea, the Ammonites near the wilderness, and the Edomites on the south — they would soon forget the Lord and begin to worship idols.

There was great danger that all the people would be led into this sin, so God sent a plague on the people, and many died. Then Moses took the men who were leading Israel into sin and put them to death. After this, the Israelites made war on the Moabites and the Midianites. They beat them in a great battle, and killed many of them. Among the men of Moab, they found Balaam the prophet, and they killed him too, because he had given advice to the Moabites that brought harm to Israel.

It would have been better for Balaam to have stayed at home and not to have gone when King Balak called him. Or it would have been good for him to have gone back home when the angel met him. He might have lived in honor, but he knew God's will and tried to go against it, and he died in disgrace with the enemies of God's people.

Discussion Questions: *1. Why did God want Balaam to say only the words he gave him? 2. What did the king offer Balaam to try to change his mind? 3. What did Balaam say about Israel? 4. How did that make the king feel? What did he say to the prophet? 5. What did the prophet do that was wrong? What happened in the end?*

DAY 62

THE LAND EAST OF JORDAN

Numbers 26:1-4, 63-65; 32:1-42

WHILE the Israelites were in their camp on the plain beside the river Jordan, God told Moses to count the number of men who were old enough and strong enough to go to war. Moses had all the men over twenty counted and found there were a little more than 600,000 fighting-age men, plus the women and children.

Among them all, only three men were over sixty years of age — men who had been more than twenty years old forty years before, when the Israelites came out of Egypt. The men who had been afraid to enter the land of Canaan the first time had all died. Some of them had been slain in war; some had died in the wilderness during the forty years; some had perished by the plague; some had been bitten by the fiery serpents. Of all those who had come out of Egypt as men, the only ones still living were Moses, Joshua, and Caleb. Moses was now 120.

He had lived forty years as a prince in Egypt, forty years as a shepherd in Midian, and forty years as the leader of Israel in the wilderness. But although he was very old, God had kept Moses strong. His eyes were bright, his mind was clear, and his arms and heart were just as strong as they had been when he was a young man.

The people of Israel now owned all the land on the east of the river Jordan, from the brook Arnon up to Mount Hermon. Much of this land was good for pasture; the grass was green and rich, and there were many streams of water. There were two of the twelve tribes, and half of another tribe, who had great flocks of sheep and goats and herds of cattle. These were the tribes descended from Reuben and Gad (the sons of Jacob) and half of the tribe of Manasseh (the son of Joseph).

The men of Reuben, Gad, and half the men of Manasseh came to Moses, and said, "The land on this side of the river is good for the feeding of sheep and cattle, and we are shepherds and herdsmen. Can't we have our land on this side of the river and give all the land beyond the river to our brothers of the other tribes?"

Moses was not pleased at this. He thought these men wanted to have their land at once in order to avoid going to war, and this may have been in their minds.

So Moses said to them, "Shall your brothers of the other tribes go to the war? And shall you sit here in your own land, and not help them? That would be wicked, and would displease the Lord your God."

Then the men of the two tribes and the half-tribe came again to Moses, and said to him, "We will build sheepfolds here for our sheep, and we will choose some cities to place our wives and our children in, but we ourselves will go armed with our brothers of the other tribes, and will help them take the land on the other side of the Jordan. We will not come back to this side of the river until the war is over and our brothers have taken their land. And we will take no part of the land on the other side of the river, because our place has been given to us here. When the land is all won and divided, we will come back here to our wives and children."

Moses was satisfied with the promise they gave, and he divided the land on the east of the Jordan to these tribes. To the men of Reuben, he gave the land on the south. To the men of Gad, the land in the middle. And to the half-tribe of Manasseh, he gave the land on the north, the country called Bashan. After their wives and children and flocks had been placed safely, the men came back to the camp, ready to go with the other tribes across the river when God called them.

_____

Discussion Questions: *1. Why were some of the Israelites trying to stay across the river from the promised land? 2. What did Moses say to them? 3. What did they promise Moses?*

DAY 63

MOSES' DEATH

Deuteronomy 31:1-34:12

OSES' work was almost done. God said to him, "Gather the children of Israel together and speak your last words, for you are not to lead the people across the Jordan. You are to die in this land, as I said to you at Kadesh."

So Moses called the leaders of the twelve tribes before his tent and said to them many things that you can read in the book of the Bible called Deuteronomy.

He told them what wonderful things God had done for their fathers and for them. He gave them all the words of God's law. He told them that they must not only keep God's law themselves, but must teach it to their children, so it might never be forgotten. Then Moses sang a song of farewell and wrote down all his last words.

Then he gave a charge to Joshua, whom God had chosen to take his place as the ruler and leader of the people, though no man could take Moses' place as a prophet of God and the giver of God's law. He laid his hands on Joshua's head, and God gave Joshua some of his Spirit that had been on Moses.

Then Moses, all alone, went out of the camp, while all the people looked at him and wept. Slowly he walked up the mountainside, until they saw him no more. He climbed to the top of Mount Nebo, stood alone up there, and looked at the Land of Promise that lay spread out before him. Far in the north he could see the white crown of Mount Hermon, where there is always snow. At his feet, but far below, the river Jordan was winding its way down to the Dead Sea. Across the river, at the foot of the mountains, stood the city of Jericho, surrounded with a high wall. On the summits of the mountains beyond, he could see Hebron, where Abraham, Isaac, and Jacob were buried. He could see Jerusalem, Bethel, and the two mountains where Shechem lay hidden in the center of the land. And here and there, through the valleys, he could see in the west the gleaming water of the Great Sea.

Then Moses — all alone — lay down on the mountaintop, and died. There was no man on Mount Nebo to bury Moses, so God himself buried him, and no man knows where God laid the body of Moses, who had served him so faithfully.

After Moses, no man ever lived so near to God, and talked with God so freely, until Jesus Christ, the Son of God, came among men.

Discussion Questions: *1. Why didn't Moses go into the promised land? 2. Who took over as leader after Moses died? 3. How do you think Moses felt about not going into the promised land? 4. Why was Moses so close to God?*

DAY 64

JOB (PART 1)

Job 1:1-22

AT some time in those early days — we do not know exactly when — there lived a good man named Job. His home was in the land of Uz, which may have been on the edge of the desert east of Israel. Job was a very rich man. He had sheep, camels, oxen, and asses by the thousand. In all the east, there was no man as rich as Job.

And Job was a good man. He served the Lord God and prayed to God every day. He tried to live as God wished him to live, and was always kind and gentle. Every day, when his sons were out in the field or having a feast together, Job went out to his altar and offered an offering for each one of his sons and daughters, praying to God for them, for he said, "It may be that my sons have sinned or have turned away from God in their hearts, and I will pray God to forgive them."

Once when the angels of God stood before the Lord, Satan also came and stood among them, as though he were one of God's angels. God saw Satan, and said to him, "Satan, where have you come from?"

"I have come," answered Satan, "from going up and down the earth and looking at the people on it."

The Lord said to Satan, "Have you looked at my servant Job? And have you seen that there is not another man like him in the earth, a good and perfect man, one who fears God and does nothing evil?"

Satan said to the Lord, "Does Job fear God for nothing? Haven't you made a wall around him, and around his house, and around everything he has? You have blessed his work and made him rich. But if you stretch out your hand and take away all he has, then he will turn away from you and curse you to your face."

Then the Lord said, "Satan, all that Job has is in your power. You can do to his sons, his flocks, and his cattle, whatever you wish. Only don't lay your hand on the man himself."

Satan left the Lord, and soon trouble began to come to Job. One day, when all his sons and daughters were eating together in the oldest brother's house, a man came running to Job, and said, "The oxen were plowing, and the asses were feeding beside them, when wild men from the desert came and drove them all away. The men who were working with the oxen and caring for the asses have all been killed; I'm the only one who escaped alive!"

While this man was speaking, another man came rushing in and said, "The lightning from the clouds has fallen on all the sheep, and on the men who were tending them. I am the only one left alive!"

Before this man had ended, another came in, and he said, "The enemies from Chaldea have come in three bands and taken away all the camels. They have killed the men who were with them; I am the only one left alive!"

Then one more man came in, and he said to Job, "Your sons and your daughters were eating and drinking together in the oldest brother's house, when a sudden wind from the desert struck the house, and it fell in on them. All your sons and your daughters are dead, and I alone have lived to tell you of it."

In one day, all that Job had — his flocks, his cattle, and his sons and daughters — were all taken away. Once rich, he was suddenly made poor. Job fell down on his face before the Lord and said, "With nothing I came into the world, and with nothing I shall leave it. The Lord gave, and the Lord has taken away. Blessed be the name of the Lord." Even when all was taken from him, Job did not turn away from God or find fault with God's doings.

Discussion Questions: *1. What kind of man was Job? 2. Who wanted to harm Job? Why? 3. How do you think Job felt when he learned he had lost his family and everything he owned? 4. What did he do? How do you think it made God feel?*

DAY 65

JOB (PART 2)

Job 2:1-42:17

AGAIN the angels of God were before the Lord, and Satan, who had done all this harm to Job, was among them. The Lord said to Satan, "Have you looked at my servant Job? There is no other man in the world as good as he; a perfect man, one that fears God and does no wrong act. Do you see how he holds fast to his goodness even after I have let you do him so great harm?"

Then Satan answered the Lord, "All that a man has he will give for his life. But if you touch his bone and flesh, he will turn from you and curse you to your face."

And the Lord said to Satan, "I will give Job into your hand. Do whatever you please to him. Only spare his life."

Then Satan went out and struck Job, and caused dreadful boils to come up all over his body, from the soles of his feet to the crown of his head. And Job sat down in the ashes in great pain, but he would not speak one word against God.

His wife said to him, "What is the use of trying to serve God? You may as well curse God and die!"

But Job said to her, "You speak like a foolish woman. Shall we take good things from the Lord and not take evil things also?"

Then three friends of Job came to see him and try to comfort him in his sorrow and pain. Their names were Eliphaz, Bildad, and Zophar. They sat down with Job, wept, and spoke to him. But their words were not words of comfort. They believed all these great troubles had come on Job to punish him for some great sin, and they tried to persuade Job to tell them what evil things he had done, to make God so angry with him.

Job's Friends Tried To Comfort Him - Job 2:11

In those times, most people believed that trouble, sickness, the loss of friends, and the loss of what they owned, came to men because God was angry with them for their sins. These men thought Job must have been very wicked when they saw such things happen to him. They made long speeches to Job, urging him to confess his wickedness.

Job said he had done no wrong, that he had tried to do right. He did not know why these troubles had come, but he would not say that God had dealt unjustly in letting him suffer. Job did not understand God's ways, but he believed God was good, and he left himself in God's hands. At last, God himself spoke to Job and his friends, telling them that it is not for man to judge God, and that God will do right by every man. The Lord said to Job's friends, "You have not spoken what is right of me, as Job has. Now bring an offering to me. Job will pray for you, and for his sake, I will forgive you."

So Job prayed for his friends, and God forgave them. And because Job had been faithful to God, the Lord blessed Job once more, took away his boils, and made him well. Then the Lord gave Job more than he had ever owned in the past — twice as many sheep, oxen, camels, and asses. And God gave Job seven more sons and three daughters, and in all the land, there were no women as lovely as the daughters of Job. After his trouble, Job lived a long time, with riches, honor, and goodness, under God's care.

Discussion Questions: *1. What did God say Satan could do to Job? 2. What did Job say when this happened to him? 3. How do you think Job felt when his friends tried to comfort him? 4. Why do you think God blessed Job in the end of the story?*

DAY 66

THE SCARLET CORD

Joshua 1:1-2:24

AFTER the death of Moses, while the children of Israel were still camped on the east bank of the river Jordan, God spoke to Joshua, saying, "Now that Moses, my servant, is dead, you are to take his place and rule this people. Don't delay. Lead them across the river Jordan and conquer the land I have given to them."

Then God told Joshua how much land the Israelites were to have, if they showed themselves worthy of it. It was to reach from the great river Euphrates, far in the north, down to the border of Egypt on the south, and from the desert on the east to the Great Sea on the west. And God said to Joshua, "Be strong and of a good courage. I will be with you, as I was with Moses. Read constantly the book of the law Moses gave you, and be careful to obey it. Do this, and you will have good success."

Then Joshua gave orders to his officers. He said, "Go through the camp and tell the people to prepare food for a journey. In three days we will pass over the Jordan and go into the land the Lord has promised us."

This was very bold, for at that time of the year, the Jordan was much larger than at other times. All its banks overflowed, and it was running as a broad, deep, swift river, down to the Dead Sea, a few miles to the south. No one could possibly walk through it. Only a strong man could swim in its powerful current. And the Israelites had no boats.

Across the river, the Israelites could see the high walls of the city of Jericho, standing at the foot of the mountains. Before the rest of the land could be won, this city had to be taken, for it stood beside the road leading up to the mountain country.

Joshua chose two careful, brave, and wise men, and said to them, "Go across the river, and get into the city of Jericho. Find out all you can about it, and come back in two days."

The two men swam across the river, walked to Jericho, and went into the city. But they had been seen, and the king of Jericho sent men to take them prisoners. They came to a house on the wall of the city, where a woman named Rahab lived. She hid them.

RAHAB SHELTERED THE SPIES - JOSHUA 2:6

But the men had been seen going into her house, and the king sent his officers after them. The woman hid the men on the roof of the house and covered them with stalks of flax (which are like long reeds) so the officers could not find them. After the officers had gone away, thinking the two spies had left the city, the woman came to the two men, and said to them, "All of us in this city know that your God is mighty and terrible, and that he has given you this land. We have heard how your God dried up the Red Sea, led you through the desert, and gave you victory over your enemies. And now all the people in this city are in fear of you, for they know your God will give you this city and all this land."

"Now," said Rahab, "promise me, in the name of the Lord, that you will spare my life, the lives of my father and mother, my brothers and sisters, when you take this city."

And the men said, "We will pledge our life for yours. No harm will come to you, for you saved our lives."

This woman's house stood on the wall of the city. From one of its windows, Rahab let down a rope, on which the men could slide down to the ground. It happened that this rope was a bright scarlet color.

The two spies said to Rahab, "When our men come to take this city, hang this rope in the window. Bring your father, mother, and family into the house, and keep them there while we are taking the city. We will tell all our men not to harm the people in the house where the scarlet cord hangs from the window."

Then the two men slid down the rope, found their way to the river, swam over it again, and told their story to Joshua. They said, "Truly the Lord has given us all the land, for all the people in it fear us, and will not dare oppose us."

One fact was a great help to the Israelites in taking the land of Canaan. It was not held by one people, or ruled over by one king, who could unite all his people against the Israelites. There were many small nations living in the land, and each little tribe was ruled by its own king. So it would be easy for the Israelites to destroy them one by one, as long as they kept apart and did not band together into one army.

The Israelites were now a strong and united people, trained for war and willing to obey one leader, so all twelve tribes were ready to fight as one man.

Discussion Questions: *1. Who was to lead the Israelites over the Jordan River? 2. Was it easy to go across the river? Why or why not? 3. What did Joshua do? 4. How did the men get out of the city? 5. What did they promise the woman who helped them?*

DAY 67

THE JORDAN DRIES UP

Joshua 3:1-4:24

AFTER the two spics came back from Jericho, Joshua commanded the people to take down their tents and move to the bank of the Jordan. Then Joshua gave the word, and they marched down toward the river, which was rolling high and strong in front of them. Joshua said, "Let the priests carry the ark of the covenant in front, and let there be a space between it and the rest of the people of three thousand feet. Do not come nearer than that to the ark."

All the people stood still, wondering, while the ark was brought far out in front of the ranks of men, until it came down to the edge of the water. They could not see the ark, for it was covered, but they knew it was under its coverings on the shoulders of the priests.

Then Joshua said to the priests, "Now walk into the water."

As soon as the feet of the priests touched the water by the shore, the river above stopped flowing. Far up the river, they could see the water rising and piling up in a great heap. And below the place they were standing, the water ran on leaving a great place dry, and the stones on the river's bed uncovered.

THE PRIESTS STOOD FIRM ON DRY GROUND - JOSHUA 3:15-17

Then, at Joshua's command, the priests carried the ark down to the middle of the dry bed of the river and stood there with it on their shoulders.

Then Joshua ordered the people to march across the river. When they had all passed over the river, Joshua called for one man from each tribe and said to them, "Go down into the river and bring up twelve stones, as large as you can carry, from where the priests are standing."

They did so, and with these stones, Joshua made a stone pile on the bank and said, "Let this heap of stones stand here in memory of what has taken place today. When your children ask you, 'Why are these stones here?' you shall say to them, 'Because here the Lord God made the river dry before the ark of the covenant, so the people could cross over into the land that God had promised their fathers.' "

Then Joshua told these twelve men to take twelve more stones and heap them up in the bed of the river where the priests stood with the ark, so those stones might remind anyone who saw them of God's wonderful help to his people.

When all this had been done, and the two heaps of stone had been piled up, Joshua said to the priests, "Come up from the river, and bring the ark to the shore."

When they did, the waters began to flow down from above, until soon the river was rolling by as it had rolled before. At last, the children of Israel were safely in the land God had promised to their fathers more than 500 years before.

They set up a new camp, with the Tabernacle in the middle, the altar before it, and the tents of the tribes in order around it.

The camp was near the river, on the plain of Jordan, and was called Gilgal. And there the main camp of the Israelites remained while they carried on the war to win the land of Canaan.

Discussion Questions: 1. What went in front of the Israelite army when they crossed the river? Do you remember what was in it? 2. What happened to the river? 3. Why did they pick up stones from the riverbed?

DAY 68

THE FALL OF JERICHO

Joshua 5:10-6:27

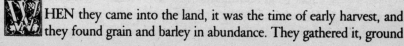 HEN they came into the land, it was the time of early harvest, and they found grain and barley in abundance. They gathered it, ground

it, and made bread of it. Some of it they roasted in the ear. On that day, the manna God had sent them from the sky through forty years ceased to fall, since it was no longer needed.

There, in full view of the new camp, stood the strong walls of Jericho. Joshua went out to look at the city, and saw an armed man coming toward him. Joshua walked boldly up to the man and said to him, "Are you on our side, or are you one of our enemies?"

The man answered, "No, I have come as captain of the Lord's army."

Then Joshua saw that he was an angel of the Lord. Bowing down before him, Joshua said, "What word has my Lord to his servant?"

The captain of the Lord's army said to Joshua, "Take off your shoes, for the ground where you are standing is holy."

Joshua did so, for the one who was speaking to him was not merely an angel, but the Lord himself, appearing as a man. And the Lord said to Joshua, "I have given you Jericho, and its king, and its mighty men of war. I will destroy the city of Jericho before you."

Then the Lord told Joshua the way the city should be taken, and Joshua went back to the camp at Gilgal and made ready to march, as God command-ed. During the next seven days, all that was done was according to the word of the Lord.

They sent out the army, as if to fight against the city. In front came the soldiers from the tribes on the east of the river. Then came a company of priests with trumpets made of rams' horns, which they blew long and loud. Then came the ark of the covenant on the shoulders of the priests. And, last of all, came the army of Israel, marching in order. No one shouted or made any noise, except for the sound of the rams'-horn trumpets. They marched around the walls of Jericho once on that day, and then marched back to the camp.

The next morning they all formed in the same order and again marched around the walls of the city. This was done for six days.

On the seventh day, they rose very early in the morning, and did not stop when they had marched around the walls once, but kept on marching round and round, until they had gone about the walls seven times. As they went by, they saw a scarlet cord at one window on the wall, and they knew this was the house of Rahab, who had saved the lives of the two spies.

When the seventh march was ended, they all stood still. Even the trumpets ceased, and there was a great silence for a moment, until the voice of Joshua rang out, "Shout, for the Lord has given you the city!"

Then a great shout went up from the host. They looked at the wall, and it was trembling, shaking, and falling! It fell down flat, except for one place — where the scarlet cord was hanging from the window. Joshua said to the two

spies, "Go and bring out Rahab and her family, and take them to a safe place."
They went into Rahab's house on the wall and brought her and her family

THE WALLS OF JERICHO FELL DOWN FLAT — SOSHUA 6:20

safely out. They cared for them and kept them safely in the camp until the war against the people of the land was ended.

While some of the soldiers were taking care of Rahab, the rest of the army was climbing over the ruined wall. The people in the city were so filled with fear when they saw the walls falling down on every side, that they did not try to defend it, but sank down helpless and were slain or taken prisoner by the Israelites.

Thus the city was taken, with all that was within it. But the Israelites were forbidden to keep any of the treasures in the city. Joshua said to them, "Nothing in this city belongs to you. It is the Lord's, and is to be destroyed as an offering to the Lord."

So they brought together all the gold, silver, precious things, and all that was in the houses. They took nothing for themselves, but kept the gold and silver and the things made of brass and iron for the Tabernacle. All the rest they burned and destroyed, leaving behind nothing but waste and desolation. And Joshua said, "Let the Lord's curse rest on any man who shall ever rebuild the city of Jericho. With the loss of his oldest born shall he lay its foundation, and with the loss of his youngest son shall he set up the gates of it."

After this, Rahab, the woman who had saved the spies, was taken in by the people of Israel, just as though she had been born one of them. One of the nobles of the tribe of Judah, whose name was Salmon, took her for his wife.

115

And from her line of descendants came King David. She was saved and blessed because she had faith in the God of Israel.

Discussion Questions: *1. How did God provide food for the Israelites? 2. Who did Joshua meet near the city of Jericho? 3. What did he tell Joshua? 4. How did Joshua and his people fight the battle of Jericho? 5. Who caused them to win?*

DAY 69

A WEDGE OF GOLD

Joshua 7:1-8:35

WHILE the Israelites were destroying the city of Jericho, one man disobeyed God's command. A man named Achan, of the tribe of Judah, found a beautiful garment that had come from Babylon, a wedge-shaped piece of gold, and some silver. He looked at it, longed to have it for his own, took it to his tent and hid it. He thought no one had seen him, but God saw it all, and Achan's robbery of God, who owned everything in Jericho, brought great trouble to Israel.

From Jericho, a road wound up the ravines and valleys into the mountain country. On one of the hills above the plain stood a little city called Ai. Joshua did not think it necessary for all the army to go and take Ai, because it was a small place, so he sent a small army of 3,000 men. But the men of Ai came out against them, killed a number of them, and drove them away, so they failed to take the city.

When the rest of the people heard of this defeat, they were filled with fear. Joshua was alarmed, not because he was afraid of the Canaanites, but because he knew that God was not with the men who went against Ai. Joshua fell on his face before the Lord, and said, "O Lord God, why have you led us across Jordan only to let us fall before our enemies? What shall I say, O Lord, now that the men of Israel have been beaten and driven away?"

And God said to Joshua, "Israel has sinned. They have disobeyed my words and broken their promise. They have taken the treasure that belongs to me, and have kept it. That is the reason I left them to suffer from their enemies. My curse shall rest on the people until they bring back that which was stolen and punish the man who robbed me." Then God told Joshua how to find the man who had done this evil thing.

The next morning, very early, Joshua called all the tribes of Israel before him. When the tribe of Judah came near, God showed Joshua that this was the tribe. Then as the divisions of Judah came by, God pointed out one division, and in that division one household, and in that household one family, and in that family one man. Achan was singled out as the man who had robbed God.

Joshua said to Achan, "My son, give honor to the Lord God and confess your sin to him. Tell me what you have done. Do not try to hide it from me."

And Achan said, "I have sinned against the Lord. I saw in Jericho a garment from Babylon, a wedge of gold, and some pieces of silver, and I hid them in my tent." Then Joshua sent messengers to the tent of Achan. They found the hidden things and brought them out before all the people.

Then, because Achan's crime had harmed all the people and because his children took part in the crime, they took them all: Achan, his sons and daughters, the treasure that had been stolen, his sheep and oxen, his tent, and all that was in it. The people threw stones at them until they all were dead, then they burned their bodies and all the things in the tent. Over the ashes they piled up a heap of stones, so all who saw it would remember what came to Achan for his sin.

By this, God showed his people how carefully they had to obey his commands, if they wanted him with them. After this, Joshua sent another army, larger than before, against Ai, and they took the city and destroyed it, as they had destroyed Jericho. This time, God allowed the people to take what they found in the city of Ai and keep it for themselves.

Then they marched over the mountains until they came near the city of Shechem, in the middle of the land of Canaan. The people of the land were so filled with fear that none of them resisted the march of the Israelites. There Joshua gathered all the people of Israel, with their wives and their children. They built an altar of stones, for they had left the Tabernacle and the brazen altar standing in the camp at Gilgal, by Jordan. On this new altar they gave offerings to the Lord and worshiped.

Then Joshua read the law that Moses had written, and all the people listened to the law of the Lord.

When they had done all this, giving the land to the Lord and pledging themselves to serve God, they marched down the mountains, past the smouldering ruins of Ai, past the heap of stones that covered Achan, past the broken walls of Jericho, back to the camp at Gilgal.

Discussion Questions: *1. Who saw what Achan did wrong? 2. Who owned everything in Jericho? 3. How did God tell Joshua to find the thief? 4. What lesson did God teach his people in this story? 5. Why do you think they worshiped God in the end of the story?*

DAY 70

THE GIBEONITES

Joshua 9:1-27

THE news of all that Joshua and the men of Israel had done at Jericho and at Ai, how they had destroyed those cities and slain their people, went through all the land. Everywhere the tribes of Canaan prepared to fight these strangers who had so suddenly and so boldly entered their country.

Near the middle of the mountain region, between Jerusalem and Shechem, were four cities of the Hivites, or the Gibeonites. These people felt they could not resist the Israelites, so they decided to make peace with them. Their cities were less than a day's journey from the camp at Gilgal, and quite near Ai, but they came to Joshua at the camp, looking as if they had made a long journey.

They were wearing old, ragged garments and worn-out shoes, and they carried dry, moldy bread and old bags of food. They met Joshua and the elders of Israel in the camp, and said to them, "We live in a country far away, but we have heard of the great things you have done, the journey you have made, and the cities you have taken on the other side of the river Jordan. We have come to offer you our friendship and to make peace with you."

Joshua said to them, "Who are you? And from what land do you come?"

"We have come," they said, "from a country far away. See this bread. We took it hot from the oven, and now it is moldy. These wineskins were new when we filled them, and you see they are old. Look at our garments and our shoes, all worn-out and patched."

Joshua and the elders did not ask the Lord what to do, but made an agreement with these men not to destroy their cities and to spare the lives of their people. A few days after making peace with them, they found that the four cities where they lived were very near.

At first the Israelite rulers were very angry and were inclined to break their agreement, but afterward they said, "We will keep our promise to these people, though they have deceived us. We will let them live, but they shall be made our servants, and shall do the hard work for the camp and for the Tabernacle."

Even this was better than being killed and having their cities destroyed, so the Gibeonite people were glad to save their lives.

From that time, the people of the four Gibeonite cities carried burdens, drew water, cut wood, and served the camp of Israel.

Discussion Questions: *1. What mistake did Joshua and the elders make when* the Gibeonites came to them? 2. What did they do to them? 3. How did the Gibeonites feel about it?

DAY 71

THE FIVE KINGS
Joshua 10:1-11:23

THE largest city near the camp at Gilgal was Jerusalem. In the days of Abraham, 500 years before, its king, Melchizedek, had been a priest of the Lord and had blessed Abraham. But now, in the days of Joshua, the people of that city worshiped idols.

When the king of Jerusalem heard that the Gibeonites, who lived near him, had made peace with Israel, he sent to the kings of Hebron, Lachish, and several other cities, and said to them, "Come, let us unite into one great army and fight the Gibeonites and destroy them, for they have made peace with our enemies, the people of Israel."

As soon as the people of Gibeon heard this, they sent to Joshua, saying, "Come quickly and help us. We are your servants, and the king of Jerusalem is coming with a great army to kill us all and destroy our cities. The whole country is in arms against us. Come at once, before it is too late!"

Joshua was a very prompt man, swift in all his acts. At once he called out his army and marched all night up the mountains. He came suddenly upon the five kings and their army at a place called Beth-horon. There a great battle was fought, Joshua leading his men against the Canaanites. He did not give his enemies time to form in line, but fell on them so suddenly that they were driven into confusion and fled before the men of Israel.

And the Lord helped his people by a storm that dropped great hailstones down on the Canaanites, so that more were killed by the hailstones than by the sword.

On that day, the land was won by the people of the Lord. If Israel had been defeated and destroyed that day, the Bible would never have been written, the worship of the true God would have been blotted out, and the whole world would have worshiped idols. The battle that day was for the salvation of the world as well as of Israel. So this was the greatest battle that the world has ever seen. There have been many battles where more men fought and more soldiers were killed, but no battle in all the world had such an effect in the times to come as this one.

After the victory, Joshua followed his enemies as they fled and killed many of them, until their armies were broken up and destroyed. The five kings who had fought Joshua were found hidden in a cave, brought out, and killed, so they could no longer trouble the Israelites. By this one victory all the south of Canaan was won, though there were a few small fights afterward.

Then Joshua turned to the north and led his army against the kings there who had united to fight the Israelites. He fell on these kings and their army near a little lake in the far north of Canaan called "the waters of Merom." There another great victory was won. After this, it was easy to conquer the land. Everywhere the tribes of Canaan were made to submit to the Israelites, until all the mountain country was under Joshua's rule.

In the conquest of Canaan, there were six great marches and six battles. Three were in the lands to the east of the Jordan (while Moses was still living): the victories over the Amorites, the Midianites, and the people of Bashan. On the west of the Jordan were the victories of Jericho, Beth-horon, and Lake Merom (under Joshua).

But even after these marchings and victories, it was a long time before all the land was taken by the Israelites.

Discussion Questions: 1. Who did the people of Jerusalem worship? 2. Why did they want to attack the Gibeonites? 3. Who won the battle that followed? Why did they win? 4. Why was the battle so important?

DAY 72

CALEB

Joshua 14:1-15

HE great war for the conquest of Canaan was now ended, though some cities were still held by the Canaanite people. Yet the Israelites were now the rulers over most of the country, and Joshua prepared to divide the land among the tribes of Israel.

One day the rulers of the tribe of Judah came to Joshua's tent at Gilgal, and with them came an old man, Caleb, one of the twelve men sent by Moses to spy on the land of Canaan years ago. Caleb was now, like Joshua, an old man, past eighty years of age. He said to Joshua, "You remember what the Lord said to Moses when we were in the desert at Kadesh-barnea, and you and I and the other spies brought back our report. On that day, Moses said to me, 'The land where your feet have trodden and over which you have walked shall be yours, because you trusted in the Lord.'

"That was forty-five years ago," Caleb went on to say, "and God has kept me alive all those years. Today, at eighty-five years of age, I am as strong as I was that day. And now I ask that the promise made by Moses be kept, and that I have my choice of the places in the land."

"Well," said Joshua, "you can take your choice. What part of it will you choose?"

Caleb answered, "The place I choose is the mountain where we saw the city with the high walls, where the giants were living — the city of Hebron. I know the walls are high and the giants live there. But the Lord will help me take the cities and drive out the people who live in them. Let me have the city of Hebron."

Choosing a city that was not yet taken from the enemies — one of the hardest cities to take — when he might have chosen some rich place already won was very bold. But Caleb showed the same spirit of courage, willingness to fight, and faith in God that he had shown in his prime, years ago.

Joshua said to Caleb, "You shall have the city of Hebron, with all its giants, if you will gather together your men and take it."

So the old soldier brought together his men and led them against the strong city of Hebron. With God's help, Caleb was able to drive out the giants, tall and mighty as they were. They fled from Caleb's men, went down to the shore on the west of the land, and lived among the people of that region, who were called the Philistines. Caleb, his children, and his descendants long after him, held the city of Hebron in the south of the land.

Discussion Questions: *1. Who was Caleb? Do you remember reading about him before? 2. Whom did Caleb depend upon to win the cities? 3. How do you think God felt about Caleb's courage?*

DAY 73

The Land Is Divided

Joshua 15:1-19:51

AFTER this, God told Joshua to divide the land among the tribes. Two tribes and half of another tribe had already received their land on the east of Jordan, which left nine and one-half tribes to receive their shares. Judah, one of the largest, had the mountain country west of the Dead Sea, from Hebron to Jerusalem. Simeon was on the south, toward the desert. Benjamin was north of Judah on the east, toward the Jordan. And Dan was north of Judah on the west, toward the Great Sea.

In the middle of the country, around the city of Shechem, was the land of the tribe of Ephraim. This was one of the best parts of the country, for the soil was rich and there were many springs and streams of water. And here, near Mount Ebal, they buried the body of their father Joseph, which they had kept in its coffin of stone ever since they left Egypt more than forty years before. As Joshua himself belonged to the tribe of Ephraim, his home was also in this land.

North of Ephraim, reaching from the river Jordan to the Great Sea, was the land of the other half of the tribe of Manasseh. The tribes of both Ephraim and Manasseh had come from Joseph, so Joseph's descendants had two tribes, as had been promised by Jacob when he was about to die.

The northern part of the land was divided among four tribes. Issacher was in the south; Asher on the west, beside the Great Sea. Zebulun was in the middle, in the mountains; and Naphtali was in the north, by the lake afterward called the Sea of Galilee.

But although all the land had been divided, it had not all been completely conquered. Nearly all the Canaanite people were there, still living on the land, though in the mountain region they were under the rule of the Israelites. But on the plain beside the Great Sea, on the west of the land, were the Philistines, a very strong people the Israelites had not yet met in war.

Even in the mountains there were many cities where the Canaanite people still lived, and in some of these cities, they were strong. Years afterward, when Joshua the great warrior was no longer living, many of these people rose up to trouble the Israelites. The time came when the tribes of Israel wished that their fathers had driven out or entirely destroyed the Canaanites before they ended the war and divided the land.

But when Joshua divided the land and sent the tribes to their new homes, peace seemed to reign over all the country. Up to this time, we have spoken of all this land as the land of Canaan, but now it was to be called The Land of Israel, or The Land of the Twelve Tribes, for it was now their home.

Discussion Questions: *1. What did Joshua do with the land? 2. Who else was living on the land? 3. What was the new name of the land?*

DAY 74

THE AVENGER OF BLOOD

Joshua 20:1-9

THE Israelites had one custom that seems strange and different from our ways. It was a rule about any man who accidentally killed another man. With us, whenever a man has been killed, the man who killed him is taken before a judge and tried. If he killed the man by accident, not wishing him harm, he is set free. If he meant to kill him, he is punished. He may be sentenced to die for the other man's death, and when he is put to death, it is by an officer of the law.

But in the lands of the East, where the Israelites lived, it was very different. There, when a man was killed, his nearest relative always took it upon himself to kill the man who had killed him. He killed this man without trial, without a judge, and by his own hand, whether the man deserved to die or not.

Two men might be working in the forest together, and one man's axe might fly from his hand and kill the other, or one man hunting might kill another hunter by mistake. No matter whether the man was guilty or innocent, the nearest relative of the one who had lost his life must find the man who had killed him and kill him in return. If he could not find him, sometimes he would kill any member of his family he could find. This man is called "the avenger of blood," because he took vengeance for the blood of his relative, whether the one he killed deserved to die or not. When Moses gave laws to the children of Israel, he found this custom of having an "avenger of blood" rooted so deeply in the habits of the people that it could not be broken up. In fact, it still remains, even to this day, among the village people in the land where the Israelites lived.

But Moses gave a law to take the place of the old custom and to teach the people to use justice in their dealings with one another, and when they came into the land of Canaan, Joshua carried out the plan Moses had commanded.

Joshua chose six cities, three on one side of the river Jordan and three on the other side. All of these were well-known places and easy to find. Most of them were on mountains, and could be seen far away. They were chosen so that from almost any part of the land, a man could reach one of these cities in a day, or at the most in two days. These cities were called Cities of Refuge, because in them, a man who had killed another by mistake could find refuge from the avenger of blood.

When a man killed another by accident, wherever he was, he ran as quickly as possible to the nearest of these cities of refuge. The avenger of blood followed him, and might overtake him and kill him before he reached the city. But almost always the man, having a head start, would get to the city of refuge first.

_____

Discussion Questions: *1. What strange custom did the Israelites have? 2. What did Moses say about this custom? 3. What did Joshua do to follow Moses' new teaching?*

DAY 75

_____

THE CITIES OF REFUGE

Joshua 21:1-45

IN the cities of refuge, the elders looked into the case. They learned all the facts, and if the man was really guilty and deserved to die, they gave him up to be killed by the avenger. But if he was innocent, and did not mean to kill the man, they forbade the avenger to touch him and kept him safe.

A line was drawn around the city, at a distance from the wall, beyond which the avenger could not come.

Within this line were fields where the man could work and raise crops so he had food.

And there at the city of refuge the innocent man, who had killed another without meaning to kill, lived until the high-priest died. After the high-priest died and another high-priest took his place, the man could go back to his own home and live in peace.

This law taught the Israelites to be patient, to control themselves, to protect the innocent, to seek justice and not yield to sudden anger.

Among the tribes was one that had no land given to it. This was the tribe of Levi, to which Moses and Aaron belonged. The men of this tribe were priests, who offered the sacrifices, and Levites, who cared for the Tabernacle and its worship. Moses and Joshua did not think it good to have all the Levites living in one part of the country, so he gave them cities — and in some places, the fields around the cities — in many parts of the land. From these places they went up to the Tabernacle to serve for part of the year. The rest of the year they stayed in their homes and cared for their fields.

When the war was over and the land was divided, Joshua fixed the Tabernacle at a place called Shiloh, not far from the center of the land, so the people could come up at least once a year for worship. They were told to come from their homes three times in each year and worship the Lord at Shiloh.

These three times were for the feast of the Passover in the spring; the feast of the Tabernacles in the fall; and the feast of Pentecost, fifty days after the Passover. These three great feasts were kept at the place of the altar and the Tabernacle.

At Shiloh, before the Tabernacle, they placed the altar, on which the offerings were laid twice every day.

God had kept his promise, and brought the Israelites into a land of their own, and had given them rest from all their enemies.

Discussion Questions: *1. What did the elders in a city of refuge do? 2. What did the law Moses gave the people teach them? 3. Which tribe did not have any land? What did the men of this tribe do? 4. How many times during the year did the people go to the Tabernacle?*

DAY 76

THE ALTAR BY THE RIVER

Joshua 22:1-34

WHEN the war for the conquest of Canaan was ended and the tribes were about to leave for their new homelands, Joshua broke camp at Gilgal, which had been the meeting place of the Israelites through the war.

You remember that two of the tribes and half of another tribe had received their land on the east of Jordan, but their soldiers crossed the Jordan with the men of the other tribes. Joshua now called these soldiers and said to them, "You have done all that Moses the servant of the Lord commanded you. You have stood faithfully by your brothers in the other tribes. Now the time has come for you to go back to your wives and your children in your own land on the other side of Jordan. Only remember, always keep the commandments of the Lord, be true to the Lord, and serve him with all your heart and all your soul."

Then Joshua gave them the blessing of the Lord and sent them away. They left Shiloh, where the Tabernacle was standing, and came to the river Jordan. There on a great rock, where it could be seen from far, they built a high altar of stone.

Soon it was told among the tribes that the men of the two tribes and half-tribe had built themselves an altar. God had commanded the people to have but one altar for all the tribes, one high-priest, and one offering for all the tribes. This was to keep all the people together as one family, with one worship. The people of Israel were greatly displeased when they found these tribes had built an altar, so upset that they were almost ready to go to war.

But before going to war, they sent one of the priests, Phinehas, and ten princes of Israel (one from each tribe) to ask the men why they had built this altar. These men came to the men of Reuben and Gad, and the half-tribe of Manasseh, and said to them, "What is this you have done, building for yourselves an altar? Do you mean to turn away from the Lord and set up your own gods? Do not rebel against God by building an altar while God's altar is standing at Shiloh."

The men of the two tribes and a half answered, "The Lord knows we have not built this altar for the offering of sacrifices. We have built this altar so our children may see it standing on your side of the river, and not on our side. Then we can say to them, 'Let that altar remind you that we are all one people, we and the tribes on the other side of Jordan.' This altar stands as a witness between us that we are all one people and worship the one Lord God of Israel."

Then the princes were satisfied and pleased to know it was an altar for witness, and not for offerings. They named the altar Ed, a word that means witness. "For," they said, "it is a witness between us that the Lord is our God, the God of us all."

_____

Discussion Questions: *1. What did the men of the tribe and a half on the other side of the river do? 2. Why did the rest of the tribes feel this was wrong? 3. Why had the men on the other side of the river build the altar? 4. Did the other tribes understand when they told them this? 5. What did they call the altar? What does that mean?*

DAY 77

_____

JOSHUA'S LAST DAYS

Joshua 23:1-24:33

JOSHUA was now a very old man, more than 100 years old. He knew he must soon die, and he wished to give the people his last words. So he called the elders and rulers and judges of the tribes to meet him at Shechem, in the middle of the land near his home.

When they were all together before him, Joshua reminded them of all that

God had done for their fathers and for them. He told them the story of Abraham, how he left his home at God's call; the story of Jacob and his family going down to Egypt; and how after many years the Lord had brought them out of that land. How the Lord had led them through the wilderness and had given them the land where they were now living at peace. Joshua then said, "You are living in cities that you did not build, and you are eating of vines and olive trees that you did not plant. It is the Lord who has given you all these things. Now, therefore, fear the Lord, and serve him with all your hearts.

"And if any of you have any other gods, put them away, and serve the Lord only. If you are not willing to serve the Lord, then choose today the god you will serve. But as for me and my house, we will serve the Lord."

Then the people answered Joshua, "We will not turn away from the Lord to serve other gods. We will serve the Lord, for he is the God of Israel."

"But," said Joshua, "you must remember that the Lord is very strict in his commands. He will be angry if you turn away from him after promising to serve him, and will punish you if you worship images, as the people do around you."

And the people said, "We pledge ourselves to serve the Lord, and the Lord only."

JOSHUA SET UP A GREAT STONE - JOSHUA 24:26

Then Joshua wrote down the people's promise in the book of the law, so others might read it and remember it. And he set up a great stone under an oak tree in Shechem, and he said, "Let this stone stand as a witness between you and the Lord, that you have pledged yourselves to be faithful to him."

127

Then Joshua sent the people away to their lands, telling them not to forget the promise they had made. After this, Joshua died, at the age of 110. And as long as people lived who remembered Joshua, the people of Israel continued serving the Lord.

Discussion Questions: *1. Why do you think Joshua reminded the people of what God had done for them? 2. What things had God given them? 3. What did the people promise Joshua? 4. What two things did Joshua do to help the people remember their promise to God?*

DAY 78

ISRAEL FORGETS THE LORD

Judges 1:1-3:7

YOU would think that after all God had done for the Israelites and their promises to serve him faithfully, they would never turn to worshiping idols, as the Canaanites did. Yet, when Joshua and the men who knew Joshua died, the people began to forget their own God and to worship images of wood and stone.

Perhaps it was not so strange, after all. In all the world, as far as we know, the Israelites were the only people at that time who did not worship idols. All the nations around them — the Egyptians, the Edomites, the Moabites, the Philistines — all bowed down to images.

Then, too, the Canaanites had not been driven out of the land. They were there still, in their own cities and villages everywhere, and their idols were standing under the trees on many high places. So the Israelites saw idols all around them and people bowing down before them, while they had no God that could be seen. The Tabernacle was far away from some parts of the land, and the people were so busy with their fields and their houses that few of them went up to worship.

And so it came to pass that the people began to neglect their own worship of the Lord, and then to begin to worship the idols around them. And from idol worship they sank lower still, into wicked deeds. For all this, the Lord let them to suffer. Their enemies attacked them and became their masters, for when God left them, they were helpless. They were made poor, for these rulers who conquered them robbed them of all their grain, grapes, and olive oil.

After a time of suffering, the Israelites would think of what God had done for them in other times. Then they would turn away from the idols and would call on God. God would hear them and raise up some great man to lead them to freedom. This great man they called "a judge," and under him they would serve God and be happy and successful once more.

As long as the judge lived and ruled, the people worshiped God. But when the judge died, they forgot God again and worshiped idols and fell under the power of their enemies as before, until God sent another judge to deliver them. This happened over and over again in the 300 years after Joshua died. Seven nations in turn ruled over the Israelites, and after each "oppression," as this rule was called, a "deliverer" arose to set the people free.

Discussion Questions: *1. What had God already done for the Israelites? 2. What did the people do after Joshua died? 3. Why was it hard for the people to remember to be faithful to God? 4. What was a judge? What did a judge do for the people?*

DAY 79

EHUD'S PRESENT

Judges 3:8-31

THE first nation to come from another land against the Israelites was Mesopotamia. Their king led his army into the land and made the Israelites serve him eight years. Then they cried to the Lord, and the Lord sent them Othniel.

He set the people free from the Mesopotamians, ruling as long as he lived, and kept them faithful to the Lord. Othniel was the first of the judges of Israel.

But after Othniel died, the people again began to worship images, and again fell under the power of their enemies. This time it was the Moabites who attacked Israel. Their king was named Eglon, and he was very hard in his rule over the Israelites. Again they cried to the Lord, and God called a man named Ehud to set the people free.

One day Ehud came to visit King Eglon, who was ruling over the land. He said, "I have a present from my people to the king. Let me go into his palace and see him."

They let Ehud into the palace, and he gave the king a present. Then he went out, but soon he came back, and said, "I have a message to the king that no one else can hear. Let me see the king alone."

As he had just brought a present, they supposed he was a friend of the king.

129

Then, too, he had no sword on the side, where men carried their swords. But Ehud was left-handed, and he carried a short, sharp sword out of sight under his garment.

He went into the room where King Eglon was sitting alone, and said, "I have a message from the Lord to you, and this is the message." He drew out his sword and drove it into the king's body so suddenly that the king died without a sound. Ehud left the sword in the body of the king, and went out quietly by the rear door. The servants of the king thought he was asleep in his room, and for a while did not go in to see why he was so still. When they found him dead, Ehud was far away.

Ehud blew a trumpet, called his people together, and led them against the Moabites. They were so helpless without their king that Ehud and his men easily drove them out of Israel and set the people free. Ehud became the second judge over the land.

After that, it was many years before someone else ruled over Israel.

The next enemies of Israel were the Philistines, who lived on the shore of the Great Sea on the west. They came up from the plain against the Israelites, but Shamgar, the third judge, met them with a company of farmers, who drove the Philistines back with their ox goads, and kept them from ruling over the land.

Discussion Questions: *1. Who was the first judge of Israel? 2. What did he do for the Israelites? 3. Who was Ehud? 4. What did he do? 5. What was the difference between the kings and the judges?*

DAY 80

DEBORAH AND JAEL

Judges 4:1-5:31

AGAIN many Israelites began to live like the people around them, praying to idols and sinning. And again the Lord left them to suffer for their sins. A Canaanite king in the north whose name was Jabin sent his army, under the command of Sisera, to conquer them. Sisera had many iron chariots drawn by horses, while soldiers in the chariots shot arrows and threw spears at the Israelites. The men of Israel were not used to horses and were afraid of these chariots. All the northern tribes of Israel fell under the power of King Jabin and his general, Sisera, and their rule was very harsh and severe.

At that time a woman was ruling as judge over a large part of the land; the only woman judge ever to rule the Israelites. Her name was Deborah. She sat under a palm tree north of Jerusalem and gave advice to all the people who came to her. She was so wise and good that men came from all over the land with their problems and the disputes that arose between them. She didn't rule because of an army or some kind of appointment, but because people saw that God's Spirit was with her.

THE PEOPLE CAME TO DEBORAH FOR ADVICE - JUDGES 4:4,5

Deborah heard of the troubles in the north under the Canaanites. She knew a brave man living in the land of Naphtali, a man named Barak, and sent this message to him: "Barak, call out the tribes of Israel who live near you. Raise an army, and lead the men to Mount Tabor. The Lord has told me he will give Sisera and the Canaanite army to you."

But Barak was afraid to take on this job by himself, so he told Deborah, "If you will go with me, I will go. But if you will not go with me, I will not go."

"I will go with you," said Deborah, "but because you did not trust God and did not go when God called you, the honor of this war will not be yours. God will deliver Sisera into the hands of a woman."

Together Deborah and Barak sent out a call for men of the north, and 10,000 men joined them on Mount Tabor. When the time was right, Deborah sent Barak and his small army down the mountain to attack the large Canaanite army.

The Canaanites were attacked so suddenly that they had no time to prepare their chariots. They were frightened and ran away, trampling one another underfoot — chariots, horses, and men all in wild flight.

And the Lord helped the Israelites, for at that time the brook Kishon was swollen into a river, and the Canaanites crowded into it. While many were killed in the battle, many were also drowned in the river.

Sisera, the general of the Canaanites, saw the battle was lost. He leaped from his chariot and fled on foot. On the edge of the plain, he found a tent standing alone, and he ran to it for shelter and hiding.

It was the tent of a man named Heber, and Heber's wife, Jael, was in front of it. She knew Sisera, and said to him, "Come in, my lord. Come into the tent. Do not be afraid."

Sisera entered the tent, and Jael covered him with a rug, so no one would find him. Sisera said to her, "I am very thirsty. Can you give me a little water to drink?"

Instead of water, she brought out a bottle of milk and gave him some. Then Sisera lay down to sleep, for he was very tired from the battle and from running. While he was in a deep sleep, Jael crept into the tent quietly with a tent peg and a hammer, placed the point of the peg on the side of his head, and killed Sisera. Jael and Deborah set the people of Israel free by their bravery. After this, there was peace for many years.

Discussion Questions: *1. Who was judge when King Jabin attacked the Israelites? 2. Why did Deborah rule the Israelites? 3. Who was Barak? 4. Who helped the Israelites win the battle? How? 5. Who killed Sisera?*

DAY 81

GIDEON AND THE ANGEL

Judges 6:1-32

AGAIN the people of Israel did evil in the sight of the Lord, and the Lord made them suffer for their sins. This time it was the Midianites who attacked the tribes in the middle of the country. The two tribes that suffered the hardest were Ephraim and the part of Manasseh on the west side of the Jordan. For seven years the Midianites swept over their land every year, just at the time of harvest, and carried away all the crops of grain, until the Israelites had no food for themselves or their sheep and cattle. The Midianites brought in their own flocks, which ate all the grass in the fields. These Midianites were Arabs living on the border of the desert, who made sudden, swift attacks on the people of Israel. The people of Israel were driven away from their villages and farms and hid in the caves in the mountains.

One day a man named Gideon was threshing wheat in a hidden place, when he saw an angel sitting under an oak tree. The angel said to him, "You are a brave man, Gideon, and the Lord is with you. Go out boldly, and save your people from the power of the Midianites."

Gideon answered the angel, "O Lord, how can I save Israel? Mine is a poor family in Manasseh, and I am the least in my father's house."

The Lord said to him, "Surely I will be with you, and I will help you drive out the Midianites."

Gideon felt it was the Lord talking with him, in the form of an angel. He brought an offering and laid it on a rock before the angel. Then the angel touched the offering with his staff. At once, a fire leaped up and burned the offering, then the angel vanished. Gideon was afraid when he saw this, but the Lord said to him, "Peace be unto you, Gideon. Do not fear, for I am with you."

Then the Lord told Gideon that before setting his people free from the Midianites, he must first set them free from the two idols most worshiped by them. Near the house of Gideon's own father stood an altar to Baal and the image of Asherah.

That night, Gideon went out with ten men, threw down the image of Baal, cut up the wooden image of Asherah, and destroyed the altar before these idols. In their place, he built an altar to the God of Israel, and on it he laid the broken pieces of the idols and offered a young ox to God.

The next morning, when the people of the village went out to worship their idols, they found them cut in pieces, the altar taken away, and its place, an altar of the Lord.

The people looked at the broken, burning idols, and they said, "Who has done this?"

Someone said, "Gideon, the son of Joash, did this last night." Then they came to Joash, Gideon's father, and said, "We are going to kill your son because he has destroyed the image of Baal, who is our god."

Joash answered, "If Baal is a god, he can take care of himself, and he will punish the man who destroyed his image. Why should you help Baal? Let Baal help himself." When they saw that Baal could not harm the man who had broken down his altar and his image, the people turned back to their own Lord God.

Discussion Questions: *1. Who did Gideon see sitting under a tree? 2. What did God tell Gideon? 3. Why did God tell Gideon to destroy the idols? 4. Why couldn't the idols harm Gideon? 5. What did the people do when they saw that the idols could not harm him?*

DAY 82

GIDEON'S FLEECE

Judges 6:33-40

IDEON sent men through his own tribe of Manasseh and the other tribes in that part of the land to say, "Come and help us drive out the Midianites." The men gathered around Gideon. Very few of them had swords and spears, for the Israelites were not a fighting people and were not trained for war. They met beside a great spring on Mount Gilboa.

On the plain, stretching up the side of another mountain, was the camp of a vast Midianite army. As soon as the Midianites heard Gideon was trying to set his people free, they came against him with a mighty army. Just as Deborah and her little army had looked down from Mount Tabor on the great army of the Canaanites, so now, on Mount Gilboa, Gideon looked down on the army of the Midianites in their camp on the same plain.

Gideon was a man of faith. He wanted to be sure God was leading him, so he prayed to God, "O Lord God, give me some sign that you will save Israel through me. Here is a fleece of wool. If tomorrow morning the fleece is wet with dew while the grass around it is dry, then I will know you are with me and will give me victory over the Midianites."

Very early the next morning, Gideon came to look at the fleece. He found it wringing wet with dew, while all around, the grass was dry. But Gideon was not satisfied. He said to the Lord, "O Lord, don't be angry with me, but give me just one more sign. Tomorrow morning, let the fleece be dry, and let the dew fall all around it, and then I will doubt no more."

The next morning, Gideon found the grass, bushes, and the trees wet with dew, while the fleece of wool was dry. And Gideon was sure that God had called him and would give him victory over the enemies of Israel.

Discussion Questions: *1. How did Gideon know God was with him in the battle? 2. Do you think Gideon showed much faith? Why or why not?*

DAY 83

GIDEON'S ARMY

Judges 7:1-15

OW the Lord said to Gideon, "Your army is too large. If Israel should win the victory, they would say, 'We won it by our own might.' Send home all those who are afraid to fight." Many of the people were frightened as they looked at their enemy's army, and the Lord knew these men would only hinder the rest.

So Gideon sent word through the camp. "Whoever is afraid of the enemy may go home," and 22,000 people went away, leaving only 10,000 in Gideon's army. But the army was stronger, because the cowards had gone and only the brave men were left.

But the Lord said to Gideon, "The people are still too many. You need only a few of the bravest and best men to fight this battle. Bring the men down the mountain, beside the water, and I will show you how to find the men you need."

In the morning, Gideon called his 10,000 men out and made them march down the hill, just as though they were going to attack the enemy. When they were beside the water, he noticed how they drank, and he divided them into two companies, according to their way of drinking. As they came to the water, most of the men threw aside their shields and spears and knelt down to scoop up water with both hands. These men Gideon commanded to stand in one company.

There were a few men who did not stop to take a large drink of water. Holding their spears and shields in their right hands, to be ready for the enemy if one should suddenly appear, they merely caught up a handful of water in passing and marched on, lapping water from one hand.

God said to Gideon, "Set apart these men. These are the men I have chosen to set Israel free."

Gideon counted these men and found there were only 300 of them. The difference between them was that these 300 were earnest men, purposeful, not turning aside from their aim even to drink, as the others did. Then, too, they were watchful men, always ready to meet their enemies. No enemy could have surprised the 300 who held their spears and shields ready while they were taking a drink.

Then Gideon, at God's command, sent back to the camp on Mount Gilboa all the rest of his army, nearly 10,000 men, keeping only his little band of 300. Before the battle, God gave Gideon one more sign, to encourage him.

God said to Gideon, "Go down with your servant into the camp of the Midianites, and hear what they say. It will cheer your heart for the fight."

Gideon crept down the mountain with his servant and walked around the edge of the Midianite camp, just as though he were one of their own men. He saw two men talking, and stood near to listen. One man said to the other, "I had a strange dream last night. I dreamed that I saw a loaf of barley bread come rolling down the mountain. It struck the tent and threw it down in a heap on the ground. What do you suppose that dream means?"

"That loaf of bread," said the other, "means Gideon, a man of Israel, who will come down and destroy this army. The Lord God has given us all into his hand."

Gideon was glad when he heard this, for it showed that the Midianites, for all their number, were in fear of him and of his army, even more than his men had feared the Midianites. He gave thanks to God, hastened back to his camp, and made ready to lead his men against the Midianites.

Discussion Questions: *1. Why did God send away some of the army? 2. Who did God want to fight the battle? 3. How did God show Gideon who should fight? 4. What did the men in the enemy camp dream? 5. What did that mean?*

DAY 84

GIDEON'S VICTORY

Judges 7:16-8:23

GIDEON'S plan did not need a large army, but it needed a few careful, bold men who would do exactly as their leader commanded them. He gave each man a lamp, a pitcher, and a trumpet, and told the men just what was to be done with them. The lamp was lighted, but was placed inside the pitcher, so it could not be seen. He divided his men into three companies and very quietly led them down the mountain in the middle of the night and arranged them all around the camp of the Midianites.

All at once, a great shout rang out in the darkness: "The sword of the Lord and of Gideon!" After came a crash of breaking pitchers, and then a flash of light from every direction. The 300 men had given the shout and broken their pitchers, so that on every side, lights were shining. The men blew their trumpets with a mighty noise, and the Midianites woke up to see enemies all around them, lights beaming, swords flashing in the darkness, and the loud sound of the trumpets.

They were filled with terror and thought only of escape, not of fighting. But wherever they turned, their enemies seemed to be standing. They trampled one another to death, fleeing from the Israelites. Their own land was in the east, across the river Jordan, and they ran in that direction.

Gideon thought the Midianites would turn toward their own lands if they were beaten in the battle, and he had made plans to cut off their flight, placing the 10,000 men in the camp on the sides of the valley leading to the Jordan.

They killed many of the Midianites as they fled down the steep pass toward the river. Gideon had also asked the men of Ephraim, who had so far taken no part in the war, to hold the only place at the river where men could wade across. The Midianites who escaped from Gideon's men in the valley were now met by the Ephraimites at the river, and many more of them were slain. Among the slain were two princes of the Midianites, Oreb and Zeeb.

A part of the Midianite army was able to get across the river and continue its flight toward the desert, but Gideon and his brave 300 followed closely after them, fought another battle with them, destroyed them utterly, and killed their two kings. After this great victory, the Israelites were freed forever from the Midianites, who never again ventured to leave their home in the desert to make war on the tribes of Israel.

The tribe of Ephraim was one of the most powerful of the twelve tribes. Its leaders were quite displeased with Gideon because their part in the victory had been so small. They said to Gideon, "Why didn't you send word to us, when you were calling for men to fight the Midianites?"

But Gideon knew how to make a kind answer. He said to them, "What have I done, compared to you? Didn't you kill thousands of the Midianites at the crossing of the Jordan? Didn't you take their two princes? What could my men have done without the help of your men?" By gentle words of praise, Gideon made the men of Ephraim his friends.

After this, as long as Gideon lived, he ruled as judge in Israel. The people wanted him to make himself a king. "Rule over us as king," they said, "and let your son be king after you, and his son king after him." But Gideon said, "No. You have a king already, for the Lord God is the King of Israel. No one but God shall be king over these tribes."

Of all the fifteen judges of Israel, Gideon, the fifth judge, had the most courage, wisdom, and faith in God.

If all the people of Israel had been like him, there would have been no worship of idols. Israel would have been strong and faithful to God. But as soon as Gideon died (and even before his death), his people began once more to turn away from the Lord to seek the idols that could give them no help.

_____

Discussion Questions: *1. When did Gideon attack the Midianite army?*
2. What did the men carry with them? 3. How did Gideon make the Ephraimites his friends? 4. Why did Gideon refuse to be made king?

DAY 85

JEPHTHAH'S PROMISE

Judges 8:33-11:40

ALTHOUGH Gideon had refused to become a king, after his death, one of his sons, whose name was Abimelech, tried to make himself a king. He began by killing all his brothers, except one who escaped. But his rule was only over Shechem and a few places near it, and lasted only a few years, so he was never named among the kings of Israel.

After this, the Israelites again began to worship the idols of the Canaanites, and again fell under the power of their enemies. The Ammonites came against them from the southeast and ruled over the tribes on the east of Jordan. This was the sixth of "the oppressions," and the man who set Israel free was Jephthah. He called together the men of the tribes on the east of Jordan — Reuben, Gad, and the half-tribe of Manasseh — and fought against the Ammonites.

Before Jephthah went to the battle, he said to the Lord, "If you will give me victory over the Ammonites, when I come back from the battle, whatever comes out of the house to meet me shall be the Lord's, and I will offer it up as an offering."

This was not a wise promise, or a right one. God had told the Israelites long before what offerings were commanded (oxen and sheep) and what were forbidden. But Jephthah had lived on the border near the desert, far from the house of God at Shiloh, and he knew very little about God's law.

Jephthah fought the Ammonites, won a victory, and drove them out of the land. Then, as he was going back to his home, his daughter, who was his only child, came out to meet him. When Jephthah saw her, he cried out in sorrow, "Oh, my daughter, what trouble you bring with you! I have given a promise to the Lord, and now I must keep it!"

As soon as his daughter learned what promise her father had made, she met it bravely. She said, "My father, you have made a solemn promise to the Lord, and you shall keep it, for God has given you victory over the enemies of your people. But let me live a little while and weep with my young friends over the death I must suffer."

For two months she stayed with the young girls on the mountains, then she gave herself up to death, and her father did as he had promised.

In all the history of the Israelites, this was the only time a living man or woman was offered in sacrifice to the Lord.

JEPHTHAH'S DAUGHTER COMES OUT TO GREET HIM - JUDGES 11:34

If Jephthah had lived near the Tabernacle at Shiloh and had been taught God's law, he would not have given such a promise (for God did not like it) and his daughter's life would have been saved.

Discussion Questions: *1. Who became king after Gideon's death? 2. Do you think he made God happy? Why or why not? 3. Why wasn't Jephthah's promise to God wise? 4. Why did he make it? Did God want him to do that?*

DAY 86

SAMSON

Judges 13:1-15:8

AFTER Jephthah, three judges ruled in turn, named Ibzan, Elon, and Abdon. None of these were men of war, and in their days the land was quiet.

But the people of Israel again began to worship idols, and as a punishment, God allowed them to fall under the power of their enemies. The seventh oppression was by far the hardest, the longest, and the most widely spread of any, for it was over all the tribes. It came from the Philistines, a strong and warlike people who lived to the west of Israel, on the plain beside the Great Sea. They worshiped an idol called Dagon, which had a fish's head on a man's body.

The Philistines took away all the Israelites' swords and spears, so they could not fight, and they robbed their land of all the crops, so the people starved. As before, the Israelites cried to the Lord, and the Lord heard their prayer.

In the land of Dan, which was next to the country of the Philistines, lived a man named Manoah. One day an angel came to his wife and said, "You shall have a son, and when he grows up, he will begin to save Israel from the hand of the Philistines. But your son must never drink any wine or strong drink as long as he lives. And his hair must be allowed to grow long, and must never be cut, for he shall be a Nazarite, under a vow to the Lord."

The child was born, and was named Samson. He grew up to become the strongest man in the Bible. Samson was no general, like Gideon or Jephthah, calling out his people and leading them in war. He did much to set his people free, but all he did was by his own strength, without help from other men.

When Samson became a young man, he went down to Timnath, in the land of the Philistines. There he saw a young Philistine woman he loved and wanted to marry. His father and mother were not pleased that he wanted to marry one of his people's enemies, but they did not know that God would make this marriage the means of bringing harm to the Philistines and help the Israelites.

As Samson was going down to Timnath to see this young woman, a hungry young lion came down the mountain, growling and roaring. Samson seized the lion, tore him to pieces easily, and then went on his way. He made his visit and came home, but said nothing to anyone about the lion.

SAMSON KILLS THE LION - JUDGES 14:6

After a time, Samson went again to Timnath, for his marriage to the Philistine woman. On his way, he stopped to look at the dead lion, and in its body he found a swarm of bees and honey they had made. He took some of the honey, ate it as he walked, but told no one of it.

At the wedding feast, which lasted a whole week, there were many Philistine young men. They amused one another with questions and riddles.

"I will give you a riddle," said Samson. "If you answer it during the feast, I will give you thirty suits of clothing. And if you cannot answer it, then you must give me thirty suits of clothing."

"Let us hear your riddle," they said. And this was Samson's riddle for the young Philistines:

> Out of the eater came forth meat.
> And out of the strong came forth sweetness.

They could not find the answer, though they tried to figure it out for three days. At last they went to Samson's wife and said to her, "Coax your husband to tell you the answer. If you do not find it out, we will set your house on fire and burn you and all your people."

Samson's wife urged him to tell her the answer. She cried and pleaded with him, and said, "If you really loved me, you would not keep this a secret from me."

At last Samson yielded and told his wife how he had killed the lion and later found the honey in its body. She told her people, and just before the end of the feast, they came to Samson with the answer. They said, "What is sweeter than honey? And what is stronger than a lion?"

Now Samson had to give them thirty suits of clothing. He went out among the Philistines, killed the first thirty he found, took off their clothes, and gave them to the guests at the feast. But all this made Samson very angry. He left his new wife and went home to his father's house, and the parents of his wife gave her to another man.

But after a time, Samson's anger went away, and he went to Timnath, to see his wife. Her father said to him, "You went away angry, and I thought you didn't care for her. I gave her to another man, and now she is his wife. But here is her younger sister. You can take her for your wife, instead."

Samson would not take his wife's sister. He went out very angry, determined to do harm to the Philistines because they had cheated him. He caught all the wild foxes he could find, until he had 300 of them. Then he tied them together in pairs by their tails. Between each pair of foxes, he tied a piece of dry wood, which he set on fire, then he let the foxes loose in the Philistines' fields when the grain was ripe. They ran wildly over the fields, set the grain on fire, and burned it, along with the olive trees in the fields.

When the Philistines saw their harvests destroyed, they said, "Who has done this?"

People said, "Samson did this, because his wife was given to another man."

The Philistines saw Samson's father-in-law as the cause of their loss. They came, set his house on fire, and burned the man and the daughter Samson had married. Then Samson came down again, fought a company of Philistines, and killed them all, as punishment for burning his wife.

Discussion Questions: 1. What was different about Samson? 2. How did Samson's parents feel when he wanted to marry a Philistine woman? Why? 3. Why did the Philistine men want to know the answer to the riddle? How did Samson get the clothes he had promised to give them?

DAY 87

SAMSON'S CAPTURE

Judges 15:9-16:21

AFTER this, Samson went to live in a hollow place in a split rock, called the rock of Etam. The Philistines came in a great army and overran the fields of Judah.

"Why do you come against us?" asked the men of Judah. "What do you want from us?"

"We have come," they said, "to bind Samson and to deal with him as he has dealt with our people."

The men of Judah said to Samson, "Don't you know the Philistines are our rulers? Why do you make them angry by killing their people? We suffer because of you. Now we must bind you and give you to the Philistines, or they will ruin us all."

Samson said, "I will let you bind me, if you promise not to kill me yourselves, but only give me to the Philistines."

They made the promise, and Samson gave himself up to them. The Philistines shouted for joy as they saw their enemy brought to them by his own people. Little did they know what was to happen. For as soon as Samson came to them, he broke the bonds as though they were light strings, picked up the jawbone of an ass, and struck out with it.

He killed almost a thousand of the Philistines with this strange weapon.

After this, Samson saw another Philistine woman and fell in love with her. The name of this woman was Delilah. The rulers of the Philistines came to Delilah, and said to her, "Find out what makes Samson so strong, and tell us. If you help us get control of him, we will give you a great sum of money."

So Delilah coaxed and pleaded with Samson to tell her what made him so strong. Samson said to her, "If they tie me with seven green twigs from a tree, then I will not be strong anymore."

DELILAH PLEADED WITH SAMSON - JUDGES 16:6

They brought her seven green twigs, and she bound Samson with them while he was asleep. Then she called out to him, "Wake up, Samson! The Philistines are coming for you!"

Samson rose up, broke the twigs easily, and escaped.

Delilah tried again to find his secret. She said, "You are only making fun of me. Now tell me how you can be bound."

Samson said, "Let them bind me with new ropes that have never been used before, and then I cannot get away."

While Samson was asleep again, Delilah bound him with new ropes. Then she called out as before, "Get up, Samson! The Philistines are coming!" And when Samson rose up, the ropes broke as if they were thread.

Again Delilah urged him to tell her, and he said, "You notice that my long hair is in seven locks. Weave it together in the loom, just as if it were the threads in a piece of cloth."

Then, while he was asleep, she wove his hair in the loom and fastened it

143

with a large pin to the frame. But when he awoke, he got up and carried away the pin and the beam of the weaving frame, for he was as strong as before.

Now Delilah said, "Why do you tell me that you love me? You deceive me, and keep from me your secret!" And she pleaded with him day after day, until at last he yielded to her and told her the real secret of his strength. He said, "I am a Nazarite, under a vow to the Lord not to drink wine and not to allow my hair to be cut. If I should let my hair be cut short, then the Lord would forsake me, and my strength would go from me, and I would be like other men."

Delilah knew she had found the truth at last. She sent for the rulers of the Philistines, saying, "Come up now, and you will have your enemy. I am sure he has told me all that is in his heart."

Then, while the Philistines watched outside, Delilah let Samson go to sleep with his head on her knees. While he was sound asleep, they took a razor and shaved off all his hair. Then she called, "Rise up, Samson! The Philistines are after you!"

He awoke and got up, expecting to find himself as strong as before, for he did not know his long hair had been cut off. But he had broken his vow to the Lord, and the Lord had left him. He was now as weak as other men, and helpless in the hands of his enemies. The Philistines easily made him their prisoner. So he might never do them harm, they put out his eyes, then they chained him and sent him to prison at Gaza. In the prison, they made Samson turn a heavy millstone to grind grain, just as though he were an animal.

Discussion Questions: *1. Why were the Philistines angry at Samson? Why did Samson tell the men of Judah to give him to the Philistines? 3. What kind of weapon did Samson use against his enemies? 4. Why did Delilah want to know the secret of Samson's strength? Do you think she was a very good wife?*

DAY 88

SAMSON'S DEATH

Judges 16:22-31

BUT while Samson was in prison, his hair grew long again, and with his hair, his strength came back to him, for Samson renewed his vow to the Lord.

One day a great feast was held by the Philistines in the temple of their fish-god Dagon. They said, "Our god has given Samson to us. Let us be glad together and praise Dagon."

The temple was thronged with people, and the roof over it was also crowded with more than 3,000 men and women. They sent for Samson, to rejoice over him, and Samson was led into the court of the temple, before all the people, to amuse them.

After a time, Samson said to the boy who was leading him, "Take me up to the front of the temple, so I may stand by one of the pillars, and lean against it."

While Samson stood between two of the pillars, he prayed to the Lord God of Israel, and said, "O Lord God, remember me, I pray thee, and give me strength only this once. Help me, that I may obtain vengeance on the Philistines for my two eyes!"

Then he placed one arm around the pillar on one side, and the other arm around the pillar on the other side, and he said, "Let me die with the Philistines."

Then he bowed forward with all his might, and pulled the pillars over, bringing down the roof. Samson himself was among the dead, but in his death, he killed more Philistines than he had killed during his life.

SAMSON TORE DOWN THE TEMPLE - JUDGES 16:30

In the terror that came upon the Philistines, the men of Samson's tribe came down and found his dead body, and buried it in their own land. After that, it was years before the Philistines tried to rule the Israelites.

Discussion Questions: *1. Why did Samson's strength come back? 2. Who did the Philistines think had given them Samson? 3. What did Samson do to the Philistines? Who helped him?*

145

DAY 89

THE IDOL TEMPLE

Judges 17:1-18:31

WHILE the judges were ruling in Israel, a man named Micah lived in the mountains of Ephraim. His mother, who was living with him, found that someone had stolen a large sum of money from her. Now, the money had been taken by her son Micah, and after a time he said to her, "Those eleven hundred pieces of silver you lost are with me. I took them myself."

His mother answered, "May the blessing of God rest on you, my son, for bringing my silver back. This money will be the Lord's. I give it back to you, to be used in the service of the Lord."

But instead of taking the money to the Tabernacle of the Lord at Shiloh, Micah used it to make two images of silver, one carved and the other cast in metal. These he set up in his house to be worshiped. He appointed one of his sons a priest, and made his house an idol's temple.

One day a man on a journey was passing by Micah's house. Micah saw from his dress that he belonged to the tribe of Levi, the tribe of priests. He said to him, "Who are you? Where do you come from?"

The young man said, "I am a Levite, from Bethlehem in Judah, and I am trying to find a place to earn my living."

"Stay here with me," said Micah, "and be a priest in my house. I will give you your food, and a place to sleep, and each year, a suit of clothes and ten pieces of silver."

The Levite was pleased at this, so he stayed in Micah's house and became his priest.

The tribe of Dan was living at that time between the Philistines and the tribe of Benjamin, with Judah on the south and Ephraim on the north. The Philistines were very close, so they looked for someplace else to live in peace. They sent out five men as spies, to go through the country and find a better place for their tribe. These five men soon came to the house of Micah, who took them into his house, as was the custom. These men from Dan (who were called Danites) met Micah's priest, who took them into the temple, showed them the images and the altar, and offered a sacrifice and prayed for them.

Then the five men went on their way and, far in the north, they found a little city called Laish which they could easily take over.

So a large part of the tribe of Dan, with their wives and their children, went up toward this place. Among them were 600 men with shields, swords, and spears for war. As they passed Micah's house, the five men remembered its temple. They took the silver idols and convinced Micah's priest to be their priest, then went on their way.

When Micah came home, he found his temple had been robbed and his images and his priest taken away.

He gathered some of his neighbors, and they hastened after the people of Dan. When he caught up to them, Micah saw that the men of Dan were too strong to fight, so he went back to his house without his priest and without his images. The Danites went up to the little city of Laish in the north. They took it, and killed all the people living there. Then they built the city again and changed its name to Dan, the name of the father of their tribe.

There, at Dan, they built a temple, and in it they set up the images, and this Levite became their priest. The strangest part of all the story is, this Levite was Moses' grandson. The people of Israel fell into sin so soon that the grandson of Moses became the priest in a temple of idols. At this time, the house of God was at Shiloh, yet at Dan there was a temple of idols, and within its walls, a line of priests descended from Moses were worshiping and offering sacrifices to images.

Since the temple of idols in Dan was much nearer to the people in the northern part of the land than the house of the Lord at Shiloh, many of those who lived in the north went to this idol temple to worship. So the people of Israel fell away from God and served idols. This was very displeasing to God.

Discussion Questions: *1. Who did Micah steal money from? 2. What did he do with the money? 3. Who robbed Micah's temple? 4. Who became a priest in the temple of idols?*

DAY 90

NAOMI GOES HOME
Ruth 1:1-22

IN the time of the judges, a man named Elimelech was living in the town of Bethlehem, in the tribe of Judah, about six miles south of Jerusalem. His wife's name was Naomi, and his two sons were Mahlon and Chilion. For some years the crops were poor and food was scarce in Judah, so Elimelech and his family went to live in the land of Moab.

They stayed there ten years, and in that time, Elimelech died. His two sons married women from Moab, one named Orpah, the other Ruth. But the two young men also died in Moab, so Naomi and her two daughters-in-law were all widows.

Naomi heard that God had again given good harvests and bread to the land of Judah, and she decided to go back to her own land and her own town of Bethlehem. Before she left, she said to her daughters-in-law, "Go back, my daughters, to your own mothers' homes. May the Lord deal kindly with you, as you have been kind to your husbands and me. May the Lord grant that each of you may find another husband and a happy home." Then Naomi kissed them farewell, and the three women all wept together. The two young widows said to her, "You have been a good mother to us, and we will go with you, and live among your people."

"No, no," said Naomi. "You are young, and I am old. Go back and be happy among your own people."

Orpah kissed Naomi and went back to her people, but Ruth would not leave her. She said, "Do not ask me to leave you, for I never will. Where you go, I will go. Where you live, I will live. Your people shall be my people, and your God shall be my God. Where you die, I will die and be buried. Nothing but death itself shall part you and me."

When Naomi saw that Ruth was firm about this, she stopped trying to persuade her, and the two women went on together. They walked around the Dead Sea, crossed the river Jordan, climbed the mountains of Judah, and came to Bethlehem.

Naomi had been absent from Bethlehem for ten years, but her friends were all glad to see her again. They said, "Is this Naomi, whom we knew years ago?" The name *Naomi* means "pleasant." And Naomi said, "Call me not Naomi. Call me Mara, for the Lord has made my life bitter. I went out full, with my husband and two sons. Now I come home empty, without them. Do not call me 'Pleasant.' Call me 'Bitter.' "

Discussion Questions: *1. Why did Elimelech and his family go to live in Moab? 2. Who stayed with Naomi? 3. What does* **Naomi** *mean?* **Mara?** *4. Why do you think Ruth stayed with her mother-in-law?*

DAY 91

BOAZ

Ruth 2:1-4:22

THERE was a very rich man named Boaz living in Bethlehem at that time. He owned large fields that were very fertile, and he was related to the family of Elimelech, Naomi's dead husband.

It was the custom in Israel not to gather all the stalks at harvest, but to leave some for the poor people, who followed after the reapers and gathered what was left. When Naomi and Ruth came to Bethlehem, it was the time of the barley harvest, and Ruth went out into the fields to glean the grain the reapers had left. It so happened that she was gleaning in the field that belonged to Boaz, this rich man.

Boaz came out from town to see his men reaping, and he said to them, "Who is the young woman I see gleaning in the field?"

They answered, "It is the young woman from the land of Moab, who came with Naomi. She asked to glean after the reapers, and has been here gathering grain since yesterday."

RUTH GLEANED IN THE FIELD OF BOAZ - RUTH 2:8

Boaz said to Ruth, "Listen to me, my daughter. Do not go to any other field. Stay here with my young women. No one shall harm you, and when you are thirsty, go and drink from our water jugs."

Ruth bowed to Boaz and thanked him for his kindness to a stranger in Israel.

Boaz said, "I have heard how true you have been to your mother-in-law, Naomi, in leaving your own land and coming with her to this land. May the Lord, under whose wings you have come, give you a reward!" At noon, when they sat down to rest and eat, Boaz gave her some of the food. He said to the reapers, "When you are reaping, leave some of the sheaves for her, and drop some sheaves from the bundles, so she may gather them."

That evening Ruth showed Naomi how much she had gleaned and told her of the rich man who had been so kind to her.

Naomi said, "This man is a relative of ours. Stay in his fields as long as the harvest lasts." And so Ruth gleaned the fields of Boaz until the harvest had been gathered.

At the end of the harvest, Boaz held a feast on the threshing floor. After the feast, following Naomi's advice, Ruth went to him, and said, "You are a near relation of my husband and of his father, Elimelech. Please be kind to us for his sake."

Boaz soon fell in love with Ruth and married her. After the wedding, Naomi and Ruth went to live in his home, so Naomi's life was no longer bitter, but pleasant. Boaz and Ruth had a son named Obed. Later, Obed had a son named Jesse, and Jesse was the father of David, the shepherd boy who became king. So Ruth, the young woman of Moab who chose the people and God of Israel, became the mother of kings.

Discussion Questions: *1. What does it mean to glean grain? Why did Ruth do it? 2. How did Boaz act toward Ruth? 3. What happened to Ruth and Boaz? 4. Who was related to them?*

DAY 92

LITTLE SAMUEL

1 Samuel 1:1-3:21

WHILE Eli was the priest and judge of Israel, a man named Elkanah lived at Ramah. He had two wives, as did many men in that time. One of these wives had children, but the other wife, Hannah, had no child.

Every year Elkanah and his family went up to worship at the house of the Lord in Shiloh, and at one of these visits, Hannah prayed to the Lord, saying, "O Lord, if you will give me a son, he shall be given to the Lord as long as he lives."

The Lord heard Hannah's prayer and gave her a little boy, and she named him Samuel, which means "Asked of God." While he was still a little child, she brought him to Eli, the priest, and said to him, "My lord, I asked God for this child and promised he would be the Lord's as long as he lives. Let him stay here with you and grow up in God's house."

So little Samuel stayed at Shiloh and lived with Eli, the priest, in one of the tents beside the Tabernacle. As he grew up, he helped Eli in the work of the Lord's house.

Samuel was a comfort to Eli because his own sons, who were priests, were very wicked young men. Eli's heart was very sad over the sins of his sons, but now that he was old, he could do nothing to control them.

One night little Samuel, who was lying down on his bed, heard a voice calling him by name. (It was the Lord's voice, but Samuel did not know it.)

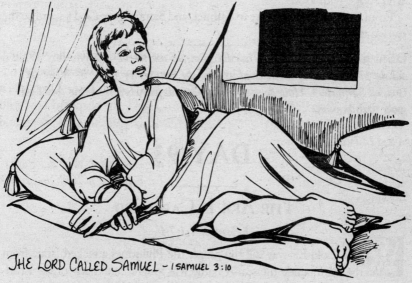

THE LORD CALLED SAMUEL — I SAMUEL 3:10

He answered, "Here I am!" and ran to Eli, saying, "Here I am. You called me. What do you want me to do?"

Eli said, "My child, I did not call you. Go and lie down again."

Samuel lay down, but soon heard the voice calling him again. Again he got up and went to Eli. "Here I am. I'm sure you called me."

"No," said Eli, "I did not call you. Lie down again."

A third time the voice was heard, and now Eli realized the Lord was calling Samuel. He said, "Go, lie down once more. And if the voice speaks to you again, say 'Speak, Lord, for thy servant heareth.'"

Samuel went and lay down, and waited for the voice. "Samuel! Samuel!" Samuel said to the Lord, "Speak, Lord, for thy servant heareth."

And the Lord said to Samuel, "Listen to what I say. I have seen the wickedness of Eli's sons. And I have seen that their father did not punish them when they were doing evil. I am going to give them such a punishment that the story will make everyone's ears tingle."

Samuel lay in his room until morning. Then he got up and went about his work as usual, saying nothing of God's voice until Eli asked him.

"Samuel, my son, tell me what the Lord said to you last night. Hide nothing from me."

So Samuel told Eli all that God had said, though it was a sad message for Eli. And Eli said, "It is the Lord. Let him do what seems good to him."

Then the news went through all the land that God had spoken again to his people. And Hannah, the lonely mother, heard that her son was the prophet who spoke with God.

From that time, God spoke to Samuel, and Samuel gave God's word to the twelve tribes.

Discussion Questions: *1. What did Hannah ask the Lord to give her? What did she promise God if she received it? Did she keep her promise? 2. What did God tell Samuel? 3. How do you think Hannah felt when she knew that God spoke with her son?*

DAY 93

THE ARK IS CAPTURED

1 Samuel 4:1-7:1

WHILE old Eli was still the judge, the Philistines attacked Israel from the plain beside the sea. A battle was fought, and many of the Israelites were slain. Then the chiefs of the people said, "We have been beaten in battle because the Lord was not with us. Let's take the ark of the covenant from the Tabernacle, and then the Lord will be among us." So they went to Shiloh, and they took the ark of the covenant, and the two sons of Eli went with the ark, to care for it. When the ark was brought into the camp of the Israelites, all the men gave a great shout, so the earth rang with the sound.

The next day, there was a great battle. The Philistines overcame the Israelites, killing thousands of them. They killed the two sons of Eli and took the ark of the Lord into their own land.

On the day of the battle, Eli, old and blind, was sitting beside the door of the Tabernacle, his heart trembling for the ark of the Lord. A man came running from the army with his garments torn and earth on his head as a sign of sorrow. The man came before Eli, and said, "I have just come from the army. There has been a great battle. Israel has fled before the Philistines, and many of the people have been killed. Your two sons are dead, and the ark of God has been taken by the enemy."

When the old man heard that the ark of God was taken, he fell backward from his seat and dropped dead too.

The Philistines took the ark of God down to Ashdod, one of their chief cities. They set it in the temple of Dagon, their fish-headed idol. The next morning, when they came into the temple, the image of Dagon was lying on its face before the ark of the Lord. They stood the image up again, but on the next morning, not only had Dagon fallen down again, but the hands and head of Dagon had been cut off and were lying on the floor.

Besides all this, all the people began to have boils and sores. They saw the hand of the God of Israel in this, and sent the ark to Gath, another of their cities. There, too, the people broke out with boils and sores. They sent the ark to Ekron, but the people of that city said, "We will not have the ark of God among us. Send it back to its own land, or we will all die."

Then the rulers of the Philistines decided to send the ark back. They placed it on a wagon drawn by two cows.

The cows drew the ark up to the village of Beth-shemesh, where the people were reaping their wheat harvest on the hillsides. They saw the ark, and were glad. The men of Beth-shemesh cut up the wagon, made a fire with it, and offered the two cows to the Lord.

But the men of Beth-shemesh opened the ark and looked into it, which was against God's command, for no one but a priest was allowed to touch the ark. God sent a plague on the people of that place, and many of them died because they did not treat the ark with respect.

They were filled with fear and sent to the men of Kirjath-jearim, asking them to take the ark away. They did so, and for twenty years the ark stood in the house of a man named Abinadab in Kirjath-jearim.

They did not take the ark back to Shiloh, for after the death of Eli, the place was deserted, the Tabernacle fell into ruins, and no man lived there again.

_____

Discussion Questions: *1. Why did the Israelites want to take the ark of the covenant into battle? Were they right? How do you know? 2. What happened when the Philistines put the ark into their temple? 3. What happened to people who did not believe in God when the ark came to their cities?*

DAY 94

The Last of the Judges
1 Samuel 7:2-17

AS soon as Samuel grew up, he began to go among the tribes and tell the people what God wanted. "If you will really come back with all your heart to the Lord God of Israel, put away the false gods, and seek the Lord, then God will set you free from the Philistines."

After Samuel's words, the people began to throw down the idols and pray to the God of Israel. Samuel called all the people to one place, named Mizpah, close to Jerusalem. There he prayed for the people, and asked God to forgive them for turning away from him. They confessed their wrongdoings, and made a solemn promise to serve the Lord.

When the Philistines on the plain beside the Great Sea heard of this meeting, they feared the Israelites were about to break away from their rule, so they sent an army to drive the Israelites away to their homes and keep them under the rule of the Philistines.

When the Israelites saw the Philistines coming against them, they were very afraid. The Philistines were men of war, with swords, shields, and spears, and they were trained in fighting. It was more than twenty years since the Israelites had fought the Philistines and been beaten by them. They had no weapons or training, and they felt helpless.

Samuel took a lamb and offered it to the Lord as an offering for the people, and he prayed mightily for God to help Israel. God heard his prayer.

Just as the Philistines were rushing on the helpless men of Israel, there came a great storm, with rolling thunder and flashing lightning. Such storms are rare in that area, and this one was so heavy it frightened the Philistines. They threw down their spears and swords in terror and ran away.

The men of Israel picked up these arms and followed the Philistines, killing many of them and winning a great victory.

After this defeat, the Philistines stayed away from the land of Israel as long as Samuel ruled as judge over the tribes. He was the fifteenth of the judges, and the last. Samuel lived many years, and ruled the people wisely.

He taught the Israelites to worship the Lord God and to put away their idols.

While Samuel ruled, there was peace in all the tribes, and no enemies came from the lands around to do harm to the Israelites.

DAY 95

THE PEOPLE ASK FOR A KING

1 Samuel 8:1-22

WHEN Samuel had grown old, the elders of the tribes of Israel came to him and said, "You are growing old, and your sons do not rule as well as you have ruled. All the lands around us have kings. Let us have a king also, and you choose the king for us."

This was not pleasing to Samuel, because he felt that if Israel had a king, they would be turning away from the Lord. Samuel prayed to the Lord, and the Lord said to him, "Listen to the people. They have not turned away from you; they have turned away from me in asking for a king. Let them have a king, but tell them the wrong they are doing, and show them the trouble their king will bring to them."

So Samuel called the elders of the people together and said to them, "If you have a king, he will take your sons away from you, and will make some of them soldiers, and horsemen, and men to drive his chariots. He will take other sons to wait on him, to work in his fields, and to make his chariots and his weapons for war. Your king will take the best of your fields and your farms, and will give them to the men of his court. He will make your daughters cook for him, and make bread, and serve in his palace. He will take a part of your sheep, your oxen, and your asses. He will be your master, and you will be his servants."

But the people would not follow Samuel's advice. They said, "No, we want a king to reign over us, so we are like other nations. Our king will be our judge and lead us to war."

It was God's will that Israel should be a quiet, plain people, living alone in the mountains, serving the Lord, and not trying to conquer other nations. But they wanted to be a great people, to be strong in war, and to have riches and power. And the Lord said to Samuel, "Do as the people ask, and choose a king for them."

So Samuel sent the people to their homes, promising to find a king for them.

_____

Discussion Questions: *1. Why did the people want a king? 2. Did God want*

155

them to have a king? Why or why not? 3. What would have happened if the Israelites had conquered other nations? 4. What did God finally say to Samuel?

DAY 96

SAUL IS CHOSEN

1 Samuel 9:1-27

THERE was at that time in the tribe of Benjamin a young man named Saul. He was a very large man and good-looking. His father, Kish, was a rich man, with large fields and many flocks. Some asses that belonged to Kish had strayed away, and Saul went out with a servant to find them. While they were looking for the asses, they came near to Ramah, where Samuel lived. The servant said to Saul, "There is in this city a man of God whom all men honor. They say he can tell what is about to happen, for he is a seer. Let us go to him and give him a present. Perhaps he can tell us where to find the asses."

The day before this, the Lord had spoken to Samuel, and said, "Tomorrow, about this time, I will send you a man out of the tribe of Benjamin, and you shall make him the prince of my people, and he shall save my people from the Philistines."

When Samuel saw this tall and noble-looking young man coming to meet him, he heard the Lord's voice, saying, "This is the man I told you about. He is the one that will rule over my people."

Saul came up to Samuel, not knowing who he was, and said, "Can you tell me where the seer's house is?"

And Samuel answered Saul, "I am the seer. Come with me up to the hill. We are to have an offering and a feast there. As for the asses that were lost three days ago, do not be troubled about them, for they have been found. But on whom is the desire of all Israel? Is it not on you and on your father's house?"

Saul could not understand what the seer meant. He said, "Is not my tribe of Benjamin the smallest of all the tribes? And is not my family the least of all the families in the tribe? Why do you say such things to me?"

But Samuel led Saul and his servant into the best room at his house. At the table with thirty others, he gave Saul the best place, the choicest of the meat.

Discussion Questions: *1. Why did Saul go to Samuel? 2. What did God tell Samuel about Saul? 3. How did Saul react when Samuel told Saul that he found favor with God? Do you think God was pleased?*

DAY 97

SAUL IS ANOINTED

1 Samuel 10:1-27

THE next morning, Samuel sent the servant on ahead, while he spoke with Saul alone. He brought a vial of oil and poured it on Saul's head, and said, "The Lord has anointed you to be prince over his land and his people."

SAUL ANOINTED KING BY SAMUEL—1 SAMUEL 10:1

Then he told Saul just what he would find on the way, where he would meet certain people, and what he must do. He said, "When you come to the tomb where Rachel is buried, two men will meet you and will say to you, 'The asses for which you were looking have been found, and now your father is looking for you.' Then under an oak you will meet three men carrying three kids, three loaves of bread, and a bottle full of wine. These men will give you two loaves of bread as a present. Next you will meet a company of prophets, men full of God's Spirit, with instruments of music, and the Lord's Spirit will come upon you, and a new heart will be given to you. All these things will show you that God is with you. Now go, and do whatever God tells you to do."

And it came just as Samuel had said. These men met Saul, and when the prophets came near, singing and praising God, Saul joined them and also sang and praised the Lord. And in that hour, a new spirit came to Saul. He was no more the farmer's son, but a king.

He came home and told how he had met Samuel and Samuel told him the asses had been found. But he did not tell them that Samuel had poured oil on his head and said he was to be the king of Israel.

Samuel called all the people to the meeting place at Mizpah. He told them that since they had wished for a king, God has chosen one for them.

"Now," said Samuel, "let the men of the tribes pass by, each tribe and each family by itself."

The people passed by Samuel, and when the tribe of Benjamin came, out of all the tribes, Benjamin was taken. Out of Benjamin, one family, and out of that family, Saul's name was called. But Saul was not with his family; he had hidden himself. They found him and brought him out, and when he stood among the people, his head and shoulders rose above them all. And Samuel said, "Look at the man the Lord has chosen! There is not another like him among all the people!"

And all the people shouted "God save the king! Long live the king!"

Then Samuel told the people the laws the king and the people must obey. He wrote them down in a book, and placed the book before the Lord. Then Samuel sent the people home, and Saul went back to his own house in Gibeah.

So after 300 years under the fifteen judges, Israel now had a king. But among the people there were some who were not pleased with the new king, because he was an unknown man from a farm. They said, "Can such a man as this save us?" They showed no respect to the king, and in their hearts they looked down on him. But Saul said nothing and showed his wisdom by appearing not to notice them.

Discussion Questions: *1. How did Samuel know what to tell Saul? Did everything he told him happen? 2. Why did Saul hide? 3. How did the people feel when they saw their new king? How did they feel later?*

DAY 98

SAUL TAKES OVER

1 Samuel 11:1-12:25

AUL was now the king of all twelve tribes of Israel, but he lived at home and worked in the fields just as he had always done.

One day, while Saul was plowing in the field, a man came running with sad news. He said that the Ammonites, a fierce people living near the desert beyond the Jordan, had attacked Jabesh in Gilead.

The people in that city were too few to fight the Ammonites, and they said, "We will submit to your rule, if you will promise to spare our lives."

Nahash, the king of the Ammonites, said to the people of Jabesh, "You shall live, but within seven days I will come with my soldiers, and put out the right eye of every man in your city."

When a city was taken by its enemies in those times, cruel punishments were common. Often all the people in it, young and old, were slain without mercy.

When Saul heard this, the spirit of a king rose within him. He killed the oxen he was driving, cut them into twelve pieces, and sent swift messengers through the land, saying to every fighting man in the twelve tribes, "This is what will happen to the oxen of anyone who doesn't come and fight with me."

At once a great army gathered with Saul, and he sent word to Jabesh, saying, "Tomorrow, by the time the sun is hot, you will be set free from all fear of the Ammonites."

Saul and his men marched down into the Jordan valley and up the mountains of Gilead. There they attacked the Ammonites early in the morning, killed many of them, and scattered the rest.

Samuel was with Saul, and after the battle, he said, "Let's go to Gilgal, where Joshua camped long ago when our fathers crossed the Jordan, and we will set up the kingdom again."

They came to Gilgal, offered sacrifices to the Lord, and worshiped. Then Samuel gave up the kingdom to Saul and said good-bye to all the people.

Samuel reminded them all that God had done for them since he had led them out of Egypt: how he had saved them from their enemies and given them judges. "Now the Lord has set a king over you. If you fear the Lord and will serve him, it will go well with you. But if you disobey the Lord, then God will punish you, as he punished your fathers."

Then Samuel called on God, and God sent thunder and rain to show his power. The people were filled with fear, and they cried to Samuel, "Pray to the Lord for us, for we have done wrong in asking for a king."

"Yes," said Samuel, "you have done wrong. But if you do right, and seek the Lord, God will not forsake you. He will forgive you and bless you. I will always pray for you, and will teach you the right way. But if you do evil, God will destroy you and your king. So fear the Lord, and serve him in truth with all your heart."

After this, Samuel went back to his house at Ramah, and Saul ruled the people from Gibeah, the home of his family.

Discussion Questions: *1. Why were the people of Jabesh afraid of the Ammonites? 2. What did Saul do when he heard that the city had been attacked? 3. Why was it important for the people to worship God after the battle? 4. What did Samuel tell the people about having a king? What lesson do you think they learned from this?*

DAY 99

SAUL'S DISOBEDIENCE

1 Samuel 13:1-14

THE people had hoped that when they had a king to lead them in war, they would be able to free themselves from the Philistines, who ruled part of the land. But after Saul had been king for two years, the Philistines seemed to be stronger than ever.

Saul gathered together a little army, part of which was with him at Michmash, and part with his son Jonathan at Gilbeah, five miles to the south. Jonathan, who was a very brave young man, led his band against the Philistines at Geba, and took that place from them. The news of this fight went through the land, and the Philistines came up the mountains with a great army of chariots and horsemen. Saul blew a trumpet and called the Israelites to war. Although many came, they came trembling in fear of the Philistines.

Samuel had told Saul not to march from Gilgal until he had come to offer a sacrifice and call on God. But Samuel was late, and Saul grew impatient, for he saw his men scattering. At last Saul could wait no longer. He offered a sacrifice himself, though he was no priest. While the offering was still burning on the altar, Samuel arrived. He said to Saul, "What have you done?"

And Saul answered, "I saw my men were scattering, and I feared the enemy might attack, so I offered the sacrifice myself, since you were not here."

"You have done wrong," said Samuel. "You have not kept God's commands. If you had obeyed and trusted the Lord, he would have kept you safe. But now God will find some other man who will do his will — a man after his own heart — and God will someday take the kingdom from you and give it to him."

Discussion Questions: *1. What did the Israelites hope a king would do for them? Had that happened? 2. What did Saul do that was wrong? Why did he do it? 3. What did Samuel have to say about what he did?*

160

DAY 100

JONATHAN

1 Samuel 13:15-14:46

AFTER Samuel left, Saul led his 600 men up the mountains to Geba, the place Jonathan had taken. Across the valley near Michmash, the army of the Philistines camped in plain sight.

One morning Jonathan and the young man who waited on him went down the hill toward the camp of the Philistines. Jonathan could see the Philistines just across the valley. He said, "If the Philistines say to us, 'Come over,' we will go and fight them, even though we two are alone. We will take it as a sign that God will help us."

The Philistines saw the two Israelites standing on a rock across the valley, and they called to them, "Come over here, and we will show you something."

Then Jonathan said to his armor bearer, "Come on. The Lord has given them to us."

They crossed the valley, ran up to the Philistines, and struck them down right and left, without giving them a chance. Some fell down, but others ran away, and soon everybody began to run around. Before long, the Israelites on the hill across the valley could see the Philistines fighting and killing each other, men running in every direction, and the whole army melting away.

Soon Saul and his men came across the valley and joined in the fight. The Israelite prisoners in the camp of the Philistines rose against them, and the tribes near at hand came out and chased them as they fled. A great victory was won over the Philistines that day.

But Saul made a great mistake that day. He was afraid his men would stop following the Philistines to seize the things in their camp, so when the battle began, King Saul said, "Let the curse of God light on any man who takes food until the evening. Whoever takes any food before the sun goes down shall die, so there may be no delay in destroying our enemies."

So that day, no man ate any food until it was evening, and they were faint and feeble from hunger. They were so worn out that they could not chase the Philistines any further, and many of the Philistines escaped. That afternoon, as they were driving the Philistines through a forest, they found honey on the trees, but no one ate it, because of Saul's oath.

But Jonathan had not heard of his father's command. He took some honey and was made stronger by it. When Jonathan heard what his father said, he said, "My father has given us all great trouble. For if the men had some food, they would have been stronger."

That night, Saul found that Jonathan had innocently broken his command. He said, "I have taken an oath before the Lord, and now, Jonathan, you must die, though you are my own son."

But the people would not allow Jonathan to be put to death, even to keep Saul's oath. They rescued Jonathan and set him free. A great victory had been won, but Saul had already shown that he was not fit to rule, because he was too hasty in his acts and words, and because he was not careful to obey God's command.

_____

Discussion Questions: *1. How did Jonathan know whether or not to attack the Philistines? 2. Who caused Jonathan to win? 3. Why did Saul tell his soldiers not to eat that day? What happened because he made them swear that oath? 4. What did Saul show by his actions?*

DAY 101

_____

Saul Is Disobedient

1 Samuel 15:1-35

AFTER the great victory over the Philistines, Saul led his men against all the enemies of Israel. He drove back the Moabites and the Ammonites, then he fought the Edomites and the kings of Zobah, until Israel was free of its oppressors.

To the south of the land, in the desert where the Israelites had lived for forty years, were the wild and wandering Amalekites, who had killed many Israelites when they were helpless on their journey. To punish them for doing this, God told the Israelites to fight the Amalekites until they destroyed them. The time had now come for God's curse against the Amalekites to be fulfilled, and Samuel said to Saul, "God says you should go down and make war against the Amalekites, and destroy them utterly."

So Saul called out the men of war and marched southward into the desert, where he made war on the Amalekites, took their city, and destroyed it. But he did not do what God had commanded him. Instead, he brought Agag, the king of the Amalekites, and many of his people as prisoners, plus their large flocks of sheep and oxen.

Then the Lord came to Samuel, saying, "It would have been better never to have chosen Saul as king, for he does not obey my commands." All that night,

Samuel prayed to the Lord, and the next day he went to meet Saul. When Saul saw him, he said, "I have done what the Lord commanded me to do."

Samuel replied, "If you have obeyed God's command and destroyed all the Amalekites and all they possessed, what is this bleating of sheep and bellowing of oxen I hear?"

"They bought them from the Amalekites," answered Saul. "The people spared the best of the sheep and oxen to offer in sacrifice to the Lord. All the rest we destroyed."

Samuel said, "God told you to go and utterly destroy the Amalekites and leave nothing of them. Why didn't you obey God's word?"

And Saul said, "I have done as God commanded, and have destroyed the Amalekites. But the people took some things that should have been destroyed, to offer in sacrifice to the Lord."

Samuel asked, "Is the Lord as happy with offerings as he is with obeying his words? To obey is better than sacrifice, and to listen to God's word is more precious than to place offerings on his altar. To disobey God's word is as evil as to worship idols. You have refused to obey the voice of the Lord, and the Lord will take away your kingdom from you."

Saul saw now what he had done, and he said, "I have sinned in not obeying God's word. But I was afraid of the people, and yielded to them. Forgive my sin. Come with me, and I will worship the Lord."

"No," said Samuel, "I will not go with you, for God will refuse you as king."

SAMUEL TURNED AWAY FROM SAUL - 1 SAMUEL 16:27

163

As Samuel turned away, Saul took hold of his garment, and it tore in his hand. And Samuel said, "God has torn the kingdom away from you, and he will give it to a man that is better than you are. God is not like a man, saying one thing and doing another. What God has said shall surely come to pass."

After this, Samuel never saw Saul again, but he mourned and wept for Saul, because he had disobeyed the Lord, and the Lord had rejected him as king.

Discussion Questions: *1. What did Saul and his army do next? 2. What did God tell them to do to the Amalekites? 3. Did Saul obey God? 4. What did Saul tell Samuel? Was it true? 5. What did Samuel tell Saul about obedience? Had Saul learned the lesson God had tried to teach him?*

DAY 102

DAVID IS CHOSEN •
1 Samuel 16:1-23

WHEN Samuel told Saul the Lord would take away his kingdom, he did not mean Saul would lose the kingdom at once. He was no longer God's king, and as soon as the right man was found and trained, then God would take away Saul's power and give it to the man he had chosen. But it was many years before all this happened.

Samuel, who had helped in choosing Saul, mourned for him. But the Lord said to Samuel, "Do not weep and mourn any longer over Saul. I have refused him as king. Fill the horn with oil and go to Bethlehem, in Judah. Find a man there named Jesse, for I have chosen a king from among his sons."

Samuel said to the Lord, "How can I go? If Saul hears of it, he will kill me."

Then the Lord said to Samuel, "Take a young cow with you, and tell the people you have come to make an offering to the Lord. Call Jesse and his sons to the sacrifice. I will tell you what to do, and you will anoint the one I point out to you."

At the sacrifice, seven of Jesse's sons passed before Samuel, but God didn't choose any of them. Finally, Samuel said to Jesse, "None of these is the man God has chosen. Are these all your children?"

"There is one more," said Jesse. "The youngest of all. He is a boy in the field, caring for the sheep."

"Send for him." After a time, the youngest son was brought in. His name was David, a word that means "darling," and he was a beautiful boy, perhaps fifteen years old, with fresh cheeks and bright eyes.

As soon as David came, the Lord said to Samuel, "Arise. Anoint him, for this is the one I have chosen."

Then Samuel poured oil on David's head in the presence of all his brothers. But no one realized that the anointing meant David was to be the king. Perhaps they thought David was chosen to be a prophet, like Samuel.

DAVID TENDING THE SHEEP -
I SAMUEL 16:11

From that day, the Spirit of the Lord was with David, and he began to show signs of coming greatness. He went back to his sheep on the hillsides around Bethlehem, but God was with him. David grew up strong and brave, not afraid of the wild beasts that prowled around and tried to carry away his sheep. More than once he fought with lions and bears and killed them. And, young as he was, David thought of God, and prayed to God. And God talked with David, and showed to him his will.

But while the Spirit of God came to David, it left King Saul, because he no longer obeyed God's words. Then Saul became very unhappy and gloomy, even seeming to lose his mind at times because he was no longer at peace with God.

The servants around Saul noticed that when someone played the harp and sang, Saul's gloominess passed away, and he became cheerful. One time, Saul said, "Find someone who can play well, and bring him to me. Let me listen to music, for it drives away my sadness."

One of the young men said, "I have seen a young man, a son of Jesse in Bethlehem, who can play well. He is handsome and pleasant, and the Lord is with him."

So Saul sent a message to Jesse, David's father. He said, "Send me your son David, who is with the sheep. Let him come and play before me."

DAVID WOULD PLAY THE HARP FOR SAUL - 1 SAMUEL 16:23

When Saul saw David, he loved him, just as everyone else did. David played on the harp and sang for Saul driving away the king's sadness. Saul liked David so well he made him his armor bearer, and David carried his shield, spear, and sword when the king was with his army. But Saul did not know that David had been anointed by Samuel. If he had, he would have been jealous of David.

After a time Saul seemed well, and David left him and went back to being a shepherd.

Discussion Questions: *1. Did God take away Saul's kingdom quickly? 2. Where did God send Samuel to find a new king? 3. What happened to Saul? 4. How did David come to Saul's court? Did Saul like him?*

DAY 103

DAVID AND GOLIATH
1 Samuel 17:1-54

ALL through the reign of Saul, there was constant war with the Philistines, who lived west of Israel. A few years after David had been anointed by Samuel, the Philistines and the Israelites were on opposite sides of a valley, ready to fight each other again.

Every day a giant came out of the camp of the Philistines and dared someone to come from the Israelites' camp and fight with him. The giant's name was Goliath. He was nine feet tall, and he wore armor from head to foot. His spear was twice as long as any other man could hold, and every day, he called out, "I am a Philistine, and you are servants of Saul. Choose one of your men, and let him come out and fight with me. If I kill him, then you will submit to us. If he kills me, we will give up to you. Send out your man!"

But no man in the army, not even King Saul, dared go out and fight the giant. The Israelites were mostly farmers and shepherds, and were not fond of war. Besides, few of the Israelites had swords and spears. Most of their weapons were made out of their farming tools. For forty days, the Philistine giant continued his call.

One day David's father sent him to visit his three brothers in the army. David came, spoke to his brothers, and gave them a present from his father. While he was talking with them, Goliath came out and called for someone to fight him.

David asked, "Who is this man, speaking this way to the army of the living God? Why doesn't someone go out and kill him?"

While all the men were in terror, this boy thought of a plan. He believed he knew how to bring down the big warrior, with all his armor. Finally, David said, "If no one else will go, I will go out and fight this enemy of the Lord's people."

They brought David before King Saul. Years had passed since Saul had met David, and he had grown from a boy to a man, so Saul did not recognize him. "You cannot fight with this giant," Saul said. "You are very young, and he is a man of war, trained from his youth."

David replied, "I am only a shepherd, but I have fought with lions and bears when they tried to steal my sheep. I'm not afraid to fight this Philistine. The Lord saved me from the lion's jaw and the bear's paw, and he will save me from this enemy, for I shall fight for the Lord and his people."

Then Saul put his own armor on David: a helmet on his head, a coat of mail on his body, and a sword at his waist. But Saul was almost a giant, and his armor was far too large for David. David said, "I am not used to fighting with weapons like these. Let me fight my own way."

David's plan was very wise. He would look very weak, which would relax Goliath's guard. Then, from far enough away that the giant could not reach him with sword or spear, he'd strike him down with a weapon the giant would not expect.

David took his shepherd's staff in his hand, as though that was his weapon. But out of sight, in a bag under his clothes, he had five smooth stones and a slingshot. The giant looked down at David and laughed at him.

DAVID CAME OUT TO MEET THE GIANT, GOLIATH — I SAMUEL 17:42

"Am I a dog," he said, "that this boy comes to me with a stick?"

And David answered him, "You come against me with a sword and a spear and a dart. But I come to you in the name of the Lord of hosts, the God of the armies of Israel. This day the Lord will give you into my hand. I will strike you down, and take off your head, and the army of the Philistines will die and be

DAVID KILLED GOLIATH WITH THE GIANT'S OWN SWORD — I SAMUEL 17:51

eaten by the birds and the beasts, so all may know there is a God in Israel, and he can save in other ways besides with sword and spear."

Then David ran toward the Philistine, as if to fight him with his shepherd's staff. But when he was just near enough for a good aim, he took out his sling and hurled a stone at the giant's forehead. David's aim was good; the stone struck the Philistine in his forehead. It stunned him, and he fell to the ground.

While the two armies stood wondering what had happened, David ran forward, drew out the giant's sword, and cut off his head. When the Philistines knew their great warrior was dead, they turned to run to their own land. The Israelites followed after them and killed them by the thousand.

David had won a great victory, and was known all over the land as the one who had saved his people from their enemies.

Discussion Questions: *1. Who was Goliath? Why were the Israelites afraid of him? 2. Who decided to fight Goliath? How did he do it? Why did he win? 3. What happened to the Philistines?*

DAY 104

SAUL'S JEALOUSY

1 Samuel 17:55-19:6

AFTER David had slain the giant, he was brought before King Saul, still holding the giant's head. Saul took David into his own house and made him an officer of his soldiers. David was as wise and brave in the army as he had been when facing the giant, and very soon he was in command of a thousand men, who all loved him.

When David was returning from his battle with the Philistines, the women of Israel came to meet him, singing:

> Saul has slain his thousands,
> And David his ten thousands.

This made Saul very angry, for he was a jealous, suspicious man. He thought of Samuel saying that God would take the kingdom from him and give it to someone more worthy of it. He began to think that perhaps this young man might try to make himself king.

Saul became very sad and depressed, raving around the house, talking like a crazy man. By this time, the others knew David was a musician, and they called him to play on his harp and sing before the troubled king. But in his madness, Saul would not listen to David's voice. Twice he threw his spear at him, but each time David leaped aside and the spear went into the wall of the house.

Saul was afraid of David, for he saw the Lord was with him. He wanted David dead, but did not dare kill him, because everybody loved him. Saul said to himself, "Though I cannot kill him myself, I can have him killed by the Philistines." And he sent David out on many dangerous errands of war. But each time, David came home safely.

One day, Saul said, "I will give you my daughter Merab for your wife, if you will fight the Philistines for me."

David fought the Philistines, but when he came home from war, he found that Merab, who had been promised to him, had been given to another man. Saul had another daughter, named Michal, who loved David. So Saul sent word to David, saying, "You shall have Michal, my daughter, for your wife when you have killed 100 Philistines."

David went out, fought the Philistines, and killed 200 of them, and Saul gave him Michal as his wife. But he was all the more afraid of David as he saw him growing in power and drawing nearer to the throne of the kingdom.

Unlike his father, Saul's son Jonathan loved David with all his heart. It saddened Jonathan that his father was so jealous of David. He spoke to his father about it, saying, "Don't harm David. He has been faithful to you and has done great things for the kingdom. Why should you kill an innocent man?"

For a while, Saul listened to Jonathan, even making a promise not to hurt David.

Discussion Questions: *1. Why did Saul make David an officer over his soldiers? 2. How did Saul feel when people praised David more than they praised him? 3. What did Saul try to do to David? 4. Who loved David?*

DAY 105

DAVID IS DRIVEN AWAY

1 Samuel 19:11-20:42

N a little while, Saul's hatred of David made him forget his promise not to hurt him, and he sent men to David's house, to capture him. But Michal, David's wife, let David down out of the window, so he escaped. She placed an image on David's bed and covered it with the bedding. When the men came, she said, "David is sick in bed, and cannot go."

They brought the word to Saul, who said, "Bring him to me in the bed, just as he is."

By the time the image was found in David's bed, David was in a safe place, far away. David went to Samuel and stayed with him and other prophets, worshiping God and singing and speaking God's word. Saul heard that David was there and sent men to take him, but when they came and saw Samuel and the prophets praising God and praying, the same spirit came on them, and they began to praise and to pray.

Finally, Saul said, "If no other man will bring David to me, I will go myself and take him." And Saul went to Ramah. But when he came near the worshipers, the same spirit came on Saul. He, too, began to join in the songs and the prayers, and stayed there all that day and night, worshiping God very earnestly. For a while after this, Saul treated David nicely.

But David knew that Saul was still his bitter enemy and would kill him the next time his madness came upon him. He met Jonathan out in the field, away from the palace. Jonathan said to David, "Stay away from the king's table for a few days. I'll find out how he feels about you, and will tell you. Maybe he'll become your friend. But if he is to be your enemy, I know the Lord is with you, and Saul will not win against you. Promise that as long as you live, you will be kind to me, and when I die, you'll treat my children kindly."

Jonathan believed, as many others believed, that David would become the king of Israel, and he was willing to give up the kingdom to him, even though Jonathan was next in line to be king.

Jonathan said to David, "In three days, I will be here with my bow and arrows, and I will send a little boy out near your place of hiding, and I will shoot three arrows. If I call out to the boy, 'The arrows are away beyond you,' that will mean there is danger, and you must hide from the king."

So David stayed away from Saul's table for two days. At first Saul said nothing of his absence, but at last he said, "Why hasn't the son of Jesse come to meals yesterday and today?"

And Jonathan said, "David asked my permission to go to visit his oldest brother."

Saul was very angry. He cried out, "You are a disobedient son! Why have you chosen this enemy of mine as your best friend? Don't you know that as long as he is alive, you can never be king? Send for him, and have him brought to me, for he shall surely die!" Saul was so mad that he threw his spear at his own son, Jonathan!

The next day Jonathan went out into the field with a little boy. He said to the boy, "Run out and be ready to find the arrows I shoot."

As the boy was running, Jonathan shot arrows beyond him and called out, "The arrows are away beyond you. Run quickly and find them."

The boy ran, found the arrows, and brought them to Jonathan. He gave the bow and arrows to the boy, saying to him, "Take them back to the city. I will stay here a while."

As soon as the boy was out of sight, David came from his hiding place and ran to Jonathan. They fell into each other's arms and wept together, for David knew he must leave his home, wife, friends, and his father's house, and hide wherever he could from the hate of King Saul.

Jonathan said to him, "Go in peace, for we have sworn together, saying, 'The Lord shall be between you and me, and between your children and my children forever.'"

Then Jonathan went back to his father's palace, and David began looking for a safe place to hide from Saul.

_____

Discussion Questions: *1. What did Michal do to keep David safe from the king? 2. Why couldn't any of Saul's men take David? 3. Why did Jonathan help David? 4. What did he do for David?*

DAY 106

_____

DAVID'S HIDING PLACE

1 Samuel 21:1-22:5

AFTER his meeting with Jonathan, David became a wanderer without a home for as long as Saul lived. He went away so suddenly that he had no bread to eat and no sword. On his way, he stopped at a little city named Nob, where the Tabernacle was then.

The chief priest, Ahimelech, was surprised to see David coming alone. David said to him, "The king has sent me on a secret errand. Can you give me a few loaves of bread?"

"There is no bread here," said the priest, "except the holy bread from the table in the holy house. The priests have just taken it away to put new bread in its place."

"Let me have that bread," said David, "for we are the Lord's, and are holy."

So the priest gave David the holy bread. Then David asked, "Have you a spear, or a sword I can take with me? The king's errand was so sudden that I had no time to bring my weapons."

"There is no sword here," said the priest, "except the sword of Goliath, who you killed. It is wrapped in a cloth, in the closet with the priest's robe. If you want that sword, you can have it."

"There is no sword like that," said David. "Give it to me." So David took the giant's sword and five loaves of bread and went away. But where should he go? Nowhere in Saul's kingdom would be safe.

So David went to live in the wilderness of Judah. He found a great cave and hid in it. Many people heard where he was, and from all parts of the land — especially from his own tribe of Judah — men who were not satisfied with the rule of King Saul gathered around David. Soon he had a little army of 400 men who stayed with him.

All of these men with David were good fighters, and some of them were very brave in battle. Once, three of these men did a great deed for David. While David was in the great cave with his men the Philistines were holding the town of Bethlehem, which had been David's home. David said one day, "How I wish I could have a drink of water from the well that is beside the gate of Bethlehem!" This was the well from which he had drunk when he was a boy, and no water tastes better than that.

Those three brave men went out together, walked to Bethlehem, fought their way through the Philistines who were on guard, drew a vessel of water from the well, and then fought their way back to David's cave.

But when they brought the water to David, he would not drink it. He said, "This water was bought by the blood of three brave men. I will not drink it, but I will pour it out as an offering to the Lord, for it is sacred." So David poured out the water as a precious gift to the Lord.

Discussion Questions: *1. How long did David have to wander? 2. What did the chief priest give David? 3. Where did David and the men who followed him live? 4. What did David ask for? Why?*

DAY 107

SAUL AND THE PRIESTS
1 Samuel 22:6-23

AUL soon heard that David was hiding in the mountains of Judah. One day while Saul was sitting in Gibeah, outdoors under a tree with his nobles around him, he said, "You are men of my own tribe of Benjamin, yet none of you will help me find this son of Jesse, who had made an agreement with my own son against me, and who has gathered an army, and is waiting to rise against me. Isn't one of you with me and against my enemy?"

One man, whose name was Doeg, said, "I was at the city of the priests some time ago, and I saw the son of Jesse come to the chief priest, Ahimelech. The priest gave him loaves of bread and a sword."

"Send for Ahimelech and all the priests," commanded King Saul. They took all the priests as prisoners — eighty-five men in all — and brought them before King Saul. Saul said to them, "Why have you priests joined with David, the son of Jesse, to rebel against me? You have given him bread and a sword, and have shown yourselves to be his friends."

Then Ahimelech the priest answered the king. "There is no one among all the king's servants as faithful as David. He is the king's son-in-law, living in the palace and sitting in the king's council. What wrong have I done by giving him bread? I knew nothing of any evil he had done against the king."

Then the king was very angry. He said, "You shall die, Ahimelech, and all your father's family, because you helped this man, who is my enemy. You knew he was hiding from me and did not tell me of him."

And the king ordered his guards to kill all the priests. But they would not obey him, for they felt it was a dreadful deed to kill the Lord's priests. This made Saul all the more furious, and he turned to Doeg. "You are the only one of my servants who is true to me. You kill these priests who have been unfaithful to their king."

Doeg obeyed the king and killed eighty-five men who wore the priestly garments. He went to the city of the priests, killed all their wives and children, and burned the city. Only one priest escaped, a young man named Abiathar, the son of Ahimelech. He came to David with the terrible news that Saul had slain all the priests, and he brought the high-priest's breastplate and robes.

David said to him, "I saw this man Doeg, the Edomite, there on that day, and I knew he would tell Saul. Without intending to do harm, I have caused the death of all your father's house. Stay with me. I will protect your life with my own."

Abiathar was now the high-priest, and he was with David, not with Saul. The news of Saul's dreadful deed spread all through the nation, and more people began to look to David as their leader and pray he would end Saul's reign as their king.

Discussion Questions: *1. Who had seen David with the chief priest? 2. What did Saul accuse the priests of doing? 3. How did the chief priest answer Saul? 4. What happened to the priests? 5. When Abiathar came to David and stayed with him, what was God showing the people?*

DAY 108

DAVID SPARES SAUL'S LIFE

1 Samuel 23:1-27:12

DAVID and his men hid in many places in the mountains of Judah, often hunted by Saul, but always escaping from him.

Once David was hiding with a few men in a great cave near the Dead Sea. They were far back in the darkness of the cave when they saw Saul come into the cave alone and lie down to sleep. David went very quietly toward Saul, his sword in his hand. His men watched to see him kill Saul, but instead, he only cut off part of Saul's long robe. His men were not pleased at this, but David said to them, "The Lord forbid that I should do harm to the man the Lord has anointed as king." David would not allow his men to harm Saul either.

After a time, Saul woke up and left the cave. David followed him at a distance, then called out to him, "My lord the king!"

DAVID SPARES SAUL'S LIFE - 1 SAMUEL 24:11

Saul looked around, and there stood David, bowing to him and holding up a piece of his royal robe. David said to Saul, "My lord, O king, why do you listen to the words of men who tell you that David is trying to do you harm? This very day the Lord gave you into my hand in the cave, and some told me

175

to kill you, but I would not. See this piece of your robe? I cut it off to prove to you that I won't harm you, though you are trying to kill me. May the Lord judge between you and me, and may the Lord give me justice. But my hand will not touch you."

When Saul heard these words, his old love for David came back to him, and he cried out, "Is that your voice, my son David?" And Saul wept, and said, "You are a better man than I am, for you have done good to me, while I have been doing harm to you. I know it is God's will that you shall be king, and you will rule over this people. Now give me your word, in the name of the Lord, that you will not destroy my family but will spare their lives."

David gave this promise to Saul in the name of the Lord, and Saul led his men away from David.

But David still kept his hiding place, for he could not trust Saul's promise not to kill him. And it was not long before Saul was again looking for David in the wilderness of Judah, with Abner, the commander of his army, and 3,000 men. From his hiding place in the mountains, David looked down on the plain and saw Saul's camp almost at his feet. That night David and Abishai, one of his men, came down quietly and walked into the middle of Saul's camp while all his guards were asleep. Saul himself was sleeping with his spear standing in the ground at his head, a bottle of water tied to it.

Abishai, David's follower, knew that David would not kill King Saul, and he said to David, "God has given your enemy into your hand again. Let me strike him through to the ground at one stroke. Only once. I will not need to strike twice."

But David said, "You can't kill him. Let the Lord strike him, or let him die when God wills it, or let him fall in battle, but he will not die by my hand. Take his spear and water bottle, and let's go."

So David took Saul's spear and his bottle of water, and David and Abishai walked out of the camp without awakening anyone. In the morning, David called out to Saul's men and to Abner, the chief of Saul's army. "Abner, where are you?"

Abner answered, "Who are you?"

Then David said, "Why haven't you kept watch over the king? You deserve to be put to death for your neglect! See, here is the king's spear and his bottle of water!"

Saul knew David's voice, and he said, "Is that your voice, my son David?"

And David answered, "It is my voice, my lord, O king. Why do you pursue me? What evil have I done? I am not worth all the trouble you are taking to hunt for me."

Saul answered, "I have done wrong. Come back, my son David, and I will no longer try to harm you, for you have spared my life today!"

David said, "Let one of the young men come and take the king's spear. As I have spared your life today, may the Lord spare mine."

So David went his way, for he would not trust himself in Saul's hands, and Saul led his men back to his home at Gibeah. David was now leading quite an army and was a powerful ruler. He made an agreement with the king of the Philistines and went down to the plain by the Great Sea, to live among the Philistines. They gave him a city called Ziklag, to the south of Judah, and David and his followers lived there during the last year of Saul's reign.

Discussion Questions: *1. Why wouldn't David harm King Saul? Do you think he was right? 2. What two things did David promise Saul? 3. What else did David do to show Saul he was safe from him? 4. Did David believe Saul's promises to him? Why or why not?*

DAY 109

THE ROBBERS

1 Samuel 28:1-30:31

NCE again the Philistines gathered to make war on King Saul and the land of Israel. The king of the Philistines sent for David and said to him, "You and your men shall go with me in the army and fight the men of Israel."

David was now living in the Philistine country and was under their rule, so he came from Ziklag with his 600 men, and they joined the army of the Philistines. But when the lords of the Philistines saw David and his men, they said, "Why are these Israelites here? They can't fight with us in this war against their own people. We can't trust them."

Achish, the king of the Philistines, sent David and his men away, so David was not made to fight against his own people. But when he came to his own city, Ziklag, he found it had been burned and destroyed. All the people in it — the wives and children of David's men, and David's own wives — had been carried away into the desert by the Amalekites.

David followed the Amalekites into the wilderness. His march was so swift that some of his men could not keep up. They stopped to rest at the brook Bezor, while 400 men went on with David. He found the Amalekites in their camp, without guards, feasting on the food they had taken. David and his men fell on them suddenly and killed all of them, except 400 of them who escaped on camels far into the desert, where David could not follow them. David freed all the women and children that had been carried away from Ziklag, including his own two wives. He also took a great amount of treasure that these men had taken from many other towns.

David divided all these things between himself and his men, giving as much to those who had stayed at the brook Bezor as to those who had fought the Amalekites. This treasure made David very rich, and he sent part of it to many of his friends in Judah.

Discussion Questions: *1. Why didn't the Philistines trust David when they went to war? 2. What had happened to his city while David was away? 3. What did David do?*

DAY 110

THE DEATH OF SAUL

1 Samuel 31:1-13

WHILE David was chasing the robbers in the south, the Philistines were gathering a great army to fight Saul. King Saul was old and weakened by disease and trouble. Samuel had died many years before. David was no longer by his side, and Saul had killed the priests.

Saul was utterly alone and didn't know what to do when he saw the mighty army of the Philistines. The Lord had left Saul, and would give him no advice at all.

Saul heard that there was a woman nearby who could call up the spirits of the dead. Whether she could really do this or not, we do not know, for the Bible doesn't say. But Saul was so anxious to have some message from the Lord that he went to this woman. He took off his kingly robes and came dressed as a common man, and said to her, "Bring me the spirit of a man I greatly long to meet."

"What spirit shall I call up?" she asked.

"Bring me the spirit of Samuel, the prophet."

The Lord allowed the spirit of Samuel to rise up from the dead to speak to King Saul. Out of the darkness came a voice saying, "Why have you troubled me and called me out of my rest?"

Saul answered Samuel, "I am in great distress, for the Philistines make war on me, and God has forsaken me. I have called you to tell me what to do."

The spirit of Samuel said to Saul, "If the Lord has forsaken you and has become your enemy, why do you call on me to help you? Because you would not obey the Lord, he has taken the kingdom away from you and has given it to David. The Lord will give Israel to the Philistines, and tomorrow you and your three sons shall be as I am, among the dead.''

On the next day, a great battle was fought on the side of Mount Gilboa. Many of the men of Israel were slain in the fight, and many more fled away. Saul's three sons were killed, including the brave and noble Jonathan.

When Saul saw that the battle had gone against him, his sons were slain, and the enemy was close to him, he called to his armor bearer, and said, "Draw your sword and kill me. It would be better to die by your hand than for the Philistines to slaughter me.''

But the armor bearer would not draw his sword on the king, the Lord's anointed, so Saul took his own sword and killed himself.

Saul had reigned for forty years. At the beginning of his reign, the Israelites were almost free from the Philistines, and for a time Saul seemed to have success in driving the Philistines out of the land. But after Saul left the Lord and refused to listen to Samuel, God's prophet, he became gloomy and full of fear, and the land fell under the power of its enemies. David could have helped him, but he had driven David away, and there was no other strong man to stand by Saul and win victories for him. When Saul fell in battle, the Philistines oppressed Israel more than ever before.

Discussion Questions: 1. Why did Saul feel so alone? 2. When the Lord would not answer Saul, who did he go to? Who did he want to talk to? 3. What lesson did Saul never seem to learn? 4. What happened to Saul and his sons? 5. Why were the Philistines so powerful by the time Saul died?

DAY 111

DAVID THE KING

2 Samuel 1:1-4:12

N the third day after the battle on Mount Gilboa, David was at home when a young man came running into the town. He hastened to David and fell down before him. "The men of Israel have been beaten in the battle. Many of them are dead, and the rest have run away. King Saul is dead, and so is Jonathan, his son.''

"How do you know that Saul and Jonathan are dead?'' asked David.

The young man said, "I saw Saul leaning on his spear wounded, and near death, with his enemies close to him. And he said to me, 'Come and kill me, for I am suffering great pain.' So I stood beside him and killed him, for I saw he could not live. And I took the crown that was on his head, and the bracelet on his arm, and I have brought them to you, my lord David."

Then David and all the men that were with him tore their clothes, and mourned, and wept, and took no food that day, in honor of Saul, Jonathan, and the people of Israel who had fallen by the sword.

And David said to the young man who had brought to him the news, "Why weren't you afraid to slay the king of Israel, the anointed of the Lord? You shall die for this deed."

And David commanded one of his men to kill him because he said he had slain the king. He may have told the truth, but it is more likely that he was not in the battle. After the fighting, he went into the field to rob the dead bodies and then lied about killing Saul, hoping to get a reward. But David — who refused to kill Saul — did not give the man the reward he expected.

After this, at the command of the Lord, David and his men went up from Ziklag to Hebron. The men of Judah met together at Hebron, and they made David king over their tribe. David reigned in Hebron, over the tribe of Judah, for seven years.

Saul's uncle, Abner, was not willing to have the kingdom go out of Saul's family. He made a son of Saul king over all the tribes in the north of the land. This king was called Ish-bosheth, a name that means "a worthless man." He was weak and helpless, except for the strong will and power of Abner, who had made him king. For six years (seemingly under Ish-bosheth, but really under Abner) the kingdom was kept up, so for a time, there were two kingdoms in Israel: that of the north under Ish-bosheth, and that of the south under David. But all the time, David's kingdom was growing stronger, and Ish-bosheth's kingdom was growing weaker.

After a time, Abner was slain by one of David's men, and at once Ish-bosheth's power faded. Then two men of his army killed him, cut off his head, and brought it to David. They looked for a reward, since Ish-bosheth had been king against David, but David said, "As the Lord lives, who has brought me out of trouble, I will give no reward to wicked men who have slain a good man in his own house. Take these two murderers away and kill them!"

So the two slayers of Ish-bosheth were punished, and his head was buried with honor. David had not forgotten his promise to Saul to deal kindly with his children.

Discussion Questions: *1. What did David do when he heard about Saul's death? Do you think he truly loved his enemy? 2. What did David do to the*

DAY 112

DAVID DEFEATS THE PHILISTINES

2 Samuel 5:1-25

AFTER David had reigned over the tribe of Judah for seven years and Saul's son, Ish-bosheth, died, all the men in Israel saw that David was the one man fit to be king. The rulers and elders of all twelve tribes came to David and said to him, "We are all your brothers; now we are ready to make you king over all the land." David was now thirty-seven, and he reigned over all Israel for thirty-three years.

DAVID WAS MADE KING AT HEBRON - 2 SAMUEL 5:3

He found the land in a helpless state, under the power of the Philistines, with many of its cities still held by the Canaanite people. The city of Jerusalem had been held as a stronghold by a Canaanite tribe called the Jebusites ever since the days of Joshua. David led his men of war against it, but the Jebusites just laughed at him. To mock him they placed on the top of the wall the blind and lame people, and they called out to David, "Even blind and lame men can keep you out of our city."

181

This made David very angry, and he said to his men, "Whoever climbs up the wall and strikes down the blind and the lame on it will be the chief captain and general of the whole army."

All David's soldiers rushed the wall, each trying to be first. The man who first reached the enemies and struck them down was Joab, the son of David's sister Zeruiah. He became the commander of David's army, a job he held as long as David lived. After the fortress on Mount Zion was taken from the Jebusites, David made it larger and stronger, then decided to live there himself. The city of Jerusalem grew to be the chief city in David's kingdom.

The Philistines soon found that there was a new king in Israel, a ruler very different from King Saul. They gathered their army to fight David, who met them a little to the south of Jerusalem and won a great victory over them.

Once again, the Philistines came up and encamped in the valley of Rephaim. When David asked the Lord what he should do, the Lord said to him, "Do not go against them openly. Turn to one side, and be ready to come against them from under the mulberry trees. Wait there until you hear a sound overhead in the tops of the trees. When you hear that sound, it will be a sign that the Lord goes before you. Then march forth and fight the Philistines."

David did as the Lord commanded him, and again he defeated the Philistines. But David did not rest, once he had driven the Philistines back to their own land. He marched into the Philistines' country and took their chief city, Gath, conquered all their land, and ended the war of 100 years by making all the Philistine plain subject to Israel.

Discussion Questions: *1. Why did the people ask David to be king? 2. What was Israel like when he first became king? 3. How did David decide who would be chief captain of the army? 4. How did David know when to attack the Philistines? 5. How was David's reign different from Saul's?*

DAY 113

THE ARK IS MOVED

2 Samuel 6:1-7:16

NOW the land was free, David thought it was time to bring the holy ark out of its hiding place, where it had remained all through the rule of Samuel and the reign of Saul. He prepared a new Tabernacle on Mount Zion, chose men from all the tribes, and went to bring the ark to Mount Zion. They did not have the ark carried by the priests, as had been done in earlier days. Instead, they stood it on a wagon drawn by oxen, followed by David and the men of Israel, who made music on all kinds of musical instruments.

At one place the road was rough, the oxen stumbled, and the ark almost fell off the wagon. Uzza, one of the men driving the oxen, took hold of the ark to steady it. God's law forbid anyone but a priest to touch the ark, and God was displeased with Uzza for his carelessness. Uzza fell dead by the ark of the Lord. This death alarmed David and all the people. David was afraid to have the ark in his city. He stopped the procession and placed the ark in the house of a man named Obed-edom, where it stayed for three months. They were afraid that it might bring harm to Obed-edom and his family, but instead it brought a blessing on them all.

When David heard of the blessings that had come to Obed-edom from the ark, he resolved to bring it into his own city on Mount Zion. This time the priests carried it, as the law commanded, and sacrifices were offered on the altar. They brought the ark up to its new home on Mount Zion, where a Tabernacle was ready to receive it. Then the priests began to offer the daily sacrifices and the services of worship were held, after having been neglected for many years.

DAVID DANCED BEFORE THE ARK -
2 SAMUEL 6:14,15

David was now living in his place on Mount Zion, and he wanted to build a temple to take the place of the Tabernacle. He said to Nathan, who was a prophet, "I live in a house of cedar, but the ark of God stands in a tent."

"Do all that is in your heart," answered Nathan, "for the Lord is with you."

And that night, the voice of the Lord came to Nathan, saying, "Go and tell my servant David that I said, 'Since the children of Israel came out of Egypt, my ark has been in a tent. I have never said to the people, build me a house of cedar.' Say to my servant David, 'I took you from the sheep pasture where you were following the sheep, and I have made you a prince over Israel, and I have given you a great name and great power. And now, because you have done my will, I will give you a house. Your son shall sit on the throne after you, and he shall build me a house and a Temple. And I will give you and your children and your descendants a throne and a kingdom that shall last forever.' "

This promise of God — that from David's line would come an everlasting kingdom — was fulfilled in Jesus Christ, who came from the family of David and reigns as King of heaven and earth.

Discussion Questions: 1. What happened to the man who touched the ark? 2. Why was David afraid to bring the ark into his city? How did he decide to take care of this? 3. What did David want to do for God? 4. What did God promise David? Who fulfilled that promise?

DAY 114

DAVID AND JONATHAN'S SON
2 Samuel 8:1-9:13

AS soon as the kings around Israel saw that a strong man was ruling over Israel, they began to make war on David, because they didn't want Israel to be strong. So David had to fight many wars. The Moabites, who lived on the east of the Dead Sea, went to war with David, but David conquered them and made Moab submit to Israel. Far in the north, the Syrians came against David, but he won great victories over them, took Damascus, their chief city, and held it as part of his kingdom. In the south, he made war on the Edomites and brought them under his rule.

For a number of years, David was constantly at war, but at last he was at peace, the ruler of all the land from the Euphrates to the wilderness and from the great desert to the Great Sea. All these lands were under the rule of King David except the people of Tyre and Sidon, who lived beside the Great Sea on the north of Israel. These people never made war on Israel, and their king, Hiram, was one of David's best friends. The men of Tyre cut down cedar trees for David, brought them to Jerusalem, and built the palace that became David's home.

Once David's wars were over, he remembered the promise he had made to his friend Jonathan, Saul's son, and he asked the men at his court, "Are any of Saul's family living, so I can show them kindness for the sake of Jonathan?"

They told David of Saul's servant, Ziba, who was in charge of Saul's farm in the country, and David sent for him. Ziba had become a rich man from caring for the lands that had belonged to Saul. David said to Ziba, "Are any of Saul's family living, to whom I can show some of the kindness God has shown toward me?"

Ziba replied, "Saul's son Jonathan left a little boy named Mephibosheth, who is now grown up and lives to the east of Jordan."

This child was in the arms of his nurse when the news came that Jonathan was dead. The nurse fled with him, to hide from the Philistines, and in running, she fell. The child's feet were injured, and he grew up lame.

David sent for Mephibosheth, who was afraid he was going to be killed, until David said to him, "Mephibosheth, you need have no fear. I will be kind to you because I loved Jonathan, your father, and he loved me. You shall have all the land that ever belonged to Saul and his family, and you shall always sit at my table in the royal palace."

Then the king called Ziba, Saul's servant, and said to him, "All the lands and houses that once belonged to Saul I have given to Mephibosheth. You care for them and bring the harvests to him. Mephibosheth will live here with me and eat at the king's table with the princes of the kingdom."

So Mephibosheth, Jonathan's lame son, was taken into David's palace and sat at the king's table. And Ziba, with his fifteen sons and twenty servants, waited on him and obeyed his orders.

This kindness might have brought trouble to David, for Mephibosheth might have been the king, if David had not won the crown. By giving Saul's grandson a place at his table and showing him honor, David might have helped him take the kingdom away from himself, if Mephibosheth had wanted the throne of Israel. But David was generous, and Mephibosheth was happy with his place in the palace.

Discussion Questions: *1. What did David have to do when the kings of other nations found out that he was a strong king? 2. What had David promised Saul? Did he remember that promise? 3. Why was it dangerous for David to be kind to Mephibosheth? 4. Do you think David's kindness pleased God?*

DAY 115

DAVID AND BATHSHEBA

2 Samuel 11:1-27

WHEN David first become king, he went into battle with his army, but eventually he left Joab to lead his warriors while he stayed in his palace on Mount Zion.

One evening, about sunset, David was walking on the roof of his palace. He looked down into a garden nearby and saw a very beautiful woman. David asked one of his servants who this woman was, and was told, "Her name is Bathsheba, and she is the wife of Uriah."

Uriah was an officer in David's army, and at that time, he was fighting the Ammonites near the desert on the east of Jordan. David sent for Uriah's wife, Bathsheba, and talked to her. He loved her, and wanted to take her as one of his own wives (in those days it was not thought a sin for a man to have more than one wife). But David could not marry Bathsheba while her husband was living. Then a wicked thought came to David, and he formed a plan to have Uriah killed so he could have Bathsheba.

David wrote a letter to Joab, the commander of his army. In the letter he said, "When there is a fight with the Ammonites, send Uriah into the middle of it, where it will be the hottest, and manage to leave him there, so he will be killed by the Ammonites."

Joab did as David commanded him. He sent Uriah with some other brave men to a place near the wall of the city, where he knew the defenders would rush out and attack. Uriah was killed.

After Bathsheba had mourned her husband's death for a time, David took her into his palace, and she became his wife. And a little child was born to them, whom David loved greatly. Only Joab, David, and perhaps a few others, knew that David had caused the death of Uriah. But God knew it, and God was displeased with David.

Discussion Questions: *1. Who was Bathsheba? 2. Why did David want to have Uriah killed? How did he plan to do it? 3. Who else knew what David had done?*

DAY 116

DAVID'S PUNISHMENT

2 Samuel 12:1-24

THEN the Lord sent Nathan, the prophet, to David to tell him that God would surely punish David for his sin. Nathan said, "There were two men in one city. One was rich, and the other poor. The rich man had great flocks of sheep and herds of cattle, but the poor man had only one little lamb he had bought. It grew up in his home with his children, drank out of his cup, sat on his lap, and was like a little daughter to him. One day a visitor came to the rich man's house for dinner but he did not kill one of his own sheep to feed his guest. He robbed the poor man of his lamb, killed it, and cooked it for his friend."

When David heard this, he was very angry. He said to Nathan, "The man who did this thing deserves to die! He shall give his poor neighbor four lambs to replace the one he took. How cruel, to treat a poor man like this!"

Nathan said to David, "You are the man who did this. The Lord made you king in place of Saul and gave you a kingdom. You have a great house, and many wives. Why, then, have you done this wickedness in the sight of the Lord? You had Uriah killed by the Ammonites, then you took his wife. You shall suffer for this, and your wives shall suffer, and your children shall suffer, because you have done this."

NATHAN REBUKES DAVID — 2 SAMUEL 12:7

When David heard all this, he realized how he had sinned. He showed such sorrow for his sin that Nathan said to him, "The Lord has forgiven your sin, and you shall not die because of it. But the child that Uriah's wife has given you will die."

Soon after this, the little child of David and Bathsheba was taken very ill. David prayed to God for the child's life. He ate no food, but lay face down on the floor in sorrow. For seven days, the child grew worse and worse, and David mourned. When the child died, the nobles were afraid to tell David, saying, "If he was in such grief while the child was living, what will he do when he hears the child is dead?"

And they said to him, "Yes, the child is dead."

Then David rose up from the floor where he had been lying. He washed his face and put on his kingly robes. He went first to the house of the Lord and worshiped, then he came home, sat down at his table, and ate. His servants wondered at this, but David said to them, "While the child was still alive, I fasted, and prayed and wept. I hoped that by prayer to the Lord, and through the Lord's mercy, his life might be spared. But now he is dead, my prayers can't help him. I cannot bring him back again. He will not come back to me, but I shall go to him."

After this, God gave David and Bathsheba another son, whom they named Solomon. The Lord loved Solomon, and he grew up to be a wise man.

Discussion Questions: *1. Who did God send to David? How did he tell David that God knew what he had done? 2. What did David do? 3. When David knew his child's life was in danger, what did he do? When he heard the child had died, what did he do? Why?*

DAY 117

Absalom's Plan

2 Samuel 13:1-15:12

NOT long after David's sin, the sorrows Nathan had predicted began to fall on David. He had many wives, and his wives had many sons, but most of his sons had grown up wild and wicked, because David had not watched over them and taught them to love God and do God's will. He had been too busy being king to do his duty as a father.

The oldest of David's sons was Absalom, who was said to be the most beautiful young man in all the land. He had long hair, of which he was very proud, because all the people admired it. Absalom became very angry with Amnon (another of David's sons) because Amnon had been cruel to Absalom's sister, Tamar.

But Absalom hid his anger against Amnon, and one day he invited Amnon, and all the other sons of David, to a feast at his house in the country. While they were all at the table, Absalom's servants rushed in and killed Amnon. The other princes were alarmed, afraid they all would be killed, and they ran away. But no harm was done to the other princes, and they arrived home safely.

David was greatly displeased with Absalom, though he loved him more than any other son. Absalom ran away to his grandfather, his mother's father, the king of Geshur. He stayed there for three years, and all the time, David longed to see him. After three years, David allowed Absalom to come back to Jerusalem. But for a while, he would not see him, because he had caused his brother's death. At last David's love was so strong that he could no longer refuse to see his son. He sent for Absalom and let him back into the palace.

But Absalom was ungrateful and cruel. He formed a plan to take the throne and the kingdom away from his father and make himself king.

He began by living like a king, with a royal chariot, and horses, and fifty men to run before him.

He would rise early in the morning, stand at the gate of the king's palace, and meet those who came to see the king. He would speak to each man about his problem, then say, "Your cause is good and right, but the king will not hear you. Now if I were a judge, I'd see that right was always done!"

This way, Absalom won the hearts of everyone he met, from every part of the land, until many wished he was king instead of David, because David no longer led the army in war, or sat as judge, or went among the people. He lived apart in his palace, scarcely knowing what was being done in the land.

Discussion Questions: *1. Why had David's sons grown up wild and wicked? 2. What did Absalom do that was wrong? Did his father still love him? How do you know? 3. What did Absalom want from David? How did he try to get it?*

DAY 118

DAVID RUNS AWAY

2 Samuel 15:7-16:4

 VENTUALLY, Absalom thought he was strong enough to seize the kingdom. He said to David, "Let me go to Hebron to worship the

189

Lord and keep a promise I made to the Lord while I was in Geshur."

David was pleased at this, so Absalom went to Hebron with a large number of his friends. A few of these knew Absalom's plans, but most of them knew nothing. At Hebron, Absalom was joined by Ahithophel, one of David's most trusted advisors.

Suddenly the word was sent through all the land: "Absalom has been made king at Hebron!" Those who were in on the secret helped lead others, and soon it seemed as though all the people were on Absalom's side and ready to accept him as king.

The news came to David that Absalom had made himself king, that many of the rulers were with him, and that the people really wanted Absalom. David did not know who he could trust, so he decided to escape before it was too late. He took a few of his servants and his wives — including Bathsheba and little Solomon.

As they were going out of the gates, they were joined by Ittai, who was the commander of the guard and brought along 600 trained men of war. Ittai was not an Israelite, and David was surprised that he wanted to go with him. He said to Ittai, "Why do you, a stranger, go with us? I don't know where we will go, or the problems we will meet. It would be better for you and your men to go back to your own land."

Ittai answered the king, "As the Lord God lives, and as my lord the king lives, wherever you are — in life or death — we will be with you."

So Ittai and his 600 soldiers went with David toward the wilderness. Soon they were joined by Zadok and Abiathar, the priests, and the Levites, carrying the holy ark of the Lord. David said, "Take the ark of God back. If I find favor in the sight of the Lord, he will bring me back to it. But if the Lord says, 'I have no pleasure in David,' then let the Lord do whatever he wants to me."

David also thought the priests might help him more in the city than if they went away with him. He said to Zadok, "Go back to the city and watch, then send word to me. I will wait at the crossing of the river Jordan for news from you."

So Zadok and Abiathar, the priests, carried the holy ark back to its Tabernacle on Mount Zion and watched closely, so they could tell David anything that would help his cause.

David walked up the steep side of the Mount of Olives with his head covered and his feet bare, weeping as he walked. And all the people who were with him, and those who saw him, were weeping in sorrow over David's having to run away.

On the top of the hill, David found another man waiting to see him. It was Hushai, one of his best friends. He stood there in sorrow, with his garments torn and earth on his head, ready to go into the wilderness with David. But David said to Hushai, "If you go with us, you can't help me in any way. But if you stay in the city and pretend to be Absalom's friend, then perhaps you can hear the advice Ahithophel gives Absalom, and prevent Absalom from following it. The priests will help you, and through their sons, you can send word to me about everything you hear."

A little past the top of the hill, another man was waiting for David. It was Ziba, the servant of Mephibosheth. You remember how kindly David had treated Mephibosheth, his friend Jonathan's lame son. Ziba had two saddled donkeys with him, plus 200 loaves of bread, 100 clusters of raisins, a quantity of fruit, and a goatskin full of wine. David said to Ziba, "Why are all these things here?"

And Ziba said, "The asses are for the king. Here is food for the journey, and wine for those who may need it in the wilderness."

David asked Ziba, "Where is Mephibosheth, your master?"

"He is in Jerusalem," said Ziba. "He says the kingdom may be given back to him, since he is Saul's heir."

David felt very sad to hear that Mephibosheth had forsaken him, and he said to Ziba, "Whatever has belonged to Mephibosheth shall be yours from now on."

But David did not know that Ziba was lying and Mephibosheth had not forsaken him.

———————

Discussion Questions: *1. What did Absolom do? 2. What did David do? 3. Why do you think Ittai went with David? 4. Why didn't David take the ark with him? 5. Why didn't David take all his friends with him?*

DAY 119

———

HUSHAI'S ADVICE

2 Samuel 16:15-17:23

DAVID and his wives, his servants, and the soldiers who were faithful to him, went on toward the wilderness and the valley of the Jordan. Soon after David had escaped from the city, Absalom came into it with his friends and followers. As Absalom drew near, Hushai, David's friend, stood by the road, crying, "Long live the king! Long live the king!"

Absalom said to Hushai, "Is this the way you treat your friend? Why haven't you stayed beside your friend David?"

Hushai said to Absalom, "Whoever the Lord and his people have chosen, I will follow, and with him I will stay. As I have served the father, so I will serve the son." So Hushai went into the palace with the followers of Absalom.

And Absalom said to Ahithophel, "Tell me what to do next."

Now Ahithophel was a very wise man. He knew what was best for Absalom's success, and he said, "Let me choose out twelve thousand men, and I will catch David tonight. We will come on him when he is tired, while only a few people are with him, and before he has time to form any plans or gather an army. I will kill David, and will harm no one else, and then you can reign as king in peace, and all the people will submit to you when they know that David is no longer living."

Absalom thought this was wise advice, but he sent for Hushai. He told him what Ahithophel had said and asked for his advice, too.

Hushai said, "The advice that Ahithophel gives is not good for now. You know that David and his men are very brave, and just now they are as savage as a bear robbed of her cubs. David is with his men in some safe place, hidden in a cave or among the mountains, and they will watch for anyone chasing them and will ambush them. Then, as soon as the news goes through the land that Absalom's men have been beaten, everybody will turn away from Absalom to David. The better plan would be to wait until you can gather all the men of war in Israel. Then you will have enough men to defeat him, wherever you find him."

Absalom and the rulers with him said to one another, "The advice of Hushai is better than the advice of Ahithophel. Let's do what Hushai suggests."

So Absalom sat down in his father's palace and began to enjoy himself while they were gathering his army. This was just what Hushai wished, for it would give David time to gather his army, and he knew that the hearts of the people would soon turn back to David.

Hushai told the priests of Absalom's plans, and they sent word to David, who was waiting beside the river Jordan. David and his men found a safe refuge across the Jordan, and his friends began to come to him.

When Ahithophel saw his advice had not been taken and Hushai was listened to, he knew at once that Absalom's cause was going to fail. He went to his home, put all his affairs in order, and hanged himself, for he thought it was better to die by his own hand than to be put to death as a traitor by David.

For a while, Absalom had his wish. He sat on the throne, wore the crown, and lived in the palace at Jerusalem as king of Israel.

———————

Discussion Questions: *1. What did Hushai say to Absalom, when the king's son asked why he had not followed David? 2. Had God really made Absalom king? 3. Why did Hushai tell Absalom not to attack his father right away?*

DAY 120

ABSALOM'S DEATH

2 Samuel 17:24-18:33

THE land on the east of the Jordan where David found a refuge was called Gilead, a word that means "high," because it is higher than the land on the west of the Jordan. There, in the city of Mahanaim, the rulers and the people were friendly to David.

David's friends gathered from all the tribes of Israel, until he had an army. It was not as large as the army of Absalom, but in it were the brave warriors who had fought under David in other years. David divided his army into three parts and placed Joab, Abishai, and Ittai in command of the parts. Then David said to the chiefs of his army, "I will go out with you in battle."

But the men said to David, "No, you must not go with us. If half of us should lose our lives, no one will care, but you are worth ten thousand of us, and your life is too precious. You must stay here in the city and be ready to help us if we need help."

So the king stood by the gate of Mahanaim while his men marched out. And as they went past the king, the men heard him say to the three chiefs (Joab, Abishai, and Ittai), "For my sake, deal gently with Absalom." Even now, David loved his son and wanted his life spared.

A great battle was fought on that day. Absalom himself went into battle, riding on a mule, as kings always did. David's soldiers won a great victory and killed thousands of Absalom's men. The armies were scattered in the woods, and many men were lost, so it was said that the woods swallowed up more men than the sword. When Absalom saw that his cause was hopeless he rode away, hoping to escape. But as he was riding under the branches of an oak, his head, with its great mass of long hair, was caught in the tree's branches. He struggled to free himself, but couldn't. His mule ran away, and Absalom was left hanging in the air by his head.

One of David's soldiers saw him and said to Joab, "I saw Absalom hanging in an oak."

"Why didn't you kill him?" asked Joab. "If you had killed him, I would have given you a reward."

"If you gave me a thousand pieces of silver," answered the soldier, "I would not touch the king's son. I heard the king tell all the generals and the men, 'Let no one harm the young man Absalom.' And if I had killed him, even you couldn't protect me from the king's anger."

"I cannot stay to talk with you," said Joab, and with three darts in his hand, he hastened to the place where Absalom was hanging. He thrust Absalom's heart through with the darts, and after that his followers, finding that Absalom was still living, pierced his body until they were sure he was dead. Then they took down his body, threw it into a deep hole in the forest, and heaped a great pile of stones on it.

After the battle, Ahimaaz, the son of the priest Zadok, came to Joab. Ahimaaz was one of the two young men who brought news from Jerusalem to David at the river Jordan. He said to Joab, "Let me run and take news of the battle to the king."

But Joab knew that the message of Absalom's death would not be pleasing to King David, and he said, "Some other time you shall bear news, but not to-day, because the king's son is dead." Joab called another man and said to him, "Go, and tell the king what you have seen."

The man bowed to Joab and left. But after a time Ahimaaz, the son of Zadok, said again to Joab, "Let me also run and take news."

"Why do you wish to go, my son?" said Joab. "The news will not bring you any reward."

"Let me go anyhow," said the young man, and Joab gave him permission. Ahimaaz ran with all his might and went by a better road, so he was the first man the watchman on the wall saw. King David was waiting below, in the little room between the outer and inner gates, anxious for news of the battle, but more anxious for his son, Absalom.

The watchman on the wall called down to the king, "I see a man running alone."

And the king said, "If he is alone, he is bringing a message." He knew that if men were running away after a defeat, there would be a crowd of them.

Then the watchman called again, "I see another man running alone."

And the king said, "He is also bringing some news."

The watchman spoke again. "The first runner is coming near, and he runs like Ahimaaz, the son of Zadok."

David said, "He is a good man, and he comes with good news."

Ahimaaz came near, and cried out as he ran, "All is well!"

The first words the king spoke were, "Is Absalom all right?"

Ahimaaz was too wise to bring the king word of Absalom's death. He left that to the other messenger, and said, "When Joab sent me, there was a great noise over something that had taken place, but I did not stop to learn what it was."

A little later, the other man arrived. "News for my lord the king! This day the Lord has given you victory over your enemies!"

And David said again, "Is Absalom all right?"

This messenger, who knew nothing of David's feelings, answered, "May all the enemies of my lord the king, and all that try to do him harm, be as that young man is!"

THE MESSENGER TELLS DAVID OF ABSALOM'S DEATH – 2 SAMUEL 18:32

David's sorrow over Absalom made him forget the victory that had been won. Slowly he walked up the steps to the room in the tower over the gate, and as he walked, he said, "O my son Absalom! My son, my son Absalom! I wish that I had died for you, my son, my son!"

Discussion Questions: *1. Why didn't the chiefs of his army want David to go into battle? 2. What did David say to his men before they went into battle? What does that show you about David? 3. One soldier would not kill the king's son. Do you think he was right? 4. Who killed Absalom? 5. How did David feel when he heard of Absalom's death?*

195

DAY 121

AFTER THE VICTORY

2 Samuel 19:1-20:26

HE word soon went out that the king, instead of rejoicing over the victory, was weeping over his son. The soldiers came stealing back to the city as if they had been defeated. Everyone felt sorry for the king, who sat in the room over the gate with his face covered, crying out, "O Absalom, my son! my son, my son Absalom!"

But Joab saw that such great sorrow was not good for his cause. He came to David, and said to him, "You have put to shame this day all who fought for you and saved your life. You have shown that you love those who hate you, and that you hate those who love you. You have said by your actions that those who have been true to you are nothing to you. Get up and act like a man, and show regard for those who have fought for you. I swear to you in the name of the Lord, that unless you do this, not a man will stay on your side."

Then David rose up, washed away his tears, put on his robes, and took his seat in the gate as a king. After this he returned to the river Jordan, and there all the people met him, to bring him back to his throne in Jerusalem.

Ziba, the servant of Mephibosheth, was there with his sons and his followers, and Mephibosheth was also there to meet the king. Mephibosheth had not dressed his lame feet, or trimmed his beard, or washed his clothes, from the day David had left Jerusalem. David said to him, "Mephibosheth, why didn't you offer to go with me?"

"My lord," said Mephibosheth, "my servant deceived me. He said, 'You are lame, and cannot go, but I will go in your name with the king, and will help him.' He has done me wrong. But what does that matter, now that the king has come again?"

David said, "You and Ziba may divide the land and the property."

And Mephibosheth said, "Let him have it all, now that the king has come in peace to his own house!"

The army of Absalom had melted away, and was scattered all over the land. David was still displeased with Joab because he had disobeyed and killed Absalom.

He sent a message to Amasa, who had been the commander of Absalom's army, and who was his nephew. "You are of my own family, of my bone and my flesh, and you shall be the general in place of Joab."

196

Joab and his brother were strong men, not willing to submit to David's rule, and David thought he would be safer on his throne if they did not hold so much power.

At the river Jordan, almost the whole tribe of Judah gathered to bring the king back to Jerusalem. But this did not please the men of the other tribes. They said to the men of Judah, "You act as though you were the only friends of the king in all the land! We, too, have some right to David."

The men of Judah said, "The king is of our own tribe, and is one of us. We come to meet him because we love him."

But the people of the other tribes were still offended, and many of them went home angry. The tribe of Ephraim was very jealous of the tribe of Judah and unwilling to come under David's rule. One man in Ephraim, Sheba, began a new rebellion against David, which for a time threatened to overthrow David's power.

Amasa, the new commander of the army, called out his men to put down Sheba's rebellion. But he was slow in gathering his army, and Joab, the old general, went out with a band of his own followers. Joab met Amasa, preing to be his friend, killed him, and then took command. He shut up Sheba in a city far in the north, and finally had him killed. So at last every enemy was put down, and David sat again in peace on his throne. But Joab, whom David feared and hated because of many evil deeds he had done, was still the commander of the army and held great power. Joab was faithful to David, and without Joab's courage and skill, David might have failed in some of his wars, especially the war against Absalom's followers. But Joab was cruel and wicked, and was so strong that David could not control him. David felt he was not fully the king while Joab lived.

But few people knew how David felt toward Joab. In appearance, the throne of David was now as strong as it had ever been, and David's last years were years of peace and power.

Discussion Questions: *1. Why did Joab tell David to stop weeping for his son? 2. What kind of man was Mephibosheth? How do you know? 3. Why was David angry with Joab? 4. What kind of man was Joab? Do you think David was right not to trust him?*

DAY 122

The Altar on the Rock

2 Samuel 24:1-25
1 Chronicles 21:1-27

AFTER the death of Absalom, David ruled in peace over Israel for many years. His kingdom stretched from the Euphrates to the border of Egypt, and from the Great Sea on the west to the great desert on the east. But again David did something that displeased God. He gave orders to Joab to count all the men in the kingdom of fighting age.

Maybe David wanted to gather a great army for some new war, but even Joab knew it was not right to do this. He said to David, "May the Lord God make his people a hundred times as great as they are. But aren't they all your servants? Why does the king command this to be done? Surely it will bring sin on the king and on the people."

But David was firm, and Joab obeyed him. He sent men through all the twelve tribes to count those in every city and town who were fit for war. They went throughout the land until they had counted 800,000 men in ten of the tribes and nearly 500,000 men in the tribe of Judah, all of fighting age. The tribe of Levi was not counted, because all its members were priests and Levites in the service of the Tabernacle, and Benjamin was not counted, because the numbering was never finished.

It was left unfinished because God was angry with David and the people because of this sin.

The Lord sent a prophet to David, a man named Gad. Gad said to him, "Thus saith the Lord, 'You have sinned in this thing, and now you and your land must suffer for your sin. I will give you the choice of three troubles. Shall I send seven years of famine? Or shall your enemies overcome you and win victories over you for three months? Or shall there be three days of pestilence, with people dying everywhere?' "

David said to the prophet, "Let me fall into the hand of the Lord, and not into the hands of men, for God's mercies are great and many. If we must suffer, let the three days of pestilence come upon the land."

Then the Lord's angel of death passed through the land, and in three days, 70,000 men died. But when the angel of the Lord stretched out his hand over the city of Jerusalem, the Lord had pity on the people and said to him, "It is enough. Hold back your hand, and cause no more people to die."

Then the Lord opened David's eyes, and he saw the angel standing on

Mount Moriah with a drawn sword in his hand. David prayed to the Lord, "O Lord, I alone have sinned and have done this wickedness. These people are like sheep. They have done nothing. Lord, let your hand fall on me, and not on these poor people."

Then the Lord sent the prophet Gad to David, and Gad said to him, "Go and build an altar to the Lord on the place the angel was standing."

David and the men of his court went out from the city and walked up Mount Moriah. They found the man who owned the rock on the top of the mountain threshing wheat on it. When the owner saw David and his nobles coming toward him, he bowed down and said, "Why does my lord come to his servant?"

"I have come," said David, "to buy your threshing floor and build an altar to the Lord, so I may ask God to stop the plague that is destroying the people."

The man said to David, "Take it as a gift, and with it these oxen for an offering, and the threshing tools and the yokes of the oxen for the wood on the altar. I give it all to you."

"No," said King David. "I cannot take it as a gift. But I will pay you for it. I will not make an offering to the Lord that costs me nothing." So David paid full price for the land, the oxen, and the wood. And there on the rock he built an altar and offered burnt offerings and peace offerings. The Lord heard David's prayer and took away the plague. Later, the altar of the temple of the Lord stood on that very same rock.

Discussion Questions: *1. What did David do that displeased God? 2. What did the prophet Gad say to David? 3. Which choice did David make? Why? 4. Why did God not harm the people of Jerusalem? 5. What did God tell David to do?*

DAY 123

DAVID'S LAST YEARS

1 Kings 1:1-53

DURING the last years of David's reign, he laid up a great treasure to build a house for the Lord on Mount Moriah. This house was to be called the Temple, and it was to be the most expensive building in all the land. David wanted to build this house while he was the king of Israel, but God said to him, "You have been a man of war, and have fought many battles, and shed much blood. My house shall be built by a man of peace. When you die, your son Solomon shall reign, and he shall have peace and shall build my house."

So David made ready a great store of precious things for the temple and said to Solomon, "God has promised that there shall be rest and peace while you are king. The Lord will be with you, and you will build a house where God will live with his people."

But David had other sons who were older than Solomon, and one of these sons, Adonijah, formed a plan to make himself king. David was now very old, and he was no longer able to go out of his palace and be seen by the people.

Adonijah gathered his friends. Among them were Joab, the general of the army, and Abiathar, one of the two high priests. They met at a place outside the wall, had a great feast, and were about to crown Adonijah as king, but David heard about it. David, though old and feeble, was still wise. He said, "Let us make Solomon king at once, and thus put an end to the plans of these men."

At David's command, they brought out the mule on which no one but the king was allowed to ride, and they placed Solomon on it. Then, with the king's guards, the nobles, and the great men, they brought Solomon down to the valley of Gihon, south of the city. Zadok the priest took the horn filled with holy oil that was used for anointing the priests when they were set apart for their work. He poured oil from this horn on the head of Solomon, and then the priests blew the trumpets, and all the people cried aloud, "God save King Solomon."

Adonijah and his friends were nearby, feasting and celebrating, planning to make Adonijah king. They heard the sound of trumpets and the shouting of the people. Joab said, "What is the cause of all this noise and uproar?"

A moment later, a messenger came running up to Adonijah's group. "King David has made Solomon king, and he has just been anointed in Gihon. All the princes and the heads of the army are with him, and the people are shouting, 'God save King Solomon!' And David has sent a message to Solomon, saying, 'May the Lord make your name greater than my name has been! Blessed be the Lord, who has given me a son to sit on my throne!' "

When Adonijah and his friends heard this, they were filled with fear. Adonijah ran to the altar of the Lord, knelt before it, and took hold of the horns that were on its corners. This was a holy place, and he hoped that Solomon might have mercy on him.

Solomon said, "If Adonijah will do right and be true to me, no harm shall come to him. But if he does wrong, he shall die."

Adonijah came and bowed down before King Solomon, promising to be true to him and was allowed to go home.

Not long after this, David sent for Solomon. From his bed, he gave his last advice to Solomon. And soon after that David died, having reigned in all forty years. He was buried on Mount Zion, where his tomb remained standing for many years.

Discussion Questions: 1. Why didn't God let David build the Temple? 2. Why did David make Solomon king while he was still alive? 3. What did Solomon say about Adonijah?

DAY 124

SOLOMON'S WISDOM

1 Kings 3:1-4
2 Chronicles 1:1-13

SOLOMON was a very young man, not more than twenty years old when he became king, and he ruled much more than the twelve tribes of Israel. On the north he ruled over all Syria. On the east, Ammon and Moab were under his power, and in the south, all the land of Edom. He had no wars, as David did; his great realm was at peace as long as Solomon reigned.

Soon after Solomon became king, he went to Gibeon, a few miles north of Jerusalem, where the altar of the Lord stood before the Temble was built. There Solomon made offerings and worshiped the Lord God of Israel.

That night, the Lord God came to Solomon and said, "Ask whatever you choose, and I will give it to you."

And Solomon said to the Lord, "I am only a child, Lord. I don't know how to rule this great people. Give me wisdom and knowledge, that I may know how to rule them properly."

The Lord was pleased with Solomon's choice and said to him, "Since you have not asked for a long life, or great riches for yourself, or victory over your enemies, or great power, but have asked wisdom and knowledge to judge this people, I have given you wisdom greater than that of any king before you, and greater than that of any king that shall come after you. And because you have asked this, I will give you not only wisdom, but all honor and riches. If you obey my words as your father David obeyed, you shall have a long life and rule for many years."

Soon after this, Solomon showed his wisdom. Two women came before him with two little babies, one dead and the other living. Each of the two women claimed the living child as her own and said the dead child belonged to the other woman. One of the women said, "We were sleeping with our children in one bed. And this woman in her sleep lay on her child, and it died. Then she placed her dead child beside me while I was asleep, and took my child. In the morning I saw that it was not my child, but she says it is mine, and the living child is hers. Command this woman to give me my own child."

SOLOMON JUDGED WISELY — I KINGS 3:27

Then the other woman said, "That is not true. The dead baby is hers, and the living one is mine, which she is trying to take from me."

The young king listened to both women. Then he said, "Bring me a sword." They brought a sword, and Solomon said, "Take this sword, cut the living child in two, and give half of it to each one."

Then one of the women cried out, "O my lord, do not kill my child! Let the other woman have it, but let the child live!"

The other woman said, "No, cut the child in two and divide it between us!"

Solomon said, "Give the living child to the woman who would not have it slain, for she is its mother."

And all the people wondered at Solomon's wisdom and saw that God had made him very wise for his age.

Discussion Questions: *1. What was the kingdom like under Solomon? 2. What did Solomon ask God to give him? Did that make God happy? 3. How did Solomon show his wisdom?*

DAY 125

SOLOMON'S TEMPLE

1 Kings 5:1-9:9
2 Chronicles 3:1-7:22

THE great work of Solomon's reign was the building of the house of God, the Temple. This stood on Mount Moriah and covered the whole mountain. King David had prepared for it by gathering great stores of gold, silver, stone, and wood. The walls were made of stone, and the roof of cedar.

All the cedar was brought from Mount Lebanon, where there were many large cedar trees. The trees were cut down and carried to Tyre, on the seacoast. There they were made into rafts and were floated down to Joppa. At Joppa, they were taken ashore and carried up to Jerusalem. All this work was done by the men of Tyre on orders of their king, Hiram, who was a friend of Solomon.

All the stones for the building of the Temple were cut into shape and fitted together before they were brought to Mount Moriah. And all the beams for the roof and the pillars of cedar were carved and made to join each other, so that as the walls were built, there was no noise from its construction. The Temple was just like the Tabernacle, except it was much larger and was built of stone and cedar, instead of a tent.

THE BUILDING OF THE TEMPLE - 1 KINGS 6

Seven years were spent in building the Temple, but at last it was finished, and a great service was held to dedicate it to the worship of the Lord. Many offerings were burned on the great altar; the ark was brought from Mount Zion and placed in the Holy of Holies; then King Solomon knelt in front of the altar and offered a prayer to the Lord in front of all the people, who filled the courts of the Temple.

One night after the Temple was finished, the Lord appeared to Solomon and said, "I have heard the prayer you offered to me, and I have made this house holy. It shall be my house, and I will dwell there. And if you will walk before me as David, your father, walked, doing my will, then your throne shall stand forever. But if you turn aside from following the Lord, then I will leave this house, and will turn from it, and will let the enemies of Israel come and destroy this house that was built for me."

Discussion Questions: *1. What did Solomon build? Why was it important? 2. What did God say to Solomon about the Temple? 3. What else did he promise Solomon?*

DAY 126

SOLOMON'S REIGN

1 Kings 10:1-11:43

UNDER King Solomon, the land of Israel rose to greatness as never before. All the countries around Israel, and some that were far away, sent their princes to visit Solomon, and everyone who saw him wondered at his wisdom and his skill in answering hard questions. It was said that King Solomon was the wisest man in the world. He wrote many of the sayings in the Book of Proverbs, and many more that have been lost, plus more than a thousand songs. People came from many lands to see Solomon's riches and listen to his wise words.

In a land more than a thousand miles from Jerusalem, in southern Arabia, the Queen of Sheba heard of Solomon's wisdom. She left her home, riding on a camel and bearing rich gifts, and came to visit King Solomon. While they were together, she asked him many difficult questions. Solomon answered all her questions, then showed her all the glory of his palace: his throne, his servants, the richness of his table, and the steps from his palace to the house of the Lord.

When she had heard and seen all, she said, "All I heard of your wisdom and your greatness was true. But I did not believe it until I came and saw your kingdom. And not half was told me, for your wisdom and splendor are far greater than I heard. Happy are those who hear your wisdom! Blessed be the Lord your God, who has set you on the throne of Israel!"

THE QUEEN OF SHEBA CAME TO VISIT KING SOLOMON — I KINGS 10:1

The Queen of Sheba gave Solomon great treasures of gold, and sweet-smelling spices, and perfumes, then Solomon gave her rich presents before she went back to her own land.

Solomon's great palace stood on the southern slope of Mount Moriah, a little lower than the Temple. It had so many cedar pillars that they looked like a forest, so the palace was called "The House of the Forest of Lebanon." From this palace, a wide staircase of stone led up to the Temple, and Solomon and his princes walked up these stairs when they went to worship.

But there was a dark side to the reign of Solomon. His palaces, and the walled cities he built to protect his kingdom, and the splendor of his court, cost money. To pay for these, he laid heavy taxes on his people, and he compelled many of the men to work on buildings, become soldiers in his army, labor in his fields, and serve in his household. Before the close of Solomon's reign, the cry of the people rose up against Solomon and his rule because of the heavy burdens he laid on the land.

Solomon was very wise in affairs of the world, but he had no feeling for the poor of the land, nor did he love God with all his heart. He chose for his queen a daughter of Pharaoh, the king of Egypt, and he built her a splendid palace. He also married many other women who were the daughters of kings. These women had worshiped idols in their own homes, and to please them, Solomon built a temple of idols on the Mount of Olives. Many idols stood on the hill in front of Jerusalem, and King Solomon himself offered sacrifices to these images.

The Lord was very angry with Solomon for all this, and said to Solomon, "Since you have done these wicked things and have not kept your promise to serve me, and because you have ignored my commands, I will take away the kingdom of Israel from your son and give it to one of your servants. But for the sake of your father, David, who loved me and obeyed my commands, I will not take away all the kingdom. I will leave him and his children one tribe."

The servant of King Solomon was a young man of the tribe of Ephraim named Jeroboam, a very able man. One day a prophet of the Lord named Ahijah met Jeroboam as he was going out of Jerusalem. Ahijah took off his own cloak and tore it into twelve pieces. Ten of these pieces he gave to Jeroboam, saying, "Take these ten pieces, for thus saith the Lord, the God of Israel: 'I will tear the kingdom out of the hand of Solomon's son and will give ten tribes to you. But Solomon's son shall have one tribe for David's sake and the sake of Jerusalem. You shall reign over ten of the tribes of Israel, and shall have anything you desire. And if you do my will, then I will be with you, and will let your children and children's children rule over this land.' "

When King Solomon heard what the prophet had said, he tried to kill Jeroboam, but Jeroboam fled to Egypt and stayed there until the end of Solomon's reign.

Solomon reigned forty years, as David had reigned before him. He died and was buried on Mount Zion, and Rehoboam, his son, became king.

Sometimes the reign of Solomon has been called "the Golden Age of Israel," because it was a time of peace and great riches. But it would be better to call it "the Gilded Age," because under all the show and glitter of Solomon's reign there were many evil things.

Discussion Questions: *1. Why did the queen of Sheba visit Solomon? 2. Why were the people unhappy during Solomon's rule? 3. Why was God angry with Solomon? 4. What did God promise Jeroboam? 5. What lay under the peace in Solomon's reign?*

DAY 127

THE KINGDOM DIVIDED

1 Kings 12:1-24
2 Chronicles 10:1-19

WHEN the strong rule of King Solomon was ended by his death and his weak son, Rehoboam, followed him as king, all the people of Israel rose up against the heavy burdens Solomon had laid on them. They sent for Jeroboam, who was in Egypt, and he became their leader. They said to Rehoboam, "Your father laid on us heavy burdens of taxes and work. If you will promise to take away our load, then we will receive you as king and serve you."

"Give me three days," said Rehoboam, "then I will tell you what I will do."

So Jeroboam and the people waited for three days while Rehoboam talked with the rulers and his friends. Rehoboam first called together the old men who had advised Solomon, asking them, "What answer shall I give the people?"

These old men said to King Rehoboam, "If you will be wise today, yield to the people, and speak good words to them, then they will submit to you and serve you always. Tell them that you will take off the heavy burdens and rule the land in kindness."

But Rehoboam would not heed the advice of these wise old men. He talked with the young princes who had grown up with him in the palace, and cared nothing for the people or their troubles.

And the young nobles said to Rehoboam, "Say to the people: 'My father made your burdens heavy, but I will make them heavier still. My father beat you with whips, but I will sting you with scorpions. My little finger shall be thicker than my father's waist.'"

On the third day, Jeroboam and all the people came to Rehoboam for his answer. And the foolish young king did not follow the good advice of the old men who knew the people and their needs. He did as the haughty young princes told him to do, and spoke harshly to the people.

Now the people of Israel were very angry at the king. They said, "Why should we submit any longer to the house of David? We will choose a king of our own!" That day, ten of the twelve tribes of Israel broke away from the rule of King Rehoboam and the house of David. They made Jeroboam their king. His kingdom was all the land northward from Bethel to Dan, and also all the tribes on the east of the river Jordan.

Rehoboam was still a king, but only over the tribe of Judah and part of Benjamin. Rehoboam ruled over the mountain country on the west of the Dead Sea, but he had no control over the Philistine cities on the plain beside the Great Sea. So the kingdom of Judah, as it was called, was less than one-third the size of the kingdom of Israel. When the kingdom was divided, all the empire of Solomon was broken up. The Syrians formed a kingdom of their own, with Damascus as its chief city. The Ammonites, the Moabites, and the Edomites all had their own kings, so the great empire founded by David and held by Solomon fell apart and became six small, struggling states.

Yet all this was the will of the Lord, who did not wish Israel to become a great nation, but a good people. The Israelites were growing rich and living for the world, while God wanted them to be his people and worship him.

Discussion Questions: *1. What kind of king was Rehoboam? 2. What did he tell the people? 3. What did the people do? 4. Why did God let the kingdom break up like that?*

DAY 128

JEROBOAM DOES EVIL

1 Kings 12:25-13:10

THE Lord had told Jeroboam that he would become king over the Ten Tribes, and that if he would serve the Lord, his kingdom would become great and his descendants would rule for a long time. But Jeroboam was not faithful to the Lord God of Israel.

He saw that his people still went up to Jerusalem to worship in the Temple, because that was the only altar in the land. Jeroboam said to himself, "If my people go up to worship at Jerusalem, they will become friends of Rehoboam and his people. Then they will leave me or kill me, and let Rehoboam rule over all the land. I will build places for worship and altars in my own kingdom, then my people will not need to go away to worship."

Jeroboam forgot that the Lord would care for him and keep him if he was faithful. Because he would not trust the Lord, he did something very evil. He chose two places — Bethel in the south and Dan in the north — and made these places of worship for his people. At each place, he made a calf of gold, set it up, and said to the people of Israel, "It is too far for you to go to Jerusalem to worship. Here are gods for you, gods that brought you out of Egypt. Come and worship these gods."

Since the priests of Levi would not serve in Jeroboam's idol temples, he took men out of all the tribes and made them his priests. And all through the land, he had images set up to lead the people in worshiping idols.

In the fall of every year, there was a feast in Jerusalem that all the people went to. Jeroboam made a great feast at Bethel, to draw people to his temple and keep them away from the Temple of the Lord at Jerusalem. Jeroboam led his people away from the Lord to idols, which is why the Bible calls him "Jeroboam, who made Israel to sin."

One day when Jeroboam was offering incense at the altar, a prophet came from Judah and cried out against the altar, saying, "O altar, altar, thus saith the Lord: 'Behold, in the time to come there shall rise up a man of the house of David, Josiah by name. And Josiah shall burn upon this altar the bones of the priests that have offered sacrifices to idols in this place. And this altar and this temple shall be destroyed.' "

The prophet from Judah also said to Jeroboam, "I will prove that I am speaking for God. This altar shall fall apart, and the ashes on it shall be poured out."

When King Jeroboam heard this, he was very angry. He stretched out his arm toward the prophet and called to his guards, "Take hold of that man!"

Instantly, the hand Jeroboam held out toward the prophet dried up and became helpless. Then the altar was torn apart, and the ashes fell onto the ground. The king saw this was the work of the Lord, so he said to the prophet, "Pray to the Lord your God for me, so he will make my hand well again."

The prophet prayed to the Lord, and the Lord heard his prayer and made the king's hand well once more. Then King Jeroboam said to the prophet, "Come home with me, eat, and rest. I will give you a reward."

But the man of God said to the king, "The Lord came to me, saying, 'Eat no bread, and drink no water in this place. Go to your home in the land of Judah by another way.' "

So the man of God left Bethel by another road and started home to Judah.

Discussion Questions: *1. What did God promise Jeroboam? 2. What evil thing did Jeroboam do? 3. What did the prophet tell Jeroboam? 4. Why wouldn't the prophet go home with Jeroboam?*

DAY 129

JEROBOAM AND THE PROPHET
1 Kings 13:11-14:20

AT that time, another old prophet lived in Bethel. His sons told him about the man of God from Judah, what he had said, and what the Lord had done. The old man learned which road the prophet had taken, followed after him, and found him resting under an oak tree. He said to him, "Are you the man of God that came from Judah?"

He replied, "I am."

Then the old man said, "I am a prophet of the Lord, as you are, and an angel spoke to me, saying, 'Bring the prophet from Judah back to your house, and let him eat and drink with you.' " Now this was not true, but the prophet from Judah went home with him and ate a meal at his house. This also was not right, for he should have obeyed what the Lord had said to him, even though another man claimed to have heard a different message.

While they were sitting at the table, a word came from the Lord to the old prophet who had told the lie, and he cried out to the prophet from Judah, "Thus saith the Lord: 'Because you have disobeyed my command, and have come back to this place, and have eaten bread and drunk water here, you shall die, and your body shall not be buried with your fathers.' "

After dinner the prophet started back to his own home. On the way, a lion came out and killed him, but did not eat the man's body. This was told to the old prophet whose lies had led him to disobey the Lord. The old prophet came, took up his body, laid it in his own tomb, and mourned over him. And he said to his sons, "When I am dead, bury me beside the body of the prophet from the land of Judah. For I know that what he spoke against the altar at Bethel shall surely come to pass."

Once a child of King Jeroboam was taken very ill. His mother went to the prophet Ahijah, who was now old and blind, to ask if the child would get well.

Ahijah said to her: "Tell King Jeroboam the Lord says: 'You have done evil, and have made graven images, and have cast the Lord behind your back. Therefore the Lord will bring evil on you and your house. Your sick child shall die. Every other child of yours shall be killed, and your family shall be swept away. In times to come, God will smite Israel, and carry them into a land far away, because of the idols they have worshiped.' "

After this, Jeroboam died, and his son Nadab began to reign in his place. But after two years Baasha, one of his servants, rose up against Nadab, killed him, and made himself king over Israel. Baasha killed every child of Jeroboam, as Ahijah the prophet had said.

So, although Jeroboam was made king, as God had promised him, the kingdom was taken away from his family because he did not obey the word of the Lord, but led his people into sin.

Discussion Questions: *1. What did the old prophet do that was wrong? What did God tell the prophet from Judah, whom he mislead? 2. What lesson was God teaching in this story? 3. Why didn't God heal the king's child? 4. What lesson was God teaching the king?*

DAY 130

OTHER KINGS OF ISRAEL

1 Kings 15:33-16:34

AFTER Jeroboam and Nadab, Baasha reigned as king of Israel. But he did as Jeroboam had done before him, disobeying the word of the Lord and worshiping idols. The Lord sent a prophet to Baasha, saying, "The Lord says to Baasha, king of Israel: 'I lifted you up from the dust and made you the prince over my people Israel. But you have walked in the way of Jeroboam and have made Israel sin. Therefore your family shall be destroyed, like the family of Jeroboam.' "

When Baasha died, his son Elah became king, but his servant, Zimri, killed him and all his family. Not one of them was left alive. Zimri tried to make himself king, but his reign was short — only seven days. Omri, the general of the Israelite army, made war on him and shut him up in his palace. Whem Zimri found he could not escape, he set his palace on fire and was burned up with it. After this, there was war in Israel between Omri and another man named Tibni, each trying to win the kingdom. But at last Tibni was slain, and Omri became king.

Omri was not a good man, for he worshiped idols, like the kings before him. But he was a strong king, and made his kingdom great. He made peace with the kingdom of Judah, for there had been war between Judah and Israel ever since Jeroboam had founded the kingdom. Omri bought a hill in the middle of the land from a man named Shemer, and on the hill he built a city he named Samaria. The city of Samaria became in Israel what Jerusalem was in Judah, the chief city and capital. Before Omri, the kings of Israel had lived in different cities, but after Omri, all the kings lived in Samaria, so the kingdom itself was often called "the kingdom of Samaria."

After Omri, Ahab reigned in Samaria. He was worse than any of the kings before him. Ahab married Jezebel, and she brought along the worship of Baal and of the Asherah, which was far more wicked than the worship of the golden calves. Jezebel was so bitter against the worship of the Lord God of Israel that she sought out the prophets of the Lord everywhere, and killed them. To save their lives, the prophets hid in caves in the mountains.

You remember that when Joshua destroyed and burned the city of Jericho he cursed any man who ever rebuilt the walls of Jericho. Five hundred years after Joshua, the walls of Jericho were rebuilt by a man named Hiel, who came from Bethel. When he laid the foundation of the wall, his oldest son died. When he set up the gates of the city, his youngest son died, and Joshua's words came true.

Discussion Questions: *1. What did God tell Baasha? Did God do what he said? 2. What were all the kings after Baasha like? 3. What did Jezebel do to the prophets?*

DAY 131

Elijah and the Widow

1 Kings 17:1-24

DURING the reign of King Ahab, a great prophet suddenly appeared — Elijah. He came from the land of Gilead beyond the Jordan, and he lived alone out in the wilderness. His clothing was made of skin, and his hair and beard were long and rough. Without any warning, Elijah came to King Ahab and said, "As the Lord God of Israel lives, no dew or rain shall fall until I call for it."

Then he went away as suddenly as he had come. At God's command, he hid himself in a wild place by the brook Cherith, which flows down from the mountains into the river Jordan. There he drank the water in the brook, and ate food brought to him every day by ravens.

As Elijah said, no rain fell on the land, and there wasn't even any dew on the grass in the morning. Every day the brook from which Elijah drank grew smaller, until at last it was dry, and there was no water. Then the Lord spoke to Elijah again and said, "Go to Zarephath. I have commanded a widow woman there to care for you."

So Elijah left the brook and walked north until he came near the city of

THE RAVENS BROUGHT ELIJAH BREAD AND MEAT — 1 KINGS 17:6

Zarephath. There, beside the gate of the city, he saw a woman picking up sticks. Elijah said to her, "Will you bring me some water to drink?"

She went to bring him the water, and Elijah said, "Bring me a little piece of bread to eat."

The woman said to Elijah, "As sure as the Lord your God lives, I don't even have a loaf of bread. I have one handful of meal in the barrel and a little oil in a bottle, and now I am gathering a few sticks to make a fire, to bake it for me and my son. When we have eaten it, there is nothing left for us except to die."

Then the word of the Lord came to Elijah, and he said to the woman, "Fear not. Go and do as you have said, but first make me a little cake, then cook for yourself and your son. God says you will have grain and oil until the rains come."

The widow woman believed Elijah's word. She made a little cake for the prophet and then found enough left for herself and her son. The barrel always had meal in it, and the bottle held oil every day. The prophet, the woman, and her son had food as long as they needed it.

One day the little boy was taken very ill and died. His mother said to Elijah, "O man of God! have you come here to cause my son to die?"

Elijah said to her, "Give me your son."

Elijah carried the boy up to his own room, and put him on the bed. Then he cried to the Lord, "O Lord God, have you brought trouble to this woman by taking away her son?" Then he stretched himself over the child's body three times and cried to the Lord again, "O Lord God, please let this child's soul come into him again!"

ELIJAH SAID, "SEE, YOUR SON IS ALIVE." - 1 KINGS 17:23

The Lord heard Elijah's prayer, and the child came alive. Elijah carried the living boy back to his mother, and she said, "Now I am sure you are a man of God and the word of the Lord you speak is the truth."

Discussion Questions: *1. What did Elijah tell King Ahab? 2. Why did Elijah hide from the king? 3. What did Elijah promise the woman? 4. Do you think the woman had much faith, when she did what he commanded? 5. What did Elijah do for the woman's son?*

DAY 132

ELIJAH'S CHALLENGE (PART 1)
1 Kings 18:1-24

FOR three years after Elijah gave God's message to King Ahab, no rain fell on Israel. The brooks didn't flow, the springs became dry, the ground was parched, and the fields produced nothing. There was no grass for the cattle and the flocks, and there was scarcely any food for the people.

King Ahab was in trouble. He knew Elijah had the power to call down rain, but Elijah was nowhere to be found. He sent men to search for him and asked the kings of the nations around to look for him, for he hoped to persuade the prophet to end the drought. During the drought's third year, Ahab called Obadiah, his chief servant. Unlike Ahab, he was a good man, worshiping the Lord and trying to do right. Once, when Queen Jezebel tried to kill all the prophets of the Lord, Obadiah hid a hundred of them in two caves, gave them food, and kept them safe.

Ahab said to Obadiah, "Let's go through all the land — you in one part and I in another — and look for running streams and springs. Perhaps we can find enough water to save some of the horses and mules."

As Obadiah was going through his part of the country looking for water, suddenly Elijah met him. Obadiah knew Elijah at once. He fell on his face before him and said, "Is this my lord Elijah?"

Elijah answered him, "Yes, it is I, Elijah. Go and tell your master that Elijah is here."

Obadiah said, "Oh, my lord, why do you want King Ahab to kill me? When I go tell him you are here, the Lord will send you away to some other place. If Ahab cannot find you, he will be angry at me, and kill me. Don't you know I fear the Lord and serve him?"

Elijah said, "I promise I will show myself to King Ahab today."

So Obadiah went to meet Ahab and told him of Elijah's coming, and Ahab went to meet Elijah. When Ahab saw Elijah, he said to him, "Are you here, you who brought all this trouble to Israel?"

And Elijah answered the king, "I am not the one that has brought trouble on Israel. It is you and your house. You have turned away from the commands of the Lord and have worshiped the images of Baal. Bring all the people to Mount Carmel, along with the four hundred and fifty prophets of Baal and the four hundred prophets of Asherah who ate at Jezebel's table."

Ahab did as Elijah commanded and brought all the people to Mount Carmel. Elijah stood before the multitude and said to them, "How long will you go halting and limping back and forth between two sides, not choosing either? If the Lord is God, follow him; but if Baal is god, then follow him. I am alone, the only prophet of the Lord here today, but Baal's prophets are four hundred and fifty men. Now, let the people give us two young oxen, one for Baal's prophets and one for me. Let the prophets of Baal take one ox, cut it up, and lay it on the altar, but let no fire be placed under it. I will do the same. Then you call on your god, and I will call on the Lord. And the God who sends down the fire to his altar will be the God of Israel."

And the people said, "What you have spoken is right. We will do as you say, and will see who is the true God."

DAY 133

ELIJAH'S CHALLENGE (PART 2)

1 Kings 18:25-46

THEN the two oxen were brought, and one was cut in pieces and laid on the altar of Baal. The prophets of Baal stood around the altar and cried, "O Baal, hear us!" But there was no answer. After a time, the worshipers of Baal became furious. Elijah laughed at them. "Call out louder, for surely he is a god! Perhaps he is thinking, or he has gone on a journey, or perhaps he is asleep, and must be awaked!"

But it was all in vain. The middle of the afternoon came, and there was no answer. The altar stood with its offering, but no fire came to it. Then Elijah said to all the people, "Come closer to me."

And they came near. He found an old altar to the Lord that had been thrown down, and he took twelve stones, one for each of the twelve tribes, and piled them up. Around the altar he dug a trench, to carry away water. Then he cut wood, and laid it on the altar, and on the wood he placed the young ox, cut into pieces for a sacrifice. Then he said, "Fill four barrels with water, and pour it on the offering."

The Great Sea was nearby, so they brought four barrels of water and poured it on the altar. He told them to do it again, and a third time, until the offering, the wood, and the altar were soaked through and through, and the trench was filled with water.

Then, in front of all the people, Elijah prayed: "O Lord, the God of Abraham, of Isaac, and of Israel, let it be known this day that you are God in Israel, and that I am your servant, and I have done all these things at your command. Hear me, O Lord, hear me, so this people will know thou are God."

Suddenly, fire fell from the sky and burned up the offering, the wood, the stones, and the dust, and licked up the water that was in the trench. And when the people saw it, they fell on their faces, and cried, "The Lord, he is God! The Lord, he is God!" Elijah said to the people, "Seize the prophets of Baal. Let not one of them escape!"

THE FIRE OF THE LORD FELL AND BURNED THE OFFERING- 1 KINGS 18:38

They took them all, 450 men. At Elijah's command, they brought them down to the dry bed of the brook Kishon and killed them for leading Israel into sin.

Ahab had seen all of this happen, and Elijah now said to him, "Rise up. Eat and drink, for there is a sound of a great rain."

While Ahab was eating and drinking, Elijah was praying. He bowed down and prayed to the Lord to send rain. After a time, he sent his servant up to the top of the mountain, saying, "Go up and look toward the sea."

The servant went up and came back, saying, "I can see nothing."

Elijah sent him up seven times. At the seventh time, his servant said, "I see a cloud rising out of the sea as small as a man's hand."

Then Elijah sent to Ahab, saying, "Hurry. Get your chariot ready before the rain stops you." In a little while, the sky was covered with black clouds, and rain began to fall.

In one day, Baal was defeated and the people turned to the true God.

Discussion Questions: *1. Why didn't Baal answer the calls of those who worshiped him? 2. Why did Elijah soak his altar with water? 3. How did God answer his prayer? What did Elijah ask God to do? 4. Why did the people kill the prophets of Baal? 5. What did God do after the people had turned back to him?*

DAY 134

Elijah's Assignments
1 Kings 19:1-18

WHEN King Ahab told his wife, Jezebel, everything Elijah had done — how fire had fallen from heaven to his altar and how he had killed all the prophets of Baal — Jezebel was very angry. She sent a messenger to Elijah with these words: "May the gods do to me as you have done to the prophets of Baal, if I do not kill you by tomorrow, as you have killed them!"

Elijah saw his life was in danger, and he found that no one in the kingdom dared to stand by him, so he ran for his life. He traveled south to Beersheba, which is on the edge of the desert, eighty miles away from Samaria. Then he went out alone into the desert.

After he walked all day under the sun over the burning sand, he sat down to rest under a juniper tree. He was tired, hungry, and discouraged. He felt his work had all been in vain and he had shown weakness in running away. Elijah cried out to the Lord, "O Lord, I have lived long enough! Take away my life, for I am no better than my people!" Then, tired out, he lay down to sleep under the tree. But the Lord was very kind to Elijah. While he was sleeping, an angel touched him and said, "Arise, and eat."

He opened his eyes and saw a little fire, with a loaf of bread baking on it, and a bottle of water. He ate and drank, then lay down to sleep again. Again he felt the angel touch him. "Arise, and eat. The journey is too long for you."

He ate once more, then he went on his way and walked through the desert for forty days. He came at last to Mount Horeb, found a cave in the side of the mountain, and went in to rest. While he was in the cave, he heard God's voice saying, "What are you doing here, Elijah?"

Elijah said to the Lord, "O Lord God, I have worked hard for you. The people of Israel have turned away from their promise to serve you. They have thrown down your altars and killed your prophets. Only I am left, and now they are trying to kill me."

Then the Lord said to Elijah, "Go out and stand on the mountain before the Lord."

While Elijah was standing on the mountain, a great wind swept by and broke the rocks in pieces, but the Lord was not in the wind. Then came an earthquake, shaking the mountain. But the Lord was not in the earthquake. After the earthquake, a fire passed by, but the Lord was not in the fire. After the fire, there was silence and stillness, and Elijah heard a low, quiet voice that he knew was the voice of the Lord.

The Lord told Elijah, "Go back to the land you came from, then go to Damascus and anoint Hazael king of Syria. Jehu you shall anoint king of Israel, and you shall anoint Elisha to take your place as prophet. Many people will die, but seven thousand good men will remain in Israel."

This work would take all the rest of Elijah's life. Some of it was not completed until after Elijah died, but it gave Elijah what he needed most: work to do, a friend to stand beside him, and the knowledge that he had not lived in vain, since there were still 7,000 faithful men in Israel.

Discussion Questions: *1. What did Jezebel want to do to Elijah? How did Elijah feel when he found out? 2. How did God take care of Elijah in the desert? 3. What did God tell Elijah? What did God give him? Why did Elijah need that?*

DAY 135

ELIJAH CALLS ELISHA

1 Kings 19:19-21

ONE of God's commands, Elijah obeyed at once. He left Mount Horeb, journeyed north through the wilderness, across the kingdom of Judah, and into the land of Israel. There he found Elisha plowing a field with twelve yoke of oxen. Elisha was a rich man's son, and he cared for a large farm.

Elijah came to the field where Elisha was at work, and without a word, took off his own cloak of skin, threw it on Elisha's shoulders, then walked away. Elisha knew who this strange man was, and he knew what it meant when Elijah cast his mantle on him. It was a call for him to leave his home, go out into the wilderness with Elijah, take up the life of a prophet, face the danger of the queen's hate, and maybe be killed, as many prophets had been killed before. But Elisha was a man of God, and he did not hesitate to obey God's call. He left his oxen standing in the field, ran after Elijah, and said to him, "Let me kiss my father and my mother, and then I will go with you."

Then Elisha went back to the field, killed the oxen, made a fire with the yokes and the wooden plow, roasted the flesh of the oxen, and gave the meat to the people on the farm. He did this to show that he was leaving forever. Then he kissed his father and mother and went to live with Elijah and be Elijah's helper.

Discussion Questions: *1. Why did Elijah go to see Elisha? 2. What did the prophet mean when he cast his mantle around Elisha? 3. Why did Elisha go with him? 4. What did killing the oxen and giving the meat to the people on the farm mean?*

DAY 136

AHAB'S ERROR

1 Kings 20:1-43

THE country nearest Israel on the north was Syria. Its chief city and capital was Damascus, and its king was named Benhadad. His kingdom was far greater and stronger than Israel, and when he went to make war on King Ahab, Ahab could bring only 7,000 men against the Syrian army. The army of the Syrians filled all the valleys and plains around Samaria, but Benhadad and his chief rulers were drinking wine when they should have been making ready for the battle, and the little army of Israel won a great victory over the Syrians, driving them back to their own land.

Again the Syrians attacked Israel, but again God gave Ahab and the Israelites a victory, and the Syrian army was destroyed. King Benhadad ran away to his palace, and King Ahab might easily have taken him prisoner and conquered all Syria. But Benhadad dressed himself in sackcloth, and put a rope around his waist, and came as a beggar to Ahab, pleading for his life and his kingdom. Ahab felt very proud to have Benhadad kneeling before him. He spared his life and gave him back his kingdom, which turned out to be a bad mistake.

By this time, through the teaching of Elijah and Elisha, there were many prophets of the Lord in Israel. The word of the Lord came to one of these prophets, and he said to a fellow prophet, "Strike me, and give me a wound."

But the man refused, and the prophet said, "Because you have not obeyed the voice of the Lord, as soon as you go away from me, a lion will kill you." And as the man was going away, a lion rushed out on him and killed him.

Then the prophet said to another man, "Strike me, I beg you!" The man struck him and wounded him, so blood flowed. Then the prophet — all bloody, with his face covered — stood by the road as King Ahab passed by, and he cried out to the king. The king saw him, stopped, and asked what had happened to him.

The prophet said, "I was in the battle and a soldier brought me a prisoner, and said to me, 'Keep this man. If you lose him, your life shall go for his life, or you shall pay me a talent of silver for him.' And while I was busy, the prisoner escaped. O king, do not let my life be taken for the man's life."

But the king said, "You gave yourself your punishment: Your life for your prisoner's life."

Then the prophet threw off the covering on his face, and the king saw he was one of the prophets. The prophet said to the king, "The Lord says, 'Because you have let go the king I wanted destroyed, your life shall go for his life, and your people for his people.' "

When Ahab heard this, he was greatly troubled and displeased. He went to his palace in Samaria full of alarm, for he saw he had made a mistake by sparing his kingdom's greatest enemy.

Discussion Questions: *1. Who gave Ahab a victory over the Syrian army? 2. How did Ahab disobey God? 3. What happened when people did not obey a prophet? 4. Why didn't the prophet immediately tell the king what he had done wrong? 5. What did the prophet say would happen to the king?*

DAY 137

NABOTH'S VINEYARD

1 Kings 21:1-29

KING Ahab's home was at Samaria, but he had also a palace at Jezreel. And beside Ahab's palace at Jezreel was a vineyard belonging to a man named Naboth. Ahab wanted this vineyard, so he said to Naboth, "Let me have your vineyard. I would like to make it a garden for vegetables. I will give you a better vineyard in place of it, or I will pay you in money."

But Naboth answered the king, "This vineyard has belonged to my father's family for many generations, and I am not willing to give it up or leave it."

Ahab was very angry when he heard this. He went to his house, refused to eat, lay down on his bed, and turned his face to the wall. His wife Jezebel came to him and said, "Why are you so sad? What's troubling you?"

Ahab answered her, "I asked Naboth to sell me his vineyard, or to trade another vineyard for it, and he would not."

Then Jezebel said to him, "Don't you rule over the kingdom of Israel? Get up, eat your dinner, and enjoy yourself. I will give you the vineyard of Naboth."

Queen Jezebel sat down and wrote a letter in Ahab's name, sealing it with the king's seal. She wrote: "Let the word be given out that a meeting of the men of Jezreel is to be held, and set Naboth up before all the people. Have two men ready to swear they heard Naboth curse God and the king. Then take Naboth out and stone him until he is dead."

Everyone was so afraid of Jezebel that they did as she ordered. When they sent word to Queen Jezebel that Naboth was dead, Jezebel said to Ahab, "Now you can go and take the vineyard of Naboth in Jezreel, because he's dead."

Ahab rode in his chariot from Samaria to Jezreel. As he was riding in the vineyard that had been Naboth's, suddenly Elijah stood before them.

Ahab was startled, and he called out, "Have you found me, my enemy?"

"I have found you," answered Elijah, "because you did evil in the sight of the Lord. I will bring evil on you and sweep you away. I will kill all your sons and will make your family like the family of Jeroboam, who made Israel to sin. And because your wife, Jezebel, has stirred you up to sin, she shall die, and the wild dogs of the city shall eat the body of Jezebel by the wall of Jezreel."

ELIJAH REBUKED AHAB AND JEZEBEL – 1 KINGS 21

When Ahab heard these words of Elijah, he saw how badly he had acted, and he felt sorrow for his sin. He put on sackcloth, fasted, and sought mercy. And the word of the Lord came to Elijah, saying, "Do you see how Ahab has humbled himself before me and shows sorrow for his sin? Because of this, I will not bring the evil in his lifetime. But after he is dead, I will bring it on his children."

———————

Discussion Questions: *1. What did Ahab want from Naboth? What did his*

222

wife do to get it? 2. What was wrong with the king's attitude? 3. What did Elijah promise him would happen because of this act? 4. Why did God forgive Ahab? Did God change the punishment?

DAY 138

AHAB'S DEATH

1 Kings 22:1-40

AFTER the two victories King Ahab won over the Syrians, there was peace between Syria and Israel for three years. But in the third year, the Syrians became strong again and seized a city called Ramoth-gilead. At that time there was peace and friendship between the kingdoms of Israel and Judah, and Ahab (the king of Israel) said to Jehoshaphat (the king of Judah), "Do you know that Ramoth-gilead is ours and we have done nothing to take it out of the hands of the king of Syria? Will you go with me to take it back?"

King Jehoshaphat sent word to the king of Israel, "I am with you." So the kings gathered their armies for war against the Syrians, and King Jehoshaphat came to Samaria to meet King Ahab.

Jehoshaphat was a good man, and he worshiped the Lord. He said to Ahab, "Let's ask the prophets to give us the word of the Lord before we go to battle."

The king of Israel called together his prophets, 400 false prophets of the idols, and asked them, "Shall I go up to battle at Ramoth-gilead, or shall I remain at home?" And the prophets of the idols said, "Go up. The Lord will give Ramoth-gilead to you."

But Jehoshaphat was not satisfied with the words of these men. He asked, "Isn't there a prophet of the Lord we can ask?"

"There is one prophet," answered Ahab. "His name is Micaiah. But I hate him; he never prophesies any good for me, only evil."

King Ahab sent one of his officers to bring the prophet. The officer said to Micaiah, "All the prophets have spoken good to the king. Let your words be like theirs."

Micaiah said, "Whatever the Lord says to me, I will say, and nothing else."

King Ahab said to Micaiah, "Micaiah, tell me the truth, in the name of the Lord."

Micaiah said, "I saw all Israel scattered on the mountains, like sheep that have no shepherd. And the Lord said, 'These have no master. Let every man go back to his own house.'"

Ahab knew this meant he would be killed in the battle. He said to his guards, "Put this fellow in prison and let him have nothing to eat but dry bread and water until I come again in peace."

So the kings of Israel and Judah led their armies to battle at Ramoth-gilead. Ahab felt afraid after the prophecy of Micaiah and he said to Jehoshaphat, "I will dress as a common soldier before going into the battle, but you wear your royal robes."

Now the king of Syria had given word to all his captains to look for the king of Israel and kill him. When they saw Jehoshaphat standing in his chariot, they thought he was King Ahab, and they turned the battle toward him. But Jehoshaphat cried out, and when they found he was not the king of Israel, they left him.

In the battle, one soldier of the Syrians drew his bow and shot an arrow, not knowing he was aiming at the king of Israel. Ahab was badly wounded and died that evening. They brought his body to Samaria, and buried him there, washing his chariot and armor at a pool. And the wild dogs of the city licked up Ahab's blood, according to the word of the Lord spoken by Elijah.

Discussion Questions: *1. Why did King Ahab go to battle? Who did he go with? 2. What did the false prophets tell Ahab? 3. What did Micaiah tell him? 4. Why did the king hate Micaiah? 5. What happened to Ahab? Was the faithful prophet right?*

DAY 139

ELIJAH IS TAKEN AWAY

2 Kings 1:1-2:15

AFTER the death of Ahab, his son Ahaziah reigned for two years as king of Israel. He fell out a window in his palace and died. Since he had no son, his brother, Jehoram, became king.

The work of Elijah the prophet was now over, and the Lord was about to take him up to heaven. Elijah and Elisha went together to a place called Gilgal in the mountains, not far from Bethel. Elijah said to Elisha, "Stay here, because the Lord has sent me to Bethel."

Elisha knew that Elijah would be taken from him very soon, and he said, "I will not leave you." So Elijah and Elisha walked together to Bethel. Many worshipers of the Lord, called "sons of the prophets" because they followed the teaching of the prophets, lived in Bethel, and some of them became prophets themselves. These men came to Elisha and said to him, "Do you know that the Lord will take away your master very soon?"

Elisha answered them, "Yes, I know it. But don't talk about it."

At Bethel, Elijah said to Elisha, "Elisha, stay here. The Lord has sent me to Jericho."

But Elisha again refused to leave Elijah, so they walked together to Jericho. From there, they walked together to the Jordan River.

When they came to the bank of the Jordan, Elijah took his mantle, wrapped it together, and hit the water. The water divided on each side, a path was made across the river, and the two prophets walked across on dry ground. As they walked, Elijah said, "Ask what I should do for you before I am taken away from you."

Elisha answered him, "All I ask is that your spirit come upon me in greater power than on any other man."

Elijah said to him, "You have asked a great blessing. If you see me when I am taken away, it shall come to you. But if you do not see me, it shall not come."

As they still went on, suddenly a chariot of fire and horses of fire came between them, and parted them, and Elijah went up in a whirlwind on the fiery chariot to heaven.

ELIJAH WENT UP BY A WHIRLWIND INTO HEAVEN
2 KINGS 2:11

Elisha saw him going up toward heaven, and he cried out, "My father, my father, the chariot of Israel, and the horsemen thereof!" He meant that in losing Elijah, the kingdom had lost more than an army of chariots and horsemen. After this, he saw Elijah no more, but he picked up Elijah's cloak that had fallen from him. With the mantle, he struck the waters of Jordan, saying, "Where is the Lord God of Elijah?" As he struck the water with Elijah's mantle, it parted on either side, and Elisha walked across the Jordan. The sons of the prophets who were standing near the river had not seen Elijah go up, but now they saw Elisha walking through the river alone and knew God had taken Elijah away. They said, "The spirit of Elijah now rests upon Elisha," and they came to meet him, and bowed down before him as their chief. So Elijah was taken away, but Elisha stood in his place as the Lord's prophet.

Discussion Questions: *1. What was going to happen to Elijah? How did Elisha feel about it? 2. Elisha would not leave Elijah. What does that show you about him? 3. What did Elisha ask for? Do you think it was a good thing to ask? 4. Did Elisha see Elijah taken away? What did that mean?*

DAY 140

THE MOABITE REBELLION

2 Kings 3:1-27

AFTER Elijah had been taken up to heaven, Elisha stayed for a time at Jericho. Elisha did not live in the wilderness like Elijah had. He lived in the cities and helped many by the power the Lord gave to him.

The people of Jericho came to Elisha, "This city is in a pleasant place, but the water of its spring is very bitter. It causes disease and death, and the land around it doesn't produce fruit."

Elisha said to them, "Bring me a small new bottle, and fill it with salt." They brought it to him, and he poured the salt into the fountain that gave water to the city, saying, "The Lord says, 'I have healed these waters. From them there shall be no more death or unfruitfulness to the land.' " The waters became pure and sweet from that time onward.

At this time Jehoram was king of Israel. He reigned twelve years, not as wickedly as his father, Ahab, had ruled, but still doing evil in the sight of the Lord. From the days of King David, the land of Moab had been under the control of Israel. The land was governed by its own king, but every year he paid a large sum to Israel. The king of Moab in the time of Jehoram was named Mesha.

When King Ahab died, the king of Moab rose against Israel and tried to set his land free. King Jehoram sent for King Jehoshaphat of Judah and the king of Edom, and all three armies marched toward Moab to put down the rebellion.

While they were on their march, they found no water, and the king of Israel said, "The Lord has brought together these three kings to let them fall into the hands of the king of Moab!"

But good King Jehoshaphat said, "Isn't there a prophet of the Lord we can speak to?"

And one man said, "Elisha is here."

So the three kings went to find Elisha, who told them, "If Jehoshaphat, the king of Judah, were not here, I would not look at you or speak to you." While a minstrel made music on his harp, the power of the Lord came on Elisha, and he said, "The Lord says, 'Make this valley full of ditches.' The Lord tells me you shall not see any rain or hear any wind, yet the valley shall be filled with water. You shall drink, and your cattle and your horses. And the Lord shall give the Moabites into your hand. You shall take their cities, cut down their trees, stop their wells, and conquer their land."

And it came to pass as Elisha had said.

After defeating the Moabites in battle, they destroyed the land of Moab.

The story of this war between Israel and Moab is written not only in the second Book of Kings in the Bible, but also on a stone pillar, which was set up by the king of Moab afterward. This pillar was found in the land of Moab not many years ago, and the writing on it was read, showing that the history of this war as given in the Bible is true.

Discussion Questions: *1. Where did Elisha live? How was that different from what Elijah had done? 2. What did the prophet do at the well in Jericho? 3. Why did the three kings call for Elisha? What did Elisha tell them?*

DAY 141

ELISHA'S WORKS

2 Kings 4:1-7; 38-44; 6:1-7

IN many places throughout Israel, families still listened to the teaching of the prophets and worshiped the Lord. Elisha went through the land meeting these people, teaching them, and leading them in their worship.

The wife of one of these men came to Elisha and said, "O man of God, my husband is dead, and you know he served the Lord while he lived. He owed some money when he died, and now the man he owed has come, and he says he will take my two sons to be his slaves, unless I pay the debt."

In those lands, when a man owed a debt, he could be sold to pay the debt.

Elisha said to the woman, "What can I do to help you? What do you have in the house?"

"I have nothing in the house," answered the woman, "except a pot of oil."

Elisha said to her, "Go to your neighbors and borrow all the empty jars you can. Then go into the room and shut the door on yourself and your sons. Pour the oil into the vessels, and as each vessel is filled, set it aside."

The woman did as he said, until all the containers she could find were full. If she had borrowed more vessels, there would have been more oil. She came and told Elisha, and he said, "Go and sell the oil. Pay the debt, and keep the rest of the money for yourself and your sons to live on."

Another time, Elisha came to Gilgal when food was scarce, and they looked in the field for vegetables and green things to eat. One man brought a number of wild gourds that were poisonous, and threw them into the pot with the rest of the food.

While they were eating, they felt suddenly that they had been poisoned, and they cried out, "O man of God, there is death in the pot! The food is poisoned!"

Elisha took some meal and threw it into the pot with the poisoned food. And he said, "Now take the food out of the pot, and let the people eat of it."

They did so; and there was no longer any poison in the food.

Another time, a man came bringing a present of bread and corn in the husks. There were 100 men with Elisha that day, and Elisha said to his servant, "Give this to the people for their dinner."

The servant said, "This won't feed one hundred men!"

Elisha said, "Set it before them, and let them eat. The Lord says, 'They shall eat, and shall have enough, and shall leave some of it.' "

So he gave them the food. Every man took as much as he wanted, and some was left over, as God had said.

Once a company of these sons of the prophets went down from the mountains to a place near the river Jordan and began to build a house. Elisha was with them. As one of the men was cutting down a tree, the head fell off his axe and dropped into the water. In those times, iron and steel were very scarce and costly. The man said, "Master, what shall I do? This was a borrowed axe!"

Elisha asked to be shown just where the axehead had fallen into the water. He cut off a stick of wood and threw it into the water at the place. At once, the iron axehead rose to the surface of the water and floated, as if it were wood. The prophet said, "Reach out and take it," and the man took the iron, fitted it to the handle, and went on with his work.

By these works of power, all the people came to know that Elisha was a true prophet of the Lord and spoke God's words to Israel.

Discussion Questions: *1. What did Elisha do for the widow? 2. How did Elisha take care of the poisoned food? 3. What happened when Elisha gave the men bread and corn to eat? 4. How did Elisha save the man's axe? 5. What did all these miracles show people?*

DAY 142

THE LITTLE BOY AT SHUNEM

2 Kings 4:8-37

THE prophet Elisha traveled through Israel, meeting the people who worshiped the Lord and teaching them. On one of his journeys he visited the little city of Shunem, and a rich woman living there asked him to come to her house and eat there whenever he was nearby. After a time, the lady said to her husband, "I see this is a holy man of God who comes to our house so often. Let's build a little room for him on the side of the house, with a bed, table, stool, and candlestick, so when he comes, it will be a home for him, and he can sleep there."

So they built the room, and whenever Elisha passed by, he stayed there with his servant, Gehazi. On one visit, Elisha said to the woman, "You have been very kind to me and my helper, and have done much for us. Now, what can I do for you? Shall I ask the king to show you some favor? Or would you like anything the chief of the army can do for you?"

The woman said, "I live among my own people, and there is nothing else I want."

Then Gehazi said to Elisha, "This woman has no son."

And Elisha said to her, "A year from now, God will give you a little boy."

The promise made the woman very happy, but she didn't really believe it until the little child came. He grew up and became old enough to go out into the field with the men reaping grain. Suddenly, the child cried out to his father, "O my head, my head!"

His father saw he was very ill, and he told one of his men to take him to his mother. He lay in his mother's arms until noon, and then he died. The mother did not tell her husband the boy was dead. Instead, she rode as quickly as she could to the prophet, who was on the other side of the plain, near Mount Carmel.

Elisha saw her coming, and he said to Gehazi, "Run to meet this lady of Shunem, and ask her, 'It is well with you? It is well with your husband? It is well with the child?' "

She answered, "It is well," but she did not stop until she met the prophet, and then she fell down before him and took hold of his feet. Gehazi did not think it was proper for her to hold him this way, and was about to take her away. But Elisha said to him, "Let her alone. She is in deep trouble, and the Lord has not told me about it!"

The woman said, "Did I ask for a son? Didn't I ask you not to lie to me?"

Then Elisha knew what had happened. He said to Gehazi, "Take my staff and go at once to this woman's house. Go and lay my staff on the face of the child."

But the mother was not content to have the servant go to her house. She wanted Elisha himself to go, so Elisha followed her back to Shunem. On the way they met Gehazi coming back. He had laid the staff, as he had been told to lay it, on the face of the child, and he said, "The child did not wake up."

When Elisha came, he found the child dead. He shut the door and prayed beside the bed. After his prayer, he lay with his face on the child's face and his hands on the child's hands, and as he lay, the child's body began to grow warm. Then Elisha walked up and down in the house, and again he lay on the child and put his arms around him. Suddenly the child began to sneeze, and then he opened his eyes, alive again. Elisha told his servant to call the mother, and when she came, he said to her, "Pick up your son."

The mother saw her son was alive, fell at Elisha's feet to show how thankful she was, took her son in her arms, and went out.

Discussion Questions: *1. What kind of woman was the one in Shunem? What did she do for the prophet? 2. What did Elisha do to repay her? 3. How did this woman show her faith? Name at least two ways. 4. What did the prophet do for her son?*

DAY 143

NAAMAN (PART 1)

2 Kings 5:1-8

AT one time while Elisha was living in Israel, the general of the Syrian army was named Naaman. He was a great man in rank and power, and a brave man in battle, winning many victories for Syria. But one terrible trouble came to Naaman: He was a leper. Leprosy was a horrible disease then, before the days of our modern medicine. In those days, people always died from leprosy.

There was a little girl living in Naaman's house, who waited on Naaman's wife. She had been stolen from her mother's home in Israel and carried away as a captive to Syria. Even when there was no open war between Syria and Israel, parties of men went out from both sides, destroying villages on the border, robbing the people, and carrying them away to be killed or sold as slaves. But this little girl, even though she was a slave, felt sorry for her master, Naaman. One day she said to her mistress, "I wish Naaman might meet the prophet who lives in Samaria. He could cure his leprosy."

Someone told Naaman what the little girl had said, and Naaman spoke of it to the king of Syria. Now the king of Syria loved Naaman and wanted Naaman's leprosy cured. He said, "I will send a letter to the king of Israel, and I will ask him to let his prophet cure you."

So Naaman, with a great train of followers, rode in his chariot from Damascus to Samaria, about a hundred miles. He took with him presents of gold and silver and many beautiful robes and garments. He came to the king of Israel and gave him the letter from the king of Syria. This was written in the letter: "With this letter I have sent you Naaman, my servant. I wish you to cure him of his leprosy."

The king of Syria supposed that the prophet who could cure leprosy was under the orders of the king of Israel and had to do whatever his king told him to do. Since he didn't know the prophet, but did know the king, he wrote to him.

But the king was greatly alarmed when he read the letter. "Am I God," he said, "to kill men and to make men live? Why should the king of Syria ask me to cure a man of leprosy? He must be trying to find an excuse for making war by asking me to do what no man can do!" The king of Israel tore his garments, as men did when they were in deep trouble.

Elisha heard of the letter and the king's alarm, and he sent a message to the king. "Why are you so frightened? Let this man come to me, and he shall know that there is a prophet of the Lord in Israel."

Discussion Questions: 1. What had happened to Naaman? Who tried to help him? 2. What did the king of Syria do for Naaman? 3. Why was the king of Israel afraid? 4. Why was Elisha willing to heal Naaman?

231

DAY 144

NAAMAN (PART 2)

2 Kings 5:9-27

S O Naaman came — with his chariots, his horses, and his followers — and stood before the door of Elisha's house. Elisha did not come out to meet him, but sent his servant out to him to say, "Go and wash in the river Jordan seven times, and your skin will become pure, and you will be free from the leprosy."

Naaman was very angry because Elisha had not treated him with more respect. He forgot, or did not know, that by the laws of Israel, no man could touch or even come near a leper, and he said, "Why, I thought he would come out and meet me, and would wave his hand over the leper spot, and would call on the name of the Lord his God, and that would cure my leprosy. Are not Abana and Pharpar, the two rivers of Damascus, better than all the water in Israel? Can't I wash in them and be clean?" Naaman went away in a rage.

But his servants were wiser than he was. They came to him and said, "If the prophet had told you to do something difficult, wouldn't you have done it? Then why not do it when he says, 'Wash and be clean'?"

After a little while, Naaman's anger cooled, and he rode down the mountains to the river Jordan. He washed in its water seven times, as the prophet had told him. The scales of leprosy left his skin, and his flesh became like the flesh of a little child, pure and clean. Naaman went back to Elisha's house and said, "Now I know that there is no God in all the earth, except in Israel. Let me make you a present in return for what you have done for me."

But the true prophets of God never gave their messages or did their work for pay, and Elisha refused to take anything.

"From this time I will offer no sacrifice to any other God except the God of Israel," said Naaman. Then Naaman went on his way back to his own land.

But Gehazi, the servant of Elisha, said to himself, "My master has let this Syrian go without taking anything from him. I will run after him and ask for a present." So Gehazi ran after Naaman. Naaman saw him following, stopped his chariot, and stepped down to meet him.

Gehazi said to him, "My master has sent me to you to say that just now two young men have come to his house. Will you give them a talent of silver and two suits of clothing?"

Naaman said, "Let me give you two talents of silver." He put two talents of silver in two bags, a talent in each bag, and gave them to Gehazi, along with two suits of fine clothing.

Gehazi hid the presents before going to see Elisha, who said, "Gehazi, where have you been?"

Gehazi answered, "I didn't go anywhere." And Elisha said to him, "My heart went with you, and I saw you. Because you have done this, Naaman's leprosy will come to you, and shall cling to you and your children forever!"

Gehazi left Elisha a leper, with skin as white as snow.

Discussion Questions: *1. Why did Naaman think the prophet had not treated him well? 2. What did Naaman start to do? Why did he change his mind? 3. What happened when Naaman obeyed Elisha? What did he have to do?*

DAY 145

CHARIOTS OF FIRE

2 Kings 6:8-23

HERE was constant war between Israel and Syria through all Elisha's life, and the king of Israel found Elisha a greater help than all his horses and chariots. Whenever the king of Syria told his officers to attack the land of Israel, Elisha would send word to the king of Israel, saying, "Watch carefully that place, and send men to guard it, for the Syrians are coming to attack it."

When the Syrian army came to the place, they were sure to find it strongly guarded, so their soldiers could do nothing. This happened so many times that the king of Syria at last said to his nobles, "Someone is secretly helping the king of Israel by sending him word of all our plans. Won't anyone tell me who the traitor is?"

And they said, "No one has made known your plans. Elisha, the prophet in Israel, tells the king of Israel everything you say."

Then the king of Syria said, "Go and find where that man is, so I can send an army to take him."

After a time, the king of Syria heard that Elisha was staying in Dothan. He sent out a great army, with horses and chariots, who came by night and stood in a ring all around the city, ready to seize the prophet. In the morning, the prophet's helper got up and saw the city surrounded by men with swords and spears. He called Elisha and asked him, "Master, what shall we do?"

"Fear not," answered Elisha, "there are more men on our side than on theirs." Elisha prayed to the Lord, saying, "O Lord, open the eyes of this young man and let him see who are with us."

Then the Lord opened the eyes of the young man, and he saw what other men could not see. The mountain on which the city stood was covered with horses and chariots of fire sent by the Lord to keep his prophet safe. But this the Syrians could not see, and they came up to the gates of the city to take Elisha. Then Elisha prayed to the Lord, saying, "Lord, make these men blind for a little while." A mist came over the eyes of the Syrians, and they could not see clearly. Elisha went out to them and said, "This is not the right city, but I will show you the way. Follow me."

Elisha led them from Dothan to Samaria, inside the walls of the city, where the army of Israel stood all around them. Then Elisha prayed, "O Lord, open the eyes of these men, that they may see."

And the Lord opened their eyes, and they saw the walls of Samaria and the army all around them. The king of Israel was glad to have his enemies in his power and said to Elisha, "Shall I kill them?"

Elisha said to him, "You shall not kill them. Would you kill helpless men you had taken as prisoners? Give them bread to eat and water to drink, and send them home to their master."

So, instead of killing the Syrian soldiers or holding them as prisoners, the king of Israel set plenty of food before them and gave them all they needed. Then he sent them home to their master, the king of Syria. It was a long time before the Syrian armies came back to the land of Israel.

Discussion Questions: *1. How useful was Elisha to the king of Israel? 2. How did Elisha know what the Syrians were going to do? 3. What did the king of Syria try to do to Elisha? How did God protect him? 4. How did Elisha win over the Syrians?*

DAY 146

THE SYRIAN CAMP

2 Kings 6:24-7:8

AFTER a time, there was another great war between Syria and Israel. Benhadad, the king of Syria, led a mighty army into the land of Israel and laid siege to the city of Samaria. So hard and long was the siege that the people in Samaria could find nothing to eat, and many died from lack of food.

Through all the siege, Elisha encouraged the king of Israel not to give up the city. When it seemed there was no hope, Elisha said to the king, "Hear the word of the Lord: 'Tomorrow at this hour, a peck of flour shall be sold for sixty cents, and two pecks of barley for sixty cents.' " (This was very cheap.)

One of the nobles said scornfully, "If the Lord makes windows in heaven and rains down wheat and barley, then this might be."

"You shall see it with your own eyes," answered Elisha, "but you will not eat any of the food."

The next morning, about daybreak, four lepers were standing outside the gate of Samaria. Being lepers, they were not allowed inside the walls of the city. They said to one another, "What shall we do? If we go into the city, we will die there from starvation. If we stay here, we will die. Let's go to the camp of the Syrians. Perhaps they will let us live. At the worst, they can do no more than kill us."

THE FOUR MEN FOUND THE ENEMY GONE – 2 KINGS 7:8

So the four men went toward the Syrian camp. As they came near, they were surprised to find no one standing guard. They went into a tent and found it empty, as though it had been left very suddenly, for there were food, drink, garments, gold, and silver. As no one was there, they ate and drank all they needed, then they took away the valuable things and hid them. They looked into another tent, and another, and found them like the first, but not a man was in sight. They walked through the camp, but not one soldier was there, and the tents were left just as they had been when men were living in them.

In the night, the Lord had caused the Syrians to hear a great noise, like the rolling of chariots and the trampling of horses and the marching of men. They

235

said to one another, in great fear, "The king of Israel has sent for the Hittites and the Egyptians to come fight us."

So great and sudden was their terror that they got up and ran away, leaving everything in their camp: their horses, their asses, all their treasure, and all their food.

Discussion Questions: *1. What happened to the Samaritans when the king of Syria fought another war with them? 2. What did Elisha promise the king? 3. Did everyone believe the prophet? Who didn't? 4. Did God do as the prophet said? Who discovered it?*

DAY 147

THE STARVATION ENDS

2 Kings 7:9-20

AFTER a time, the lepers said to one another, "We do wrong by not telling this good news in the city. If they find it out, they will blame us for not letting them know, and we may lose our lives on account of it."

So they went up to the gate, called the men on guard, and told them how they had found the camp of the Syrians with its tents standing, horses tied, but not a man left. The men on guard told the king's palace. But the king, when he heard it, thought it was a trick of the Syrians to hide themselves and draw the men out of the city, so they might take it.

The king sent out two men with horses and chariots, and they found that not only had the camp been left, but the road down the mountains to the river Jordan was covered with garments, arms, and treasures that the Syrians had thrown away in their wild flight.

The news soon spread through the city of Samaria, and in a few hours, all the city was at the gate. When the food was brought in from the camp, there was plenty for all the people. And as Elisha had said, a peck of grain and two pecks of barley were sold for sixty cents in the gate of Samaria by noon of that day.

The king chose the noble who had laughed at Elisha to be in charge of the gate, so he saw with his own eyes what the prophet had foretold. But he did not eat any of it himself because the huge, starving crowd knocked him down and killed him in their rush to get to the food. Now the king and all Samaria knew Elisha had indeed spoken the word of the Lord.

We have seen how different Elijah was from Elisha. Elijah lived alone in the wilderness, never coming before kings except to tell them of their evil deeds and warn them of punishment. But Elisha lived in the city — at times in the capital — often sent helpful messages to the king, and seemed to be his friend. Both these men were needed, one to destroy the evil in the land and the other to build up the good.

_____

Discussion Questions: *1. What happened to the man who did not believe the prophet? 2. What did this show the people? 3. What was different about Elijah and Elisha? Did God use them both?*

DAY 148

_____

JEHU AND HAZAEL MADE KINGS

2 Kings 8:7-9:15

YOU remember that when the Lord came to Elijah at Mount Horeb in the wilderness, he gave Elijah a command to anoint Hazael king of Syria and Jehu king of Israel. But to prepare the way for these changes of rule, a long time was needed, and Elijah was taken home to heaven before these men were called to be kings.

The time to call these men had now come, and Elisha undertook the work that had been left him by Elijah. He went to Damascus, the chief city of Syria. Benhadad, the king of Syria, heard that the great prophet of Israel had come, for the fame of Elisha's deeds had made his name known through all those lands.

At that time, King Benhadad was ill. He sent one of his chief princes, Hazael, to ask Elisha whether he would get well again. Hazael came to meet Elisha with forty camels loaded with gifts and spoke to Elisha with great respect, saying, "Your son, Benhadad, king of Syria, has sent me to you to ask, 'Shall I become well again from this sickness?'"

Elisha said to Hazael, "You may tell Benhadad that he will get well. Nevertheless, the Lord has shown me that he will die."

Then Elisha stared at Hazael's face until Hazael felt ashamed, and Elisha wept as he looked at him. Hazael said, "Why does my lord weep?"

"I weep," said Elisha, "because I know the evil you will do to the people of Israel. You will take their castles and set them on fire. You will kill their young men, and you will destroy their children."

Hazael was surprised at this. "I am nothing but a dog. How can I do such great things?"

Elisha answered him, "The Lord has shown me that you will be king over Syria."

Then Hazael went to King Benhadad and said to him, "The man of God told me that you will surely be well from your sickness." But on the next day, Hazael took the cover from the bed, dipped it in water, and pressed it tightly over Benhadad's face, so he died, and Hazael reigned in his place as king of Syria.

Elisha returned from his visit to Syria. He knew the time had come to finish the work left to him by Elijah, so he called one of the sons of the prophets to him, and said, "Go to the camp at Ramoth-gilead, and take this little bottle of oil. When you reach Ramoth-gilead, find one of the captains of the army — Jehu. Lead him into a room alone, pour the oil on his head, and say, 'Thus saith the Lord, I have anointed you as king over Israel.' When you have done this, come back to me at once, without waiting."

The young man, who was a prophet like Elisha, took the bottle of oil in his hand and went to Ramoth-gilead. In the camp of Israel, he found the captains of the army sitting together.

"O captain, I have a message for you," he said.

Jehu replied, "For which one of us?"

"My message is for you, captain."

Jehu went with the young prophet into the house, and he poured the oil on his head and said, "The Lord says, 'I have anointed you as king over my people Israel. You shall destroy the family of Ahab, because they destroyed the prophets of the Lord.'"

After he said this, the prophet opened the door and went away as suddenly as he had come.

Jehu came back to the other captains and sat down again. When they asked him what had happened, Jehu told them he had been anointed king, which pleased all the captains. At once they took off their outer garments and spread them as a carpet on the stairs of the house. At the head of the stairs, they placed Jehu, then they blew the trumpets and called out to the army, "Jehu is the king!"

Jehu said to the captains, "Do not let anyone go out of the camp to tell Jehoram. I will go myself."

Discussion Questions: *1. Why did Benhadad send a message to Elisha? 2. What did Elisha tell the messenger? 3. Who did the prophet anoint the king of Israel? 4. What did God want Jehu to do?*

DAY 149

THE DEATH OF AHAB'S FAMILY
2 Kings 9:16-10:31

JEHU rode swiftly toward Jezreel, his men riding after him. When he saw it was Jehu coming, Jehoram thought they were bearing news of the war with the Syrians. He sent for his chariot and went out to meet Jehu. With him went Ahaziah, the king of Judah, each in his own chariot. As Jehoram drew near to Jehu, he called to him, "Is all well, Jehu?"

"Can anything be well," answered Jehu, "as long as your mother Jezebel lives, with all her wickedness?"

When Jehoram heard this, he knew Jehu was his enemy. He cried out to King Ahaziah, turned his chariot, and fled. But he was too late, for Jehu drew his bow with all his strength and sent an arrow to his heart. Jehoram fell dead in his chariot. Then Jehu said to his chief captain, "Take away the body of Jehoram and throw it into the field where the body of Naboth was thrown."

When Ahaziah, the king of Judah, saw Jehoram fall, he, too, turned and fled. But Jehu pursued him and ordered his followers to kill him. So Ahaziah, the grandson of Ahab, also died at the hand of Jehu. His servants took the body of Ahaziah to Jerusalem and buried it.

THE WATCHMAN SAW JEHU DRIVING FURIOUSLY - 2 KINGS 9:20

239

When Jehu rode into the city of Jezreel, Queen Jezebel knew her end had come, but she met it boldly, like a queen. She put on her royal robes and a crown and sat by the window, waiting for Jehu to come.

Jehu looked up to the window and called out, "Throw her out the window!" They threw her down, and her blood splattered on the wall and on the horses. When they later went to find her body, they saw the wild dogs of the city had eaten it, as Elijah had said would happen.

Obeying God's orders, Jehu slew all the sons of Ahab and their children, so not one of Ahab's family was left alive.

When Jehu saw he was safe and strong on the throne, he sent out a message to all the worshipers of Baal, telling them to gather in the temple of Baal in Samaria. They came by hundreds, hoping Jehu would be their friend as Ahab and his family had been. But when they were all in the temple, he brought an army of his soldiers and had every priest of Baal killed.

Though Jehu broke up the worship of Baal, he did not worship the Lord God of Israel as he should. He continued to serve the golden calves Jeroboam had set up long before. The Lord sent a prophet to Jehu, who said to him, "Because you have done my will in destroying the house of Ahab and destroying those that worshiped Baal, your children to the fourth generation shall sit on the throne of Israel."

Discussion Questions: *1. Did Jehu do what God told him to? 2. What did Jehu do to the priests of Baal? 3. What did Jehu do wrong? 4. What did God promise Jehu?*

DAY 150

ELISHA AND THE BOW

2 Kings 13:1-25

AFTER Jehu, his son Jehoahaz reigned in Israel. He was not only wicked, but also a weak king. Under him, Israel became helpless in the hands of its enemies — Hazael, the fierce king of Syria, and his son, Benhadad the second. But when Jehoahaz died, his son Joash became king, and under his rule, Israel began to rise again.

Elisha the prophet was now an old man, very feeble and near death. The young king Joash came to see him, wept over him, and said to him (as Elisha had said to Elijah), "My father, my father, you are more to Israel than its chariots and horsemen!"

But Elisha, though weak in body, was still strong in soul. He told King Joash to bring him a bow and arrows, then open the window to the east, looking toward the land of Syria. Then Elisha had the king draw the bow, and he placed his hands on the king's hands. As the king shot an arrow, Elisha said, "This is the Lord's arrow of victory over Syria, for you shall attack the Syrians in Aphek and destroy them."

Then Elisha told the king to take the arrows and hit the ground with them. The king struck them on the ground three times, and then stopped. The old prophet was displeased at this, and said, "Why did you stop? You should have struck the ground five or six times, then you would have won that many victories over Syria. But now you shall beat the Syrians three times, and no more."

Soon after this, Elisha died, and they buried him in a cave. In the spring of the next year, bands of Moabites came on the place just as they were burying another man, and in their haste to escape from their enemies, they placed the body in the cave where Elisha was buried. When the body of this man touched the body of the dead prophet, life came back to it, and the dead man stood up. Even after Elisha was dead, he still had power.

After the death of Elisha, Joash, the king of Israel, made war on Benhadad the second, the king of Syria. Joash beat him three times in battle and took back all the cities that Hazael had taken away from Israel. After Joash, his son Jeroboam the second reigned, who became the greatest of all the kings of the Ten Tribes. Under him, the kingdom grew rich and strong. He conquered nearly all Syria and made Samaria the greatest city in the whole area.

Discussion Questions: *1. What kind of king was Jehu's son? 2. What kind of king was Joash? 3. What did Elisha tell Joash? 4. Why did the man come back to life when his body touched Elisha's? 5. What happened to the kingdom under Joash? Why?*

DAY 151

JONAH'S ORDERS

Jonah 1:1-7

ALTHOUGH Syria was losing its power, another nation was rising to power — Assyria, on the eastern side of the Tigris River. Its capital was Nineveh, a great city so large that it would take three days for a man to walk around its walls. The Assyrians were beginning to conquer all the lands near them, and Israel was in danger of falling under their power. At this time another prophet named Jonah was giving the word of the Lord to the Israelites. The Lord spoke to Jonah, saying, "Go to Nineveh, that great city, and preach to it, for its wickedness rises up before me."

But Jonah did not want to preach to the people of Nineveh, because they were the enemies of his land, the land of Israel. He wanted Nineveh to die in its sins, not turn to God and live. So Jonah tried to go away from the city where God had sent him. He went down to Joppa, on the shore of the Great Sea. There he found a ship about to sail to Tarshish, far away in the west. He paid the fare and went on board, intending to go as far as possible from Nineveh.

But the Lord saw Jonah on the ship, and the Lord sent a great storm on the sea, so the ship was in danger of sinking. The sailors threw everything on the ship overboard, and when they could do no more, every man prayed to his god to save the ship and themselves. Jonah was now lying fast asleep under the deck of the ship, and the ship's captain came to him, and said, "What do you mean by sleeping at such a time as this? Awake, get up, and call to your God. Perhaps your God will hear you and save our lives."

But the storm continued to rage around the ship, and they said, "There is some man on this ship who has brought us this trouble. Let's cast lots, and find who it is."

_____

Discussion Questions: *1. What did God tell Jonah? Why didn't Jonah obey? 2. Why did the ship Jonah was on run into a storm? 3. What does it mean to cast lots?*

DAY 152

———

JONAH IN THE FISH

Jonah 1:8-2:10

WHEN the sailors cast their lots, the lot fell on Jonah. They said to him, "Tell us, who are you? From what country do you come? What is your business? To what people do you belong? Why have you brought all this trouble on us?"

Then Jonah told them the whole story: how he came from the land of Israel and had run away from the presence of the Lord.

And they said to him, "What must we do to you to end this storm?"

Jonah said, "Pick me up and throw me into the sea. Then the storm will stop and the waters will be calm, because I brought this storm on you.''

But the men were not willing to throw Jonah into the sea. They rowed hard to bring the ship to land, but they couldn't. Then they cried to the Lord, saying, ''We pray thee, O Lord, don't make us die for this man's life.''

At last, when they could do nothing else to save themselves, they threw Jonah into the sea. At once the storm ceased and the waves became still. Then the men on the ship feared the Lord greatly. They offered a sacrifice to the Lord, and made promises to serve him.

Now the Lord caused a great fish to swallow Jonah, and Jonah was alive inside the fish for three days and three nights. Long afterward, when Jesus was on the earth, he said that as Jonah was three days inside the fish, so he would be three days in the earth. Jonah in the fish was like a prophecy of Christ. In the fish, Jonah cried to the Lord, and the Lord heard his prayer and made the great fish spit out Jonah on the dry land.

THE GREAT FISH SPIT JONAH OUT ON DRY LAND - JONAH 2:10

Discussion Questions: *1. Who did the lot fall on? 2. What did Jonah tell the men in the boat to do? 3. What did they do after the storm stopped? 4. How did God save Jonah? 5. What is this story a prophecy of?*

243

DAY 153

JONAH IN NINEVEH

Jonah 3:1-4:11

BY now, Jonah had learned that some men who worshiped idols were kind and were loved by the Lord. This was the lesson that God meant Jonah to learn, and now he knew this, the Lord called Jonah again. "Arise. Go to Nineveh, that great city, and preach to it what I command you."

So Jonah went to the city of Nineveh, and as he entered it, he called out to the people, "Within forty days, Nineveh will be destroyed." And he walked through the city all day, crying out, "Within forty days shall Nineveh be destroyed."

The people of Nineveh believed Jonah. They turned away from their sins, fasted, and sought the Lord, every one of them. The king of Nineveh left his throne, put aside his royal robes, covered himself with sackcloth, and sat in ashes, as a sign of his sorrow. And the king ordered his people to fast, seek the Lord, and turn from sin.

God saw the people of Nineveh were sorry for their wickedness, and he forgave them and did not destroy their city. But this made Jonah very angry. He did not want to have Nineveh spared, because it was the enemy of his own land. He also feared that men would call him a false prophet when his words did not come true.

So Jonah said to the Lord, "O Lord, I was sure it would be like this and you would spare the city. That's why I tried to run away. I know you are a gracious God, full of pity, slow to anger, and rich in mercy. Now, Lord, take away my life, for it is better for me to die than to live."

Jonah went out of the city, built a little hut on the east side of it, and sat under its roof, to see whether God would keep the word he had spoken. Then the Lord caused a plant with thick leaves, called a gourd, to grow up and shade Jonah from the sun. Jonah was glad, and sat under its shadow. But a worm destroyed the plant, and the next day a hot wind blew, and Jonah suffered from the heat. Again Jonah wished that he could die. And the Lord said to Jonah, "You were sorry to see the plant die, though you did not make it grow, and though it came up in a night and died in a night. Shouldn't I have pity on Nineveh, that great city where there are more than a hundred thousand little children, all helpless and knowing nothing?"

And Jonah learned that men, women, and little children are all precious in the sight of the Lord, even if they don't know God.

DAY 154

THE TEN TRIBES LOST

2 Kings 15:8-17:18

THE power and peace that Judah enjoyed under Jeroboam the second did not last after his death. His great kingdom fell apart, and his son Zechariah reigned for only six months. He was killed in front of his people by Shallum, who made himself king. But after only a month of rule, Shallum himself was killed by Menahem, who reigned during ten years of wickedness and suffering, for the Assyrians spoiled the land and took away the riches of Israel. Then came Pekahiah, who was slain by Pekah, and Hoshea, who in turn killed Pekah. So nearly all the last kings of Israel won the throne by murder and were themselves murdered. The land was helpless, and its enemies, the Assyrians from Nineveh, won victories, carried away many of the people, and robbed those who were left. All these evils came upon the Israelites because they and their kings had forsaken the Lord God of their fathers and worshiped idols.

Hoshea was the last of the kings over the Ten Tribes. There were nineteen kings in all from Jeroboam to Hoshea. In Hoshea's time, the king of Assyria, whose name was Shalmanezer, came up with a great army against Samaria. He laid siege to the city, but it was in a strong place, and hard to take, for it stood on a high hill. The siege lasted three years, and before it was ended, Shalmanezer, the king of Assyria, died, and Sargon, a great warrior and conqueror, reigned in his place. Sargon took Samaria and killed Hoshea, the last king of Israel. He carried away nearly all the people from the land, and led them into distant countries in the east, to Mesopotamia, to Media, and the lands near the great Caspian Sea. Sargon did this to keep the Israelites from breaking away from his rule.

Discussion Questions: *1. How did the last kings of Israel win the throne? 2. What happened to Hoshea, the last king? 3. What did King Sargon do to the people? 4. Why did Sargon do that?*

DAY 155

THE SAMARITANS

2 Kings 17:24-41

JUST as in their own land the children of Israel had forsaken the Lord and worshiped idols, so after they were taken to these distant lands, they worshiped the gods of the people they lived with. They married the people of those lands and ceased to be Israelites. After a time, they lost all knowledge of their own God, who had given them his words and sent them his prophets. This was the end of the Ten Tribes of Israel, for they never came back to their own land, and were lost among the people of the Far East.

But a small number of the people of Israel were left in their own land. The king of Assyria brought new people from other countries and placed them in the land, but they were too few to fill the land and care for it. The wild beasts began to increase in Israel, and many of these new settlers were killed by lions who lived in the mountains and valleys. They thought the lions attacked them because they did not worship the God who ruled the land, and they sent to the king of Assyria, saying, "Send us a priest who can teach us how to worship the God who owns this land, for he has sent lions among us, and they are destroying us."

They supposed that each land had its own God, since Philistines worshiped Dagon; the Moabites, Chemosh; and the Tyrians and Zidonians, Baal and the Asherah. They did not know there is only one God who rules all the world and who is to be worshiped by all men.

Then the king of Assyria sent these people a priest from the Israelites in his land, and this priest tried to teach them how to worship the Lord. But with the Lord's worship, they also worshiped idols and did not serve only the Lord, as God wanted. Later, these people were called Samaritans, from Samaria, which was their chief city.

Discussion Questions: *1. What happened to the people Sargon took away to other lands? 2. What happened to the people who moved into Samaria? 3. Why did they want to worship God? Did they really understand God? How do you know?*

DAY 156

REHOBOAM AND ABIJAH

2 Chronicles 12:1-13:20

NOW we turn from the story of the kingdom of Israel in the north to the story of the kingdom of Judah in the south. You remember how the Ten Tribes broke away from the rule of King Rehoboam and set up a kingdom of their own under Jeroboam. This division left the kingdom of Judah very small and weak. It reached from the Dead Sea westward to the land of the Philistines on the shore of the Great Sea, and from Beersheba on the south not quite to Bethel on the north, but it held some control over the land of Edom on the south of the Dead Sea. Its chief city was Jerusalem, with the Temple of the Lord and the palace of the king.

After Rehoboam found he couldn't rule over the Ten Tribes, he tried to make his own little kingdom strong by building cities and raising an army of soldiers. But he did not look to the Lord, as his grandfather David had looked. He allowed his people to worship idols, and soon almost every hill and every grove of trees had an image of stone or wood. God was not pleased with Rehoboam and his people, because they had forsaken him for idols. He brought on the land of Judah a great army from Egypt, led by Shishak, the king of Egypt. They marched over all the land of Judah, took the city of Jerusalem, and robbed the Temple of all the great treasure of gold and silver Solomon had stored up. This evil came on Judah because its king and people had turned away from the Lord their God.

After Rehoboam had reigned seventeen years, he died, and his son Abijah became king of Judah. When Jeroboam, the king of Israel, made war on him, Abijah led his army into the land of Israel. But Jeroboam's army was twice as large as Abijah's, and his men stood not only in front of the men of Judah, but also behind them, so the army of Judah was in great danger of being destroyed. But Abijah told his men to trust in the Lord and fight bravely in the Lord's name. And God helped the men of Judah against Israel, so they won a great victory, and Jeroboam never again attacked Judah.

Discussion Questions: *1. Where was the kingdom of Judah? What was it like? Why? 2. Who conquered Judah? What did they do to the Temple? 3. Why did Abijah's army win against Israel?*

DAY 157

Asa

2 Chronicles 14:1-16:14

ABIJAH'S reign was short — only three years. After him came Asa, his son, who was a great warrior, a great builder of cities, and a wise ruler.

A great army attacked Asa from Ethiopia, which was south of Egypt. Asa drew out his little army against the Ethiopians at a place called Mareshah, in the south of Judah near the desert. He had no hope of his soldiers winning because they were so few and the enemies were so many. But Asa called on the Lord and said, "O Lord, it makes no difference to you whether there are few or many. Help us, O Lord, for we trust in you and fight this vast multitude for you. O Lord, you are our God. Don't let men defeat you."

The Lord heard Asa's prayer and gave him a great victory over the Ethiopians. Asa retook the cities in the south that had gone over to the side of the Ethiopians, and he brought back to Jerusalem great riches, flocks of sheep, heads of cattle, and camels he had taken from his enemies.

Then the Lord sent Asa a prophet named Azariah. He said, "Hear me, King Asa, and all Judah and Benjamin. The Lord is with you while you are with him. If you seek him, you shall find him, but if you forsake the Lord, he will forsake you. Now be strong, and put away the wickedness out of the land, and the Lord shall reward your work."

Then Asa rebuilt the altar of the Lord, which had rotted away, and he called his people to worship. He went through the land, broke down the idols, and burned them. He found his own mother, the queen, had made an idol, and he cut it down and broke it in pieces. Then he would not allow her to be queen any longer, because she had worshiped idols.

Until Asa was old, he served the Lord, but in his old age, he became sick, and in his sickness he did not seek the Lord. He turned to men who called themselves physicians or doctors, but they were men who tried to cure by the power of idols. This led many of Asa's people to worship images, so that when he died, there were idols throughout the land again.

Discussion Questions: *1. What kind of king was Asa? 2. How did he win over the Ethiopians? 3. What did the prophet Azariah tell Asa? 4. What did Asa do after he heard the prophet's words? 5. How did the idols come into the land again?*

DAY 158

JEHOSHAPHAT

2 Chronicles 20:1-21

ASA'S son, Jehoshaphat, was the next king, the wisest and strongest of all the kings of Judah, ruling over the largest amount of land. When Asa became king of Judah, Ahab was king of Israel. Jehoshaphat made peace with Israel and united with the Israelites against the kingdom of Syria. He fought against the Syrians in the battle at Ramoth-gilead, where King Ahab was killed, and joined Ahab's son, Jehoram, to fight against the Moabites.

Jehoshaphat served the Lord with all his heart. He took away the idols in the land, called on his people to worship the Lord, and sent princes and priests throughout all Judah to read the law of the Lord and teach the people how to serve the Lord.

JEHOSHAPHAT HAD THE LAW TAUGHT TO THE PEOPLE - 2 CHRONICLES 17:9

The Lord gave Jehoshaphat great power. He ruled over the land of Edom, over the wilderness on the south, and over the cities of the Philistines on the coast. When Jehoshaphat chose judges for the cities, he said to them, "Remember that you are not judging for men, but for the Lord. The Lord is with you, and sees all your acts. Therefore fear the Lord, and do his will. Do not allow men to make you presents, so you will favor them, but be just toward all, and be strong in doing right."

At one time news came to King Jehoshaphat that the Moabites, Ammonites, and Syrians had banded together against him and were camped with a great army at Engedi, near the Dead Sea. Jehoshaphat called out his soldiers, but before they went to battle, he led them to the Temple to worship the Lord. Jehoshaphat called on the Lord for help, saying, "O Lord, the God of our fathers, aren't you God in heaven? Don't you rule over the nations of earth? Don't you have so much power that no one can defeat you? Now, Lord, look at the army that has come against your people. We have no might against this great company, and don't know what to do. Our eyes look to you for help."

Then the Spirit of the Lord came upon one of the Levites, a man named Jahaziel, and he said, "Hear, men of Jerusalem and Judah, and hear, King Jehoshaphat. The Lord says, 'Fear not this great army of your enemies, for the battle is not yours, but the Lord's. Go out against them, but you will not need to fight. You shall stand still and see how the Lord will save you. Do not fear, for the Lord is with you.' "

Then Jehoshaphat and all his people worshiped the Lord, bowing with their faces on the ground. And the next day, when they marched against the enemies, the Levites walked in front, singing and praising the Lord, while all the people answered, "Give thanks to the Lord, for his mercy endureth forever."

Discussion Questions: *1. Was Jehoshaphat a good king? 2. Did Jehoshaphat please God by his actions? How? 3. What did Jehoshaphat tell the judges over the cities? 4. What did the king do when the Moabites, Ammonites, and Syrians banded together against him? 5. What did God say to the king?*

DAY 159

THE LORD FIGHTS FOR JUDAH

2 Chronicles 20:22-37

HEN the men of Judah came to the camp of their enemies, they found that a quarrel had broken out among them. The Ammonites and the Moabites began to fight with the rest of the bands, and soon all the armies were fighting and killing each other. And when the men of Judah came, part of the army was lying dead, and the rest had fled away into the desert, leaving behind them great treasure. So it came to pass as the prophet Azariah had said. They did not fight, but the Lord fought for them and saved them from their enemies.

The place where this strange battle had taken place they named the valley of Berachah, which means "blessing," because there they blessed the Lord for the help he had given them. And afterward they came back to Jerusalem with songs, praises, and the great riches they had taken. And God gave King Jehoshaphat peace and rest from his enemies and great power as long as he lived.

Discussion Questions: *1. Who saved the army of Judah? How? 2. What blessing did God give the army? 3. How did the people react to this? 4. What did God give the king for the rest of his life?*

DAY 160

JEHORAM
2 Chronicles 21:1-20

JEHOSHAPHAT, the king of Judah, was a good man and a wise king, but he made one mistake that later brought great trouble to his family and his land. He married his son Jehoram to Athaliah, the daughter of Ahab and the wicked Jezebel. When Jehoshaphat died and Jehoram became king of Judah, his wife led him into all the wickedness of the house of Ahab. Jehoram killed all his brothers, the sons of Jehoshaphat, so none of them could rise up against him. His queen Athaliah set up idols all around Jerusalem and throughout Judah, and led the people in worshiping them.

The prophet Elijah was still living in Israel when Jehoram began to reign in Judah. He sent King Jehoram a letter containing a message from the Lord. "Thus saith the Lord, the God of David, 'Because you have not walked in the ways of your father, Jehoshaphat, but have walked in the ways of the kings of Israel, and have led the people of Jerusalem and Judah to turn from the Lord to idols, and because you have slain your brothers, who were better than you, therefore the Lord will strike you and your house, and your people, and you will have a terrible disease that none can cure.' "

After this, great troubles came to Jehoram and his land. The Edomites on the south, who had been under the rule of Judah since the days of David, broke away from King Jehoram and set up a kingdom of their own. The Philistines on the west and the Arabians of the desert made war on him. They broke into his palace, carried away his treasures, and killed all his children except one, the youngest.

Jehoram caught a sickness that lasted many years and caused him great suffering. No cure could be found, and after long years of pain, Jehoram died. So evil had been his reign of eight years that no one was sorry to have him die, and they would not allow his body to be buried with the kings of Judah.

Discussion Questions: *1. What mistake did Jehoshaphat make? 2. What kind of king was Jehoram? 3. What did Elijah tell the new king? 4. What happened to Judah during Jehoram's rule?*

DAY 161

AHAZIAH, ATHALIAH, AND JOASH

2 Chronicles 22:1-23:21

AFTER Jehoram died, his youngest son, Ahaziah, became king. His mother was the wicked Athaliah, the daughter of Jezebel. Ahaziah reigned only one year. While he was visiting King Jehoram of Israel (his uncle), he was slain by Jehu. This was the time when Jehu rose against the house of Ahab, killed Jehoram, Ahab's son, and Jezebel, Ahab's widow, and made himself king of Israel. But Jehu gave the body of Ahaziah a king's burial, for he said, "He was the son of Jehoshaphat, who sought the Lord with all his heart."

When Athaliah, the mother of Ahaziah, heard her son was dead, all the fierceness of her mother Jezebel arose in her. She seized the princes who belonged to the family of David and killed them, so there was not one man of the royal line left alive. She made herself the queen and ruler over the land of Judah. She shut up the house of the Lord, built a temple for Baal, and for six years led the people of Judah in idol worship.

In the slaughter of the royal family by Athaliah, one of Ahaziah's sons survived — Joash. He was a baby, only a year old when his grandmother seized the throne. His aunt hid him in the Temple of the Lord and kept him safe from Queen Athaliah. There he lived for six years while Jehoida the priest prepared to make him king.

When everything was ready and little Joash was seven years old, Jehoiada the priest brought him out of his hiding place and showed him to the people and the rulers in the Temple, putting the crown on his head. All the people shouted, "Long live the king! Long live the king!"

Queen Athaliah heard the noise of the shouting and came out of her palace to see what had taken place. She saw the little boy king standing by a pillar in the Temple with the crown on his head and everyone shouting, "Long live the king!"

Athaliah was very angry when she saw all this. She called for her servants and her soldiers to break up this gathering of the people and take the boy king. But no one would follow her, for they were tired of her cruel rule and wanted a king who came from the line of David.

Jehoiada said to the soldiers, "Take this woman prisoner and carry her out of the Temple of the Lord. Don't let her blood be spilled in the holy house."

So they seized Athaliah, dragged her out of the Temple, and killed her. Then Jehoiada and all the people made a promise to serve only the Lord. They tore down the house of the idol Baal, destroyed the images, and broke its altar in pieces. They made the Temple holy once more, set the house in order, offered the sacrifices, and held the daily worship before the altar. And all the people were glad to have a descendant of David — one of the royal line — once more on the throne of Judah.

Discussion Questions: *1. What kind of king was Ahaziah? 2. Who ruled after Ahaziah? 3. Why did the people put Joash on the throne? 4. What did the people promise to do?*

DAY 162

THE TEMPLE RESTORED

2 Chronicles 24:1-27

AS long as Jehoiada the good priest lived, Joash ruled well and his people served the Lord. When King Joash grew up, he wanted to have the Temple of the Lord made new and beautiful. In the years since the Temple had been built by Solomon, it had grown old and had fallen into decay. Then, too, Queen Athaliah and the men who worshiped Baal had broken down the walls in many places and carried away the gold and the silver of the Temple to use in the worship of Baal.

At first King Joash told the priests and Levites who served in the Temple to go through the land and ask the people for money to fix up the Temple. But the priests and the Levites were slow in the work, and the king tried another plan for getting the money that was needed.

He had a large box made, and had it placed at the door of the Temple, so everyone would see it when they went to worship the Lord. In the lid of the box was a hole through which they dropped money into the box. The king sent word through all the land that the princes and the people should bring gifts of money and drop it into the chest whenever they came to the Temple.

ALL THE PRINCES AND PEOPLE GLADLY GAVE TO THE CHEST - 2 CHRONICLES 24:10

The people were glad, and brought their gifts willingly, for they all wanted to have God's house made beautiful. In a short time, the box was full of gold and silver. Then the king's officers opened the box, tied up the money in bags, and placed the bags of money in a safe place. The box was filled with gold and silver many times, until there was enough money to pay for all the work needed in the Temple and for making new ornaments of gold and silver for the house.

When Jehoiada the good priest was very old, he died, and after his death there was no one to teach King Joash the proper way to act. The princes of the land loved to worship idols, and they led King Joash astray after he had done so well. God was not pleased with Joash after he abandoned him, so he allowed the Syrians from the north to attack the land. They robbed the cities and left Joash sick and poor. Soon after the coming of the Syrians, his own servants killed him and made Amaziah, his son, king in his place.

Discussion Questions: *1. What had happened to the Temple? 2. How did Joash collect money to rebuilt the Temple? 3. What happened to the king after Jehoiada died?*

DAY 163

AMAZIAH

2 Chronicles 25:1-28

AMAZIAH was the ninth king of Judah. Amaziah worshiped the Lord, but he did not serve the Lord with a perfect heart. He gathered an army of 300,000 men to make war on Edom and bring its people back under the rule of Judah. He also hired an army from Israel to help him in this war, until a prophet said to him, "Don't let the army of Israel go with you against Edom, for the Lord is not with the people of Israel. Go with your own men, be strong and brave, and the Lord will help you."

"But how will I get back the money I paid to the army of Israel?" Amaziah asked the prophet.

"Fear not," said the prophet. "The Lord is able to give you much more than you have lost."

Amaziah obeyed the Lord, sent home the men of Israel, and fought the Edomites just with the men of Judah. The Lord gave him a great victory in the land of Edom, but Amaziah was cruel to the people he conquered and killed many of them in his anger.

When he came back from Edom, he brought with him the idols of that land, set them up as his own gods, burned incense to them, and bowed down before them. When a prophet of the Lord came to him and warned him that God was angry with him and would surely punish him for this wickedness, Amaziah said to the prophet, "Who asked you to give advice to the king? Keep still, or you will be put to death!"

The prophet answered him, "I know it is God's will that you be destroyed, because you will not listen to the word of the Lord."

Amaziah's punishment came soon. In a little while, he made war on Joash, the king of Israel, whose kingdom was far greater and stronger than his own. The two armies met at Bethshemesh, northwest of Jerusalem. Amaziah was beaten in a great battle, many of his men were slain, and Amaziah himself was taken prisoner by Joash, the king of Israel. Joash took the city of Jerusalem, broke down the wall, and carried away all the treasures in the palace and the Temple of the Lord.

After this, Amaziah lived fifteen years, but he never regained the power he had lost. His nobles made a plan to kill him, and Amaziah fled from the city to escape them, but they caught him, killed him, and brought his body back to Jerusalem to be buried in the tombs of the kings. His reign began well, but it ended badly because he failed to obey the word of the Lord.

Discussion Questions: *1. Why did Amaziah gather an army? 2. What did the prophet tell him? 3. What did the king bring back from Edom? Was he right to do that? Why or why not? 4. How did God punish him?*

DAY 164

UZZIAH AND JOTHAM
2 Chronicles 26:1-27:9

AFTER Amaziah came his son Uzziah, who was also called Azariah. He was the tenth king of Judah. Uzziah was only sixteen years old when he began to reign, and he was king for fifty-two years. He did right in the sight of the Lord during most of his reign. Uzziah found the kingdom weak and made it strong, for the Lord helped him. He won back the land of the Philistines, the land of the Ammonites, and of the Arabians. He built cities and made strong walls around them, with towers full of weapons for defense against enemies. He loved the fields, planted trees and vineyards, and raised crops of wheat and barley.

But when Uzziah was strong and rich, his heart became proud and he no longer tried to do God's will. He wanted to have the power of the high priest as well as that of the king, so he went into the Holy Place in the Temple to offer incense on the golden altar, which only priests were allowed to do. The high priest Azariah followed Uzziah into the Holy Place with the other priests, and said to him, "It is not for you to offer incense, King Uzziah, or to come into the Holy Place. This belongs to the priests alone. Go out of the Holy Place for you have disobeyed the Lord's command, and it will not bring you honor, but trouble."

Uzziah was standing before the golden altar with a censer of incense in his hand. Instantly the white scales of leprosy rose on his forehead. The priests saw right away that God had given Uzziah leprosy. He felt it, and turned to leave the Holy Place. But they would not wait for him to go out — they drove him out, for a leper's presence made the house unholy. From that day until he died, Uzziah was a leper. He could no longer sit as king, but his son Jotham took his place. He was not allowed to live in the palace, but stayed in a house alone. And when he died, they would not give him a place among the tombs of the kings, but buried him in a field outside.

KING UZZIAH WAS SMITTEN WITH LEPROSY - 2 CHRONICLES 26:19

Jotham, the eleventh king, ruled after his father's death for sixteen years. He served the Lord, but he did not stop his people from worshiping idols. He was warned by his father's fate and was content to be a king, without trying at the same time to be a priest and offer incense in the Temple. God was with Jotham, and gave his kingdom some success.

Discussion Questions: *1. What did Uzziah do for Judah? 2. Why did he want to be high priest as well as king? 3. What did Uzziah do that was wrong? 4. What happened to him? 5. What kind of king was Jotham?*

DAY 165

AHAZ

2 Chronicles 28:1-27

THE next king, the twelfth, was Ahaz, who was the wickedest of all the kings of Judah. He left the service of God and worshiped the images of Baal. Worse than any other king, he even offered some of his own children as offerings to the false gods. In his reign the house of the Lord was shut up, its treasures were taken away, and it was left to fall into ruin. For his sins and the sins of his people, God brought great suffering to the land.

The king of Israel, Pekah, attacked Ahaz and killed more than 100,000 men of Judah, among them the king's own son. The Israelites also took away many more — men, women, and children — as captives.

But a prophet of the Lord in Israel, whose name was Oded, came out to meet the rulers and said to them, "The Lord God was angry with Judah and gave its people into your hand. But do you now intend to keep your brothers as slaves? Haven't you also sinned against the Lord? Now listen to the word of the Lord and set your brothers free."

The rulers of Israel gave clothing and food to their captives from Judah, then sent them home, even giving those who were weak donkeys to ride on. They brought them to Jericho, in the valley of the Jordan, and gave them to their own people.

When the Edomites attacked Judah, King Ahaz asked the Assyrians, a great people far away, to come and help him. The Assyrians came, but they did not help him, for they made themselves the rulers of Judah, robbed Ahaz of everything he had, and laid heavy burdens on the land. At last Ahaz died, leaving his people worshipers of idols under the power of the king of Assyria.

Discussion Questions: 1. What kind of king was Ahaz? What happened to his country? 2. What did the prophet Oded tell the Israelites? 3. What did they do when they heard this message? 4. Why did God put Judah in the hands of the Assyrians?

DAY 166

ISAIAH'S VISION

Isaiah 6

IN the days of Uzziah, Jotham, and Ahaz, God raised up a great prophet in Judah whose name was Isaiah. The prophecies he spoke in the name of the Lord are given in the book of Isaiah. The year King Uzziah died, Isaiah was a young man. One day, while he was worshiping in the Temple, a wonderful vision came to him. He saw the Lord God on a throne, with the angels around him. He also saw strange creatures called seraphim standing before the throne of the Lord. Each of these had six wings. With two wings, he covered his face before the glory of the Lord. With two other wings, he covered his feet. And with the last two, he flew through the air to do God's will. And these seraphim called out to one another, "Holy, holy, is the Lord of hosts. The whole earth is full of his glory!"

Young Isaiah felt the walls and the floor of the Temple shaking at these voices, and he saw a cloud of smoke covering the house. Isaiah was filled with fear. He cried out, saying, "Woe has come to me! I am a man of sinful lips, and I live among a people of sinful lips, and now my eyes have seen the king, the Lord of hosts!"

Then one of the seraphim took into his hand the tongs that were used in the sacrifices. He flew to the altar, and with the tongs took up a burning coal. Then he flew to the place where Isaiah was standing, pressed the fiery coal to Isaiah's lips, and said, "This coal from God's altar has touched your lips, and now your sin is taken away and you are made clean."

Then Isaiah heard the voice of the Lord saying, "Whom shall I send to this people? Who will carry the message of the Lord to them?"

Isaiah said, "Here I am, Lord. Send me!"

And the Lord said to Isaiah, "You shall be my prophet, and shall go to this people, and shall give them my words. But they will not listen to you or understand you. Your words will do them no good, but will seem to make their hearts hard, their ears heavy, and their eyes shut. For they will not hear with their ears, or see with their eyes, or understand with their hearts, or turn to me and be saved."

Isaiah said, "How long must this be, Lord?"

And the Lord said, "Until the cities are left waste without people, and the houses without men to live in them. The land shall become utterly desolate, and the people shall be turned far away into another land. But out of all this there will be a few people — a tenth — who will come back and rise like a new tree from the roots of the tree that was cut down. This tenth shall be the seed of a new people in times to come."

This told Isaiah that although his words might seem to do no good, yet he was to go on preaching, for long afterward, a new Judah would rise out of the ruins of the old kingdom and serve the Lord.

Isaiah lived for many years and spoke the word of the Lord to his people until he was a very old man. He preached while at least four kings ruled. Some of these kings were friendly and listened to his words, but others were not willing to obey the prophet and do the will of God. The kingdom of Judah gradually fell away from the worship of the Lord and followed the people of the Ten Tribes in the worship of idols.

_____

Discussion Questions: *1. What did the prophet Isaiah speak? What did he see? 2. Why do you think Isaiah was afraid when he saw the vision? 3. What did God tell Isaiah would happen?*

DAY 167

HEZEKIAH

2 Chronicles 29:1-31:21

AFTER Ahaz, the most wicked king of Judah, came Hezekiah, who was the best of the kings. He listened to the words of the prophet Isaiah and obeyed the commands of the Lord.

In the first month of his reign, when he was a young man, he called together the priests and the Levites who had charge of the house of the Lord and said to them, "My sons, give yourselves again to the service of the Lord and be holy, as God commands you. Now open the doors of the house of the Lord, which have been shut all these years. Take out all the idols that have been placed in it, and make the place clean and pure from all evil things. Because the people have turned away from the Lord, he has been angry with us, and has left us to our enemies. Now let us go back to the Lord and promise to serve him. God has chosen you to lead his worship. Do not neglect the work the Lord has given you."

So the Temple was opened, the idols were taken away, the altar was made holy, and the daily offering was laid on it. The lamps were lit in the holy place. The priest stood before the golden altar offering incense. The Levites in their robes sang the psalms of David while the silver trumpets made music, and the people came up to worship in the Temple, which they had not done in many years.

You remember that the great Feast of the Passover reminded the people how the children of Israel had come out of Egypt. For a long time, the people had not kept this feast, both in Judah and Israel. King Hezekiah sent commands through all Judah for the people to come up to Jerusalem and worship the Lord at this feast. He also sent men through the land of Israel — the Ten Tribes — to ask them to come up with their brothers of Judah to Jerusalem and keep the feast.

At that time Hoshea, the last king of Israel, was on the throne, the land was overrun by the Assyrians, and the kingdom was very weak and nearing its end.

Most of the people in Israel were worshipers of idols and had forgotten God's law. They laughed at Hezekiah's messengers, and would not come to the feast. But in many places in Israel there were some who had listened to the prophets of the Lord, and these came up to worship with the men of Judah.

For each family, they roasted a lamb, and with it they ate unleavened bread

(bread made without yeast). They praised the Lord who had led their fathers out from Egypt to their own land.

After the feast, when the people had given themselves to the service of God, King Hezekiah began to destroy the idols that were everywhere in Judah. He sent men to break down the images, to tear in pieces the altars to the false gods, and to cut down the trees under which the altars stood. You remember that Moses made a serpent of brass in the wilderness. This image had been brought to Jerusalem and was still there in the days of Hezekiah. The people were worshiping it as an idol and burning incense before it. Hezekiah said, "It is nothing but a piece of brass," and he commanded that it should be broken up. Everywhere he called on his people to turn from the idols, to destroy them, and to worship the Lord God.

Discussion Questions: 1. What kind of king was Hezekiah? 2. What did Hezekiah do to the house of the Lord? 3. What did the feast of Passover remind the people of? 4. What did the king command his people to do? What happened when he asked the people of Israel to join them? 5. How do you think God felt when the king destroyed all the idols?

DAY 168

The Lord Saves Judah

2 Chronicles 32:1-22

WHEN Hezekiah became king, the kingdoms of Israel, Syria, Judah, and all the lands near them were under the power of the great kingdom of the Assyrians. Each land had its own king, but he ruled under the king of Assyria, and every year a heavy tax was paid to the Assyrians.

After a few years, Hezekiah thought he was strong enough to set his kingdom free from Assyrian rule. He refused to pay the tax any longer, gathered an army, built the walls of Jerusalem higher, and made ready for a war with the Assyrians. But Sennacherib, the king of Assyria, came into the land of Judah with a great army, took all the cities in the west of Judah, and threatened to take Jerusalem.

Then Hezekiah saw that he had made a mistake. He was not able to fight the Assyrians, the most powerful of all the nations in that part of the world. He sent word to the king of Assyria, saying, "I will not resist your rule. Forgive me for the past, and I will pay whatever you ask."

Then the king of Assyria laid on Hezekiah and his people a tax heavier than before. **To obtain** the money, Hezekiah took all the gold and silver in the Temple, all that was in his own palace, and all that he could find among the people, and sent it to the Assyrians. But even then, the king of Assyria was not satisfied. He sent his princes to Jerusalem with this message, "We are going to destroy this city and take you away into another land, as we have taken the people of Israel. The gods of other nations have not been able to save them, and your God will not be able to save you. Surrender yourselves to the king of Assyria and go wherever he sends you."

When King Hezekiah heard this, he was filled with fear. He took the letter into the house of the Lord, spread it out before the altar, and called on the Lord to help him save his people. Then he sent his princes to the prophet Isaiah, to ask him to give them some word from the Lord. And Isaiah said, "The Lord says, 'The king of Assyria shall not come to this city, nor shall he shoot an arrow against it. But he shall go back to his own land the same way he came. And I will cause him to fall by the sword in his own land. For I will defend this city and will save it, for my own sake and for my servant David's sake.' "

Just at that time, Sennacherib, the king of Assyria, heard that a great army was marching against him from another land. He turned away from the land of Judah and went to meet these new enemies. And the Lord sent a sudden and terrible plague to the army of the Assyrians, so that in one night nearly 200,000 of them died in their camp. King Sennacherib hurried back to his own land and never again came into the land of Judah.

Discussion Questions: *1. What did Hezekiah decide to do about the Assyrians? 2. What did the king of Assyria do? 3. Why was Hezekiah afraid? 4. Who saved Judah? How?*

DAY 169

GOD SPARES HEZEKIAH

2 Kings 20:1-11

WHILE the Assyrians were in the land and the kingdom was in great danger, King Hezekiah was suddenly stricken with a deadly disease, a cancer that no doctor could cure. The prophet Isaiah said to him, "The Lord says, 'Set your house in order and prepare to leave your kingdom, for you shall die.' "

But King Hezekiah felt he could not be spared, especially since he had no son to take charge of the kingdom. Hezekiah prayed to the Lord, asking to be allowed to live. "O Lord, I beg you, remember now how I have walked before you in truth and with a perfect heart and have done good in your sight. Let me live, Lord!"

The Lord heard Hezekiah's prayer, and before Isaiah had reached the middle of the city on his way home, the Lord said to him, "Turn again, and say to Hezekiah, 'I have heard your prayer. I have seen your tears. I will heal you, and in three days you shall go up to the house of the Lord. I will add to your life fifteen years, and I will save this city from the king of Assyria.' "

Then Isaiah the prophet came back to Hezekiah and told him the words of the Lord. "Lay on the tumor a plaster made of figs, and you will be cured."

When Hezekiah heard the words of Isaiah, he said, "What sign will the Lord give, to show that he will cure me and I shall again go up to the house of the Lord?"

Isaiah said, "The Lord will give you a sign, and you shall choose it yourself. Shall the shadow on the dial go forward ten degrees, or go back ten degrees?" Near the palace stood a sundial on which the time of day was shown, for there were no clocks in those years.

Hezekiah said, "It is easy for the shadow to go forward ten degrees. Let it go back ten degrees."

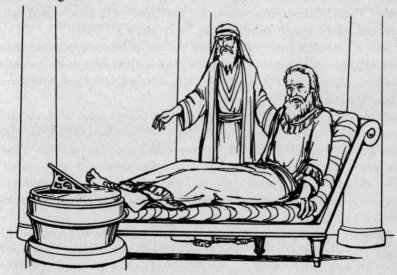

THE LORD MADE THE SHADOW GO BACKWARDS - ISAIAH 38:8

Then Isaiah the prophet called on the Lord. The Lord heard him, and caused the shadow to go backward on the sundial ten degrees. Within three days, Hezekiah was well, and he went to worship in the house of the Lord. After this, Hezekiah lived fifteen years in honor. When he died, all the land mourned for him as the best of the kings.

Discussion Questions: *1. What happened to King Hezekiah? 2. What did he ask God to do? Did God hear him? 3. How did God show the king he would do what he promised? 4. What did Hezekiah do when the Lord made him well? 5. Why were the people sad when Hezekiah died?*

DAY 170

MANASSEH

2 Kings 21:1-26

MANASSEH, the fourteenth king of Judah, followed the sins of his grandfather Ahaz, not the good deeds of his father, Hezekiah. He was only twelve years old when he began to reign, too young for such responsibility. In his youth, he turned away from the teachings of the prophet Isaiah and the service of the Lord. He rebuilt the altars to Baal and the Asherah that his father, Hezekiah, had thrown down. He worshiped the sun, moon, and stars. He even set up images in the Temple, the house of the Lord.

When Manasseh grew older and had children of his own, he made them walk through fire to please the false gods. He would not listen to the prophets the Lord sent to warn him, and there is reason to believe — though the Bible does not say it — that he killed Isaiah.

Manasseh reigned a long time, longer than any of the wicked kings who had gone before him. He led his people further away from God than Ahaz, who had been as wicked as Manasseh. Because of Manasseh's sins and the sins of his people, the Lord brought the Assyrians against Judah with a great army. They took Manasseh a prisoner, bound him with chains, and carried him to the city of Babylon, where the king of Assyria was living. There Manasseh was kept a prisoner for a time.

While he was in prison, Manasseh saw how wicked he had been and he sought the Lord. He prayed to be forgiven for his sins, and the Lord heard him. Afterward, the king of Assyria allowed Manasseh to rule over his land again. Then Manasseh knew the Lord was the only true God, and from that time he worshiped the Lord only. He took the altars and the images of the false gods out of the Temple, built the altar of the Lord, and caused offerings to be laid on it. He commanded his people to worship the Lord and leave the idols. But they had gone too far to come back, and only a few of them followed their king's example in seeking the Lord. He could easily lead his people into sin, but he could not bring them back to God.

After a long reign of fifty-five years, Manasseh died, and his son Amon became king. He reigned only two years, but they were years of wickedness and worshiping idols. Then his servants killed Amon. The people killed them in turn, and made his son Josiah king.

Discussion Questions: *1. What kind of king was Manasseh? 2. Whom did he worship? 3. What happened to the people of his country? Why? 4. How did Manasseh learn that he had done wrong? 5. What did Manesseh ask God to do? Did God? What does that tell you about God?*

DAY 171

JOSIAH

2 Kings 22:1-14

JOSIAH, the sixteenth king, was only eight years old when his father Amon was killed. At first he was too young to rule the land, and the princes of his court governed in his name. But when Josiah was sixteen years old, he chose the Lord God of his father David, the God Hezekiah had worshiped, and he served the Lord better than any of the kings before him.

When he was twenty years old, he began to clear away the idols and the idol temples from the land of Judah. He did this work more thoroughly than it had ever been done before, by Jehoshaphat or by Hezekiah, for he left not one place where idols were worshiped. He went even beyond his own borders, into the land that had been the land of Israel, from which most of the people had been carried away long before. And in every place, he broke down the altars, burned the images, and even dug up the bones of the idol priests and burned them with their images.

He came to Bethel, twelve miles north of Jerusalem, where Jeroboam of Israel had built the temple for the worship of the golden calves 200 years before.

As he was burning the bones of the idol priests on the ruins of their own altars, he found a tomb, and asked who was buried there. They said, "This is the tomb of the man of God who came from Judah and warned King Jeroboam that someone would do these very things you are doing."

"Let his bones rest," said King Josiah. "Let no man touch the bones of the prophet."

While the men of King Josiah were at work in the Temple on Mount Moriah, making the house pure once more, they found an old book written on rolls of leather. It was the book of the law of the Lord given by Moses, but it had been hidden so long that men had forgotten it. They brought the book and read it aloud to the king.

SHAPHAN READ THE BOOK TO KING JOSIAH - 2 CHRONICLES 34:18

When King Josiah heard the words of the law, the warnings about disobeying them, the king was filled with alarm. He said to the rulers, "Go and ask about the Lord for me and all the people. Great is the anger of the Lord against us, because our fathers have disobeyed the words written in this book."

They looked for a prophet to give them the word of the Lord, and they found a woman named Huldah living in Jerusalem, to whom the word of the Lord came. She was called a prophetess, and they brought her the king's message.

Discussion Questions: *1. Who did Josiah choose to worship? 2. Why did he clear the idols from the land? 3. What did the men cleaning the Temple find? 4. How did Josiah feel when he found out that he and his people had not done all God commanded? 5. What did he do?*

DAY 172

Josiah's Death

2 Kings 22:15-23:30

THE prophetess told them the Lord's message: " 'Behold, I will bring evil on this place and on the people living in it, because they have forsaken the Lord and have worshiped other gods. My anger will fall on this city and on this land.' But because King Josiah has sought the Lord and has done God's will and called on the Lord, therefore the Lord says he will hold back his anger against this land as long as Josiah lives. He shall go down to his grave before all these evils come upon Judah and Jerusalem."

When Josiah heard this, he called all the princes, priests, and people to meet in the Temple of the Lord. There the king stood by a pillar and read the words of the book that had been found. Then the king and all his people made a promise to serve the Lord and do his will, and to keep his law with all their hearts. They kept this promise while Josiah lived, but that was only a few years.

All this time, the kingdom of Judah, like all the kingdoms around, was part of the greater kingdom of Assyria. But the great kings of Assyria had passed away, and now the empire of Assyria was becoming weak and falling apart. Pharaoh Nechoh, the king of Egypt, went to war with the Assyrians, and on his way, he passed through the land of Judah and what had once been Israel before its people were carried away captive. Josiah thought that since the king of Assyria was his overlord, he had to fight the king of Egypt.

Pharaoh Nechoh sent a message to King Josiah, saying, "I have nothing against you, king of Judah, and I am not coming to make war on you, but on the king of Assyria. God has sent me, and commanded me to make haste. Do not stand in my way, or you may be destroyed."

But Josiah would not heed the message of the king of Egypt. He went out against him with his army and met him in battle on the great plain of Esdraelon, where so many battles had been fought before and since. There the Egyptians won a victory, and in the fight, the archers shot King Josiah. He died in his chariot, and they brought his dead body to Jerusalem. And all the land mourned and wept for the king they loved because he had ruled wisely and well. With good King Josiah, the last hope of the kingdom of Judah died.

Discussion Questions: *1. Why did God promise not to harm Judah? How long did he promise not to harm them? 2. Why did Josiah fight Pharaoh? 3. What happened to Josiah?*

267

DAY 173

JEHOIAKIM

2 Kings 23:31-24:1
2 Chronicles 36:1-7
Jeremiah 22:10-12

WHEN the good King Josiah fell in battle, the people of the land made his son Jehoahaz king. At that time all the kingdoms around Judah were in confusion. The great empire of Assyria had been the ruler of nearly all that part of the world, but now it had been broken up. Nineveh, its chief city, had been destroyed, and Egypt, Babylonia, and other lands were at war, each striving to take the place of Assyria as the ruler of the nations.

Pharaoh Nechoh, the king of Egypt whose warriors had slain King Josiah, became for a time the master of the lands between Egypt and the Euphrates River. He felt he could not trust young King Jehoahaz, so he took his crown from him and took him as a captive down to Egypt. Jehoahaz, the seventeenth king, reigned only three months. The prophet Jeremiah said this about the young king: "Weep not for the dead King Josiah, nor sorrow over him, but weep for him that goeth away, the King Jehoahaz, for he shall return no more, nor shall he again see his own land. In the place where they have led him captive, there shall he die, and he shall look upon this land no more."

The man Pharaoh Nechoh set up as king over Judah in place of Jehoahaz was his brother Jehoiakim, another son of Joshia. But he was not like his father, because he led his people back to the idols Josiah had tried to destroy. Jeremiah the prophet warned him that his evil ways would surely ruin himself and the people, which made King Jehoiakim very angry. He tried to kill the prophet, but Jeremiah was hidden by his friends.

Jeremiah could no longer go out among the people or stand in the Temple to speak the word of the Lord. So he wrote God's message and gave it to his friend Baruch to read before the people. While Baruch was reading it, some officers of the king came, took the message away, and brought it to the king. King Jehoiakim was sitting in his palace with the princes around him, a fire burning before him, for it was wintertime. The officer began to read the scroll to the king and the princes, but when he had read a few pages, the king took up a knife and began cutting up the pages and throwing them into the fire. Even the princes were shocked at this, for they knew the writing on the scroll was God's word to the king and the people. They begged the king not to destroy the scroll, but he would not listen to them. He went on cutting up the scroll and throwing it in the fire until it was all burned.

The king told his officers to capture Jeremiah and Baruch, and he would have killed them if he found them. But they were hidden, and he could not find them, for the Lord kept them safe.

Jehoiakim reigned a few years as the servant of the king of Egypt. But soon the Egyptians lost all the lands they had gained outside their own country. The Babylonians, under Nebuchadnezzar, rose to power over the nations and took the place of the empire that had been held by the Assyrians. Nebuchadnezzar was the son of the king of Babylon, and at first was the general of his army. He attacked Judah and Jerusalem, but Jehoiakim did not dare to fight with him. He promised to serve Nebuchadnezzar, and on that condition was allowed to remain king. No sooner had the Babylonian army gone away than he broke his promise, rose up against Babylon, and tried to make himself free.

But he did not succeed. Instead, he lost his kingdom and his life, for either the Babylonians or his own people killed him, and his dead body was thrown outside the gate of the city. He had reigned in wickedness for eleven years, and he died in disgrace.

Discussion Questions: *1. What happened to King Jehoahaz? 2. Who did Pharaoh Nechoh make king in Jehoahaz's place? 3. What was the new king like? 4. Why did the king dislike Jeremiah? 5. What did he do to the prophet's message?*

DAY 174

JEREMIAH'S VISION

Jeremiah 24:1-10

JEHOIAKIM'S young son Jehoiachin, who was also called Coniah or Jeconiah, was then made king by the people. But he reigned only three months, for Nebuchadnezzar, who was now the king of Babylon, came with his army and took the city of Jerusalem. He took the young king as a captive to Babylon, just as Nechoh had taken Jehoahaz to Egypt eleven years before. They also took away many of the nobles, rulers, and the best people of the land.

Most of these were worshipers of the Lord, who took to Babylonia their love for the Lord and served him there, for their troubles drew them closer to their God.

After these captives had been taken away, the Lord gave Jeremiah a vision of what would come to pass. Jeremiah saw two baskets of figs. One basket was full of fresh, ripe figs, the best that could be found. The other basket was full of poor, decayed figs, not fit to be eaten. The Lord said, "Jeremiah, what do you see?"

Jeremiah said, "Figs. The good figs very good, and the bad figs very bad — so bad they cannot be eaten."

Then the Lord said to Jeremiah, "The captives who have been taken away to the land of Babylon are like these good figs. I will care for them, keep them, and bring them back to this land. I will give them a heart to know me. I will be their God, and they shall be my people. And the bad figs are like those who are left in this land, the king who shall reign over them, his princes, and his people. They shall suffer and die by the sword, by famine, and by plague, until they are destroyed."

This showed Jeremiah that the captives in Babylon were the hope of the nation. Jeremiah sent a letter to these captives, saying, "The Lord says this to those who have been carried away captive: 'Build houses, and live in them. Plant gardens, and eat the fruit of them. Have sons and daughters, and let your children be married in that land when they grow up. And pray the Lord to give peace to the city and the land where you are living, for you and your children shall stay there seventy years, and after seventy years, shall come again to your own land in peace. For my thoughts are thoughts of peace and kindness toward you. You shall call on me, and I will hear you. You shall seek me and find me, when you seek me with all your heart.' "

Discussion Questions: *1. What kind of people did the king of Babylon bring to Babylonia? 2. What did God show Jeremiah with the figs? 3. How did Jeremiah tell the captives to pray?*

DAY 175

JEREMIAH IMPRISONED
2 Chronicles 36:10-14
Jeremiah 37:1-38:13

AFTER Jehoiachin and the captives had been taken away, Nebuchadnezzar set up Zedekiah as the king of Judah. He was the twentieth and last king of the kingdom of Judah. He began by promising to be true and faithful to Nebuchadnezzar, the king of Babylon who had made him king. But very soon he was convinced to break his promise and throw off the rule of Babylon. Also, he left the worship of the Lord and began to pray to the idols of wood and stone that could give him no help.

Jeremiah the prophet told King Zedekiah that he was doing wrong by breaking his promises and turning from the Lord to idols. He told Zedekiah that he would fail and bring his kingdom to ruin. He said, "It is better to obey the king of Babylon than to fight against him, for God will not bless you and your people for breaking your word. The king of Babylon will come and destroy this city. You shall see him face-to-face, and he will take you away a captive to his own land, and this city shall be destroyed."

This made the princes and nobles very angry with Jeremiah. They said, "This man is an enemy of his land and a friend to the king of Babylon. He is a traitor, and should be put to death." Zedekiah said to his nobles, "Jeremiah is in your hands; you can do with him what you choose. The king cannot help him against you."

These men seized Jeremiah, took him to the prison, threw him into a dungeon below the floor, and left him to die.

JEREMIAH WAS THROWN INTO THE DUNGEON - JEREMIAH 37:15,16

But in the court of the king there was one kind man, a black man named Ebedmelech. He found Jeremiah in the dungeon, let down a rope, drew him up, and brought him to a safe, dry place in the prison.

Discussion Questions: *1. What did King Zedekiah promise? 2. What did God say about the king's breaking his promises? 3. How did the princes and nobles feel about Jeremiah? 4. Why did the king let them put the prophet in prison? 5. Had God forgotten Jeremiah? How do you know?*

271

DAY 176

THE END OF JUDAH

Jeremiah 39:1-10

BY this time, Nebuchadnezzar, the king of Babylon, was laying siege against Jerusalem. No one could go out or come in. No food could be found for the people, and many of them starved to death. The soldiers of Nebuchadnezzar built forts, threw darts and stones, broke down the gates, and made great openings in the walls of the city.

When King Zedekiah saw the city would fall to its enemies, he tried to escape. But the men of Babylon followed him and took him prisoner, along with all his family, his wives, and his sons. They were all brought before King Nebuchadnezzar, so just as Jeremiah had said, Zedekiah saw the king of Babylon.

But he also saw something more terrible: All his sons were killed in front of him. Then Zedekiah's eyes were put out and he was dragged away to Babylon. The Babylonian soldiers killed all the leaders of the people who had led Zedekiah to rebel against Nebuchadnezzar. The rest of the people, except for the very poorest in the land, were carried away to the land of Babylon.

The king of Babylon was friendly to Jeremiah the prophet because of the advice he had given Zedekiah and his people. The ruler Nebuchadnezzar set over the city opened the door of Jeremiah's prison and allowed him to choose between going to Babylon with the captives or staying with the poor people in the land. Jeremiah chose to stay, but not long after, he was taken down to Egypt by enemies of the king of Babylon. In Egypt, Jeremiah died; some think he was killed. His life had been sad, for he had seen nothing but evil come to his land, and his message from the Lord had been a message of trouble and sadness. Because of his sorrow, Jeremiah has been called the weeping prophet.

Nebuchadnezzar carried away all that was left of the valuable things in the Temple, and then he burned the buildings. He tore down the walls of Jerusalem and set the city on fire. All that was left of the city of David and the Temple of Solomon was a heap of ashes and blackened stones. So the kingdom of Judah ended, nearly 400 years after Rehoboam became its first king.

Discussion Questions: *1. What did King Nebuchadnezzar do? 2. What happened to King Zedekiah when he tried to run away? 3. Why did the king of Babylon like Jeremiah? What did he do for the prophet? 4. Why was Jeremiah so sad?*

DAY 177

CAPTIVITY IN BABYLONIA

Ezekiel 37

ALL that was left of the people of Judah was a company of captives carried away from their own land to the land of Babylon. Theirs was a long, sorrowful journey, dragged by cruel soldiers over mountains and valleys for almost a thousand miles. They could not go straight across the vast desert between Judah and the plains of Babylonia. They were led around this desert, through Syria, up to the Euphrates River, and then — following the great river in all its windings — down to the land of their captivity. There in the land of Babylonia (or Chaldea) at last they found rest.

When they were in their new home, the captives met with less trouble than they had feared. The people of the land treated them kindly and gave them their own fields to farm. The soil was rich, so they raised large crops of wheat, barley, and other grains. They planted gardens and built themselves homes. Some of them went to live in the cities and became rich, and some were in the court of King Nebuchadnezzar as nobles and princes standing next to the king in rank and honor.

Best of all, these captives did not worship idols. They saw the images of the Babylonian gods all around them, but they did not bow down to them. They worshiped only the Lord God of their fathers. The idol worshipers in Judah had been slain, and most of the captives were good men and women, who taught their children to love and serve the Lord.

These people did not forget their homeland. They loved the land of Israel, and they taught their children to love it by singing songs about it. Some of these songs are in the Book of Psalms. Here is part of one of these songs:

By the rivers of Babylon,
There we sat down, yea, we wept,
When we remembered Zion.
Upon the willow trees in the midst of that land
We hanged up our harps

For there they that led us captive asked us to sing;
And they that wanted us asked us to be glad, saying,
"Sing us one of the songs of Zion."
How shall we sing the Lord's song
In a foreign land?

273

If I forget thee, O Jerusalem,
Let my right hand forget her skill.
Let my tongue cleave to the roof of my mouth,
If I do not remember thee
If I do not prefer Jerusalem
Above my chief joy.

From this time on these people were called Jews, a name that means "people of Judah." The Jews all over the world belong to this people, for they came from the men who once lived in the land of Judah. And because they had once belonged to the twelve tribes of Israel, and ten of the tribes had been lost, and their kingdom had been destroyed, they were also spoken of as Israelites. So from this time on "people of Judah," "Jews," and "Israelites" all mean the people who had come from the land of Judah, and their descendants.

Discussion Questions: *1. How was the journey to Babylon? 2. What was it like when the people got to Babylon? 3. Whom did the captives worship? Did they forget their homeland? 4. What does Jews mean?*

DAY 178

EZEKIEL

Ezekiel 37

GOD was good to his people in the land of Babylon. He sent them prophets who showed them the way of the Lord. One of these prophets was Daniel, a young man who lived in the court of King Nebuchadnezzar. Another was a priest named Ezekiel, who lived among the captive people beside a river called the river Cheban. God gave Ezekiel wonderful visions. He saw the throne of the Lord and the strange creatures with six wings that the prophet Isaiah had seen long before. And he heard the voice of the Lord telling him what would happen to his people in the years to come.

Once the Lord lifted up Ezekiel and brought him to the middle of a great valley. The prophet looked around and saw the valley was covered with the bones of men, as though a great battle had been fought in it and the bodies of those killed had been left there.

"Son of man," the Lord said to Ezekiel, "can these dry bones live again?" Ezekiel answered, "O Lord God, you know if these dry bones can live." Then the Lord said to Ezekiel, "Preach to these dry bones, O son of man, and say to them, 'O ye dry bones, hear the voice of the Lord. Thus saith the Lord, I will send breath into you, and you shall live, and I will put flesh upon you, and cover you with skin, and you shall be alive again, and know that I am the Lord.' "

Ezekiel spoke to the army of dry bones spread over the valley, as the Lord told him to. And while he was speaking, he heard the sound of rolling thunder. All through the field, the bones began to come together, one part attaching to another part, until they were no longer loose bones, but skeletons of bones fitted together. Then another change came. Suddenly flesh grew over all the bones, and they lay on the ground like an army of dead men, a lifeless army.

Then the Lord said to Ezekiel, "Speak to the wind, O son of man. Speak, and say, 'Come from the four winds, O breath, and breathe upon these slain, that they may live.' "

Ezekiel called the wind, and while he was speaking, the dead bodies began to breathe. Then they stood up on their feet, a great army of living men, filling the whole valley.

The Lord said to Ezekiel, "Son of man, these dry bones are the people of Israel. They seem to be lost, and dead, and without hope. But they shall live again, for I, the Lord, will put life into them. And they shall go back to their own land, and be a people once more. I, the Lord, have spoken it, and I will do it."

When Ezekiel told the captives this vision, they were filled with hope that they would see their own land again.

Discussion Questions: *1. What did God give Ezekiel? 2. What did Ezekiel see in the valley? What did God ask him? 3. What lesson was God teaching Ezekiel?*

DAY 179

The King's Students

Daniel 1:1-7

EARLIER we read about Jehoiakim, the wicked son of the good King Josiah. While Jehoiakim was ruling the land of Judah, Nebuchadnezzar, the great conqueror of the nations, came from Babylon with his army of Chaldean soldiers. He took the city of Jerusalem and made Jehoiakim promise to submit to him as his master, a promise that Jehoiakim soon broke. And when Nebuchadnezzar went back to his own land, he took with him all the gold and silver he could find in the Temple. He also carried away as captives many of the princes and nobles, the best people in the land of Judah.

When these Jews were brought to the land of Chaldea (or Babylon), King Nebuchadnezzar gave orders to the prince who had charge of his palace to choose from these Jewish captives some young men that were of noble rank, good-looking, and bright — young men who would be able to learn new things. These young men were to be placed under the care of wise men who would teach them all they knew and make them capable of carrying out the king's orders. The king wanted them to be wise so they could give him advice about ruling the people.

THE FOUR YOUNG MEN WERE PRESENTED BEFORE THE KING -DANIEL 1:18

Among the young men chosen were four Jews who had been brought from Judah. By order of the king, the names of these men were changed. One of them, named Daniel, was to be called Belteshazzar. The other three young men were called Shadrach, Meshach, and Abednego. These four young men were taught all the knowledge of the Chaldeans, and after three years of training, they were taken into the king's palace to stand before the king.

Discussion Questions: *1. What kind of people did Nebuchadnezzar take with him as captive? 2. What did the king want the young men of noble rank to learn? 3. How did the king want them to help him?*

DAY 180

DANIEL'S DIET

Daniel 1:8-21

AFTER they came to the palace, the chief of the palace princes sent these men — as a special honor — some of the food from the king's table and some of the wine that was set apart for the king and his princes to drink. But both the meat and the wine of the king's table had been offerings to the idols of wood and stone that were worshiped by the Chaldeans. These young Jews felt that if they ate the food they, too, would be worshiping idols. Then, too, the laws of the Jews were very strict about what kind of food could be eaten and how it should be cooked. Certain foods were considered unclean, and the Jews were forbidden to touch it.

These young Jews, far away from their own land and from their Temple, felt they must be very careful to do nothing forbidden by the laws God had given to their people. They said to the chief of the nobles in the palace, "We cannot eat this meat and drink this wine, for it is forbidden by our laws."

The chief of the nobles said to Daniel, "If you do not eat the food that is given you, the king will see that you are not healthy. He will be angry with me for not giving you better care. What shall I do? I am afraid the king will command me to be put to death."

Daniel said, "Give us vegetables and bread. Let us eat no meat and drink no wine for ten days, and see if we don't look healthy."

The chief of the nobles to whose care these young men had been given liked Daniel. Everyone who knew him liked him. So he did as Daniel asked. He took away the meat and the wine, and gave these young Jews only vegetables and bread. At the end of ten days, the four young men were brought into the room where the great King Nebuchadnezzar sat. They bowed low before him. King Nebuchadnezzar was pleased with these four young men, more than with any others who came before him. He found them wise, faithful in the work given to them, and able to rule over men under them. These four men were given important places in the kingdom of the Chaldeans.

Discussion Questions: *1. Why didn't the young Jews want to eat the meat from the king's table? 2. Why was the chief noble afraid to do what they asked? 3. What did Daniel ask him to do? 4. Why did the king like the four young Jews? What did he do for them?*

DAY 181

DANIEL VOLUNTEERS
Daniel 2:1-16

DANIEL was more than a wise man: He was a prophet, like Elijah, Elisha, and Jeremiah. God let him know many things that would happen, and when God sent any man a dream that had a deep meaning, like Joseph, Daniel could tell the meaning of the dream.

Once King Nebuchadnezzar dreamed a dream that upset him. When he woke up, he knew the dream had some deep meaning, but by morning, he had forgotten what the dream was. He sent for the wise men who had before given him the meaning of his dreams, and said to them, "O ye wise men, I have dreamed a wonderful dream, but I have forgotten it. Now tell me what my dream was, and then tell me what it means, for I am sure that it has a meaning."

The wise men said, "O king, may you live forever! If you will tell us your dream, we will tell you its meaning. But we have no power to tell both the dream and its meaning. That only the gods can know."

The king became very angry, for these men had claimed their gods gave them all knowledge. He said, "Tell me the dream and its meaning and I will give you a rich reward and high honor. But if you cannot tell, I shall know you are liars, and you shall be put to death."

The wise men could not do what the king asked, and in great fury, he gave command that all of them should be slain. Among these men were Daniel and his three friends, Shadrach, Meshach, and Abednego, and these four Jews were to be killed with the rest of the wise men. Daniel said to the chief captain who had been sent to kill the wise men, "Give me a little time. I will call on my God. I know he will help me tell the king his dream and its meaning."

So time was given, and Daniel and his three friends prayed to the Lord God. That night the Lord gave Daniel the secret of the king's dream and its meaning. Daniel gave praise and thanks to the Lord, and in the morning, he said to the king's captain, "Do not kill the wise men. Take me before the king, and I will show him his dream and its meaning."

Discussion Questions: *1. What was Daniel? 2. Why didn't the king tell his wise men what he had dreamed? 3. What did he promise he would do if they could not tell him what he had dreamed? 4. What did Daniel ask the king to do?*

DAY 182

THE DREAM
Daniel 2:17-49

DANIEL was brought before King Nebuchadnezzar. The king said to him, "Are you able to tell me the dream I dreamed and the meaning of it?"

Daniel answered, "The wise men of Babylon who look to their idol gods cannot tell the king his dream. But there is a God in heaven who knows all things, and he has given me, his servant, to know your dream and the meaning of it. This is the dream, O king. You saw a great image, tall and noble-looking. The head of this image was of gold, his breast and his arms were of silver. His waist and his hips were of brass, his legs of iron, and his feet and toes were of iron and clay mixed together. And while this great image was standing, you saw a stone cut out without hands. The stone rolled and dashed against the feet of the image, and the whole image fell down and was broken in pieces. It was crushed and ground into a powder so fine that the wind blew it away like chaff. And you saw the stone that struck the image grow until it became a mountain and filled the whole world. This was your dream, O king."

And Daniel went on, and said, "And this, O king, is the meaning of the dream. God has shown you what shall come to pass in the years to come. You are that head of gold. That head means your kingdom as it is now. After your kingdom has passed away, another kingdom shall take its place — the shoulders and arms of silver. That kingdom shall be followed by another — the waist and hips of brass. After that shall come one more kingdom, that of iron. But you saw a stone cut out without hands. While the last of these kingdoms stands, the Lord God of heaven will set up his kingdom. God's kingdom, like that stone, will be small at first, but it will break down and destroy all those kingdoms. They shall pass away and perish before it. And as you saw that stone grow into a mountain, so God's kingdom shall become great and rule all the lands. And that kingdom of God shall never pass away, but shall last forever."

When King Nebuchadnezzar heard this, he was filled with wonder. He bowed down before Daniel and worshiped him, as though Daniel were a god. Then he gave him great presents and made him ruler over the part of his kingdom where the city of Babylon was standing. He gave Shadrach, Meshach and Abednego, Daniel's friends, high offices, but Daniel himself stayed in his palace, to be near him all the time.

DAY 183

THE GOLDEN IMAGE

Daniel 3:1-20

KING Nebuchadnezzar now had a great image made and covered with gold. This image he set up as an idol to be worshiped on the plain of Dura, near the city of Babylon. When it was finished, it stood almost a hundred feet high, so it could be seen from far away. Then the king sent out a command for all the princes, rulers, and nobles in the land to come to a great gathering for the dedication of the statue.

The great men of the kingdom came from far and near and stood around the image. Among them, by command of the king, were Daniel's three friends, Shadrach, Meshach, and Abednego. For some reason, Daniel himself was not there. He may have been busy with the work of the kingdom in some other place.

At one moment in the service before the image, all the trumpets sounded, the drums were beaten, and music was made on instruments of all kinds, as a signal for all the people to kneel down and worship the great golden image. But while the people were kneeling, three men stood up and would not bow down. These were the three young Jews, Shadrach, Meshach, and Abednego. They knelt down only before the Lord God.

Many of the nobles had been jealous of these young men because they had been lifted to high places in the rule of the kingdom, and these men, who hated Daniel and his friends, were glad to find they had not obeyed the command of King Nebuchadnezzar. The king had said that if anyone did not worship the golden image, he would be thrown into a furnace of fire.

These men who hated the Jews came to the king and said, "O king, may you live forever! You gave orders that when the music sounded everyone should bow down and worship the golden image, and if any man did not worship, he should be thrown into a furnace of fire. There are some Jews you have made rulers in the land, and they have not done as you commanded. Their names are Shadrach, Meshach, and Abednego. They do not serve your gods or worship the golden image you have set up."

Nebuchadnezzar was filled with rage and fury that anyone should dare to disobey his words. He sent for these three men and said to them, "Shadrach, Meshach, and Abednego, was it on purpose that you did not fall down and worship the image of gold? The music shall sound once more, and if you will worship the image, then all will be well. But if you will not, then you shall be thrown into the furnace of fire to die."

These three young men were not afraid of the king. They said, "King Nebuchadnezzar, we are ready to answer you now. The God we serve is able to save us from the fiery furnace, and we know he will save us. But if it is God's will that we die, even then we will not serve your gods or worship the golden image you have set up."

This answer made the king more furious than before. He said to his servants, "Make a fire in the furnace hotter than it has ever been before, as hot as fire can be made, and throw these three men into it."

Discussion Questions: 1. What did King Nebuchadnezzar ask the people to do? 2. Who would not do it? 3. Why did they refuse to obey the king? 4. What did the young men's enemies tell the king? 5. What were the young men willing to do for God?

DAY 184

THE FIERY FURNACE

Daniel 3:21-30

HEN the soldiers of the king's army seized Shadrach, Meshach, and Abednego as they stood in their loose robes, with their turbans on their heads. They tied them with ropes, dragged them to the mouth of the furnace, and threw them into the fire. The flames rushed from the opened door with such fury that they killed the soldiers holding these men. The men themselves fell down into the middle of the fiery furnace.

King Nebuchadnezzar stood in front of the furnace and looked into the open door. As he looked, he was filled with wonder at what he saw, and he said to the nobles around him, "Didn't we throw three tied men into the fire? Why do I see four untied men walking in the furnace, and the fourth man looks as though he were a son of the gods?"

The king went nearer the door of the furnace as the fire burned lower, and he called out to the three men inside, "Shadrach, Meshach, and Abednego — you who serve the Most High God — come out of the fire and come to me."

They came out and stood before the king in front of all the princes, nobles, and rulers. Everyone could see they were alive. Their garments had not been scorched or their hair singed. They didn't even have the smell of fire on them.

SHADRACH, MESHACH & ABED-NEGO CAME OUT OF THE FIRE - DANIEL 3:26

Nebuchadnezzar said, "Blessed be the God of these men, who has sent his angel and has saved their lives. I make a law that no man in all my kingdoms shall say a word against their God, for there is no other god who can save in this manner. And if any man speaks a word against their God — the Most High God — that man shall be cut in pieces and his house torn down."

After this, the king promoted these three young men to higher positions in the land of Babylon.

Discussion Questions: *1. What happened to the men who threw the Jews into the furnace? 2. What did the king see when he looked into the furnace? 3. What had happened to the four young men? 4. Who kept them safe? 5. What did the king do when he saw how powerful God was?*

DAY 185

Nebuchadnezzar's Dream (Part 1)

Daniel 4:1-18

HIS is the story that King Nebuchadnezzar himself told all the people in his kingdom. It's a story about a strange dream that came to him, the meaning of the dream as Daniel told it to him, and how the dream came true.

He said, "Nebuchadnezzar the king sends this message to all the people and nations that live in the world. May peace be given to you! It has seemed good to me to show you the signs and wonders that the Most High God has sent to me. How great are God's works! How mighty are his wonders! His kingdom is without end, and his rule is from age to age forever!

"I, King Nebuchadnezzar, was at rest in my house, and was living at peace in my palace. One night a dream came to me that made me afraid, and my thoughts and my visions troubled my heart. I sent for all the wise men of Babylon, to have them tell me the meaning of my dream. But they did not tell me what the meaning was, because they could not. At last came Daniel, who has the spirit of the holy gods, and I said to him: 'O Daniel, master of the wise men, I know you have the spirit of the holy gods and no secret is hidden from you. Tell me the meaning of the dream that has come to me. This was the dream. I saw a tree standing on the earth. It grew until the top of it reached up to heaven, and it was so great that it could be seen all over the earth. Its leaves were beautiful, and it had much fruit. The beasts in the field stood in its shadow, and the birds of heaven lived on its branches, and many people ate of the fruit.

" 'I saw in my dream that a Holy One came down from heaven. He cried out, "Cut down the tree, and cut off its branches. Shake off its leaves and scatter its fruit. Let the beasts get away from beneath it, and let the birds fly from its branches. But leave the stump of the tree with its roots in the ground, with a band of iron and brass around it, and the grass of the field growing about it. Let the stump be wet with the dew from heaven, and let it be among the beasts eating the grass of the field. And let seven years pass over it, so those who live may know that the Most High God rules over the kingdoms of men and gives them whatever is pleasing to his will."

" 'Now Daniel, whose name is Belteshazzar, tell me what it means.'

"Then Daniel stood surprised and wondering, and was in deep trouble. And I, Nebuchadnezzar, said to him, 'Daniel, don't let the dream give you trouble. Don't be afraid to tell me its meaning.' "

Discussion Questions: *1. What came to King Nebuchadnezzar? 2. Why did he call on Daniel? 3. What did the king dream? 4. How did Daniel feel about the dream?*

DAY 186

NEBUCHADNEZZAR'S DREAM (PART 2)

Daniel 4:19-37

" THEN Daniel said to me, 'My lord, may the dream be to those who hate you, and the meaning to your enemies! The tree you saw with green leaves, rich fruit, and height reaching to heaven in sight of all the earth — that tree is yourself. You have become great. Your power reaches up to heaven, and your rule is over all the lands.

" 'And as you saw a Holy One coming down from heaven, saying, "Cut down the tree and destroy it; but leave its stump in the earth, with a band of iron and brass until seven years pass over it," this is the meaning, O king, and it is the command of the Most High God that shall come upon my lord the king.

" 'You, O king, shall be driven away from men. You shall live with the beasts of the field. You shall be made to eat grass like oxen. You shall be wet with the dew of heaven. Seven years shall pass over you before you know that the Most High God rules in your kingdom and gives it to the one he chooses. And as the Holy One gave command to leave the stump of the tree with its roots, so it shall be with you. Your kingdom shall stand and shall come back to you when you know that he who sits in the heavens shall rule over the earth.

" 'And now, O king, take my advice. Stop your sins, do right, and show mercy to the poor. It may be that God will give to you more days of peace.'

"All this Daniel said to me, King Nebuchadnezzar; and it came to pass. Twelve months afterward, I was walking in my palace. I looked over the city and said, 'Isn't this great Babylon that I have built for my royal home built by my power and for my own glory?'

"While the words were in my mouth, a voice fell from heaven, saying, 'O King Nebuchadnezzar, the word has been spoken, and your kingdom is gone from you!'

"And in that hour my reason left me, and another heart was given to me, the heart of a beast instead of the heart of a man. I was driven out of my palace. I lived among the beasts, and ate grass as oxen eat it. My body was wet with the dew of heaven, until my hair was grown like eagles' feathers and my nails like birds' claws.

"And at the end of seven years, my mind came back to me, and my reason returned. I blessed the king of heaven and praised him that lives forever. My kingdom was given to me once more, my princes and rulers came to me again, and I was again the king over all the lands.

"Now I, Nebuchadnezzar, praise and honor the king of heaven. His words are truth and his works are right, and those who walk in pride he is able to make humble."

This was the story of the seven years' madness of King Nebuchadnezzar, and of his reason and his power coming back to him again.

Discussion Questions: *1. What did the king's dream mean? 2. Who had commanded that this happen to the king? 3. What did Daniel say the king could do to avoid it? 4. Did everything happen as Daniel said?*

DAY 187

BELSHAZZAR'S FEAST

Daniel 5:1-12

THE great empire of Nebuchadnezzar was made up of many smaller kingdoms that he had conquered. As long as he lived, his kingdom was strong, but as soon as he died, it began to fall apart. His son became king in his place, but was soon killed, and one king followed another quickly for some years. The last king was named Nabonidus. He made his son Belshazzar king with himself, and left Belshazzar to rule in the city of Babylon while he was caring for the most distant parts of the kingdom.

But a new nation was rising to power. Far to the east were the kingdoms of Media and Persia. These two peoples had become one, and were at war with Babylon under their great leader, Cyrus. While Belshazzar was ruling in the city of Babylon, Cyrus and his Persian soldiers were on the outside, around the walls, trying to take the city. These walls were so great and high that the Persian soldiers could not break through them.

But inside the city were many who were enemies of Belshazzar and friendly to Cyrus. These people opened the gates of Babylon to Cyrus. At night he brought his army quietly into the city and surrounded the palace of King Belshazzar.

On that night, King Belshazzar was holding a great feast in honor of his god. On the tables were the golden cups and vessels that Nebuchadnezzar had taken from the Temple of the Lord in Jerusalem. Around the table were the king, his many wives, and a thousand of his princes and nobles. They did not know that their city was taken and their enemies were at the very doors of the palace.

While they were all drinking wine together, a strange thing happened. On the wall there suddenly appeared a great hand, writing letters and words no one could read. Every eye was drawn to the spot, and everyone saw the fingers moving on the wall and the letters being written. The king was filled with fear. His face became pale and his knees shook. He called for the wise men of Babylon to tell him what the writing meant. He said, "Whoever can read the words on the wall shall be dressed in a purple robe, shall have a chain of gold around his neck, and shall rank next to King Belshazzar as the third ruler in the kingdom."

But not one of the wise men could read it, for God had not given them that power. At last the queen of Babylon said to Belshazzar, "O king, may you live forever! There is one man who can read this writing, a man with the spirit of the holy gods, a man whom Nebuchadnezzar, your father, made master of all the wise men. His name is Daniel. Send for him, and he will tell you what these words are and what they mean."

Discussion Questions: 1. What happened to Nebuchadnezzar's empire?
2. What were Cyrus and his soldiers trying to do? 3. What happened during King Belshazzar's feast? 4. How did the king feel? 5. Who did the queen tell him to send for?

DAY 188

DANIEL'S EXPLANATION

Daniel 5:13-31

DANIEL was now an old man. Since Nebuchadnezzar died, he no longer had his high place as ruler and chief adviser of the king. They sent for Daniel, and he came.

The king said to him, "Are you the Daniel my father brought here many years ago? I have heard of you, that the spirit of the holy gods is upon you and you have wisdom and knowledge. If you can read this writing on the wall and tell me what it means, I will give you a purple robe, a gold chain, and a place next to myself as the third ruler in the kingdom."

And Daniel answered the king, "You may keep your rewards and give your gifts to whom you please, for I do not want them. But I will read to you the writing. The Most High God gave Nebuchadnezzar this kingdom, great power, and glory. But when Nebuchadnezzar became proud and boasted of his greatness, the Lord took his crown and his throne and let him live among the beasts of the field until he knew the Most High God rules over the kingdoms of men. Belshazzar, you knew all this, yet you have not been humble. You have risen up against the Lord, have taken the vessels of his house, and have drunk wine in them in honor of your own gods of wood and stone. But you have not praised the Lord God who has given you your kingdom and power. For this reason, God has sent this hand to write these words on the wall. This is the writing: mene, mene, tekel, upharsin. And this is the meaning: numbered, numbered, weighed, divided.

"Mene: God has counted the years of your kingdom, and has brought it to an end.

"Tekel: You have been weighed in the balances and have been found wanting.

"Upharsin: Your kingdom is divided, taken from you, and given to the Medes and the Persians."

King Belshazzar could scarcely believe what he heard, but he commanded that the promised reward be given to Daniel. Almost while he was speaking, his end came. The Persians and the Medes burst into his palace, seized Belshazzar, and killed him in the midst of his feast.

That night the empire set up by Nebuchadnezzar came to an end. A new empire arose, one greater than that of Babylon — the Persian Empire. And in the place of Belshazzar, Cyrus, the commander of the Persians, made an old man named Darius king until he was ready to take the kingdom for himself.

This empire of Persia was the third of the empires we read about in the Bible. The first was the Assyrian kingdom, with Nineveh as its capital. This was the kingdom that carried the Ten Tribes of Israel into captivity. The second was the Babylonian or Chaldean kingdom, which carried the Jews into captivity. And the third was the Persian kingdom, which lasted 200 years, ruling all the lands named in the Bible.

Discussion Questions: *1. What did the king promise Daniel if he could read the writing on the wall? Did Daniel want them? 2. What did Daniel say about King Nebuchadnezzar? 3. What had King Belshazzar done wrong? 4. What did God promise to do? Did he do it?*

DAY 189

DARIUS'S DECREE

Daniel 6:1-9

 HE lands that had been the Babylonian or Chaldean empire now became the empire of Persia, with Darius as their king. King Darius gave Daniel, who was now a very old man, a position of much honor and power. He was the highest of the land's rulers, because the king saw he was wise and able to rule. This made the other princes and rulers very jealous, and they tried to find something against Daniel, so they could speak to the king about him.

These men knew that three times every day Daniel went to his room, opened the window that looked toward Jerusalem, and prayed to God. Jerusalem was in ruins, and the Temple was no longer standing, but Daniel prayed facing the place where the house of God had once stood, although it was many hundreds of miles away.

DANIEL PRAYED TO HIS GOD — DANIEL 6:10

These nobles thought that Daniel's prayers might give them a chance to do him harm, maybe even have him put to death. They came to King Darius, and said to him, "All the rulers have agreed to make a law saying that for thirty days, no one shall ask anything of any god or any man, except from you. If anyone prays to any god, or asks anything from any man during thirty days — except for you, O king — he shall be thrown into the den where the lions are kept. Now, O king, make the law, and sign the writing so it cannot be changed, for no law of the Medes and Persians can be changed."

The king was not a wise man, and being foolish and vain, he was pleased with this law, which would set him above the gods. So, without asking Daniel's advice, he signed the writing. The law was made, and the word was sent out through the kingdom that for thirty days no one could pray to any god or ask a favor of any man.

Discussion Questions: *1. Why did King Darius give Daniel much honor and power? 2. How did that make the other princes feel? 3. What did Daniel do every day? 4. What kind of law did the king make? Why did he make it?*

DAY 190

THE LIONS' DEN
Daniel 6:10-17

DANIEL knew the law had been made, but every day he went to his room three times, opened the window that looked toward Jerusalem, and offered his prayer to the Lord, just as he had always done. These rulers were watching nearby, and they saw Daniel kneeling in prayer to God. Then they came to the king and said, "King Darius, haven't you made a law that if anyone offers a prayer, he shall be thrown into the den of lions?"

"It is true," said the king. "The law has been made, and it must stand."

They said to the king, "There is one man who does not obey the law you have made: Daniel, one of the captive Jews. Every day Daniel prays to his God three times, just as he did before you signed the law."

Then the king was very sorry for what he had done, for he loved Daniel and knew that no one could take his place in the kingdom. All day, until the sun went down, he tried in vain to find some way to save Daniel's life. When evening came, these men told him again of the law he had made, and said to him that it must be kept. Very unwillingly, the king sent for Daniel and gave an order that he should be thrown into the den of lions. He said to Daniel, "Perhaps your God, whom you serve so faithfully, will save you from the lions."

They led Daniel to the mouth of the pit where the lions were kept and threw him in. Over the mouth, they placed a stone, and the king sealed it with his own seal and the seals of his nobles, so no one could take away the stone and let Daniel out of the den.

Discussion Questions: *1. What did Daniel do even though the king had passed that law? Do you think Daniel was brave? 2. Who told the king about Daniel? Why? 3. What did the king have done to Daniel? Did he want to do it?*

DAY 191

DANIEL SAVED

Daniel 6:18-28

AFTER sealing Daniel in the lions' den, the king went back to his palace, but that night he was so sad he could not eat or listen to music, as he usually did. He could not sleep, for all through the night he was thinking of Daniel. Very early in the morning he got up from his bed and hurried to the den of lions. He broke the seal and took away the stone, and in a voice full of sorrow, he called out, scarcely hoping to hear any answer except the roaring of the lions, "Daniel, servant of the living God, has your God been able to keep you safe from the lions?"

And out of the darkness in the den came the voice of Daniel, saying, "O king, may you live forever! My God has sent his angel, and has shut the mouths of the lions. They have not hurt me, because my God saw I had done no wrong. And I have done no wrong toward you, O king!"

DANIEL IN THE DEN OF LIONS - DANIEL 6:16-23

Then the king was glad. He gave his servants orders to take Daniel out of the den. Daniel was brought out safe and without harm because he had trusted fully in the Lord God. Then, at the king's command, they seized those men who had spoken against Daniel, plus their wives and their children, for the king was very angry with them. They were all thrown into the den, where the hungry lions leaped on them and tore them to pieces as soon as they fell to the floor of the den.

It was very cruel and unjust to put to death the men's wives and children who had done no wrong to King Darius or Daniel. But cruel and unjust as it was, such things were very common in all the lands of that part of the world. The lives of people weren't considered important, and children often suffered for their parent's crime.

After this, King Darius wrote all the lands and people in the many kingdoms under his rule: "May peace be given to you all abundantly! I make a law that everywhere among my kingdoms men fear and worship the Lord God of Daniel, for he is the living God, above all other gods, who only can save men."

Daniel stood beside King Darius to the end of his reign, and afterward, while Cyrus the Persian was king over all the lands. Daniel lived for a number of years after being saved from the lions. He had several wonderful dreams and visions that showed him what would happen many years later, including the coming of Jesus Christ.

Discussion Questions: *1. How did the king feel all night? 2. Who had kept Daniel safe? 3. What had Daniel done that had kept him safe? 4. Who did the king tell his people to worship? Why?*

DAY 192

CYRUS'S PROCLAMATION

Ezra 1:1-11

E have seen how the great empire of Assyria ruled all the lands and carried the Ten Tribes of Israel into captivity, from which they never came back to their own land. We saw, too, how the empire of Assyria fell and the empire of Babylon rose in its place under Nebuchadnezzar. As soon as Nebuchadnezzar died, the empire of Babylon began to fall, and in its place arose the empire of Persia, under Cyrus the Great. His empire was much greater than either the Assyrian or the Chaldean empire, for it ruled Egypt, all the lands known as Asia Minor, and also many lands in the Far East.

Cyrus was a friend to the Jews, who at this time were still living in the lands of Chaldea, between the Tigris and Euphrates rivers. It had been seventy years since the first company of captives had been taken away from Judah by

Nebuchadnezzar and fifty years since the city of Jerusalem had been burned. Now the Jews were no longer looked on as captives in the land of Chaldea. They lived in their own houses, tilled their own farms, and were at peace. Many of them were rich, and some of them, like Daniel and his three friends, held high places in the court of the king.

You remember that in the early days of the captivity, Jeremiah the prophet wrote a letter to those who had been carried away to Babylon, telling them that after seventy years they would come back to their own land. The seventy years were now over. The older men and women who had been taken away had died in the land of Chaldea, but their children, and their children's children, still loved the land of Judah as their own land, although it was far away.

The Lord put it into the heart of Cyrus, the king of Persia, to issue the following proclamation: "Thus saith Cyrus, the king of Persia, The Lord, the God of heaven, has given me all the kingdoms of the earth, and he has commanded me to build him a house in Jerusalem, in the land of Judah. Therefore, let those of the people of God who are among you go up to Jerusalem, and help to build the house of the Lord. And those who do not go to Jerusalem, but stay in the places where they are living, let them give to those who go back to their own land gifts of gold and silver, and beasts to carry them, and goods, and also a free gift toward the building of the house of the Lord in Jerusalem."

So the Jewish people prepared to go back to their own land. Those who were rich and noble in rank stayed in the land of Chaldea and other lands of the Persian Empire. But though they did not go back to the land from which their fathers had come, they gave large gifts of gold and silver to help those who did go. Cyrus took all the vessels of the Temple that had been taken away by Nebuchadnezzar and gave them to the Jews, to be used in the new Temple they were to build. These were plates, dishes, bowls, and cups of gold and silver — more than 4,000 in all. So, with the gifts of the king, and the gifts of their own people, and what was owned by those who went to the land of Judah, the company took away a vast treasure of gold and silver.

Discussion Questions: *1. How did King Cyrus treat the Jews? 2. How long had the Jews been in Babylon? 3. Why did some of the Jews go back to Jerusalem? What did God want them to do there?*

DAY 193

The Return to Judah

Ezra 2:1-3:7

T was a happy group of people that met together for the journey back to the land they still called home, though very few of them had seen it. There were 42,000 of them besides their servants. They traveled slowly up the Euphrates River, singing songs of joy, until they reached the northern end of the great desert. Then they turned toward the southwest and journeyed beside the Lebanon mountains, past Damascus, and through Syria, until at last they came to the land of their fathers, the land of Judah.

Despite their joy, they must have felt sad when they saw the city of Jerusalem in ruins, its walls broken down, its houses heaps of blackened stone, its once-beautiful Temple burned to a heap of ashes.

As soon as they arrived, they found the rock where the altar of the Lord had stood, the same rock where David had long ago offered a sacrifice. From the smooth surface of this rock they gathered up the stones and swept away the ashes and dust. Then they built upon it the altar of the Lord, and Joshua, the high priest, began to offer the sacrifices which had not been offered on that altar for the last fifty years. Every morning and every afternoon they laid on the altar the burnt offering, gave themselves to the Lord, and asked God's help.

From this time on, there were two branches of the Jewish race. Those who came back to the land of Judah, which was also called the land of Israel, were called Hebrews, which was an old name of the Israelites. Those who stayed in other countries — in Chaldea and throughout the empire of Persia — were called "the Jews of the Dispersion." There were far more Jews abroad than in their own land, and they were richer. Many of them went up to Jerusalem to visit and worship, and many others sent rich gifts, so between the Jewish people in their own land and other lands, there was a close friendship, and they all felt that wherever the Jews were, they were still one people.

The Jews who had been captives in the land of Babylon were now free to go wherever they chose. Besides those who went back to the land of their fathers, there were many who chose to visit other lands where they could find work. It was not many years before Jews were found in many cities of the Persian Empire. They went to Africa and to Europe, choosing the cities for their home rather than the country. In all the great cities, the "Jews of the Dispersion" were found, besides those who were living in their own land of Israel.

When the Jews came back to their land, their leader was named Zerubbabel, a word that means "one born in Babylon." He belonged to the family of David and was called a prince, but he ruled under Cyrus, for Judah (which now began to be called Judea) was a province of the great empire of Persia.

Discussion Questions: *1. How did the people feel as they journeyed back to their homeland? What did they find when they got there? 2. Do you think the people worked hard in their home? 3. Who were the Jews of the Dispersion? What did they do for the Jews in Jerusalem?*

DAY 194

THE TEMPLE REBUILDING BEGINS

Ezra 3:8-4:6

AFTER the Jews came back to their own land, they first built the altar on Mount Moriah, as we read in the last story. Then they built some houses for themselves, for winter was coming on. Early in the next year, they began to rebuild the Temple of the Lord. Zerubbabel, the prince, and Joshua, the priest, led in the work, and the priests and Levites helped. They gave money to masons and carpenters, and they paid men of Tyre and Sidon to float cedar trees from Mount Lebanon to Joppa, then they carried them up the mountains to Jerusalem for the building of the house.

When they laid the first stones in the new building, the priests stood ready with trumpets and the Levites with cymbals, to praise the Lord for his goodness in bringing them once again to their own land. The singers sang: "Praise the Lord, for he is good: His mercy endureth forever toward Israel his people."

All the people shouted a great shout as the first stones were laid. But some of the priests, Levites, and Jews were old men who had seen the first Temple while it was still standing, more than fifty years before. These old men wept as they thought of the house that had been burned and their friends who had been killed in the destruction of the city. Some wept, and some shouted, but the sounds mingled together, and those who heard from a distance could not tell the weeping from the shouting.

But these builders soon found enemies, and the work was slowed down. In the middle of the land lived the Samaritan people, some of whom were from the old Ten Tribes. Others were people who had been brought into the land by the Assyrians many years before.

These people worshiped the Lord, but they also worshiped other gods. They came to Zerubbabel and said, "Let us join you in building this house, for we seek the Lord as you do, and we offer sacrifices to him."

But Zerubbabel and the rulers said to them, "You are not with us, and you do not worship as we worship. You can have nothing to do with building the Lord's house. We will build by ourselves to our God, the God of Israel — as Cyrus, the king of Persia, has told us to build."

This made the people of Samaria very angry. They tried to stop the Jews from building, frightened them, and wrote letters to the king urging him to stop the work. Cyrus was a friend to the Jews, but he was far away carrying on a war, so he could not help them. Soon after this, he died.

Discussion Questions: *1. What did the Jews do when they first came back to their land? 2. What did they start to rebuild? 3. How did the people feel when they laid the first stones? 4. Why didn't Zerubbabel want the other peoples in the land to help rebuild the Temple?*

DAY 195

THE BUILDING STOPPED

Ezra 4:17-24

THEN a nobleman of another family seized the throne and held if for nearly a year. His name was Smerdis, but he is called Artaxerxes in the Bible. While this king was reigning, the Samaritan rulers wrote him a letter, saying: "Let it be known to the king that the Jews have come back to Jerusalem. They are building again the city which always refused to obey the kings when it was standing before. If that city is built and its walls finished, the Jews will not serve the king or pay their taxes. We are true to the king, and we do not wish to see harm come to his rule. In old times, this city was rebellious and was destroyed because of it. If it is built again, soon the king will have no power anywhere on this side of the Euphrates."

Artaxerxes wrote an answer to the chief men of Samaria: "The letter you sent has been read to me. I have had a search made of the records, and I find that the city of Jerusalem has been a strong city with great kings ruling in it, and also ruling the lands around it. I find, too, that this city did rise up and make war against the kings of empires in the past. Command the men who are building the city of Jerusalem to stop the work. Don't let it continue until an order is given from the king."

The Samaritans and other enemies of the Jews were glad to have this letter come from the great king of Persia. They went to Jerusalem and made the building of the Temple and the city stop. So the foundations of the Temple lay unfinished for several years.

Discussion Questions: *1. What did the Samaritans write to the new king? 2. What did King Artaxerxes command? 3. How did the Samaritans feel about that? How do you think the Jews felt? 4. What happened because of the command?*

DAY 196

THE TEMPLE COMPLETED

Ezra 5:1-6:22

SOON, two prophets arose in the land of Judea — Haggai and Zechariah — and they spoke the word of the Lord, telling the people to go ahead with the building. Haggai said, "Should you live in richly finished houses while the Lord's house lies waste? Go up to the mountains, bring wood, and build, and I will be pleased with you, and will bless you, says Lord. The glory of this house shall be greater than the glory of the other house, and in this place I will give peace."

Zechariah, the other prophet, said, "It shall not be by might nor by power, but by my spirit, says the Lord. The hands of Zerubbabel have laid the foundation of this house, and his hands shall finish it. He shall lay the headstone with shouts of 'Grace, grace unto it!'"

Then Zerubbabel, Joshua, and the rest of the Jews went on with the work. Soon after this, a new king began to reign in Persia, a wise man and great ruler whose name was Darius.

King Darius looked in the records of Persia and found that Cyrus had commanded the Temple to be built. He wrote a letter to the rulers in all the lands around Judea, telling them not to hinder the work but to help it, and to give what was needed for it. Then the Jews went on with the building in great joy, and it was finished twenty-one years after it had been begun, while Zerubbabel and Joshua were still ruling over the people.

The Temple built the second time was like the one built by Solomon nearly 500 years before, but though it was larger, it was not as beautiful or expensive. In front of it was an open court with a wall around it, where the people could go to worship. Next to the people's court, on higher ground, was the priests' court, with the altar and the bowl for washing. Within this court rose the house of God, with the Holy of Holies separated by a great veil. In the Holy Place, as before, was the table for bread, the golden lampstand, and the golden altar for incense. But there was no ark of the covenant, for this had been lost and was never brought back to Jerusalem. In place of the ark stood a marble block on which the high priest sprinkled the blood when he went into the Holy of Holies on the great day of atonement once each year.

Discussion Questions: *1. What did Haggai and Zechariah do? What did they tell the people? 2. What did the people of Jerusalem do? 3. What did King Darius do? 4. What did the new Temple look like?*

DAY 197

ESTHER

Esther 1:1-2:23

WHEN Darius, the Persian king, died, his son Xerxes, who the Bible call Ahasuerus, took his place on the throne. Ahasuerus was not, like his father Darius, a wise man. He had a bad temper and did many foolish acts.

The palace where the king of Persia lived was no longer at Babylon, but at a city named Shushan in the mountains of a region called Elam. There King Ahasuerus held a great feast with his nobles. When the king and his company were all drunk with wine, he sent for his queen, Vashti, to let all the nobles see how beautiful she was. Among the Persians, it was wrong for a woman to allow her face to be seen by any man except her husband. Queen Vashti refused to come to the feast so these drunken men might stare at her. This made the king very angry. He said that because Vashti would not obey him, she could not be queen any longer, and he sent her away.

After this, King Ahasuerus decided to choose another woman to be his queen. He sent commands throughout all the kingdom that they should find the most beautiful young women and bring them to the royal city of Shushan. There the king would see them all, choose the one that pleased him best, and take her as his queen. So from every land in the great empire of Persia the loveliest young women were brought to Shushan, and there they were left in the care of Hegai, the chief of the king's palace.

At that time many Jews were living in the cities of Persia, for only a small part of them went back to the land of Israel when King Cyrus allowed them to return.

There was a Jew living in Shushan named Mordecai. He belonged to the tribe of Benjamin, from the same family as Saul, the first king of Israel. With Mordecai lived his cousin, a young girl named Hadassah, or Esther, which means "star." Her father and mother had died, and she had been left alone, so Mordecai took her to his own house and brought her up as his own daughter. Esther was very beautiful, and was as lovely in her heart as she was in her face. With the other beautiful young women, she was taken to the palace to be brought before the king.

When King Ahasuerus saw Esther, he chose her to be his queen, and set the royal crown of Persia on her head. Esther was taken into the king's palace. Rooms and servants were given to her, and she lived as a queen. When the king wished to see her, he sent for her, and she came to his room. No one could go to the king or see him unless sent for. If anyone, man or woman, came before the king without being called, that person was led away to death unless the king held out his golden scepter and prevented it.

Mordecai could no longer meet his cousin Esther, for no man except the king could enter the rooms set apart for the women. But Esther could see Mordecai as he walked by her window, and she could send word to him and hear word from him through her servants. Mordecai loved the lovely young queen who was like a daughter to him, and every day he sat at the gate of the palace to hear from her.

While Mordecai was sitting by the gate, he often saw two men who were keepers of the gate whispering together. He watched them closely and found they had made a plan to kill King Ahasuerus. He sent word of this to Queen Esther, and Esther told the king about it. The men were captured and hung.

An account of their plan, of how they were found out by Mordecai the Jew, and how they were punished by death, was written in the records of the kingdom.

Discussion Questions: *1. What kind of king was Ahasuerus? Why did the queen refuse to come to his feasts? 2. What did the king decide to do? 3. Who did the king choose? 4. What did Mordecai do for the king?*

DAY 198

HAMAN'S DECREE

Esther 3:1-15

 man named Haman soon rose to great power in the kingdom. The king gave him a seat above all the other princes, asked his advice in all matters, and allowed Haman to do whatever he pleased. Of course everybody in the palace showed great respect to Haman because of his power. When he came near, all the men in the palace and the city bowed down before him, and many fell on their faces in the dust. But Mordecai was a worshiper of God, and he would not fall on his face before any man. Haman noticed that there was one man who did not bow down to him. He said to his servants, "Who is that man sitting by the gate who does not bow down when I pass by?"

MORDECAI REFUSED TO BOW BEFORE HAMAN - ESTHER 5:9

They answered, "That is Mordecai the Jew."

No one in the palace knew that Mordecai was the cousin of Queen Esther and the queen of Persia herself was a Jewess.

When Haman found that Mordecai was a Jew, he became very angry — not only at Mordecai, but at all his people. He hated the Jews, and he resolved to have revenge on Mordecai and to make all Mordecai's people suffer. Haman went in to the king and said to him, "O King Ahasuerus, there is a certain people scattered through your kingdom who are different from other people. Their laws are different from those of every other nation, and they do not keep the king's laws. It is not good to allow such people to live. If it is pleasing to the king, let a law be made that this strange people be destroyed. I will pay all the cost of putting them to death and will place the money in the king's treasury."

The king lived in his palace and never went out among his people, so he knew nothing of the Jews and believed Haman. He took off his ring with the royal seal and gave it to Haman, saying, "Do as you please. Write whatever law you wish and stamp it with the king's seal. The money is yours, and I give this strange people to you. You can do with them as you please."

Then Haman had a law written and sealed it with the king's seal, that on a certain day — the thirteenth day of the twelfth month — all the Jews in every part of Persia could be killed. Anyone who chose to kill them might do so and then take all the money, gold, silver, and garments they found in the houses of the Jews.

Copies of this law were sent to every city of the empire, so everyone would know that the Jews were to be destroyed. Everybody who heard of it was filled with wonder, for no one knew what the Jews had done to deserve death. They could not understand why the law had been made, but the enemies of the Jews made plans to destroy them and take their riches for themselves.

Discussion Questions: *1. Why didn't Haman like Mordecai? 2. What did Haman try to do to the Jews? 3. What did some of the people of that country decide to do to the Jews? Why?*

DAY 199

ESTHER'S DINNER
Esther 4:1-5:8

NEWS of this terrible law came to Mordecai, as it came to all the Jews in Shushan. Mordecai tore his clothes, put on garments of sackcloth, covered his head with ashes, and went out in front of the palace, crying a loud, bitter cry.

Queen Esther saw him and heard his voice. She sent one of her servants named Hatach to Mordecai, to find why he was in such deep trouble. Hatach came to Mordecai, and Mordecai told him of the law and gave him a copy of it to show to Queen Esther. He told Hatach to ask the queen to go to King Ahasuerus and beg him to spare the lives of her people.

Queen Esther heard Hatach's words and sent this message to Mordecai, "It is the rule of the palace that if any man or woman goes in to the king without being sent for, he will be killed unless the king holds out the golden scepter. But I have not been called to meet the king for thirty days."

When Mordecai heard this message, he sent word back to Queen Esther, "Do not think that you are safe and shall escape the fate of your people. If you keep still and do nothing to save your people, God will surely save them in some other way, but you and your father's family shall be destroyed. Perhaps God has given you your royal place for a time like this."

Then Esther sent this answer to Mordecai, "Go and bring together all the Jews in Shushan, and let them all pray for me, eating and drinking nothing, for three days. I and my maids will pray and fast at the same time. Then I will go in to the king, even though it is against the law. If it is God's will that I should die trying to save my people, then I will die."

When Mordecai heard these words he was glad, for he felt sure God would save his people through Queen Esther. For three days, all the Jews in Shushan met together, praying, and in the palace, Esther and her servants were praying at the same time.

The third day came, and Esther dressed herself in her robes as queen. She went out of her own rooms, across the open court, and entered the door in front of the throne where the king was sitting. The king saw her standing before him in all her beauty, and his heart was touched with love for her. He held out the golden rod that was in his hand. Esther came near and touched the top of the scepter. The king said to her, "What do you wish, Queen Esther? It shall be given to you, even half of my kingdom."

But Esther did not ask for what she wanted right away. She was very wise, and she said, "If it pleases the king, I have come to ask that the king and Haman come to a dinner I have made ready for them."

The king said, "Send word to Haman that he should come dine with the king and queen."

So that day King Ahasuerus and Haman sat at the table with the queen. She was covered with a veil, for even Haman was not allowed to look at her face. While they were sitting together, the king said, "Queen Esther, is there anything you want? It shall be given to you, whatever it is."

"My wish," answered the queen, "is that the king and Haman shall come again to eat with me tomorrow."

———————

Discussion Questions: *1. What did Mordecai do when he found out about the law? 2. Why was it dangerous for Esther to go to the king? 3. What did Mordecai tell Esther? 4. What did the queen ask the king and Haman to do? Why didn't she want to tell the king about the law right away?*

DAY 200

MORDECAI'S HONORS

Esther 5:9-6:14

HAMAN walked out of the palace that day happy at the honor that had come to him, but when he saw Mordecai sitting by the gate and not getting up to bow to him, all his happiness left him, and he was angry. When he came to his own house, he told his wife and his friends how the king and queen had honored him, and then he said, "But all this is nothing to me when I see that man, Mordecai the Jew, sitting at the king's gate."

His wife said to him, "That is nothing. Before you go to the feast tomorrow, have a gallows made, and then ask the king to command that Mordecai be hanged on it. The king will do whatever you wish, and then, when you have sent Mordecai to death, you can be happy at your feast with the king and queen."

This was very pleasing to Haman, and that very day, he had the gallows set up for hanging Mordecai on the next day.

It so happened that on that night the king could not sleep. He told them to read the records of the kingdom, hoping the reading might put him to sleep. They read in the book how Mordecai reported on the two men who planned to murder the king. The king stopped the reading and said, "What reward has been given to Mordecai for saving the life of the king from those men?"

"O king," they answered, "nothing has been done for Mordecai."

Then the king said, "Are any of the princes standing outside in the court?"

"Yes, O king. Haman is in the court."

Haman had come in at that very moment to ask the king to put Mordecai to death. The king sent word to Haman to come in, and as soon as he entered, said to him, "What shall be done to a man the king wants to honor?"

Now Haman thought the king wanted to honor him, so he said, "The man the king wants to honor should be dressed in the garments of the king, put on the horse the king rides, and the royal crown set on his head. Let him ride through the main street of the city, and let one of the nobles call out before him, 'This is the man the king delights to honor.'"

Then the king said to Haman, "Make haste and do all this to Mordecai the Jew, who sits in the king's gate. See that nothing is left out of what you have said."

Haman was astonished and cut to the heart, but he did not dare show it. He obeyed the king's command, sent for the king's horse, robes, and crown, dressed Mordecai like a king, mounted him on the horse, and went before him through the street of Shushan, calling aloud, "This is the man the king delights to honor!" After that, Haman hid his anger and sat down to the feast in the queen's palace. He had not said a word to the king about having Mordecai hanged.

Discussion Questions: *1. What did Haman want to do to Mordecai? Why? 2. What did the king find in the record books? 3. Why do you think Haman thought the king wanted to honor him? Who did the king really want to honor? 4. What did the king do for Mordecai?*

DAY 201

HAMAN'S DEATH

Esther 7:1-10:3

KING Ahasuerus knew very well that his queen had some favor to ask. At the feast, he said to her, "What do you wish, Queen Esther? Tell me, and I will give it to you, even if it's half my kingdom."

Esther saw that her time had come. She said to the king, "If I have found favor in your sight, and if it please you, let my life be given me, and the lives of my people. For we have been sold, and are all to be killed. If we had been sold as slaves, I would have said nothing, but we are to be slain in order to please our enemy."

The king asked, "Who is the man, and where is he, that has dared do this thing?"

"The enemy," said Queen Esther, "is this wicked Haman!"

When the king heard this, he was so angry that he got up from the table and walked out into the garden. In a moment he came back and saw Haman on his face, begging the queen to spare his life. The king looked at him in anger, and the servants at once covered Haman's face, as one doomed to death. One of the officers standing near said, "There are gallows, seventy-five feet high, that Haman set up yesterday to hang Mordecai."

"Hang Haman on it," commanded the king. So Haman died on the gallows he had made for Mordecai. That day, the king gave Haman's place to Mordecai, and set him over the princes. He gave Mordecai his own ring with its royal seal, and all Haman's family — his sons — were put to death for their father's acts.

The law about killing the Jews on the thirteenth day of the twelfth month

ESTHER SAID HAMAN IS HER ENEMY - ESTHER 7:6

had been made and sent out, and no law of the Persians could be changed. But though this law could not be taken back, another law was made that the Jews could defend themselves against any who tried to harm them. When the day came most of their enemies were afraid to harm the Jews, because now they were under the care of the king and Mordecai ruled next to the king.

Instead of sorrow and death on the thirteenth day of the twelfth month, the Jews had joy and gladness. And on the day following, the Jews kept a feast of thanksgiving for God's mercy in saving them from their enemies. The same feast was kept on that day every year afterward, and is still kept among the Jews. It's called the feast of Purim, when the story of Esther, the beautiful queen, is read by all the Jewish people.

Discussion Questions: *1. How did the king feel when he discovered what Haman had done? 2. How did he punish Haman? Who had Haman wanted to do that to? 3. What did the king do for Mordecai? 4. What happened to the law Haman had made?*

DAY 202

THE OLD TESTAMENT (PART 1)

Ezra 7:1-10:44

ROM the court of the great king at Shushan we turn back to the Jews at Jerusalem and Judea. For a long time after the first company came to the land under Zerubbabel, very few Jews from other countries joined them. The Jews in Judea were poor and discouraged. Many of them had borrowed money they could not repay and had been sold as slaves to richer Jews. Around them were their enemies, the idol-worshiping people in the land and the Samaritans on the north. These enemies robbed them of their crops and constantly sent false reports of them to the Persian governors. Many of the men of Israel had married women of the land who were not of the Israelite race, and their children were growing up half heathen and half Jewish, unable to speak the language of their fathers and knowing nothing of the true God.

Ninety years after the Jews had come back to the land, Jerusalem was a small town, with many of its old houses still in ruins and no wall around it. In those times no city could be safe from its enemies without a wall, so Jerusalem lay helpless against bands of robbers who came up from the desert and carried away nearly everything the people earned.

Just at the time, God raised up two men to help his people. These two men were Ezra and Nehemiah. Through Ezra, the people of Judea were led back to their God. About the same time, Nehemiah gave new hope, courage, and strength to the people by helping them build a wall around Jerusalem. The work of these two men brought Judea peace and plenty, and brought many Jews from other lands to their country.

Ezra was a priest living in the city of Babylon, though he came from the family of Aaron, the first priest. He was also a prophet through whom God spoke to his people. But above all, Ezra was a lover of God's book in a time when the book of the Lord was almost forgotten. Nearly all the books of the Old Testament had been written long ago, but in those days there were no printed books. Each copy was written separately with a pen. Since this was a lot of work, there were very few copies of the different books of the Bible. And these copies were in different places; one book of the Bible was in one place, another book was in another place. No one before Ezra had ever owned or seen the whole Old Testament in one book.

Ezra began to look everywhere for copies of these different books. Whenever he found one, he wrote it out and kept the copy. He also had other men copy the books as they found them. At last Ezra had copies of all the books in the Old Testament, except the very last books. They were written very nearly as we have them now, except that his copies were all in Hebrew, the language spoken by the men who wrote most of the Old Testament.

Ezra put all these different books together, making one book out of many. This great book was written on parchment, or sheepskin, in long rolls, as all books were written then. When the book was finished, it was called the Book of the Law, because it contained God's law for his people as given by Moses, Samuel, David, Isaiah, and all the other prophets.

Discussion Questions: *1. What were the Jews in Jerusalem doing? 2. What did Ezra and Nehemiah do for the people? 3. Why weren't there any copies of the Bible? 4. How did Ezra get copies of the whole Old Testament?*

DAY 203

The Old Testament (Part 2)

Ezra 7:1–10:44

WHEN Ezra finished writing this book of the law, he traveled from Babylon to Judea, taking with him the rolls of the book. With Ezra went a company of men he had taught to love the law, to write copies of it, to read it, and to teach it to others. These men who gave their lives to studying, copying, and teaching the law, were called *scribes*, a word that means "writers."

Ezra was the first and greatest of these scribes, but from then on, there were many scribes among the Jews, both in Judea and in other lands. For wherever the Jews lived, they began to read the Bible and love it. The time came, soon after Ezra's day, when every place where the Jews met to worship had at least one copy of all the books in the Old Testament. Then there was no danger that the Bible, or any part of it, would be lost.

You remember that there was only one Temple for all the Jews in the world, and only one altar. On this one altar, and only there, they offered the sacrifice every day. But the Jews in distant places needed to meet together for worship, and there grew up what became called *synagogues*, a word that means "coming together." At first they met in a room, but afterward they built houses for the synagogues, much like our churches. Some of these synagogues were large and beautiful, and the people met there every week to worship God, sing the psalms, hear the law and the prophets read, and talk together about what they had heard. It was something like a prayer meeting, for any Jew who wanted to speak in the meeting could do so. The men sat on mats laid on the floor. The rulers of the synagogue were on seats raised up above the rest. The women were in a covered gallery on one side, where they could see and hear but could not be seen. And on the end of the room nearest Jerusalem there was a large box called "the ark," within which were kept the copies of the books of the Old Testament. Through the synagogue, all the Jews in the world listened to the reading of the Old Testament until many of them knew every word by heart. All this happened because of Ezra's work copying and teaching the word of the Lord.

Ezra did another work almost as great as that of giving the Bible to the world. He taught the Jewish people — first in Israel, and then in other lands — that they were the people of God and must live apart from other nations. If they had gone on marrying women of other races who worshiped other gods, after a time there would have been no Jews and no worshipers of God. Ezra made some of them give up their foreign wives and taught the Jews to be a people by themselves, keeping away from those who worshiped idols. In this way, Ezra led the Jews to look on themselves as a holy people given to the service of God. He taught them to live apart from other nations, with their own customs and ways of living, and be very exact in obeying the laws of God.

Discussion Questions: *1. What is a scribe? 2. What happened when there were many scribes abong the Jews? 3. What was a synagogue? What was a synagogue meeting like? 4. How was the Temple different from a synagogue? 5. Why was Ezra's work important to the people of God?*

DAY 204

Nehemiah's Requests

Nehemiah 1:1-2:9

WHILE Ezra was at work finding the books of the Bible, copying them, and teaching them, another great man was helping God's people another way. This man was Nehemiah. He was a nobleman of high rank at the court of King Artaxerxes, who ruled after Ahasuerus.

Nehemiah was the cup bearer to the king of Persia at Shushan. It was his job to take charge of all the wine used at the king's table, to pour it out, and hand the cup to the king. This was an important job, for he saw the king every day at his meals and could speak with him, as very few of even the highest princes could speak. Then, too, the life of the king was in his hands, for if he were an enemy, he could have allowed poison to be put into the wine to kill the king. So the cup bearer was always a man the king trusted as a friend.

Nehemiah was a Jew, and like all the Jews, he felt a great love for Jerusalem. At one time a Jew named Hanani and his friends from Jerusalem visited Nehemiah. Nehemiah asked them, "How are the Jews in Jerusalem doing? How does the city look?"

They answered, "The people who are living in the land of Judea are very poor, and are looked down on by all around them. The wall of Jerusalem is broken down, and its gates have been burned."

When Nehemiah heard this, he was filled with sorrow for his city and his people. After the Jews left him, he sat down for days, and would eat nothing. He fasted, wept, and prayed. He said, "O Lord God of heaven, the great God who keeps his promises to those who love him and do his will, hear my prayer for the people of Israel, your servants. We have done very wickedly, and because of our sins you have scattered us among the nations. Now, Lord, give me grace this day in the sight of the king of Persia, and may the king help me do good and help my people in the land of Israel."

A few days after this, Nehemiah was standing beside the king's table while the king and queen were seated at their meal. As Nehemiah poured out the wine, the king saw his face was sad, which was not usual, for Nehemiah was cheerful, and generally had a happy face. The king said to him, "Nehemiah, why do you look so sad? You do not seem to be sick. I am sure there is something troubling you. What is it? Tell me."

Nehemiah was afraid the king might be displeased with him, but he said, "Let the king live forever! Why shouldn't my face be sad, when the city where my fathers are buried lies waste, with its walls broken down and its gates burned with fire?"

The king said, "Do you want to ask me a favor? Tell me what I can do to help you."

Nehemiah lifted up a silent prayer to God and said, "May it please the king, I would be glad if you would send me to Jerusalem with an order to build the walls."

The king said, "How long will the journey be? And when will you come back?"

Nehemiah told the king how long it would be, and he asked that he might have letters to the men who ruled the different provinces through which he would pass, so he would have a safe journey. He also asked for authority to cut wood for the beams of a house he wanted to build, for repairing the Temple, and for building the wall. The king was kind to Nehemiah and gave him all he asked.

Nehemiah, with a company of horsemen and many friends, made the long journey of almost 1,000 miles to Jerusalem. All the people were glad to have a visit from a man of such high rank, and the whole city rejoiced at his coming. But Nehemiah was sad to see how poor and helpless the city was.

Discussion Questions: *1. Why was Nehemiah's job important? 2. How did the cup bearer feel when he heard that his people were poor and Jerusalem was burned? 3. What did he say to God? 4. What did the king do for Nehemiah and the Jews?*

DAY 205

THE WALLS REBUILT
Nehemiah 2:12-3:32

ONE night, without telling any of the men in the city his purpose, Nehemiah got up with a few of his friends, and rode his horse around the city. He saw that in many places the walls were mere heaps of ruins, and gates were broken down and burned. He found great heaps of ashes and piles of stone, so that in some places his horse could not walk over them. The next day he called together the rulers of the city and the chief priests, and he said to them, "You see how poor and helpless this city lies without walls, or gates, open to all its enemies. Come, let us build the wall of Jerusalem, so people won't hold us in contempt." Then he told them how God had heard his prayer and had made the king friendly, and had sent gifts to help them.

The people and the rulers said, "Let's go to work and build the wall!" Each family in Jerusalem agreed to build a part of the wall. The high priest said he would build one of the gates and the wall beside it. Some of the rich men built a long space, others did very little, and some would do nothing. One man built just the part of the wall in front of his house. Another built only as much as fronted on his own room. One man and his daughters hired workers to build. The goldsmiths built some, and so did the apothecaries, the men who sold medicines. The merchants built a part. Almost all the men of the city, and some of the women, took part in the building, for the people wanted the wall completed.

Discussion Questions: *1. Why was it important to rebuild the walls of Jerusalem? 2. How did the Jews decide to do it? 3. How did the people feel about rebuilding the wall?*

DAY 206

The Walls Completed

Nehemiah 4:1-6:16

SOON the news spread that the walls of Jerusalem were rising from their ruins. There were many who were far from pleased when they heard this, for they hated the Jews and their God and did not want to see Jerusalem strong. The leader of these people was a man named Sanballat, who came from Samaria, where all the people were jealous of the Jews.

"What are these feeble Jews doing?" said Sanballat. "Do they intend to make their city strong? Will they pile up stones from the rubbish of the burned city?"

His servant Tobiah said, "Why, if a fox tried, he could break down their little wall!"

The Arabians from the desert, the Philistines from Ashdod on the plain, and the Ammonites from the east of Jordan saw that if the wall was built, they couldn't rob and plunder the city. They tried to form an army to attack the city and stop the building. But Nehemiah prayed to God for help, then chose watchmen to walk around the wall and watch for any enemies. Half of Nehemiah's men worked on the wall, while the other half held the bows, spears, and armor of the workers. In some places, a man would hold a spear in one hand while he spread mortar with the other. At other places, men worked with their swords hanging at one side, always ready for battle.

Nehemiah rode his horse around the wall, while his servant walked beside him with a trumpet. He said, "The work is large, and you are far apart from one another. Whenever you hear the sound of the trumpet, leave your work, take your arms, and go to the place where it sounds. The Lord will fight for us."

Since they were not strong enough to fight the Jews, Sanballat, Tobiah, and another of their leaders named Geshem, sent a letter to Nehemiah, saying, "Come and meet us in one of the villages on the plain near the Great Sea, and let's talk about this matter."

Nehemiah knew that to go to this place and return to Jerusalem would take more than a week, so he sent back this answer: "I am doing a great work, and I cannot come down. Why should the work stop so I can come down and talk with you?"

Over and over again, they sent for Nehemiah, but he refused to come. Finally, Sanballat sent a letter with this message: "It is told among all the people, and Geshem says it is a fact, that you are building this city to rebel against the king of Persia and set up a kingdom of your own. Talk with us, or trouble may come to you."

Nehemiah wrote back: "You know very well that there is no truth in these stories. You have made them up yourselves."

Some of the Jews in the city were friendly to these enemies outside, and these men tried to frighten Nehemiah. One of them made believe he was a prophet and said to Nehemiah, "Go into the Temple and hide, for in the night your enemies will come to kill you!"

"Should I run away and hide myself?" said Nehemiah. "No. I will not go."

So hard did the men of Judea work that fifty-two days after the work began, it was finished. The gates were hung and guards were placed inside so no enemy could enter. Now Jerusalem began to rise from its weakness and helplessness and become a strong city again.

Discussion Questions: *1. Why didn't the Jews' neighbors want the city's walls rebuilt? 2. Name two things Nehemiah did to keep out the enemies. 3. Why wouldn't Nehemiah meet with his enemies? 4. What did the people have to say about the enemies? 5. What did the people do to help?*

DAY 207

The Reading of the Law

Nehemiah 8:1-12

WHEN the wall of Jerusalem was finished, Nehemiah called all the Jews from the villages and cities to meet in Jerusalem. They met in an open place before the Temple. Ezra, the good priest and scribe who had done such a great work in bringing together and writing the books of the Old Testament, was in the city at that time. They asked Ezra to bring the book and read the law of the Lord to the people.

He came, carrying the great rolls on which the law was written, and stood up on a pulpit they had built so all the people could see him. With Ezra were men he had taught the law, so they could teach it to others.

When Ezra stood up in the pulpit and unrolled the scroll, all the people sitting on the ground stood up while Ezra gave thanks to the Lord who had given them his law. Then the people said "Amen!" with a loud voice, bowed until their heads touched the ground, and worshiped.

Then Ezra began to read the book aloud, so everyone could hear. Since the people did not all understand the old Hebrew tongue in which the book was written, men were chosen to stand by Ezra. As he read each sentence, these men explained it to the people. Many of the people had never heard God's law read before, and they wept as they listened to it. But Nehemiah, who was there as the ruler, said to them, "This day is holy to the Lord. Do not mourn or weep, but be glad, eat and drink, and send gifts of food to those who are in need, for you are strong in the Lord and should be joyful."

The Levites quieted the people, saying, "Hold your peace, for the day is holy. Do not weep, but be glad in the Lord."

And all the people went home to feast and be glad, because they could hear and understand the words of God's law.

Discussion Questions: *1. What did Ezra do when the wall was rebuilt? 2. What did the people do? 3. Why did Ezra tell the people to be glad? 4. Why were they glad?*

DAY 208

THE SABBATH KEPT HOLY
Nehemiah 13:15-31

AFTER the reading of the law, another great meeting was held. The people confessed their sins before God, and the sins of their fathers in forsaking God's law, and not doing his will. And all the people made a solemn promise that they would keep God's law and would do his will. They would be God's people, and not let their sons marry women who did not worship the Lord. They would keep the Sabbath holy, and they would give the Lord's house their offerings. They wrote these promises on a roll, then all the princes, rulers, and priests signed it and placed their seals on it.

Nehemiah had now finished his work in Jerusalem. He went back to Shushan and resumed pouring the wine at the king's table. But after some years, he went back to Jerusalem. He found that not all the people had fulfilled their promises to serve the Lord. The Sabbath day was not being kept as it should be. People were treading wine presses, bringing in loads of grain, selling wine, grapes, and figs on the Sabbath. Men from the city of Tyre, who were not worshipers of the Lord, brought in fish and sold them on the Sabbath.

When Nehemiah saw all these evils, he was greatly displeased, and he said to the rulers of the city, "Why do you allow these things to be done and the Sabbath to be broken? Weren't these the very things that made God angry with our fathers, so he let this city be destroyed? Will you bring God's anger on us again by doing such things on God's holy day?"

Then Nehemiah gave orders that before sunset on the evening before the Sabbath, the gates of the city should be shut and not opened until the morning after the Sabbath was over. The men came with their things to be sold and waited outside for the gates to be opened. Nehemiah looked over the wall, saw them, and said, "What are you doing here? If you come here again on the Sabbath, I will put you in prison!"

Then they went away and came no more on the holy day. By strong acts like these, Nehemiah led the people to faithful service of the Lord. And after this, Jerusalem grew large and strong, and was full of people. Jews from other lands began to come to live in the land, until it was filled with cities and towns. The hills of the land were covered with vineyards and oliveyards, and the plains waved with fields of grain.

Discussion Questions: *1. What did the people do at the great meeting? 2. What did they promise God? 3. Did they keep their promise to God? 4. What had they done wrong? Who told them about it?*

DAY 209

ZACHARIAS'S VISION

Luke 1:1-22

AT the time the story of the New Testament begins, the land of Israel (also called the land of Judea) was ruled by a king named Herod. He was the first of several Herods who ruled either the whole land or parts of it. But Herod was not the highest ruler. Many years before this time, the Romans had won all the lands around the Great Sea, which we call the Mediterranean. Above King Herod of Judea was the great king at Rome. So Herod, though king of Judea, obeyed his overlord, the emperor at Rome. At the time this story begins, the emperor at Rome was named Augustus Caesar.

At this time, the land where the Jews lived was full of people. Jerusalem was its largest city, and in Jerusalem was the Temple of the Lord, which King Herod had begun to rebuild to take the place of the old Temple built in the time of Zerubbabel, which had long needed repair.

There were also many other large cities besides Jerusalem. In the south was Hebron; on the shore of the Great Sea were Gaza, Joppa, and Caesarea. In the middle of the land were Shechem and Samaria; and in the north were

Nazareth and Cana. Down by the shore of the Sea of Galilee were Tiberias, Capernaum, and Bethsaida. Far up in the north, at the foot of snowy Mount Hebron, was another Caesarea. So it wouldn't be confused with the Caesarea on the seacoast, this city was called Caesarea Philippi, or Philip's Caesarea, from the name of one of Herod's sons.

One day, an old priest named Zacharias was leading the service of worship in the Temple. He was standing in front of the golden altar of incense in the Holy Place and was holding a cup full of burning coals and incense. All the people were worshiping in the court of the Temple, outside the court of the priests, where the great altar stood.

Suddenly Zacharias saw an angel of the Lord standing on the right side of the altar of incense. He felt great fear when he saw this strange being with a shining face, but the angel said to him, "Do not be afraid, Zacharias. I have come from the Lord to bring you good news. Your wife Elizabeth shall have a son, and you shall name him John. You shall be glad, for your son John shall bring joy and gladness to many. He shall be great in the sight of the Lord, and he shall never taste wine or strong drink as long as he lives, but he shall be filled with God's Holy Spirit. He shall lead many of the people of Israel to the Lord, for he shall go before the Lord in the power of Elijah the prophet, as was promised by Malachi, the last of the old prophets. He shall turn the hearts of the fathers to the children, and those who are disobeying the Lord will do his will."

As Zacharias heard these words, he was filled with wonder and could hardly believe them. He was an old man, and his wife Elizabeth was also old. They could not expect to have a child. He said to the angel, "How shall I know your words are true, for I am an old man, and my wife is old."

"I am Gabriel, who stands in the presence of God," said the angel, "and I was sent from the Lord to speak to you and bring you this good news. But because you did not believe my words, you shall become dumb and shall not be able to speak until this comes to pass."

All this time, the people outside in the court were wondering why the priest was so long in the Temple. When he came out, they found he could not speak a word, but he made signs to them, telling them he had seen a vision in the Temple.

Discussion Questions: *1. Who was the ruler in Israel? Could he rule the people any way he wanted? Why or why not? 2. What did Zacharias see in the Temple? 3. What was Zacharias told? 4. Why couldn't Zacharias speak after he left the Temple?*

DAY 210

THE ANGEL VISITS MARY
Luke 1:26-38

AFTER the days of his service were over, Zacharias went to his own home, which was near Hebron, a city of priests in the south of Judea. When his wife Elizabeth found that God was soon to give her a child, she was very happy and praised the Lord. About six months after Zacharias saw the vision in the Temple, the same angel was sent from the Lord to a city in Galilee, which was in the north. The city to which the angel was sent was Nazareth. There the angel found a young girl named Mary, who was a cousin to Elizabeth. Mary was soon to be married to a good man from the line of King David, though he was not himself a king or a rich man. He was a carpenter living in Nazareth, and his name was Joseph. The angel came into the room where Mary was and said to her, "Hail, woman favored by the Lord. The Lord is with you!"

Mary was surprised at the angel's words, and wondered what they could mean.

GOD'S ANGEL VISITED MARY - LUKE 1:28

Then the angel spoke again. "Do not be afraid, Mary. The Lord has given you his favor, and has chosen you to be the mother of a son whose name shall be Jesus, which means "salvation," because he shall save his people from their sins. He shall be great, and shall be called the Son of God. The Lord shall give him the throne of his father David. He shall be a king and shall reign over the people of God forever, and of his kingdom there shall be no end."

But Mary could not see how all this was to happen.

And the angel said to her, "The Holy Spirit shall come upon you, and the power of the Most High God shall be over you, and the holy child you shall have shall be called the Son of God."

Then the angel told Mary that her cousin Elizabeth was soon to have a child through the power of the Lord. And when Mary heard all this, she said, "I am the servant of the Lord, to do his will. Let it be as you have said."

Discussion Questions: *1. Did God keep his promise to Zacharias? 2. Who else did the angel visit? 3. What did the angel tell her? 4. How was what Mary said different from what Zacharias had said to the angel?*

DAY 211

John Is Born
Luke 1:39-80

WHEN the angel had given his message and gone away, Mary traveled to the home of Zacharias and Elizabeth, eighty miles away to the south. When Elizabeth saw Mary, she was filled with the Spirit of the Lord and said, "Blessed are you among women, and blessed among men shall be your son! And why is it that the mother of my Lord comes to visit me? Blessed is the woman who believed that the promise of the Lord shall be made true!"

Mary was filled with the Spirit of the Lord, and she broke into a song of praise. She stayed with Elizabeth for nearly three months, and then went back to her own home at Nazareth.

As the angel had said, Elizabeth was given a son. They were going to name him Zacharias, after his father, but his mother said, "No. His name shall be John."

"Why?" they said. "None of your family has ever been named John."

They asked his father Zacharias what name he wanted given to the child. He asked for something to write on, and when they brought it, he wrote, "His name is John." All at once, the power to hear and speak came back to Zacharias. He spoke, praising and blessing God, then he sang a song of thanks to God, in which he said, "You, O child, shall be called a prophet of the Most High, to go before the Lord and make ready his ways."

MARY GREETED ELIZABETH - LUKE 1:41

When John was growing up, they sent him out into the desert on the south of the land, and there he stayed until the time came for him to preach to the people, for this child became the great prophet John the Baptist.

Discussion Questions: *1. Who did Mary visit? 2. When was Zacharias able to speak again? Why? 3. What did the old man do as soon as he could talk? What do you think he had learned?*

DAY 212

THE BIRTH OF JESUS
Matthew 1:18-21
Luke 2:1-7

SOON after John the Baptist was born, Joseph, the carpenter of Nazareth and husband of Mary, had a dream. In his dream he saw an angel of the Lord standing beside him. The angel said to him, "Joseph, I have come to tell you that Mary, the young woman you are to marry, will have a son by the Lord God. You shall call his name Jesus, which means salvation, because he shall save his people from their sins."

This told Joseph that the child was to be the King of Israel the prophets of the Old Testament had spoken of so many times.

317

Soon after Joseph and Mary were married in Nazareth, a command went out from the emperor, Augustus Caesar, for all the people to go to the cities from which their families had come, for the emperor wanted a list of all the people under his rule. Since both Joseph and Mary came from the family of David, they went from Nazareth to Bethlehem, to have their names written on the list. You remember that Bethlehem was where David was born and where his father's family had lived for many years.

It was a long journey from Nazareth to Bethlehem: down the mountains to the river Jordan, along the Jordan almost to its end, and then up the mountains of Judea to the town of Bethlehem. When Joseph and Mary came to Bethlehem, they found the city full of people who had come to have their names written on the list. The inn was full, and there was no room for them. The best they could do was go to a stable where the cattle were kept. There the little baby was born and was laid in a manger, where the cattle were fed.

Discussion Questions: *1. What did the angel tell Joseph? 2. What did that mean to Joseph? 3. Why did Joseph and Mary go to Bethlehem? 4. Where did they stay when they got there?*

DAY 213

THE SHEPHERDS' VISIT

Luke 2:8-20

THAT night, some shepherds were tending their sheep in a field near Bethlehem. Suddenly a great light shone on them, and they saw an angel of the Lord standing before them. They were filled with fear when they saw how glorious the angel was. But the angel said to them, "Be not afraid. I bring you news of great joy, which shall be to all the people. There is born to you this day in Bethlehem, the city of David, a Saviour who is Christ the Lord, the anointed king. You may see him there and may know him by this sign: He is a newborn baby, lying in a manger at the inn."

And then they saw that the air around and the sky above them were filled with angels, praising God and singing, "Glory to God in the highest. And on earth peace among men in whom God is well pleased."

While they looked with wonder and listened, the angels went out of sight as suddenly as they had come. Then the shepherds said, "Let's go at once to Bethlehem, and see this wonderful thing that has come to pass, which the Lord has made known to us." As quickly as they could they went and found

An Angel Stood Before The Shepherds - Luke 2:9

Joseph, Mary, and the little baby lying in the manger. They told Mary and Joseph how they had seen the angels and what they had heard about this baby. All who heard their story wondered at it, but Mary, the mother of the child, said nothing. She thought over all these things and kept them in her heart. After their visit, the shepherds went back to their flocks, praising God for the good news he had sent them.

Discussion Questions: *1. What did the shepherds see? What did they say to the shepherds? 2. How would the shepherds know they had found the right baby? 3. What did the shepherds decide to do? 4. Who did they find?*

DAY 214

THE BABY IN THE TEMPLE

Luke 2:21-38

WHEN the little baby was eight days old, they gave him the name Jesus, a word that means "salvation," the name the angel had told Mary and Joseph he should be named. So the very name of this child told what he would do for men: He was to bring salvation to the world.

It was the law among the Jews that after the first child was born in a family,

319

he should be brought to the Temple. There an offering would be made for him, to show that the child was the Lord's. A rich man would offer a lamb, but a poor man could give a pair of young pigeons for the sacrifice. On the day Jesus was forty days old, Joseph and Mary brought him to the Temple. Since Joseph the carpenter was not a rich man, they gave as an offering a pair of young pigeons.

JOSEPH AND MARY BROUGHT JESUS TO THE TEMPLE - LUKE 2:21-38

At that time a man of God named Simeon lived in Jerusalem. The Lord had spoken to Simeon and told him that he would not die until the Anointed King would come — the Christ. On a certain day, the Spirit of the Lord told Simeon to go to the Temple. He went, and was there when Joseph and Mary brought the little child Jesus. The Spirit of the Lord said to Simeon, "This little one is the promised Christ."

Then Simeon took the baby in his arms and praised the Lord, saying,

> Now, O Lord, thou mayest let thy servant depart,
> According to thy word, in peace.
> For my eyes have seen thy salvation,
> Which thou hast given before all the peoples,
> A light to give light to the nations,
> And the glory of thy people Israel.

When Joseph and Mary heard this, they were amazed. Simeon gave them a

320

blessing in the name of the Lord and said to Mary, "This little one shall cause many in Israel to fall, and to rise again. Many shall speak against him, and sorrow like a sword shall pierce your heart, also." (You know this happened when Mary saw her son dying on the cross.)

When Simeon was speaking, a very old woman came in. Her name was Anna, and she was a prophet. She spent most of her time in the Temple, worshiping God day and night. She, too, saw that this little child was Christ the Lord and gave thanks to God.

Early in the life of Jesus, God showed a few people that this little child would become the Saviour of his people and the world.

Discussion Questions: *1. What does Jesus mean? 2. Why did Joseph and Mary bring the baby to the Temple? 3. What did Simeon do when he saw the baby? Anna? 4. What was God showing people?*

DAY 215

THE WISE MEN'S JOURNEY

Matthew 2:1-6

FOR some time after Jesus was born, Joseph and Mary stayed in Bethlehem with him. The little baby didn't have to stay in the stable for very long. After a few days, they found room in a house, and there, strange men from a land far away came to visit him.

In a country east of Judea, many miles away, lived some very wise men who studied the stars. One night they saw a strange star shining in the sky. Something told them that the coming of this star meant a king was soon to be born in the land of Judea. These men felt God telling them to go to Judea — far to the west of their own home — to see this newborn king. After a long journey on camels and horses, they came to the land of Judea just when Jesus was born at Bethlehem. As soon as they were in Judea, they assumed everyone would know all about the king, and they said, "Where is he that is born the King of the Jews? In the east we have seen his star, and we have come to worship him."

But no one they asked had ever seen this king or heard of him. News of their coming was sent to Herod the king, who was now a very old man. He ruled the land of Judea under the emperor at Rome, Augustus Caesar. Herod was a very wicked man, and when he heard of someone born to be a king, he feared he might lose his kingdom.

Herod decided to kill this new king to keep his own power. He sent for the priests and scribes, the men who studied and taught the books of the Old Testament, and asked them about this Christ for whom the people were looking. He said, "Can you tell me where Christ, the King of Israel, is to be born?"

They looked at the books of the prophets and said, "He is to be born in Bethlehem of Judea. The prophet has written, 'And thou, Bethlehem, in the land of Judah, art not the least among the princes of Judah, for out of thee shall come forth one who shall rule my people Israel.'"

Discussion Questions: *1. Who else visited the baby Jesus? Why? 2. Who heard about the men who were looking for Jesus? 3. Why was Herod afraid of the new king Jesus? 4. Who did Herod ask when he wanted to know where to find the king?*

DAY 216

THE FLIGHT TO EGYPT
Matthew 2:7-23

HEROD sent for the wise men from the east, met them alone, and found exactly when the star was first seen. Then he said to them, "Go to Bethlehem and search carefully for the little child. When you find him, bring me word so I may come and worship him."

As the wise men went on their way toward Bethlehem, they suddenly saw the star shining on the road ahead of them, so they followed the star until it led them to the house where the little child was. They came in and saw the little one with Mary, his mother. They knew at once that this was the King, and they fell down and worshiped him as the Lord. Then they brought out gifts of gold and precious perfumes, frankincense and myrrh, which were used in offering sacrifices, and they gave them as presents to the royal child.

That night God sent a dream to the wise men, telling them not to go back to Herod, but go home to their own land by another way. They obeyed the Lord and found another road to their own country without passing through Jerusalem, where Herod was living. So Herod could not learn from these men where the child was who was born to be a king.

Soon after these wise men had gone away, the Lord sent another dream to Joseph. He saw an angel, who spoke to him, saying, "Get up quickly. Take the little child and his mother, and go down to the land of Egypt, for Herod will try to find the little child to kill him."

The Visit of the Wise Men — Matthew 2:11

Joseph got up that same night, without even waiting for morning. He took his wife and her baby down to Egypt, where they all lived safely until Herod died.

King Herod waited for the wise men to come back to him from their visit to Bethlehem, but he soon found they had gone home without bringing him any word. Then Herod was very angry. He sent out his soldiers to Bethlehem.

On the king's orders, they seized all the little children in Bethlehem who were under the age of three and killed them all. What a cry went up to God from the mothers of Bethlehem as their children were torn from their arms and killed! But all this time, Jesus was safe with his mother in Egypt.

Soon after this, King Herod died, a very old man who was cruel to the end. Then the angel of the Lord came again and spoke to Joseph in a dream, saying, "You may now take the young child back to his own land, for the king who sought to kill him is dead."

Joseph took his wife and the little child Jesus and started back to the land of Judea. He probably wanted to return to Bethlehem, the city of David, to bring up the child. But he heard that Archelaus was ruling there and being just as cruel as his father, Herod, had been. So he took his wife and the child to Nazareth, which had been their home before the child was born. Nazareth was in the part of the land called Galilee, which at that time was ruled by another son of King Herod, a king named Herod Antipas. He was not a good man, but was not so cruel as his wicked father had been. They stayed in

Nazareth for many years while Jesus was growing up. Jesus was not the only child in their house, for other sons and daughters were given to them, too.

Discussion Questions: *1. What did Herod ask the wise men to do? 2. What did the wise men do when they saw the baby Jesus? 3. How did they know not to go back to Herod? 4. How did Joseph know to leave the country? Where did he go with his family? 5. How did Joseph know when to return to his country?*

DAY 217

JESUS AS A BOY

Luke 2:40-42

JESUS was brought to Nazareth when he was a little child not more than three years old. There he grew up as a boy and young man until he was thirty years old. We would like to know many things about his boyhood, but the Bible tells us very little. Since Joseph was a workingman, it's likely that he lived in a house with only one room, with no floor but the earth, no window except a hole in the wall, no pictures on the walls. They sat on the floor or on cushions; they slept on rolls of matting; and their meals were taken from a low table not much larger than a stool.

Jesus may have learned to read at the village school, which was generally held in the synagogue. The lessons were from rolls of the Old Testament, but Jesus never had a Bible of his own. From the time he was a child, he went with Joseph to worship in the synagogue twice every week. There they sat on the floor and heard the Old Testament read and explained while Mary and Jesus' younger sisters listened from a gallery behind a lattice screen. The Jewish boys of that time were taught almost the whole Old Testament by heart.

It was customary for Jews from all parts of the land to go up to Jerusalem to worship at least once every year at Passover, which was held in the spring. Some families also stayed for the feast of Pentecost, which was fifty days after Passover, and some went again in the fall, to the feast of Tabernacles, when for a week all the families slept outdoors under roofs made of green twigs and bushes.

When Jesus was twelve years old, he was taken up to the feast of the Passover and saw the holy city of Jerusalem and the Temple of the Lord on Mount Moriah for the first time. Young as he was, his soul was stirred as he walked through the courts of the Temple and saw the altar with its smoking sacrifice, the priests in their white robes, and the Levites with their silver trumpets. Though just a boy, Jesus began to feel he was the Son of God, and this was his Father's house.

Discussion Questions: *1. What was life like for the young boy Jesus? 2. What did Jesus learn by heart? 3. Where did Jesus go when he was twelve?*

DAY 218

JESUS FOUND IN THE TEMPLE

Luke 2:43-52

JESUS' heart was so filled with the worship of the Temple, with the words of the scribes teaching in the courts, and with his own thoughts, that when it was time to go home to Nazareth, he stayed behind, held by his love for the house of the Lord. A large number of people were traveling home together, and at first he was not missed. But when night came and Jesus could not be found, his mother was frightened. The next day Joseph and Mary hurried back to Jerusalem. They didn't think to go to the Temple, but looked for him among their friends and relatives who were living in the city. They didn't find him.

On the third day, they went up to the Temple with heavy hearts, still looking for their boy. And there they found him, sitting with the teachers of the law, listening to their words, and asking them questions. Everybody who stood near was surprised to find how much this boy knew about the word of the Lord.

His mother spoke to him a little sharply, for she felt her son had not been very thoughtful. "Child, why have you treated us this way? Don't you know that your father and I have been looking for you, and were worried?"

"Why did you look for me?" said Jesus. "Didn't you know I would be in my Father's house?"

They did not understand his words, but Mary thought about them afterward, for she felt her son was no common child and his words had a deep meaning. Though Jesus was wise beyond his years, he obeyed Joseph and his mother in all things. He went with them to Nazareth and lived happily with the plain life of their country home.

As the years went on, Jesus grew from a boy to a young man. He also grew in knowledge, wisdom, and the favor of God. He won the love of all who knew him, for there was something in him that drew all hearts, both young and old.

Jesus learned the trade of a carpenter from Joseph, and when Joseph died, Jesus, as the oldest son, took care of his mother and his younger brothers and sisters. And so, in the work of the carpenter's shop, the quiet life of a country village, and the worship of the synagogue, the years passed until Jesus was thirty years old.

Discussion Questions: *1. Why did Jesus stay behind? 2. Where did his parents find him? 3. Why were the people surprised at Jesus? 4. How did Jesus treat his parents?*

DAY 219

JOHN

Luke 3:1-11

JESUS was a young man about thirty years of age. John, the son of the old priest Zacharias, was six months older, but these two young men had never met, for one was in the north of Nazareth and the other was living in the desert on the south of Judea.

Suddenly the news went through the land of Israel that a prophet had risen up and was giving the people the word of the Lord. It was more than 400 years since God had sent a prophet to his people, and when it was known that again a man was speaking what God told him, and not what he had learned by studying the old writings, a thrill went through the hearts of all the people. From all parts of the land — out of cities and villages — people traveled to the wild region beside the river Jordan, where the new prophet was preaching the word of the Lord.

This prophet was John, the son of Zacharias. He lived in the wilderness alone with God and God's voice. Then he told the people the words God had given him. John didn't look or dress like other men. His clothing was made of rough cloth woven from camel's hair. Around his waist was a girdle of skin, and he ate dried locusts and wild honey from the trees.

This was John's message: "Turn from sin and do right, for the kingdom of heaven is at hand, and the King is soon to come." The people came to hear his words, and when they asked him, "What shall we do?" John said to them, "He that has two coats, let him give one to him that has none. He that has more food than he needs, let him give to him that is hungry."

Discussion Questions: *1. How did the people feel when they heard God had given them a new prophet? What did they do? 2. How was John different from other men? 3. What did John tell the people?*

DAY 220

JESUS IS BAPTIZED

Luke 3:12-22

THE men who collected the taxes, the publicans, asked John, "Master, what shall we do?" And John answered them, "Do not cheat the people or rob them or take more money than the law tells you to take from them."

And when the soldiers came to him, he said to them, "Do not harm anyone, or bring false charges against any. Be content with the wages paid to you."

Then some Pharisees came to John. These men made a great show of being good, worshiping often, and keeping the law of Moses. But in their hearts, they were not really good. John said to these men, "You brood of vipers! Who has told you to escape from the wrath of God that is soon to come? Turn from your sins to God, and do right. And do not say to yourselves, 'Abraham is our father,' for God is able to raise up children to Abraham out of these stones."

When men who heard the words of John wanted to serve God and do his will, John baptized them in the river Jordan as a sign that their sins were washed away. Because of this, he was called John the Baptist. Some of the people began to ask, "Isn't this man the Christ that God promised to send to rule over the people?"

John heard this and said, "I baptize you with water, but there is one coming after me who is greater than I. He shall baptize you with the Holy Spirit and with fire. He is so high above me that I am not worthy to stoop down and untie the strings of his shoes. This mighty one who is coming shall sift out the wheat from the chaff among the people. The wheat he will gather, but the chaff he will burn up with fire that no man can put out."

Nearly all the people in the land came to hear John in the wilderness and were baptized by him. Among the last who came was Jesus, the young carpenter from Nazareth. When John saw Jesus, something told John that here was one greater and holier than himself. He said to Jesus, "I need to be baptized by you, and you come to me?"

Jesus answered him, "Let it be so now, for it is fitting that I should do all things that are right."

Then John baptized Jesus as he had baptized others. And as Jesus came up out of the water and was praying, John saw the heavens opening and the Holy

JOHN BAPTIZED JESUS – MATTHEW 3:13-17

Spirit coming down like a dove and lighting on him. John heard a voice from heaven say, "This is my beloved Son, in whom I am well pleased."

Then John knew and told others that this was the Son of God, the Christ God had promised to send to the people.

Discussion Questions: *1. What kind of people asked John questions? 2. What did John do to people who wanted to serve God? 3. Was John the Christ God had promised? 4. Who came to John to be baptized? How did John know who he was?*

DAY 221

JESUS IS TEMPTED

Luke 4:1-13

FROM the earliest years of Jesus, the Holy Spirit of God was with him, growing as he grew. When he was baptized and a dove was seen hovering over him, Jesus was filled with the Holy Spirit as no man before him had been filled, for he was the Son of God. At that hour he knew, more fully than he had ever known before, the work he would do to save men. The Spirit of God sent Jesus into the desert to be alone with God and plan his work for men.

So earnest was the thought of Jesus in the desert, so full was his union with God, that for forty days he never once ate anything or felt any wish for food. But when the forty days were ended, then suddenly he became hungry and felt faint, as any other man would feel who had been without food for so long.

At that moment, Satan came to Jesus, just as he comes to us, and put a thought in his mind: "If you are the Son of God, you can do whatever you please and can have whatever you wish. Why don't you command that these stones be turned into loaves of bread for you to eat?"

SATAN TEMPTED JESUS IN THE DESERT— MATTHEW 4:1-11

Jesus knew he could do this, but he also knew this power had not been given for his own use, but that he might help others. He said to the evil spirit, "It is written in God's book, 'Man shall not live by bread alone, but by every word that comes from the mouth of God.'"

Then the evil spirit led Jesus to Jerusalem and took him to the top of a high tower on the Temple, saying to him, "Now show all the people that you are the Son of God by throwing yourself to the ground. You know it is written in the book of Psalms, 'He shall give his angels charge over you; and in their hands they shall bear you up, lest at any time you hit your foot against a stone.'"

But Jesus knew this would not be right, for it would not be done to please God, but as a trial of God's power that God had not commanded. He answered, "It is written again, 'You shall not tempt the Lord your God.'"

Again the evil spirit tried to lead Jesus into doing wrong (as he leads us all).

He led him to the top of a high mountain, and caused a vision of all the kingdoms of the world and their glory to stand before the eyes of Jesus. Then he said, "All these shall be yours. You shall be the king of all the earth if you will only fall down and worship me."

Then Jesus said to him, "Leave me, Satan, you evil spirit! For it is written, 'You shall worship the Lord your God, and him only shall you serve.'"

When Satan found that Jesus would not listen to him, he left him. Then the angels of God came to Jesus in the desert and gave him the food he needed.

Discussion Questions: 1. Was Jesus different from other men? How? 2. What kind of thoughts did Satan put in Jesus' mind? 3. How did Jesus answer him? 4. What did Satan do in the end?

DAY 222

ANDREW AND JOHN

John 1:29-41

AFTER this victory over Satan, Jesus went from the desert to the place at the river Jordan where he had been baptized. It was near a city called Bethabara, a word that means "a place of crossing," because it was one of the places where the river Jordan was so shallow that people could walk across it. The city was also called "Bethany beyond Jordan," so it would not be mistaken for another Bethany on the Mount of Olives, very near Jerusalem.

John the Baptist saw Jesus coming toward him and said, "Behold the Lamb of God, who takes away the sin of the world! This is the one of whom I spoke, saying, 'There is One coming after me who is greater than I.' This is the Son of God."

The next morning, John the Baptist was standing with two young men, his followers. They were fishermen who had come from the Sea of Galilee to hear him. One was named Andrew, and the other John. John the Baptist saw Jesus walking nearby, and he said again, "Behold the Lamb of God!"

When the two young men heard this, they left John and went to speak with Jesus, although they had not known him before. Jesus saw they were following him, and he said, "What is it that you wish from me?"

They said to him, "Master, we would like to know where you are staying, so we can see you and talk with you."

Jesus replied, "Come and see."

JESUS SAID, "FOLLOW ME" - MATTHEW 4:19

They went with Jesus and saw where he was staying, then they stayed and talked with him, and listened to his words all the rest of that day, for it was about ten o'clock in the morning when they first saw Jesus. These two young men went away from the meeting with Jesus believing Jesus was the Saviour and King of Israel. Andrew and John were the first two men, after John the Baptist, to believe in Jesus.

Each of these men had a brother he wanted to know Jesus. Andrew's brother was named Simon, and John's brother was named James. These four men were all fishermen on the Sea of Galilee. Andrew found his brother first and said to him, "We have found the Anointed One, the Christ, who is to be the King of Israel."

Discussion Questions: *1. Who was with John when he called Jesus the Lamb of God? 2. What did they do when they heard John's words? 3. What did they tell their brothers?*

DAY 223

PETER, PHILIP, AND NATHANAEL

John 1:42-51

NDREW brought his brother to meet Jesus. Jesus saw him coming, and without waiting to hear his name, he said, "Your name is Simon, and you are the son of Jonas. But I will give you a new name. You shall be called 'The Rock.' "

The word *rock* in Hebrew, the language of the Jews, was "Cephas," and in Greek, the language in which the New Testament was written, it is "Petros," or Peter. So from that time Simon was called Simon Peter, that is, Simon the Rock. So now Jesus had three followers: Andrew, John, and Simon Peter. The next day he was going back to Galilee when he met another man — Philip — who had also come from Galilee. He said to Philip, "Follow me."

Philip went with Jesus as the fourth of his followers. Philip found a friend named Nathanael, who came from a place in Galilee called Cana. Philip said to Nathanael, "We have found the one of whom Moses wrote in the law, and of whom the prophets spoke — the Anointed Christ. It is Jesus of Nazareth."

Nathanael lived near Nazareth, and he did not think Nazareth could be the home of the Christ. He said to Philip, in scorn, "Can there any good thing come out of Nazareth?"

Philip knew that if Nathanael could only meet Jesus and hear his words, he would believe in him, as the others believed. He said to Nathanael, "Come and see him for yourself."

And he brought Nathanael to Jesus. As soon as Jesus saw him, he said, "Here is an Israelite indeed, a man without evil."

Nathanael was surprised at this, and he said to Jesus, "Master, how did you know me?"

"Before Philip called you — when you were standing under the fig tree — I saw you," said Jesus.

At this Nathanael wondered all the more, for he saw that Jesus knew what no man could know. He said, "Master, you are the Son of God! You are the King of Israel!"

Jesus said to Nathanael, "Do you believe in me because I tell you that I saw you under the fig tree? You shall see greater things than that. The time will come when you will see heaven opened and the angels of God going up and coming down through me, the Son of God."

Jesus now had five followers. These men and others who walked with him and listened to his words were called *disciples*, a word that means "learners."

Discussion Questions: *1. What was Simon's other name? Who gave it to him? 2. What did Jesus tell Philip? 3. Who did Nathanael say Jesus was? What did Jesus promise him? 4. What were Jesus' followers called?*

DAY 224
THE WEDDING

John 2:1-11

A few days after Jesus met his first followers, he came with these men to a town in Galilee called Cana, to be present at a wedding. In those lands a feast was always held at a wedding, and often the friends of those who were married stayed several days, eating and drinking together.

The mother of Jesus was at this wedding as a friend of the family, for Nazareth, where she lived, was quite near Cana. Before the wedding feast was over, all the wine had been used, and there was no more for the guests to drink. The mother of Jesus knew her son had power to do whatever he chose, and she said to him, "They have no wine."

Jesus said to her, "O woman, what have I to do with thee? My hour is not yet come."

But his mother knew that Jesus would in some way help the people in their need, and she said to the servants who were waiting at the table, "Whatever he tells you to do, be sure to do it."

In the dining hall were six large stone jars, each about as large as a barrel, holding twenty-five gallons. These jars held water for washing. The Jews washed their hands before every meal and washed their feet when they entered a house, because they wore sandals. Jesus said to the servants, "Fill the water jars with water."

The servants obeyed Jesus and filled the jars to the brim. Then Jesus spoke to them again. "Now draw out some of the water and take it to the ruler of the feast."

They drew out water from the jars and saw that it had been turned into wine. The ruler did not know where the wine came from, but he said to the young man who had just been married, "At a feast, everybody serves his best wine at the beginning. Afterward, when his guests have drunk freely, he brings on wine that is not so good. But you have kept the good wine until now."

This was the first time Jesus used the power that God had given him to do what no other man could do. Such works as these were called *miracles*, and Jesus did them as signs of his power as the Son of God. When the disciples saw this miracle, they believed in Jesus more than before.

Discussion Questions: *1. Where did Jesus and his followers go? 2. What happened to the wine? What did Jesus do to it? 3. What kind of wine did Jesus make? Can he change our lives that way, too? 4. What is a miracle? Why did Jesus do them?*

DAY 225

JESUS AT THE TEMPLE

John 2:12-16

AFTER this, Jesus went with his mother and his younger brothers to a place called Capernaum, on the shore of the Sea of Galilee. But they stayed there only a few days, for the feast of the Passover was near, and Jesus went up to Jerusalem to attend it.

You remember that the feast of the Passover was held every year to remind people how God had led them out of Egypt long ago.

When Jesus came to Jerusalem, he found men in the Temple court selling oxen, sheep, and doves for the sacrifices. Other men sat at tables, changing the money of Jews who came from other lands into the money of Judea. All this made the courts around the Temple seem like a market, not a place for the worship of God.

Jesus picked up some cord and made a little whip. Then he began to drive out all the buyers and sellers. He was only one, and they were many, but he was so angry that they ran from him. He drove the men, the sheep, and the oxen. He overturned the tables and threw down the money. To those who were selling the doves, he said, "Take these things away. Don't make my Father's house a house for selling and buying!"

Discussion Questions: *1. What did the Passover remind the Jews of? 2. What did Jesus see the men in the Temple doing? What did Jesus do about it? 3. Why do you think Jesus was angry?*

DAY 226

NICODEMUS

Luke 2:18-3:17

JESUS' acts at the Temple didn't please the rulers of the Jews, many of whom were getting rich by this selling of sacrifices and changing of money. Some of the rulers came to Jesus and said to him, "What right have you to come here and do these things? What sign can you show that God has given you power to rule in this place?"

Jesus said to them, "I will give you a sign. Destroy this house of God, and in three days I will raise it up."

Then the Jews said, "It has taken forty-six years to build this Temple, and it is not finished yet. Will you raise it up in three days?"

But Jesus did not mean that Temple on Mount Moriah. He was speaking of himself, because He was God.

He meant that when they put him to death, he would rise again in three days. Afterward, when Jesus had died and risen again, his followers remembered what he had said and understood these words.

While Jesus was in Jerusalem, one of the rulers of the Jews, a man named Nicodemus, came to see him. He came in the night, perhaps because he was afraid to be seen coming in the daytime. He said to Jesus, "Master, we know that you are a teacher from God, for no man can do these wonderful things that you do unless God is with him."

Jesus said to Nicodemus, "I tell you, unless a man is born again, he cannot see the kingdom of God."

Nicodemus did not know that this meant that to be saved, we must have new hearts given to us by the Lord. He said, "Why, how can a man be born twice? How can one be born again after he has grown up?"

Jesus said to him, "I tell you truthfully, unless a man is born of water and of the Spirit, he cannot enter into the kingdom of God."

By this he meant we must be baptized and God must put his Spirit in us, if we are to become God's children. Jesus added, "As Moses lifted up the serpent in the wilderness, so must the Son of Man be lifted up, that everyone who believes in him may have everlasting life. For God so loved the world that he gave his only Son, that whosoever believes in him may not perish, but may have everlasting life. For God sent not his son into the world to condemn the world; but that the world through him might be saved."

Discussion Questions: *1. Why didn't the rulers of the Jews like what Jesus did? 2. What was Jesus referring to when he said, "Destroy this house of God, and in three days I will raise it up"? 3. What did Jesus tell Nicodemus he had to do? 4. What did he mean by that?*

DAY 227

JOHN IMPRISONED

John 3:22-30
Luke 3:19, 20
John 4:1-6

HILE Jesus was teaching in Jerusalem and in the country nearby, John the Baptist was still preaching and baptizing. But already people were leaving John and going to hear Jesus. Some of the followers of John the Baptist were not pleased when they saw fewer people coming to their master, and more going to Jesus.

But John said to them, "I told you I am not the Christ, but am sent before him. Jesus is the Christ, the King. He must grow greater, while I must grow less, and I am glad that it is so."

Soon after this, Herod Antipas, the king of the province of Galilee, put John in prison. Herod had taken for his wife a woman named Herodias, who had left her husband to live with Herod, which was a sin. John sent word to Herod that it was not right for him to have this woman as his wife. These words made Herodias very angry. She hated John, and tried to kill him. Herod himself did not hate John, because he knew John had spoken the truth. But he was weak, and he yielded to his wife, Herodias. To please her, he sent John the Baptist to a lonely prison in the mountains east of the Dead Sea, for the land in that region was under Herod's rule. There Herod hoped to keep John safe from the hate of his wife, Herodias.

Soon after John the Baptist was thrown into prison, Jesus left the country near Jerusalem with his disciples and went toward Galilee, the province in the north. Between Judea in the south and Galilee in the north lay the land of Samaria, where the Samaritans lived, who hated the Jews. They worshiped the Lord as the Jews worshiped him, but they had their own temple and their own priests. And they had their own Bible, which was only the five books of Moses, for they would not read the other books of the Old Testament. The Jews and the Samaritans would scarcely speak to each other, so great was the hate between them.

When Jews went from Galilee to Jerusalem, or from Jerusalem to Galilee, they would not pass through Samaria, but went down the mountains to the river Jordan and walked around Samaria. But Jesus walked over the mountains, straight through Samaria. One morning while he was on his journey, he stopped to rest beside an old well at the foot of Mount Gerizim, not far from the city of Shechem.

This well had been dug by Jacob hundreds of years before. It was an old well in the days of Jesus, and it is much older now, for the same well may still be seen there.

_____

Discussion Questions: *1. How did some of John the Baptist's followers feel when they saw people going to Jesus instead of John? How did John feel about it? 2. Why did Herodias hate John? What did she try to do? 3. How did the Jews and Samaritans feel about each other? 4. What was Jesus showing people when he went into Samaria?*

DAY 228

———

THE SAMARITAN WOMAN

John 4:7-42

I T was early in the morning, about sunrise, when Jesus sat by Jacob's well. He was very tired, for he had walked a long way. He was hungry, and his disciples had gone to a village to buy food. He was thirsty, too. As he looked into the well, he could see the water 100 feet below, but he had no rope to let down a cup or a jar and draw up some water.

Just at this moment a Samaritan woman came to the well with her water jar on her head and her rope in her hand. Jesus looked at her, and in one glance, he read her soul and saw all her life. He knew that Jews did not speak to Samaritans, but he said to her, "Please give me a drink."

The woman saw from his looks and his dress that he was a Jew, and she said to him, "How is it that you, a Jew, ask a drink of me, a Samaritan woman?"

Jesus answered her, "If you knew what God's free gift is, and if you knew who it is that says to you, 'Give me a drink,' you would ask him to give you living water, and he would give it to you."

There was something in the words and looks of Jesus that made the woman feel he was not an ordinary man. She said to him, "Sir, you have nothing to draw water with, and the well is deep. Where can you get that living water? Are you greater than our father Jacob, who drank from this well and gave it to us?"

"Whoever drinks of this water," said Jesus, "shall thirst again. But whoever drinks of the water that I give him shall never thirst. The water I give him shall be a well of water springing up unto everlasting life."

"Sir," said the woman, "give me some of this water of yours, so I will not thirst anymore or have to come all the way to this well."

Jesus looked at the woman and said to her, "Go home, bring your husband, and come back."

"I have no husband," answered the woman.

"Yes," said Jesus, "you have spoken the truth. You have no husband. But you have had five husbands, and the man you now have is not your husband."

The woman was filled with wonder when she heard this.

Here was a man who knew what a stranger could not know. She felt God had spoken to him, and she said, "Sir, I see that you are a prophet of God. Tell me whether our people or the Jews are right. Our fathers have worshiped on this mountain. The Jews say that Jerusalem is the place men should go to worship. Now, which of these is the right place?"

"Woman, believe me," said Jesus, "there is coming a time when men shall worship God in other places besides this mountain and Jerusalem. The time is near — it has even come — when true worshipers everywhere shall pray to God in spirit and in truth, for God himself is a Spirit."

The woman said, "I know that the Anointed One is coming, the Christ. When he comes, he will teach us all things."

Jesus said to her, "I that speak to you now am he, the Christ!"

Just then, the disciples of Jesus came back from the village. They wondered to see Jesus talking with this Samaritan woman, but they said nothing.

The woman had come to draw water, but in her interest in this wonderful stranger, she forgot her errand. Leaving her water jar, she ran back to her village and said to the people, "Come, see a man who told me everything I have done all my life! Isn't this the Christ we are looking for?"

When the woman left, the disciples urged Jesus to eat some of the food they had brought. A little while before, Jesus had been hungry, but now he had forgotten his own needs. He said to them, "I have food to eat that you know nothing of — the food of the soul. That food is to do the will of God and to work for him. Do you say to me that there are four months before the harvest? I tell you to look at the fields, and see them white for the harvest. You shall reap, and shall have a rich reward, gathering fruit to everlasting life."

Jesus meant that this woman, bad as she may have been before, was now ready to hear his words. So they would find the hearts of men everywhere, like a field of ripe grain, ready to be won and be saved.

Soon the woman came back to the well with many of her people. They asked Jesus to come to their town and stay there and teach them. He went with them and stayed there two days, teaching these Samaritans. And many of the people believed Jesus, and said, "We have heard for ourselves. Now we know that this is the Saviour of the world."

Discussion Questions: *1. Why wouldn't most Jews have talked to the woman at the well? Who did talk to her? 2. What kind of water did Jesus tell the woman about? 3. What did the woman do when she found out that Jesus was the Anointed One? 4. What happened to the people in that town because of the woman at the well?*

DAY 229

THE NOBLEMAN'S SON

John 4:46-53

FROM the village near Jacob's well, Jesus went north to Cana, the place where he had made the water into wine. The news that Jesus had come back from Jerusalem went through all that part of the land, and everybody wished to see the prophet who had done such wonders.

There was one man living in Capernaum — a town beside the Sea of Galilee — who was very happy that Jesus was back at Cana. He was a man of high rank, a nobleman at the court of King Herod, but he was in despair about his son, who was very sick and in danger of dying. This nobleman hurried up the mountains between Capernaum and Cana. He rode all night, and in the morning, when he found Jesus, he begged him to come down to Capernaum and cure his son. Jesus said to the man, "You people will not believe I am the Saviour unless you continually see signs and wonders."

"O my lord," said the father, "do come down quickly, or my child will die."

"You may go home," said Jesus, "for your son will live."

The man believed the words of Jesus and went home, but he did not hurry or ask Jesus to go with him. The next morning, as he was going down the mountains, his servants met him and said, "Master, your son is living, and is better."

"At what hour did he begin to grow better?" asked the nobleman.

"It was yesterday, at seven o'clock in the morning, when the fever left him," they answered.

That was the very hour Jesus had said to him, "Your son will live." After that, the nobleman believed in Jesus, and so did everyone living in his house.

Jesus had come to Galilee to preach to the people and to tell them of his gospel. He thought he would begin his preaching in the town of Nazareth, where he had lived so many years, where his brothers and sisters were still living, and where all the people knew him. He loved the men who had played with him when they were all boys together, and he longed to give them the first news of his gospel.

___

Discussion Questions: *1. Why did people want to see Jesus? 2. Why didn't Jesus go to the nobleman's house to heal his son? Was the boy healed as Jesus said? 3. How did the father know Jesus had healed the boy? What did everyone living in the house do? 4. Where did Jesus want to begin preaching? Why?*

DAY 230

JESUS IN THE SYNAGOGUE
Luke 4:16-22

S O Jesus went to Nazareth, and, since he had always worshiped in the synagogue, he went there on the Sabbath. He was no longer the carpenter, but the teacher, the prophet everyone was talking about, and the synagogue was filled with people eager to hear him and hoping to see him do some wonderful works. Seated on the floor before him were men who had known him since he was a little boy. Perhaps some of his own sisters were looking down from the gallery behind the lattice screen.

Jesus stood up to show that he wanted to read from the Scriptures, and the officer who had charge of the books handed him the roll of the prophet Isaiah. Jesus turned to the sixty-first chapter and read:

> The Spirit of the Lord is upon me,
> Because he hath anointed me to preach good tidings to
>   the poor.
> He hath sent me to proclaim freedom to the captives,
> And recovering of sight to the blind,
> To set at liberty those that are bruised,
> To proclaim the year of God's grace to men.

When Jesus had read these words, he rolled up the book, gave it back to the keeper of the rolls, and sat down. In the synagogue, a man stood up to read the Bible and sat down to speak to the people. He began by saying, "This day this word of the Lord has come to pass before you."

Then he showed how he had been sent to preach to the poor, to set the captives free, to give sight to the blind, to comfort those in trouble, and to tell men the news of God's grace. At first the people listened with deep interest and were touched by the kind, tender words he spoke.

Discussion Questions: *1. Why did the people come to see Jesus in Nazareth? 2. What did Jesus do in the synagogue? 3. What did the verses he read talk about? 4. What did the people do at first?*

DAY 231

JESUS REJECTED

Luke 4:23-31

BUT soon they began to whisper among themselves. One said, "Why should this carpenter try to teach us?" And another, "This man is no teacher! He is only the son of Joseph! We know his brothers, and his sisters are living here." And some began to say, "Why doesn't he do here the wonders they say he has done in other places? We want to see some of his miracles!"

Jesus knew their thoughts, and he said, "I know that you will say to me, 'Let us see a miracle like that on the nobleman's son in Capernaum.' Truthfully, I say to you, 'No prophet has honor among his own people.'

"You remember what is told of Elijah the prophet. The heavens were shut up, and there was no rain for three years and six months. There were many widows in the land of Israel at that time, but Elijah was not sent by the Lord to any one of them. The Lord sent him out of the land to Zarephath, a town near Zidon, to a widow there, and there he wrought his miracles.

"And in the time of Elisha the prophet, there were many lepers in Israel that Elisha might have cured, but the only leper that Elisha made well was Naaman the Syrian."

All this made the people in the synagogue very angry. They only came to see some wonderful work, not to hear the words of Jesus. They would not listen to him. They leaped up from their seats, took hold of Jesus, and dragged him outdoors. They then took him up to the top of the hill above the city, and they would have thrown him down to his death, but Jesus slipped quietly out of their hands and went away, because it wasn't time for him to die.

Very sadly, Jesus went away from Nazareth, for he had longed to bring God's blessings to his own people. He walked down the mountains to the city of Capernaum and taught there on the Sabbath.

Discussion Questions: *1. Why didn't the people believe in what Jesus said? 2. Why did the people really want to see miracles? 3. How did the people feel when they knew Jesus would not do a miracle? 4. How did that make Jesus feel? What did he do?*

DAY 232

THE FISHERMEN

Luke 5:1-10

YOU remember that when Jesus was by the river Jordan, a few young men came to him as followers. We read of these men — Andrew, John, Peter, Philip, and Nathanael, earlier. While Jesus was teaching near Jerusalem and in Samaria, these men stayed with Jesus, but when he came to Galilee, they went back to their homes and work, for most of them were fishermen from the Sea of Galilee.

One morning soon after Jesus came to Capernaum, he went out of the city, down to the sea, followed by a great throng of people who had come to see and hear him. On the shore were two fishing boats, one of which belonged to Simon and Andrew, the other to James and John and their father, Zebedee. The men were not in the boats, but were washing their nets nearby.

Jesus stepped into the boat that belonged to Simon Peter and his brother Andrew and asked them to push it out a little into the lake, so he could talk to the people without being crowded too closely. They pushed it out, then Jesus sat in the boat and spoke to the people as they stood on the beach. After he had finished speaking to the people and had sent them away, he said to Simon Peter, "Put out into the deep water and let down your nets to catch some fish."

"Master," said Simon, "we have been fishing all night and have caught nothing. But if it is your will, I will let down the net again." They did as Jesus told them, and the net caught so many fish that Simon and Andrew could not pull it up, and it was in danger of breaking. They made signs to James and John, who were in the other boat, for them to come and help them. They came, lifted the net, and poured out the fish. There were so many of them that both boats were filled and began to sink.

When Simon Peter saw this, he was struck with wonder and felt this was by the power of God. He fell down at the feet of Jesus, saying, "O Lord, I am full of sin, and am not worthy of all this! Leave me, O Lord."

But Jesus said to Simon and the others, "Fear not. Follow me, and I will make you fishers of men."

Discussion Questions: *1. Where were the followers of Jesus when he went to Galilee? 2. Why did Jesus get into a boat to preach? 3. What did Jesus tell Peter to do? What happened when the fisherman obeyed him? 4. What did Jesus promise to make Peter?*

DAY 233

The Evil Spirit

Luke 4:33-41

FROM then on, Simon, Andrew, James, and John gave up their nets and their work and walked with Jesus as his disciples.

On the Sabbath after this, Jesus and his disciples went together to the synagogue and spoke to the people. They listened to him and were surprised at his teaching. Scribes always repeated what other scribes had said before, but Jesus never spoke about what other men had said. He spoke in his own name, saying, "I say to you," as one who had the right to speak. Men felt Jesus was speaking to them as God.

On one Sabbath while Jesus was preaching, a man came into the synagogue who had an evil spirit. Sometimes evil spirits came into men, lived in them, and spoke from them. The evil spirit in this man cried out, "Let us alone, Jesus of Nazareth! What have we to do with you? Have you come to destroy us? I know you, and I know you are the Holy One of God!"

Then Jesus spoke to the evil spirit in the man. "Be still, and come out of this man!"

Then the evil spirit threw the man down, and it seemed as if he would tear him apart, but he came out and left the man lying on the ground.

All the people were amazed. They were filled with fear, and said, "What mighty word is this? This man speaks to evil spirits, and they obey him!"

After the meeting in the synagogue, Jesus went into the house where Simon Peter lived. There he saw the mother of Simon's wife, who was very ill with a fever. He stood over her and touched her hand. At once the fever left her; she got up from her bed and waited on them.

At sunset, the Sabbath was over. Then they brought Jesus all the people who were sick or had evil spirits in them. Jesus laid his hands on the sick and they became well. He drove out the evil spirits by a word, and would not allow them to speak.

Discussion Questions: *1. What did Simon, Andrew, James, and John do? 2. Why were the people surprised at what Jesus said? 3. What happened to the man with the evil spirit? What did Jesus do? 4. Why did many people come to see Jesus?*

DAY 234

THE LEPER

Matthew 8:1-4

AFTER the great day of teaching and healing, Jesus lay down to rest in the house of Simon Peter. But very early the next morning, before it was light, he got up and went out of the house to a place where he could be alone, and there for a long time he prayed to God. Soon Simon and the other disciples missed him. They looked for him until they found him, then said, "Everybody is looking for you. Come back to the city."

But Jesus said, "No, I cannot stay in Capernaum. There are other places I must preach the kingdom of God, for this is the work I have been sent to do."

And Jesus went out through all the towns in that part of Galilee, preaching in the synagogues, healing all kinds of sickness, and casting out the evil spirits. His disciples were with him, and great crowds followed him. They came to hear his wonderful words and see his wonderful works.

THE PEOPLE WERE AMAZED AS THEY LISTENED TO JESUS - MARK 1:22

While he was on this journey of preaching in Galilee, a leper came to him. You remember, from the story of Naaman the Syrian, what a terrible disease leprosy was, and that no man could cure a leper.

This poor leper fell down before the feet of Jesus and cried out, "O Lord, if

344

you are willing, I know you can make me well and clean!"

Jesus was full of pity for this poor man. He reached out his hand touched him, and said, "I am willing. Be clean!" And in a moment, all the scales of leprosy fell away, his skin became pure, and the leper stood up a well man. Jesus said to him, "Do not tell anyone. Go to the priests and offer the gift the law commands, and let them see you have been cured."

Jesus said this because he knew that if the man told everyone how he had been cured, crowds would come to him for healing, and he would have no time for preaching the word of God. Preaching God's word, not healing the sick, was Jesus' work.

But this leper did not obey the command of Jesus. He could not keep still, and he told everybody he knew that Jesus, the great prophet, had taken away his leprosy.

As Jesus had expected, great crowds gathered in all the towns and villages to see Jesus and to ask him to heal their sick. Jesus could not enter the cities to preach the gospel. He went out to the fields in the open country, followed by crowds of people.

_____

Discussion Questions: *1. Why did Jesus want to be alone? 2. Why did Jesus leave Capernaum? 3. Why did Jesus tell the healed leper not to tell anyone what he had done? 4. What else did Jesus want to do?*

DAY 235

THE MAN WITH PALSY

Matthew 9:1-9

AFTER a time, Jesus came again to Capernaum, which was now his home. As soon as the people heard he was there, they came in great crowds to see and hear him. They filled the house, the courtyard inside its walls, and even the streets around it, while Jesus sat in the open court of the house and taught them. It was spring, and warm, and a roof had been placed over the court as a shelter from the sun.

In the crowd listening to Jesus were not only his friends, but some that were his enemies: Pharisees — men making a great show of serving God, but wicked in their hearts — and scribes who taught the law, but were jealous of this new teacher whose words were so far above theirs. These men were watching to find some evil in Jesus, so they might lead the people away from him.

While Jesus was teaching and these men were listening, the roof was suddenly taken away above their heads. They looked up and saw a man being let down in a bed by four men on the walls above.

This man had a sickness called palsy, which made his arms and legs shake all the time and kept him from standing or walking. He was so eager to come to Jesus that these men, finding they could not carry him through the crowd, had lifted him up to the top of the house, opened the roof, and let him down in his bed before Jesus.

This showed that they believed without a doubt that Jesus could cure this man from his palsy. Jesus said to the man, "My son, be of good cheer. Your sins are forgiven!"

The enemies of Jesus who were sitting near heard these words, and they thought (though they did not speak it aloud), "What wicked things this man speaks! He claims to forgive sins! Who except God himself has power to say, 'Your sins are forgiven?' "

Jesus knew their thoughts, and he said, "Why do you think evil in your hearts? Which is the easier to say, 'Your sins are forgiven,' or 'Rise up and walk?' But I will show you that while I am on earth as the Son of man, I have the power to forgive sins."

Then he spoke to the palsied man on his couch before them. "Rise up, take up your bed, and go to your house!"

At once, new life and power came to the palsied man. He stood on his feet, rolled up the bed, placed it on his shoulders, and walked out through the crowd, which opened to make a way for him. The man went, strong and well, to his own house, praising God as he walked.

By this Jesus had shown that as the Son of God, he had the right to forgive the sins of men.

These enemies of Jesus could say nothing, but in their hearts they hated him more than ever, for they saw the people believed in Jesus. They praised the Lord God, and felt fear toward one who could do such mighty works, and they said, "We have seen strange things today!"

Discussion Questions: *1. Why did Jesus' enemies come to listen to him? 2. Why did the sick man's friends lower him through the roof? 3. What did Jesus say when he healed the man? Why did that upset his enemies? 4. What had Jesus shown everyone?*

DAY 236

The Pool of Bethesda

John 5:1-18

WHILE Jesus was living in Capernaum, Passover drew near, and Jesus went up to Jerusalem to keep the feast, as he had kept it a year before. You remember that at that time he drove out of the Temple the people who were buying and selling. The feast Jesus now kept was the second Passover in the three years of Jesus' preaching.

While Jesus was at Jerusalem, he saw a pool called Bethesda. Beside this pool were five arches (or porches), and in these porches were a great crowd of sick, blind, helpless, and crippled people. At certain times, the water rose and bubbled up in the pool, and it was believed that at these times it had power to cure diseases. We know there are springs of water that will cure many kinds of sickness, and this may have been one of these.

On the Sabbath, Jesus walked among these poor, helpless, suffering people who were waiting for the water to rise. Jesus looked at one man, and though no one told him, he knew this man had been a cripple for almost forty years. He said to this man, "Do you wish to be made well?"

The man did not know who Jesus was. He answered, "Sir, I cannot walk,

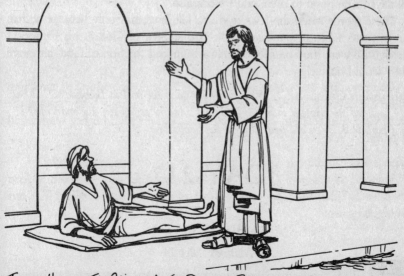

JESUS HEALED THE CRIPPLE AT THE POOL OF BETHESDA - JOHN 5:2-9

347

and I have no man to carry me down to the water when it rises in the pool. While I am trying to crawl down, others crowd in before me, and the place is full, so I cannot reach the water and be cured."

Jesus said to the man, "Rise, take up your bed, and walk!"

The cripple had never heards words like these before, but as they were spoken, he felt new power shoot through his limbs. He rose up, took the piece of matting on which he had been lying, rolled it up, and walked away toward his home!

Someone who saw him said, "Stop. This is the Sabbath, and it is against the law for you to carry your bed!"

The man did not lay down his load. He only said, "The one who made me well said to me, 'Take up your bed and walk.' "

The Jews said, "Who was this man that told you to carry your bed on the Sabbath?"

The man who had been cured did not know who it was that had cured him. There were many people standing near, and Jesus, after healing the man, had walked away without being noticed. But after this, Jesus met this man in the Temple and said to him, "You have been made well. Do not sin against God anymore, or something worse than disease will come to you."

The man went away from the Temple and told the Jews that it was Jesus who had made him well. The Jews were very angry at Jesus because he had cured this man on the Sabbath. But Jesus said to them, "My Father works on all days to do good to men, and I work also."

These words made the Jews ready to kill Jesus, not only because he had broken the Sabbath, but because he had spoken of God as his Father, as though he were the Son of God. He was indeed the Son of God, although they would not believe it.

Discussion Questions: *1. Why did people go to the pool at Bethesda? 2. What did Jesus tell the crippled man? 3. Why did someone try to stop the man after he was healed? 4. Why did Jesus heal on the Sabbath?*

DAY 237

THE SABBATH

Matthew 12:1-14

 FTER the feast of the Passover, Jesus went again to Capernaum in Galilee, beside the lake. One Sabbath he was walking with his disciples through the fields of ripe grain. The disciples, as they walked, picked the heads of grain, rubbed them in their hands, blew away the chaff, and ate the kernels of wheat. The law of the Jews allowed anyone walking through the fields to eat what he could gather with his hands, though it did not allow him to take any of the grain home. But the Pharisees, whose goodness was all for show, said it was a breaking of the Sabbath to pick the ears and rub them in the hands on the Sabbath. They said to Jesus, "Do you see how your disciples are doing on the Sabbath what is against the law?"

Jesus answered them, "Have you never read what David did when he was hungry? He went into the house of God, took the holy bread from the table, ate some of it, and gave some to his men, though the law said that only the priests might eat this bread. And do you not know that on the Sabbath the priests in the Temple work, killing and offering the sacrifices, yet they do no wrong? I say to you that one greater than the Temple is here, for the Son of man is lord of the Sabbath."

Jesus meant them to understand that he was the Son of God, that God lived in him even more fully than he lived in the Temple, and that he spoke as Lord of all.

On another Sabbath, Jesus went to the synagogue. A man was there whose hand was withered. The Pharisees watched Jesus, to see whether he would

JESUS HEALED THE MAN WITH THE WITHERED HAND – MARK 3:1-5

make his hand well on the Sabbath. Not that they felt for the poor man; they only wished to find some opportunity to speak against Jesus. Jesus knew all their thoughts, and he spoke to the man. "Rise up, and stand where all can see you!"

The man rose up from the mat where he had been sitting and stood before all the people. Then Jesus looked around them sternly, sad because their hearts were so hard and cruel, and he said, "Is it against the law to do good on the Sabbath or to do evil? to heal a man, or to try to kill a man, as you are doing? If anyone of you owns a sheep and it falls into a pit on the Sabbath, doesn't he save it? Isn't a man worth more than a sheep? I tell you that it is right to do good to men on the Sabbath."

And then, turning to the man, he said, "Stretch out your hand!"

The man obeyed the word of Jesus and held out his hand. At once it became strong and well, like his other hand. Many of the people were glad as they saw this, but the Pharisees, who hated Jesus, went out very angry and met together to make a plan for putting Jesus to death.

Discussion Questions: *1. What is a Sabbath? 2. What did the disciples do on the Sabbath? 3. Why did the Pharisees think this was wrong? 4. What did Jesus mean when he said, "One greater than the Temple is here, for the Son of man is lord of the Sabbath?" 5. Why did Jesus heal people on the Sabbath?*

DAY 238

MATTHEW CALLED

Mark 2:13-16

AMONG the Jews there was one class of men who were hated and despised more than any other: the publicans. These were the men who collected the tax the Roman rulers laid on the land. Many of these publicans were selfish, grasping, and cruel. They robbed the people, taking more than was right. Some of them were honest men, dealing fairly and taking no more than was owed, but because so many were wicked, all publicans were hated and were called sinners by the people.

One day when Jesus was going out of Capernaum to the seaside, followed by a great crowd of people, he passed a publican who was seated at his table taking money from the people who came to pay their taxes. This man was named Matthew or Levi, for many Jews had two names. Jesus could look into the hearts of men, and he saw that Matthew might help him as one of his disciples. He looked at Matthew and said, "Follow me!"

At once the publican got up from his table and left it to go with Jesus. All the people wondered when they saw one of the hated publicans with the disciples, but Jesus knew that Matthew would eventually do something that would help the world.

Many years after this, Matthew wrote the Gospel according to Matthew, a book that tells us so much about Jesus and gives us the words that Jesus spoke to the people. Jesus chose Matthew knowing he would write this book. A little while after Jesus called him, Matthew made a great feast for Jesus at his house. He invited many publicans and others the Jews called sinners. The Pharisees saw Jesus sitting among these people, and they said with scorn to his disciples, "Why does your Master sit at the table with publicans and sinners?"

Discussion Questions: *1. Why did people hate the publicans? What did many of the publicans do? 2. Why did Jesus choose the publican Matthew as a disciple? 3. What did Matthew do as soon as Jesus called him?*

DAY 239

THE APOSTLES ARE CALLED

Luke 6:12-49

JESUS heard what these men had said, and he said, "Those that are well do not need a doctor to cure them, but those that are sick do need one. I go to these people because they know that they are sinners and need to be saved. I came not to call those who think themselves to be good, but those who wish to be made better."

One evening Jesus went alone to a mountain not far from Capernaum. A crowd of people and his disciples followed him, but Jesus left them all and went up to the top of the mountain, where he could be alone. He stayed there all night, praying to God. In the morning, out of all his followers, he chose twelve men to walk with him, listen to his words, and learn to teach others in turn. Some of these men he had called before, but now he called them again, along with some others. They were called The Twelve, or the disciples.

After Jesus went to heaven, they were called the *Apostles*, a word that means "those who were sent out," because Jesus sent them out to preach the gospel to the world.

The names of the twelve disciples were: Simon Peter and his brother Andrew; James and John, the two sons of Zebedee; Philip of Bethsaida and Nathanael, who was also called Bartholomew; Thomas, who was also called Didymus, and Matthew, the publican; another James, who was called James the Less, to keep his name apart from the first James, the brother of John; and Lebbeus, who was also called Thaddeus. Lebbeus was called also Judas, but he was a different man from another Judas, whose name is always given last. The eleventh man was another Simon, who was called the Cananaen, or Simon Zelotes; and the last name was Judas Iscariot, who was the traitor. We know very little about most of these men, but some of them later did great works. Simon Peter was a leader among them, and John, when he was a very old man, wrote one of the most wonderful books in all the world: the Gospel according to John, the fourth of the gospels.

In the sight of all the people who had come to hear Jesus, Jesus called these twelve men to stand by his side. Then he preached to these disciples and the great company of people. Jesus sat down, the disciples stood beside him, and the great crowd of people stood in front, while Jesus spoke. What he said on that day is called the Sermon on the Mount. Matthew wrote it down, and you can read it in his gospel, in the fifth, sixth, and seventh chapters.

JESUS TAUGHT FROM UP ON THE MOUNTAIN - MATTHEW 5-7

Discussion Questions: *1. Who did Jesus go to? Why? 2. Why did Jesus want to be alone? What did he do? 3. Name as many of the twelve disciples as you can remember, then check back in the book if you can't remember them. Who were all twelve?*

DAY 240

The Centurion

Luke 7:1-10

There was in Capernaum an officer of the Roman army, a man who led a company of 100 men. They called him a *centurion*, a word that means "having a hundred," but we should call him a captain. This man was not a Jew, but was what the Jews called a Gentile, a foreigner, a name the Jews gave to all people outside their own race. Anyone who was not a Jew was a Gentile.

This Roman centurion was a good man who loved the Jews because they had taught him about God and how to worship him. Out of his love for the Jews, he had built with his own money a synagogue, which may have been the synagogue where Jesus taught on the Sabbath.

The centurion had a young servant he loved greatly. This boy was very sick, and near to death. The centurion had heard that Jesus could cure the sick, so he asked the chief men of the synagogue to go to Jesus and ask him to come and cure his young servant.

The elders spoke to Jesus just as he returned to Capernaum after the Sermon on the Mount. They asked Jesus to go with them to the centurion's house, and they said, "He is a worthy man, and it is fitting that you should help him, for though a Gentile, he loves our people, and he has built for us our synagogue."

Then Jesus said, "I will go and heal him."

But while he was on his way, the centurion sent some other friends to Jesus with this message, "Lord, do not take the trouble to come to my house. I am not worthy that one so high should come under my roof, and I did not think I was worthy to go and speak to you. But speak only a word where you are, and my servant shall be made well. For I also am a man under orders. I have soldiers under me, and I say to one, 'Go,' and he goes, and to another, 'Come,' and he comes, and to my servants, 'Do this,' and he does it. You, too, have power to speak and be obeyed. Speak the word, and my servant will be cured."

When Jesus heard this, he wondered at this man's faith. He turned to the people following him and said, "In truth I say to you, I have not found such faith as this in all Israel!"

Then he spoke to the friends of the centurion. "Go and say this to this man, 'As you have believed in me, so shall it be done to you.'"

Then those who had been sent went back to the centurion's house and found that in that same hour, his servant had been made perfectly well.

Discussion Questions: *1. What is a centurion? 2. What is a Gentile? 3. Why didn't the centurion go to Jesus himself? Who did he send first? 4. What did the centurion say in his second message to Jesus? 5. Why did the centurion's message surprise Jesus? What did it show about the centurion?*

DAY 241

THE WOMAN AT THE FEAST
Luke 7:36-50

N the day after this, Jesus, with his disciples and many people, traveled from Capernaum to a city called Nain. Just as Jesus and his disciples came near the gate of the city, they were met by people carrying out the body of a dead man to be buried. He was a young man, and the only son of his mother, who was a widow. All the people felt sad for this woman who had lost her only son.

When the Lord Jesus saw the mother in her grief, he pitied her and said, "Do not weep."

He drew near and touched the frame on which they were carrying the body, which was wrapped with long strips of linen. The bearers looked with wonder at this stranger, set down the frame with its body, and stood still. Standing beside the body, Jesus said, "Young man, I say to you, Rise up!"

In a moment, the young man sat up and began to speak. Jesus gave him to his mother, who now saw that her son was alive again.

Great fear came on all who looked on this wonderful work of Jesus. They praised God and said, "God has indeed come to his people and has given us a great prophet!"

And the news that Jesus had raised a dead man to life again went through all the land.

While Jesus was on this journey through southern Galilee, at one place a Pharisee whose name was Simon asked Jesus to come and dine at his house. This man did not believe in Jesus, but he wanted to watch him, and, if possible, find some fault in him. He did not show Jesus the respect due to a guest, did not welcome him or bring water to wash Jesus' feet, as was done to people when they came in from walking.

THE POOR WIDOW'S SON IS RESTORED TO LIFE BY JESUS - LUKE 7:12-15

At meals they did not sit up around the table, but leaned on couches, with their heads toward the table and their feet away from it. While Jesus was leaning on his couch at the table, a woman came into the room, bringing a flask of ointment that was used to anoint people of high rank. She knelt down at the feet of Jesus, weeping, and began to wet his feet with her tears, then to wipe them with her long hair. She anointed his feet with the ointment and kissed them over and over again.

THE WOMAN POURED THE PRECIOUS PERFUME ON JESUS - MATTHEW 26:7

This woman had not been a good woman. She had led a wicked life. But by her act, she showed that in her heart she was truly sorry for her sins. When Simon the Pharisee saw her at the Saviour's feet, he thought to himself, "If this man were really a prophet coming from God, he would have known how wicked this woman is, and he would not have allowed her to touch him."

Jesus knew this man's thoughts, and he said, "Simon, I have something to say to you."

And Simon said, "Master, say on."

Then Jesus said, "There was a certain lender of money. One man owed him 500 shillings, and the other owed him fifty. When he found that they could not pay their debts, he freely forgave them and let them both go free. Which of these two will love that man most?"

"Why," said Simon, "I suppose that the one he forgave the most will love him the most."

"You are right," said Jesus. Then he turned toward the woman, and added, "Do you see this woman? I came into your house. You gave me no water for my feet, but she has wet my feet with her tears and wiped them with her hair. You gave me no kiss of welcome, but she has not ceased to kiss my feet. You did not anoint my head with oil, but she has anointed my feet with ointment. You have acted as though you owed me little, and you have loved me little, but she feels that she owes me much, and she loves me greatly. I say to you, her sins, which are many, are forgiven."

Then he spoke to the woman, "Your sins are forgiven."

Those who were around the table whispered to one another, "Who is this man that dares to act like God and forgive sins?"

But Jesus said to the woman, "Your faith has saved you. Go in peace!"

And Jesus went through that part of Galilee, preaching and teaching in all the villages, telling the people everywhere the good news of the kingdom of God.

———————

Discussion Questions: *1. What did Jesus do for the young man from Nain? 2. How did the people feel when they saw this? 3. Why did the woman love Jesus more than Simon did? What was Jesus trying to teach Simon? 4. What was Jesus saying to the people when he told the women he had forgiven her sins?*

DAY 242

THE PARABLE OF THE SOWER (PART 1)
Luke 8:4-8

AFTER Jesus had journeyed through the southern parts of Galilee teaching and healing the sick, he went back to Capernaum. One day he went out of the city to a place where the beach rose up gently from the water. There he sat in Simon Peter's boat, as he had sat before, and spoke to a great crowd of people who stood on the beach.

At this time Jesus began teaching the people by parables — stories that showed the truths of the gospel. Everybody liked to hear a story, and the story would often lead people to think and find out the truth for themselves. The first of these parables that Jesus gave was called the Parable of the Sower.

"Listen to me," said Jesus. "A sower went out to sow his seed. And as he sowed, some seeds fell by the roadside, where the ground was hard, where some of the seeds were trodden down, and other seeds were picked up by the birds. Some of the seed fell where the soil was thin, because rocks were under it. These seeds grew up quickly, but when the sun became hot, they were scorched and dried up, because they did not have enough soil and moisture for their roots. Other seeds fell among briars and thorns, and the thorns kept them from growing. And some seeds fell into good ground, and brought forth fruit, thirty times as many as were sown, sixty times, and even 100 times. Whoever has ears to hear this, let him hear!"

Discussion Questions: *1. What is a parable? 2. Which parable did Jesus tell in this story? 3. Name some of the kinds of soil the seed fell on.*

DAY 243

THE PARABLE OF THE SOWER (PART 2)
Luke 8:9-15

WHEN Jesus was alone with his disciples, they said to him, "Why do you speak to the people in parables? What does this parable about the man sowing his seeds mean?"

Jesus said to them, "To you it is given to know the deep things of the kingdom of God, because you seek to find them out. But to many, these things are spoken in parables, for they hear the story, but do not try to find out what it means. They have eyes, but they do not see, and they have ears, but they do not hear. For they do not wish to understand with the heart, turn to the Lord, and have their sins forgiven them. But blessed are your eyes, for they see, and your ears, for they hear. Listen now to the meaning of the parable of the sower.

"The sower is the one who speaks the word of God, and the seed is the word he speaks. The seeds by the roadside are those who hear. But the evil one comes and snatches away the truth, so they forget it. The seed on the rock are those who hear the word with joy, but have no root in themselves, and their goodness lasts only for a little time. That which is sown among the thorns are they who hear, but the cares of the world, and seeking after riches and the enjoyments of this life, crowd out the gospel from their lives, so it does them little good. But that which is sown on the good ground are they who take the word into an honest and good heart, and keep it, and bring forth fruit in their lives."

Discussion Questions: *1. Why did Jesus use parables? 2. Who was the sower? What was the seed? 3. What does the parable mean? Do you understand it?*

DAY 244

MORE PARABLES OF JESUS

Matthew 13:1-50

ANOTHER parable Jesus told to the people was the Parable of the Tares.

"The kingdom of God is as a man sowing good seed in his field. But while people were asleep, his enemy came and sowed tares, or weeds, among the wheat, and then went away. When the shoots of grain began to have heads of wheat, the tares were seen among them. The servants of the farmer came to him and said, 'Sir, didn't you sow good seed in your field? How did the tares come into it?'

"He said to them, 'An enemy has done this.'

" 'Shall we go and pick out the tares from among the wheat?' asked the servants.

" 'No,' answered the farmer, 'for while you are pulling up the tares, you will also root up the wheat with them. Let both grow together until the harvest. In the time of the harvest, I will say to the reapers, "Take out the tares first, and bind them in bundles, to be burned, but gather the wheat into my barn.' ' "

Another parable was that of the Mustard Seed. He said: "The kingdom of heaven is like a grain of mustard seed, which a man took and sowed in his field. This is the smallest of all seeds, but it grows up to be a large bush, almost a tree, so the birds of the air light on its branches and rest under its shadow."

Another parable was the Leaven, or Yeast: "The kingdom of heaven is like a little leaven, or yeast, that a woman mixed with dough when she was making bread. It worked through all the dough and changed it into good, light bread."

These parables Jesus told to the people as he sat in the boat and the people stood on the shore. But he did not tell them what the parables meant, for he wanted them to think out the meaning for themselves. After giving the parables, he sent the people away and came back to the house in the city. There his disciples said to him, "Tell us the meaning of the parable of the tares growing in the field."

Jesus said to them, "The one who sows the good seed is the Son of man. The field is the world. The good seed are those who belong to the kingdom of God, but the tares are the children of the evil one. The enemy that sowed them is Satan, the devil, and the reapers are the angels. Just as the tares are gathered and burned in the fire, so shall it be at the end of the world. The Son of man shall send out his angels, and they shall gather out of his kingdom all that do evil and cause harm, and shall cast them into a furnace of fire. There shall be weeping and gnashing of teeth. But the people of God in that day shall shine as the sun in the kingdom of their Father."

And in the house Jesus gave his disciples some more parables for them to think about. He said, "The kingdom of heaven is like treasure that a man found hidden in a field. He was glad when he saw it, but hid it again. Then he went home, sold all he had, and bought that field with the treasure in it.

"The kingdom of heaven is like a merchant who was seeking precious pearls. This man found one pearl of great price. He went and sold all he had and bought the pearl.

"Once more: The kingdom of heaven is like a net that was cast into the sea and took in fish of all kinds. When it was full, they drew the net to the shore. Then they sat down and picked out the good fish from the bad. The good fish they put away for safekeeping, but the bad fish they threw away. So shall it be at the end of the world. The angels shall come and shall place the wicked apart from the good, and shall cast them into a furnace of fire. There shall be weeping and gnashing of teeth."

DAY 245

————

THE MAN WITH EVIL SPIRITS

Mark 4:35-5:20

HEN evening came, after teaching all day by the sea and in the house, Jesus saw that the crowds of people were still pressing around him and there was no time for him to rest. Jesus said, "Let's go over to the other side of the lake."

So they took Jesus into the boat and began to row across the Sea of Galilee. Other little boats were with them, for many wanted to go with Jesus. While they were rowing, Jesus fell asleep, resting on a cushion of the boat. Suddenly a storm arose and drove great waves of water into the boat, so it was in danger of sinking, but Jesus slept on. The disciples woke him, saying, "Master, Master, we are lost! Help us, or we will die!"

Jesus awoke, looked out at the sea, then said to the waves, "Peace. Be still!" At once the wind ceased, the waves died down, and there was a great calm. Jesus said to his disciples, "Why are you afraid? Why do you have so little faith in me?"

They all wondered at Jesus' power and said to one another, "Who is this man, that the winds and the sea obey him?"

They came to the land on the eastern side of the lake, and as they were landing, a man came running down to meet them. He was one of those poor men with evil spirits living in his body. When this man saw Jesus, he ran toward him and fell down on his face before him. Jesus saw his problem and spoke to the evil spirit in him: "Come out of this man, vile spirit of evil!"

The spirit within the man cried out loudly, "What have I to do with thee, Jesus, Son of the Most High God? I call on you in the name of the Lord: Do not make me suffer!"

Jesus saw that this man was more troubled than most men who had evil spirits in them. He said to the evil one, "What is your name?"

And the spirit said, "My name is Legion, because there are many of us."

On the mountainside, a great drove of hogs was feeding. The Jews were not allowed to keep hogs or eat their flesh.

The evil spirits said to Jesus, "If we must leave this man, will you let us go into the drove of hogs?"

Jesus gave them permission, and the evil spirits went out of the man and into the hogs. The whole drove — 2,000 hogs — went wild. They rushed down the steep mountain into the sea, and were all drowned.

The men who kept the hogs ran into the city nearby and told all the people how the man had been made well and what had come to the drove of hogs. The people came out to meet Jesus, and they were full of fear. They saw the man who had been filled with evil spirits sitting at the feet of Jesus, clothed and in his right mind. But they did not think of what Jesus had done to this man. They thought only of the hogs they had lost, and they begged Jesus to go away from their land.

Jesus turned away from these people and went back to the boat on the shore. The man who had been set free from the evil spirits pleaded with Jesus to take him with them, but Jesus would not take him into the boat. He said, "Go home to your friends, and tell them how the Lord has had mercy on you, and has done great things for you."

The man went home and told all the people in the land of Decapolis the great things that Jesus had done for him.

Jesus boarded the boat, crossed the lake, and went back to Capernaum.

_____

Discussion Questions: *1. What happened when the disciples and Jesus took the boat to the other side of the Sea of Galilee? 2. Would God not have cared for the disciples while Jesus was asleep? What did the disciples' fear show about them? 3. What did the evil spirit call Jesus? Did Jesus have power over evil spirits? How do you know?*

DAY 246

_____

THE WOMAN IN THE CROWD

Mark 5:22-34

WHEN Jesus and his disciples landed at Capernaum after their sail across the lake, they found a crowd of people on the shore waiting for them. A man came forward from the throng and fell down at the feet of Jesus. He was one of the chief men in the synagogue, and his name was Jairus. He said, "O Master, come to my house at once! My little daughter is dying, but if you will come and lay your hands on her, she will live."

So Jesus went with Jairus, followed by his disciples and a throng of people.

In the crowd was a poor woman who had been ill for many years with a bleeding sore. Many doctors had tried to help her, but they could not, and she had spent all her money, so she was very poor.

This woman had heard of Jesus, and she tried to speak to him, but she couldn't reach him in the throng of people. She said to herself, "If I can only touch his garment, I know the touch will make me well." As Jesus passed by, she reached out her hand and touched the hem of his robe. At that instant she felt she was cured. Jesus himself felt her touch. Turning around, he said, "Who touched me?"

Peter said to him, "Master, the crowd throngs around you and presses on you. How can you ask, 'Who touched me?' "

But Jesus said, "Someone touched me. I feel power has gone out from me."

Then the woman came forward, fearing and trembling over what she had done. She fell down before Jesus and told him how she had touched him and had been made well. Jesus said to her, "Daughter, be of good comfort. Your faith has made you well. Rise up and go in peace."

And from that hour, the woman was free from her disease.

Discussion Questions: *1. What had happened to Jairus' daughter? 2. What was wrong with the woman? What did she do? 3. What did Jesus say to the woman, when he saw her? Why did he say she had been healed?*

DAY 247

A LITTLE GIRL SAVED
Mark 5:35-43; 6:7-12

ALL this time Jairus, the father of the dying child, stood beside Jesus, afraid his child would die before Jesus reached his house. At that moment, someone came to him and said, "It is too late. Your daughter is dead. You need not trouble the Master anymore."

But Jesus said to him, "Do not be afraid. Only believe, and she will be saved."

Soon they came to the house where Jairus lived. They could hear the people inside weeping and crying. Jesus said to them, "Why do you make such a noise? The little girl is not dead, only asleep." Jesus meant that we shouldn't be too sad when our friends die, for death is only a sleep until God wakes them. But they did not understand this and would not be comforted, for they knew the child was dead.

Jesus would not allow any of the crowd to go into the room where the dead child was. He took with him three of his disciples — Peter, James, and John — and the father and mother of the child, and shut out all the rest of the people. On a couch was the dead body of a girl of twelve. Taking her hand into his own, he said to her, "Little girl, rise up!" And life returned to the little girl. She opened her eyes and sat up. Jesus told them to give her something to eat, then he said to them, "Do not tell anyone how the little girl was brought to life."

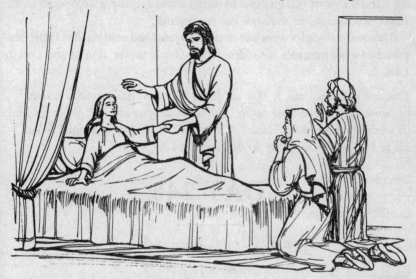

JESUS TOOK THE GIRL'S HAND AND TOLD HER TO ARISE - MARK 5:35-43

Already the crowds following him were so great that he could not teach the people in the city. If it became known that he could raise the dead to life, the throng and press of the multitudes would be greater. His great work was to teach and bring life to the souls of men, not to heal or to raise the dead.

He went out once more among the villages of Galilee, teaching in the synagogues and healing the sick people who were brought to him. He pitied the people because there was no one to give them the gospel; they were like sheep wandering and lost without a shepherd. He said to his disciples, "The harvest truly is great, but the workers to gather the harvest are few. Pray to the Lord of the harvest, that he may send out reapers into these fields."

After this, Jesus sent out his twelve disciples to different places to preach in his name to the people. He sent them out in pairs, so they could help each other, and he gave them power to heal the sick and to cast out evil spirits from men. He said to them, "Go to the lost sheep of the house of Israel, and as you go, preach, saying, 'The kingdom of heaven is at hand.' Heal the sick, cleanse the lepers, raise the dead, cast out the evil spirits. Freely you have received; freely give. Do not take any money with you. Wherever you go, ask for some good man and stay at his house.

"And if any people will not listen to your words, when you go out of that house or city, shake off the dust from your sandals, as a sign, and God will judge that house or city.

"He that hears you, hears me, and he that hears me, hears him who sent me. And if anyone will give one of these little ones a cup of cold water in the name of a disciple, he shall not lose his reward."

The twelve disciples went out in pairs, as Jesus had commanded them, and preached in all the cities of Galilee, telling people to stop sinning and turn to God.

Discussion Questions: 1. How did Jairus feel when Jesus stopped to heal the woman? How do you think he felt when the messengers came? 2. What did Jesus do when he came to Jairus' house? 3. Where did Jesus send the disciples? What did he tell them to do? What did the disciples tell the people?

DAY 248

JESUS TALKS ABOUT JOHN
Matthew 11:2-11

YOU remember that just before Jesus went from Jerusalem to Galilee, John the Baptist was put in prison by Herod Antipas. Jesus stayed in Galilee for a year, and nearly all that time John the Baptist was alone in his prison near the Dead Sea. His followers, who were now very few, came to see him and told him of the works Jesus was doing. These were wonderful, but they were not what John had expected Jesus to do and in his prison, with no one to explain what Jesus was saying and doing, John began to doubt a little whether Jesus was the Saviour who had been promised. Then, too, John's followers were inclined to feel jealous, because their master was now left alone and all the people were seeking Jesus. John sent two of his followers to Jesus, to ask him this question: "Are you really the Saviour who is to come, or are we to look for some other as the promised Christ?"

When these men came with this message from John the Baptist, they found Jesus in the midst of a great company of suffering people. They saw him make the sick well by his touch, giving sight to the blind, and casting out the evil spirits, and they listened to the words of Jesus as he taught the people.

When his work was done, Jesus turned to the men who had come from John and said to them, "Go and tell John what you have seen and heard: how the blind see, the lame walk, the lepers are made clean, the deaf hear, the dead are raised to life, and the poor have good news preached to them. And blessed is that man who believes in me without doubting."

After these men had gone to bring this message to John, Jesus spoke to the people about John the Baptist. He said, "What was it that you went out into the wilderness to see? Was it a reed shaken by the wind? Was it a man dressed in rich robes? Those who are clad in splendid garments and sit at feasts are in the houses of kings. Who was the man you went out to see? Was he a prophet of God? I tell you that he was a prophet, and more than a prophet. He was the one who came to make men ready for the coming of the king. And I say to you there has never arisen a greater man than John the Baptist. Yet he who is the least in the kingdom of God is greater than John, for he can see with his own eyes what John can only hear of from others — the works of the gospel."

All the common people who heard this were glad, for they believed that John was a prophet, and they had been baptized by him. But the Pharisees and the rulers were not pleased, because they had refused to listen to John the Baptist or to be baptized by him.

Discussion Questions: *1. Why did John begin to doubt that Jesus was the Saviour? 2. What message did he send to Jesus? What answer did Jesus send back? 3. What did Jesus say to the people about John the Baptist? 4. Why were the rulers not pleased?*

DAY 249

The Death of John the Baptist
Matthew 14:1-12

NOT long after this, John the Baptist's life ended. A great feast was held on King Herod's birthday, and all the princes and nobles of his kingdom were in the palace, eating and drinking together. While they were making merry, the young daughter of Herodias came into the room and danced before the guests. Herod was so greatly pleased with her dancing that he said to her, "Ask whatever you please, and I will give it to you."

He swore a solemn oath that he would give her whatever she might ask, even half of his kingdom. The girl went to her mother and said to her, "Tell me, what shall I ask?"

Her mother told her what to ask, and she came back to the king and said, "I will ask that you give me here on a plate the head of John the Baptist!"

The king was very sorry that he had made the promise, but he was ashamed to break his word in the presence of his princes. He sent a man to the prison with orders that the head of John the Baptist should be cut off and brought. It was done, and the young girl took it on a plate and gave it to her mother, Herodias.

So, as Herod's father had had all the little children of Bethlehem killed thirty years before, this King Herod (his son) caused John the Baptist to be put to death.

The followers of John the Baptist went to the prison, took away his body, and buried it. Then they went and told Jesus and began to follow him.

Herod the king heard of what Jesus was doing, since everybody was talking about him and wondering who he was. Some said, "This is the prophet Elijah come again to earth." Others said, "If he is not Elijah, he is surely one of the prophets who has come to life."

But Herod said, "I know who this is. It is John the Baptist, whom I killed! He has come back to life, and by him all these great works are done!" Herod was very upset, because he was afraid of the man he had killed.

Discussion Questions: *1. Why did Herodias hate John the Baptist? What did she tell her daughter to ask for? 2. Why did Herod give Herodias's daughter what she asked for? 3. Who did people say Jesus was? Who did Herod think he was?*

DAY 250

THE HUNGRY CROWD

Matthew 14:13-18

WHEN the twelve disciples came back to Jesus after preaching in his name in the villages of Galilee, they told him all they had done and what they had said to the people. The multitudes seeking Jesus were now greater than ever before, for it was again the time of the Passover, and very many on their way to Jerusalem turned aside to see and hear the great Teacher. So many people were coming and going that they could scarcely find time even to eat. Jesus said to the twelve, "Come with me into a quiet place away from the crowds, and let's rest for a while."

They went into the boat and rowed across the lake to an open place where no one lived, not far from the city of Bethsaida. But they could not be alone, for the people saw them going, watched them from the shore, then walked around the northern end of the lake and found them. When Jesus saw how eager the crowds were to hear him, he took pity on them and taught them and healed the sick.

As it began to grow toward evening, the disciples said to Jesus, "This is a lonely place, and there is nothing here for such a large crowd to eat. Send them away before it is too late and tell them to go to the towns and get food."

But Jesus said to them, "They need not go away. You can give them food to eat."

They said to him, "Shall we go into the town and buy two hundred shillings' worth of bread, so each one may have a little?"

Jesus turned to Philip and said to him, "Philip, where shall we find bread so everyone may eat?"

Jesus said this to try Philip's faith, for he knew what he would do. Philip looked at the great crowd of 5,000 men, plus women and children, and he said, "Two hundred shillings' worth of bread would not be enough to give everyone even a little piece."

Just then another of the disciples, Andrew, said to Jesus, "There is a boy here who has five loaves of barley bread and two little fish. But what use would they be with so many people?"

Jesus said to the disciples, "Go out among the people, divide them into companies of fifty and a hundred, and tell them to sit down in order."

THE FEEDING OF THE FIVE THOUSAND - JOHN 6:1-14

DAY 251

JESUS WALKS ON WATER

Matthew 14:19-29

S O the people all sat down. On the green grass, arranged in rows and squares in their garments of different colors, they looked like beds of flowers.

Then Jesus took into his hands the five loaves and the two fish the boy had brought. He looked up to heaven and blessed the food. Then he broke the loaves and the dried fish and gave the pieces to the disciples. They went among the companies of people and gave everyone bread and fish, as much as each needed. So they all ate, and had enough.

Then Jesus said, "Gather up the pieces of food that are left, so nothing may be wasted."

Each of the disciples carried a basket among the people, and when they came back to Jesus, all twelve baskets were filled with the pieces that were left over of the five loaves and the two fish.

When the people saw that here was one who could give them food, they were ready to make Jesus their king and break away from the rule of the Romans. Jesus was a King, but he would not be the kind of king they wanted. His kingdom was to be in the hearts of men who loved him, not a kingdom set up by the swords of soldiers. He found that his disciples were ready to help the people make him a king, even against his own will.

So Jesus first compelled his disciples to go on board the boat, though they were not willing, and to row across the lake to Capernaum. Then he sent away the great crowd of people who were still eager that he should be their king. And when all had gone away and he was left alone, he went up into the mountain to pray. While he was praying in the night, a great storm arose on the lake. From the mountain, Jesus could see his disciples working hard with their oars against the waves, although they could not see him. A little after midnight, when the storm was the worst, Jesus went to his disciples, walking on the water as though the sea were dry land. The men in the boat saw a strange figure approaching them on the sea and cried out with fear, for they thought it was a ghost. But Jesus called out to them, "Be of good cheer. It is I. Be not afraid!" And then they knew it was their Lord.

Peter called out, "Lord, if it's you, let me walk to you on the water." Jesus said to Peter, "Come."

_____

Discussion Questions: *1. What happened to the bread and fish the little boy had brought to eat? How much was left over? 2. What kind of kingdom did Jesus have? Why didn't he want the people to make him king? What did they want from him?*

DAY 252

_____

PETER ON THE WATER

Matthew 14:29-36
John 6:24-68

SIMON Peter leaped overboard and walked toward Jesus on the water. But when he saw how terrible the storm was, he began to be afraid, and forgetting to trust in the word of Jesus, he began to sink. He cried out, "Lord, save me!"

Jesus reached out his hand, caught hold of him, and lifted him up, saying, "O man of little faith, why did you doubt my word?"

When Jesus came on board the boat with Peter, the wind ceased and the sea calmed. The disciples wondered when they saw the power of Jesus. They fell down before him and said, "You really are the Son of God!" When they came to the shore and daybreak came, they saw they were in the land of Gennesaret, a plain a little to the south of Capernaum. They went ashore, and as soon as the people saw Jesus and knew who he was, they brought their sick to him and begged that they might touch the border of his garment. All who touched him were made well.

Soon after this, Jesus returned to Capernaum and went into the synagogue, which was full of people, some of whom he had fed a few days before. They wanted him to feed them in the same way again, but Jesus said to them, "Seek not for food that passes away, but for the food that gives everlasting life, such as the Son of man can give you."

They said to him, "What sign can you show that God has sent you? Moses gave our fathers bread from heaven — the manna in the desert. What can you do?"

Jesus said to them, "It was not Moses, but God, who gave your fathers bread. Now God is giving you the true bread from heaven — his Son, who came down from heaven to give life to the world."

As soon as the people found that Jesus would not work wonders to please them, they turned away from him and left him, although only a few days before they would have made him a king. When Jesus saw the great crowds of people were with him no longer, he said to his twelve disciples, "Will you also go away and leave me?"

Simon Peter answered, "Lord, to whom else can we go? Only you have the words that will give us everlasting life."

Discussion Questions: *1. What did it take to walk on the water with Jesus? Did Peter have it? 2. Who did the disciples say Jesus was after he had walked on the water? 3. What kind of food did the people want Jesus to give them? What kind did he want to give them? Why did the people leave?*

DAY 253

A WOMAN'S FAITH

Matthew 15:21-28

AFTER the feeding of the 5,000 and the talk that followed it in the synagogue of Capernaum, Jesus no longer tried to preach to the people in crowds, as he had preached before. He had spoken his last words to the people of Galilee, and now he wanted to be alone with his disciples so he could teach them many things they needed. Jesus knew that in a few months — less than a year — he would leave his disciples alone to carry on the work of preaching his gospel to the world. Before then, he wanted to teach and train his disciples, so he tried to be apart from the people and alone with these twelve men.

With this purpose in mind, Jesus led his disciples away from Capernaum, across Galilee to the land of Tyre and Sidon near the Great Sea. On the border of this land he came to a village and went with his disciples into a house. Jesus did not wish the people of the place to know he was there, but he could not be hidden.

A woman from town, who was not of the Jewish race but belonged to the old Canaanite people, heard of Jesus' coming. She found Jesus, fell down before him, and begged him to come to her house and cure her daughter, who had an evil spirit. At first Jesus would not answer her, for he had not come to that place to do works of healing. But she kept on crying and calling on Jesus to help her daughter until the disciples said, "Master, send this woman away. She is a trouble to us, crying out after us!"

They thought that a Gentile woman — one who did not belong to the race of Israel — was not worthy of the Lord's care. But Jesus wanted to teach his disciples that he did care for this woman, though she was a Gentile and a stranger. To show them how strong her faith was, he said to her, "I am not sent to the Gentiles, but only to the lost sheep of the house of Israel."

But the woman would not be discouraged. She kept on saying, "Lord, help me!"

Jesus said to her again, "It is not fitting to take the children's bread and throw it to the dogs!"

Then the woman said, "It is true, Lord. Yet the little dogs under the table eat the children's crumbs!"

Jesus said to her, "Woman, your faith is great! It shall be done as you ask. Go your way. The evil spirit is sent out of your daughter."

The woman believed the word that Jesus spoke. She went to her home and found her daughter resting on her bed, freed from the evil spirit.

———————

Discussion Questions: *1. Now who did Jesus want to teach? Why? 2. Why didn't the disciples want Jesus to heal the Gentile woman's daughter? 3. What lesson did Jesus want to teach the disciples? 4. What did Jesus say was great in the woman? Did he do what she wanted?*

DAY 254

———————

THE CROWD FED AGAIN

Mark 7:32-9:26

SO many people tried to see Jesus in that place that he went around Galilee and went back to the country called Decapolis, on the east of the Sea of Galilee. You remember that Jesus had visited this country before, when he cast the army of evil spirits out of a man and into the hogs. At that time the people almost drove Jesus away from their land, but now they were glad to see him and brought their sick to him to be healed. Perhaps they had heard how kind and good and helpful Jesus was.

They led up to Jesus a man who was deaf and could not speak plainly. They asked Jesus to cure him, but Jesus would not do his work to entertain the crowds. He took the man away from the crowd, and when he was alone with him, he put his fingers into the man's ears and touched his tongue. Then he looked up to heaven, gave a sigh, and said to the man, "Be opened!"

The man's ears were opened and his tongue was set free, so he heard and spoke plainly. Jesus told the man, and those with him, not to let others know what he had done, but they could not keep from telling the good news to everybody. They were full of wonder, for they had not seen the works of Jesus, and they said, "He has done all things well. He even makes the deaf to hear and the dumb to speak!"

In the land of Decapolis, as before in Galilee, great crowds of people came to see and hear Jesus. They followed him without thinking that they would need food to eat, and Jesus said to his disciples, "I feel pity for this people, for they have now been with me three days, and they have nothing to eat. If I send them home hungry, they will faint by the way, for many of them came from far away."

The disciples answered, "How can we find bread for such a great crowd of people here in the desert, so far from the villages?"

"How many loaves of bread have you?" asked Jesus. They said, "We have seven loaves and a few small fish."

Then he told all the people to sit down on the ground. When they were seated, Jesus took the seven loaves and the fish, gave thanks to God, broke them, and gave them to his disciples, who gave them to the people. Then, as before, he had them gather up the food that was left, and they filled seven large baskets with the pieces. This time 4,000 men were fed, besides women and children. After the meal, he sent the people to their homes. He and his disciples went on board a boat and sailed across the lake to a place on the western shore. He stayed there for a little time, then sailed northward to Bethsaida, at the head of the lake.

At Bethsaida they brought him a blind man and asked him to touch his eyes. But Jesus would not heal the man while a crowd was looking on. He led the man out of the village alone. Then he spat on the man's eyes, touched them with his hands, and said to him, "Can you see anything?"

The man looked up and said, "I see men. But they look like trees walking."

Again Jesus laid his hands on the man's eyes. He looked once more, and now he could see things clearly. Jesus sent him to his home and said to him, "Do not even go into the village or tell it to anyone in the village." Jesus didn't want crowds coming to him. He wanted to be alone with his disciples, for he had many things to teach them.

Discussion Questions: *1. Why was Jesus traveling so far? 2. Why did he take the deaf man away from the crowd? 3. How long did the people follow Jesus? Why did he feel pity for them? 4. What did Jesus do for the people?*

DAY 255

PETER, THE ROCK

Mark 8:27-38

FROM Bethsaida on the Sea of Galilee, Jesus led his disciples still further north to Caesarea Philippi, at the foot of Mount Hermon. The name of this place means "Philip's Caesarea." It was called that because it was under the rule of King Herod Philip, a brother of King Herod Antipas, who ruled in Galilee. There was another Caesarea on the shore of the Great Sea, south of Mount Carmel. At Caesarea Philippi, Jesus asked his disciples this question: "Who do men say that I, the Son of man, am?" "The Son of man" was the name by which Jesus often spoke of himself.

They answered him, "Some men say you are John the Baptist, risen from the dead. Some say you are the prophet Elijah or the prophet Jeremiah, come again to earth."

Then Jesus said, "But who do you say I am?"

Simon Peter answered for them all, saying, "You are the Anointed One, the Christ, the Son of the living God!"

Jesus said to Peter, "Simon, this has come to you not from men, but from my Father who is in heaven. You are Peter, the Rock. And on this rock I will build my church, and all the powers of earth shall not overcome it."

The church of Christ is made up of those who believe what Peter said, that Jesus is the Christ, the Saviour of the world.

After this, Jesus began to tell his disciples what would happen to him soon. "We are going up to Jerusalem. There the people will refuse the Son of man. He shall suffer many wrongs from the rulers and chief priests, and shall be killed, and on the third day, he shall be raised to life."

But the disciples could not believe that such sad things would happen to Jesus. They thought he would reign as a king and high places in his kingdom would be given to them. Peter took Jesus apart from the rest, and said to him, "Master, do not speak of such things. You will not suffer and die. You shall be a king!"

But Jesus saw that under Peter's words was the evil one, tempting him, and he said to Peter, "Go from me, Satan, evil one! You would be a stumbling block to make me fall! You are not seeking God's will, but men's."

Jesus knew that while men wanted him to be a king and rule over a kingdom on earth, it was God's will for him to die on the cross to save the world from sin. Then Jesus called the people to come near and said to them all:

"If any man will come after me, let him give up his own will, and take up his cross, and follow me. For whoever has a will to save his life here shall lose it hereafter. And whoever is willing to give up his life for my sake will find it again in the life everlasting. What gain will it be to a man to have the whole world, and lose his soul? For the Son of man will come in his glory, with all the holy angels, and then he will give to every man according to his acts. And if any man is ashamed to acknowledge the Lord now, the Lord will not acknowledge him that day!"

_____

Discussion Questions: *1. Who did some people think Jesus was? 2. Who did Peter say he was? 3. What is the church made up of? 4. What did the disciples expect to happen to Jesus? What did Jesus say would happen to him?*

DAY 256
_____

THE TRANSFIGURATION

Mark 9:2-10

ONE night about a week after saying these words, Jesus called three of his disciples, Peter, James, and John, and took them up the side of Mount Hermon. At a high place on the mountain, the three disciples lay down to sleep, but Jesus sought his Father in prayer. While Jesus was praying, a great change came over him. His face began to shine as bright as the sun, and his garments became whiter than snow. The three disciples awoke and saw their Lord with all this glory beaming from him.

They also saw two men talking with Jesus. These were Moses and Elijah, who had come down from heaven to meet Jesus and talk with him about his coming death in Jerusalem. As these men were leaving the sight of the disciples, Peter spoke. "Master, it is good for us to be here! Let us make here three tabernacles, one for you, one for Moses, and one for Elijah!"

While Peter was speaking, a bright cloud came over them all. The three disciples felt great fear as they found themselves in the cloud and no longer able to see their Master. Out of the cloud came the voice of God, saying these words, "This is my beloved Son, in whom I am well pleased. Hear him!"

As the disciples heard this voice, they fell on their faces on the ground in great fear. Jesus came and touched them, saying, "Rise up, and do not be afraid."

When they looked up, the bright cloud had gone away, the two men were no more in sight, and Jesus was standing alone. They walked down the moun-

MOSES AND ELIJAH APPEARED WITH JESUS — MATTHEW 17:1-9

tain, and Jesus said to them very seriously, "Do not tell any man what you have seen until the Son of man is risen from the dead."

They wondered what this "rising from the dead" could mean. Even then, they could not believe Jesus would die. But they said nothing to anyone, not even to the other disciples.

Discussion Questions: *1. Who did Jesus take with him to Mount Hermon? What did Jesus do there? 2. Who talked with Jesus there? What did they talk about? 3. What did God say about Jesus?*

DAY 257

A LITTLE BOY HEALED

Mark 9:14-32

WHEN Jesus and the three disciples came down the mountain, they found many people around the other nine disciples. As the people saw Jesus, they were filled with wonder, for some of the glory still remained on his face. They bowed before him.

One man came to Jesus, and said, "Master, look at my son, my only child, and have mercy on him, for he is terribly troubled by an evil spirit. At times he cannot speak, and then he will cry out suddenly. The spirit almost tears him in pieces, and makes him fall into the fire and the water. He foams at the mouth, grinds his teeth, and pines away. I spoke to your disciples, but they could not cast out the evil spirit."

Jesus said, "O ye people without faith and wandering from God, how long must I be with you? How long must I bear with you? Bring your child to me."

While they were bringing the boy to Jesus, the evil spirit in him threw him down and seemed to tear him apart. He lay suffering and rolling on the ground. Jesus said to the boy's father, "How long is it since this came to him?"

The father said, "Ever since he was a little child. But if you can do anything, have mercy on us and help us!"

"If I can!" said Jesus. "Don't you know that all things are possible to the one that believes in me?"

At once the father of the child cried out, "Lord, I believe! Help my lack of faith!"

Then Jesus spoke to the evil spirit in the boy, "Dumb and deaf spirit, come out of this child, and never again enter into him!"

Then the spirit gave a cry and came out, leaving the child on the ground. Many who looked at him said, "He is dead!"

But Jesus took him by the hand and lifted him up, and the boy was healthy.

When Jesus was in the house, his disciples asked him, "Why couldn't we cast out the evil spirit?"

Jesus said to them, "Because you are wanting in faith. This kind of evil spirit can be sent out only through prayer and fasting."

While all were wondering at the great things Jesus did, he said to his disciples, "Let what I say to you sink down into your hearts. The time is coming when the Son of man shall be given into the hands of men. They shall kill him, and after he is killed, on the third day he shall rise again."

But they could not understand what he meant by these words, and they were afraid to ask him.

_____

Discussion Questions: *1. What was wrong with the child? 2. What did Jesus tell the father he needed? 3. What happened when Jesus lifted the boy up? 4. Why hadn't the disciples been able to help the boy?*

DAY 258

PAYING THE TAX

Matthew 17:24-18:6

FROM Caesarea Philippi, in the far north, Jesus went with his disciples through Galilee, but not, as at other times, with a great multitude following him. This time Jesus wanted no one to know of his coming, for he had already preached to these people, and now he wanted to be alone with his disciples. They came to Capernaum, and while they were there, the officer to whom the Jews paid the tax of half a shekel (about thirty cents) for each man, said to Peter, "Does not your Master pay the half-shekel?"

Peter said, "Yes."

But when Peter came into the house, Jesus said to Peter, "Simon, do the kings of the earth take taxes of their own children, or of strangers?"

Peter said to him, "Of strangers, not of their own children."

And Jesus said, "Then the children of the King should be free from the tax. But so we may not cause trouble, go to the lake, cast in a hook, and pull up the first fish that comes. When you have opened his mouth, you shall find in it a piece of money. Take that, and pay it to them for you and for me."

While Jesus was in the house, he said to his disciples, "What was it that you were talking about among yourselves while you were on the way?"

They looked at one another and said nothing, for on the way they had been arguing which of them would have the highest places in their Lord's kingdom. Then Jesus said to them, "If anyone among you wishes to be first, let him be willing to be the last of all, and to be a servant of all."

And Jesus took a little child in his arms and held him up before all his disciples, and said to them, "Unless you turn from your ways and become like little children in spirit, you shall not enter into the kingdom of heaven. Whoever shall be gentle and lowly and willing to be taught, like this little child, shall be the greatest in the kingdom of heaven. And whoever shall receive one such little child for my sake, he receives me. Take care not to despise one of these little ones, for I say to you, that in heaven their angels always look on the face of my Father who is in heaven. For the Son of man is come to save that which was lost, and it is not the will of your Father who is in heaven that one of these little ones should perish."

Discussion Questions: *1. How did Jesus pay the tax? Why did he pay it? 2. What had the disciples been talking about on the way? Did Jesus like their talk? 3. What example was Jesus giving them, when he talked about children?*

DAY 259

FORGIVENESS

Matthew 18:21-35

NE day Peter asked Jesus, "Lord, how many times should I forgive a brother when he has sinned against me? Seven times?"

Jesus said to Peter, "I do not say that you should forgive him only seven times, but seventy times seven."

Then Jesus told his disciples the parable of the Unkind Servant: "There was once a king who had an account made with his servants of how much money they owed him. One servant was brought before the king who owed the king a great sum of money — ten million dollars. The man had nothing with which to pay his debt, and the king commanded that the man, his wife, and his children be sold as slaves for the debt. Then the servant fell down before the king and said, 'Be patient with me. Give me time, and I will pay all I owe!'

"Then the king felt a pity for his servant, set him free, and let him go without any payment, giving him all that he owed.

"But that servant went out and found another servant who owed him a small sum, only ten dollars. He came to this man, took hold of him by the throat, and said, 'Pay what you owe me!' The man fell down before him and said, 'Have patience with me, and I will pay you!' He would not wait for the man to earn the money, but threw the man in prison, to stay there until he should pay the debt. When his fellow servants heard what he had done, they were sorry for the poor debtor in prison, and came and told the king all that had been done. Then the king sent for the servant and said to him, 'You wicked servant! I forgave you all your debt when you asked me to give you time. And you should have had mercy on your fellow servant, just as I had mercy on you!' The king was angry with the unkind servant. He sent him to prison and ordered that he should be made to suffer until he paid all his debt. So also shall my heavenly Father do to you, if from your hearts you do not forgive your brothers who have sinned against you."

Discussion Questions: *1. What did Peter ask Jesus? 2. How many times did Jesus say Peter should forgive someone? 3. What did the parable Jesus told mean?*

DAY 260

"FOLLOW ME"

Luke 9:57-62

IN the fall of every year the Feast of the Tabernacles was held in Jerusalem to remind the people of the time the Israelites came out of Egypt and lived for forty years in the wilderness, more than 1,000 years before Jesus was on the earth. At this feast the people from all parts of the land came up to Jerusalem and worshiped in the Temple. Just as the Israelites had lived in tents in the wilderness, the people at the feast did not sleep indoors, but made huts on the roofs of the houses and the hills around the city, and slept in them at night.

Jesus and his disciples went from Galilee to Jerusalem to attend this feast. Just as Jesus was leaving, a man who had heard Jesus said to him, "Master, I will follow you wherever you go."

Jesus said to him, "The foxes have holes, and the birds of the air have nests, but the Son of man has not a place where he can lay his head."

There was another man to whom Jesus had said, "Follow me." This man said, "Lord, let me go and bury my father, who is very old and must die soon, and then I will follow you."

THE RICH YOUNG RULER TURNED AND WALKED AWAY - MARK 10:22

Jesus said to him, "Let the dead bury their own dead. You go and preach the kingdom of God."

And another said, "Lord, I will follow you. But first let me go home and say good-bye to those who are in my house."

Jesus said to him, "No man who has put his hand to the plow and looks back is fit for the kingdom of God."

On his way to Jerusalem, Jesus went through the country of Samaria, where the people hated the Jews. In one place the Samaritans would not let Jesus and his disciples come into their village, because they saw that they were Jews going up to Jerusalem. The disciples were very angry at such treatment, and James and John said to him, "Lord, shall we call down fire from heaven to destroy this village, as Elijah the prophet did once?"

But Jesus would not allow them to do this to their enemies. He said to them, "Your spirit is not the spirit of my kingdom. The Son of man has not come to destroy men's lives, but to save them."

And they went to another village to find a resting place.

Discussion Questions: *1. What did the Feast of the Tabernacles remind the people of? 2. Many people wanted to follow Jesus. What was he saying to the three mentioned here? 3. Why wouldn't the Samaritans let Jesus and the disciples go through their land? 4. How did Jesus help his disciples learn to love their enemies?*

DAY 261

MARY AND MARTHA

Luke 17:12-19; 10:38-42

AT one town, they met ten men with the dreadful disease of leprosy, who had heard of Jesus and his power to heal. When they saw him, they cried out aloud, "Jesus, Master, have mercy on us!"

Jesus said to them, "Go and show yourselves to the priests." If a leper became well, he went to the priest, offered a sacrifice, and then was allowed to go to his home. These men obeyed Jesus, believing he would cure them, and as soon as they started to go to the priests, they found that they were already well. All but one of the men went on their way, but one turned and came back to Jesus. He fell at his feet, giving praise to God. This man was not a Jew, but a Samaritan. Jesus said, as he saw him, "Weren't ten cleansed? But where are the nine? Were there none who came back to give glory to God except this stranger?"

Then he said to the man, "Rise up, and go your way. Your faith has saved you."

Jesus came to Jerusalem in the middle of the feast, which was held for a week. He stood in the Temple, taught the people, and all wondered at his words. On the last and greatest day of the feast, when they were bringing water and pouring it out in the Temple, Jesus cried aloud, "If any man thirst, let him come to me and drink! He that believes in me, out of him shall flow rivers of living water."

While Jesus was teaching in Jerusalem, he often went out of the city to the village of Bethany, on the Mount of Olives. There he stayed with the family of Martha, her sister Mary, and their brother Lazarus. These were friends of Jesus, and he loved to be with them. One day while Jesus was at the house, Mary sat at the feet of Jesus listening to his words, but Martha was busy with work and full of worry. Martha came to Jesus and said, "Master, don't you care that my sister has left me to do all the work? Tell her to come and help me!"

JESUS AT THE HOUSE OF MARY AND MARTHA - LUKE 10:38-42

But Jesus said to her, "Martha, Martha, you are anxious and troubled about many things. Only one thing is necessary. Mary has chosen the good part, which shall not be taken away from her."

Discussion Questions: *1. Why did one leper come back to Jesus? How did that make Jesus feel? 2. What had saved the man? 3. How is Jesus like water? Why did he compare himself to it? 4. Why did Jesus tell Martha to be like Mary?*

DAY 262

The Blind Man (Part 1)

John 9:1-12

ONE Sabbath, as Jesus and his disciples were walking in Jerusalem, they met a blind man begging. This man had been born blind. The disciples said to Jesus, "Master, whose fault was it that this man was born blind? Was it because he has sinned, or did his parents sin?"

The Jews thought that when any evil came, it was caused by someone's sin. But Jesus said, "This man was born blind, not because of his parents' sin or because of his own, but so God might show his power in him. We must do God's work while it is day, for the night is coming when no man can work. As long as I am in the world, I am the light of the world."

When Jesus had said this, he spat on the ground and mixed up the spittle with earth, making a little lump of clay. This clay Jesus spread on the eyes of the blind man, and then he said to him, "Go and wash in the pool of Siloam."

The pool of Siloam was a large cistern or reservoir on the southeast of Jerusalem, outside the wall, where the Gihon and Kedron valleys come together. To go to this pool, the blind man — with two great blotches of mud on his face — had to walk through the streets of the city, out the gate, and into the valley. He went, and felt his way down the steps into the pool of Siloam. There he washed, and then at once his lifelong blindness passed away, and he could see. When the man came back to the part of the city where he lived, his neighbors could scarcely believe that he was the same man. They said, "Isn't this the man who used to sit on the street begging?"

"This must be the same man," said some. But others said, "No it is someone who looks like him."

But the man said, "I am the very same man who was blind!"

"Why, how did this come to pass?" they asked him. "How were your eyes opened?"

"The man called Jesus," he answered, "mixed clay, and put it on my eyes, and said to me, 'Go to the pool of Siloam and wash,' and I went and washed, and then I could see."

"Where is this man?" they asked him.

"I do not know," said the man.

___

Discussion Questions: *1. What did the disciples ask Jesus? 2. What did Jesus answer? 3. Why did Jesus make the man walk to the pool of Siloam? What happened when he obeyed Jesus?*

DAY 263

THE BLIND MAN (PART 2)

John 9:13-21

SOME of the Pharisees — the men who made a show of always obeying the law — asked the man how he had been made to see. He said to them, as he had said before, "A man put clay on my eyes, and I washed, and my sight came to me."

Some of the Pharisees said, "The man who did this is not a man of God, because he does not keep the Sabbath. He makes clay and puts it on men's eyes on the Sabbath. He is a sinner."

Others said, "How can a man who is a sinner do such wonderful works?" The people were divided in what they thought of Jesus. They asked the man who had been blind, "What do you think of this man who has opened your eyes?"

"He is a prophet of God!" said the man.

But the leading Jews would not believe this man had gained his sight until they sent for his father and mother. The Jews asked them, "Is this your son, who you say was born blind? How can he now see?"

His parents were afraid to tell all they knew, for the Jews had agreed that if any man said Jesus was the Christ, he would be turned out of the synagogue and not be allowed to worship with the people. So his parents said to the Jews, "We know this is our son, and we know that he was born blind. But how he was made to see we do not know, or who has opened his eyes we do not know. He is of age. Ask him, and let him speak for himself."

Discussion Questions: *1. Who wanted to know how the man had gotten his sight? 2. Why did the Pharisees think Jesus had done wrong? Had he? 3. Who did the man think Jesus was? 4. Why wouldn't the man's parents answer the questions? How did they feel?*

DAY 264

THE BLIND MAN (PART 3)

John 9:24-38

THEN again the rulers of the Jews called the man who had been blind, and they said to him, "Give God the praise for your sight. We know this man who made clay on the Sabbath is a sinner."

"Whether that man is a sinner or not, I do not know," answered the man. "But one thing I do know: once I was blind, and now I see."

They said to him again, "What did this man do to you? How did he open your eyes?"

"I have told you already, and you would not listen," said the man. "Why do you want to hear it again? Do you intend to believe in him and be his followers?"

This made them very angry, and they said to the man, "You are his follower. We are followers of Moses. We know that God spoke to Moses. As for this fellow, we do not even know where he comes from!"

The man said, "Why, this is a very wonderful thing! You who are teachers of the people do not know who this man is or where he comes from, yet he has the power to open my eyes? We know that God does not hear sinners. God hears only those who worship him and do his will. Never before has anyone opened the eyes of a man born blind. If this man were not from God, he could not do such works as these!"

The rulers of the Jews then said to the man, "You were born in sin. Now you are trying to teach us?" They turned him out of the synagogue and would not let him worship with them.

Jesus heard of this, and when Jesus found him, he said to him, "Do you believe in the Son of God?"

The man said, "And who is he, Lord, that I may believe in him?"

"You have seen him," said Jesus, "and it is he who now talks with you!"

The man said, "Lord, I believe." And he fell down before Jesus and worshiped him.

Discussion Questions: *1. Why did the man believe Jesus was not a sinner? 2. Did the Pharisees know as much as they thought they did? What didn't they know? 3. How did the man find out who Jesus really is?*

DAY 265

THE GOOD SHEPHERD

John 10:1-40

AFTER the cure of the man born blind, Jesus told the people of Jerusalem the parable of the Good Shepherd.

"I say to you, anyone who does not go into the sheepfold by the door, but climbs up some other way, is a thief and a robber. But the one who comes in by the door is a shepherd of the sheep. The porter opens the door to him, and the sheep know him and listen to his call, for he calls his own sheep by name and leads them out to the pasture. And when he has led out his sheep, he goes in front of them, and the sheep follow him, for they know his voice. The sheep will not follow a stranger, for they do not know the stranger's voice."

The people did not understand what all this meant, so Jesus explained it to them. "I am the door that leads to the sheepfold. If anyone comes to the sheep in any other way than through me and in my name, he is a thief and a robber, and the sheep will not listen to him. I am the door. If any man goes into the fold through me, he shall be saved, and shall go in and go out, and shall find pasture.

"The thief comes to the fold to steal the sheep and kill them, but I come to the fold so they may have life and everything they need. I am the good shepherd. The good shepherd will give his own life to save his sheep, and I will give my life that my sheep may be saved.

"I am the good shepherd. Just as a true shepherd knows all the sheep in his flock, so I know my own, and my own know me, even as I know the Father, and the Father knows me. I lay down my life for the sheep. Other sheep I have, which are not of this fold. Them I also must lead, and they shall hear my voice, and there shall be one flock and one shepherd."

The Jews could not understand these words of Jesus, but they became very angry with him, because he spoke of God as his Father. They took up stones to throw at him and tried to seize him, intending to kill him. But Jesus escaped and went away to the land beyond Jordan, at the place called Bethabara, or "Bethany beyond Jordan," the same place where he had been baptized by John the Baptist more than two years before.

Discussion Questions: *1. What parable did Jesus tell? 2. What did this parable mean? 3. Why did the people get angry when Jesus said God was his Father? What did Jesus do?*

DAY 266

THE SEVENTY SENT OUT

Luke 10:1-29

 ROM Bethabara, Jesus wanted to go through the land on the east of the Jordan, a land called Perea, a word that means "beyond." But before going out through this land, Jesus sent out seventy chosen men from among his followers to go to all the villages and make the people ready for his own coming. He gave these seventy the same commands he had given to the twelve disciples he sent through Galilee, and sent them out in pairs, two men to travel and preach together.

He told them, "I send you forth as lambs among wolves. Carry no purse, no bag for food, no shoes except those you are wearing. Do not stop to talk with people by the way, but go through the towns and the villages healing the sick and preaching to the people, 'The kingdom of God is coming.' He that hears you, hears me. He that refuses you, refuses me. He that will not hear me, will not hear him that sent me."

After a time, the seventy men came back to Jesus, saying, "Lord, even the evil spirits obey our words in your name!"

Jesus said to them, "I saw Satan, the king of the evil spirits, falling down like lightning from heaven. I have given you power to tread on serpents and scorpions. Nothing shall harm you. Still, do not rejoice because the evil spirits obey you, but rejoice that your names are written in heaven."

And at that time, one of the scribes — men who wrote copies of the books of the Old Testament, studied them, and taught them — came to Jesus and asked him a question, to see what answer he would give. He said, "Master, what shall I do to have everlasting life?"

Jesus said to the scribe, "What is written in the law? You are a reader of God's law. Tell me what it says."

The man gave this answer: "Thou shalt love the Lord thy God with all thy heart, and with all thy soul, and with all thy strength, and with all thy mind. And thou shalt love thy neighbor as thyself."

Jesus said to the man, "You have answered right. Do this, and you shall have everlasting life."

But the man was not satisfied. He asked another question: "And who is my neighbor?"

———————

Discussion Questions: *1. Who did Jesus send out to the villages? 2. What did Jesus give to these men? 3. What were the men to take with them? 4. What were the men to tell the people? 5. What did Jesus say the scribe should do to receive eternal life?*

DAY 267

THE GOOD SAMARITAN

Luke 10:30-37

TO answer the scribe's question, Jesus told the parable of the Good Samaritan. He said, "A certain man was going down the lonely road from Jerusalem to Jericho. And he fell among robbers, who stripped him of all he had, beat him, and then went away, leaving him almost dead. It happened that a certain priest was going down that road. And when he saw the man lying there, he passed by on the other side. And a Levite also, when he came to the place and saw the man, went by on the other side. But a certain Samaritan, as he was going down, came where this man was, and he felt pity for him. He came to the man and dressed his wounds, pouring oil and wine into them. Then he lifted him up, set him on his own beast of burden, and walked beside him to an inn. There he took care of him all night. The next morning, he took out two shillings and gave them to the keeper of the inn, saying, 'Take care of him. If you need to spend more than this, do so, and when I come again, I will pay it to you.'

"Which one of these three do you think showed himself a neighbor to the man who fell among the robbers?"

THE GOOD SAMARITAN - LUKE 10:30-37

The scribe said, "The one who showed mercy on him."

Then Jesus said to him, "Go and do likewise."

By this parable Jesus showed that our neighbor is the one who needs the help we can give him, whoever he may be.

———

Discussion Questions: *1. What parable did Jesus tell? 2. Which man acted like a neighbor? 3. What did Jesus tell the scribe to do?*

DAY 268

———

LAZARUS (PART 1)

John 11:1-16

WHILE Jesus was at Bethabara beyond Jordan, ready to begin preaching in the land of Perea, he was suddenly called back to the village of Bethany, on the Mount of Olives near Jerusalem. Martha, Mary, and Lazarus, the friends of Jesus, were living in this place.

Word came to Jesus that Lazarus was very ill. But Jesus did not hurry away from Bethabara to Bethany. He stayed two days, and then he said to his disciples, "Let us go again into Judea, near Jerusalem."

The disciples said to Jesus, "Master, when we were in Judea before, the people tried to stone you and kill you. Do you want to go there again?"

Jesus said, "Our friend Lazarus has fallen asleep. I go to awake him out of his sleep."

The disciples said, "Master, if he has fallen asleep, he may be well." They thought Jesus was speaking of normal sleep, but Jesus meant Lazarus was dead.

Then Jesus said to them, "Lazarus is dead, and I am glad that I was not there to keep him alive. Now you will be led to believe in me all the more fully. But let us now go to him."

Then one of the disciples named Thomas said to the others, "Let us go, too, and die with our Master!"

———

Discussion Questions: *1. Why was Jesus called back to Bethany? 2. How long did Jesus stay where he was? 3. Why were the disciples afraid to go to Bethany? 4. What did Jesus mean when he said Lazarus was asleep? Did the disciples understand?*

DAY 269

LAZARUS (PART 2)

John 11:17-54

SO Jesus left Bethabara with his disciples and came to Bethany, where he found Lazarus had been buried for four days. Many of the Jews had come to comfort Martha and Mary in the loss of their brother. They told Martha that Jesus was coming, and she went to meet him, but Mary stayed at home. As soon as Martha saw Jesus, she said to him very sadly, "Lord, if you had been here, my brother would not have died. Even now, I know God will give you whatever you may ask."

Jesus said to her, "Your brother shall rise again."

"I know that he shall rise," said Martha, "when the last day comes, and all the dead are raised."

Jesus said to her, "I am the resurrection — the raising from the dead — and I am the life. Whoever believes in me, even though he may die, shall live. Whoever lives and believes in me shall never die. Do you believe this?"

She said to him, "Yes, Lord, I believe you are the Christ, the Son of God, the one who comes into the world."

Then Martha went to her home and said to her sister Mary, so no other person heard her, "The Master is here, and he asks for you!"

At once Mary got up to go to Jesus. Her friends thought she was going to her brother's tomb, and they went with her. Jesus was still at the place where Martha had met him. When Mary came to him, she fell down at his feet and said, "Lord, if you had been here, my brother wouldn't have died!"

When Jesus saw her weeping and all the Jews weeping with her, he was touched and filled with sorrow. He said, "Where have you laid him?"

They showed him where Lazarus was buried in a cave, with a stone on the door. Jesus wept as he stood near it, and the Jews said, "See how he loved Lazarus!"

But some of them said, "This man could open the eyes of the blind. Why couldn't he keep this man he loved from dying?"

Jesus, standing before the cave and still groaning within, said, "Take away the stone!"

Martha said, "Lord, by this time his body has begun to decay, for he has been dead four days."

Jesus said to her, "Didn't I say to you that if you would believe, you would see the glory of God?"

They took away the stone as Jesus commanded. Then Jesus lifted up his eyes toward heaven and said, "Father, I thank you for hearing me. I know you always hear me, but because of those who are standing here, I spoke, so they may believe that you have sent me."

JESUS SAID WITH A LOUD VOICE, "LAZARUS, COME FORTH." - JOHN 11:43

Then, with a loud voice, Jesus called out, "Lazarus, come forth!"

And the man who had been dead for four days came out of the tomb. His body, hands, and feet were wrapped round and round with grave bands, and over his face was tied a napkin.

Jesus said to those standing near, "Loose him, and let him go!"

When they saw the wonderful power of Jesus in raising Lazarus to life, many of the people believed in Jesus. But others went away and told the Pharisees and rulers what Jesus had done. They called a meeting of all the rulers, the great council of the Jews, and they said, "What shall we do, for this man is doing many works of wonder? If we let him alone, everybody will believe in him and try to make him the king. Then the Romans will make war on us and destroy our nation and our people."

But the high priest Caiphas said, "It is better for us that one man should die for the people than that our whole nation should be destroyed. Let us put this man to death."

They agreed, and from that day, all the rulers made plans to have Jesus slain. But Jesus knew their plans, for he knew all things. His time to die had not yet come, and he went away with his disciples to a city near the wilderness. And from this place he went out to preach in the land of Perea.

Discussion Questions: *1. What had happened to Lazarus? 2. What did Martha and Mary say to Jesus? 3. What did Jesus tell Martha he would do? Did she understand? 4. What did Jesus do? Why did that worry the rulers?*

DAY 270

THE RICH FOOL

Luke 12:13-21; 13:11-16

ESUS traveled with his disciples through the land of Perea, the only part of the Israelite country he had not already visited. The people had heard of Jesus from the seventy disciples he had sent through the land, and in every place great multitudes of people came to see and hear him. One time, a man called out of the crowd to Jesus, "Master, speak to my brother, and tell him to give me my share of what our father left us!"

Jesus said, "Who made me a judge over you, to settle your disputes? Let both of you — and all of you — take care and keep from being covetous, seeking what is not yours."

Then Jesus told the people the parable of the Rich Fool. He said:

"There was a rich farmer whose fields brought great harvests, until the rich man said to himself: 'What shall I do? for I have no place where I can store up the fruits of my fields. This is what I will do. I will pull down my barns and build larger ones to store all my grain and my goods. And I will say to my soul, "Soul, you have goods laid up enough to last for many years. Take your ease, eat, drink, and be merry." '

"But God said to the rich man, 'Thou foolish one; this night you will die, and your soul shall be taken away from you. And the things you have saved up; whose shall they be?' "

Jesus said, "Such is the man who lays up treasure for himself, and is not rich toward God."

One Sabbath, Jesus was teaching in a synagogue when a woman came in who had not been able to stand upright for eighteen years. When Jesus saw her, he said to her, "Woman, you are set free from your body's trouble." He laid his hands on her, and she stood up straight and praised God for his mercy.

But the chief man in the synagogue was not pleased to see Jesus healing on the Sabbath. He spoke to the people, and said, "There are six days when men ought to work. During them you should come and be healed, not on the Sabbath."

But Jesus said to him, "Doesn't each of you loose his ox or his ass from the stall and lead him away to give him water on the Sabbath? And should not this woman, a daughter of Abraham who has been bound for eighteen years, be set free from her bonds on the Sabbath?"

And the enemies of Jesus could say nothing, while all the people were glad at his glorious work.

Discussion Questions: *1. What did Jesus say to the man who wanted him to judge between him and his brother? What was the man like? 2. What parable did Jesus tell? 3. What happened when Jesus healed the woman on the Sabbath? What did Jesus tell the people?*

DAY 271

TO BE A DISCIPLE

Luke 14:12-33

AT one place Jesus was invited to a dinner. He said to the one who had invited him, "When you make a dinner or a supper, do not invite your friends or your rich neighbors; for they will invite you in return. But when you make a feast, invite the poor, the helpless, the lame and the blind. They cannot invite you again, but God will give you a reward in his own time."

And there went with Jesus great multitudes of people, and he turned, and said to them, "If any man comes after me, he must love me more than he loves his own father, and his mother, and wife and children — yes, and his own life, also — or else he cannot be my disciple.

"For who of you, wishing to build a tower, does not first sit down and count the cost, whether he will be able to finish? For if he lays the foundation and then leaves it unfinished, everyone who passes by will laugh at him, and say, 'This man began to build, and was not able to finish.'

"Or what king going out to meet another king in war will not sit down first and find whether he is able, with ten thousand men, to meet the one who comes against him with twenty thousand? And if he finds that he cannot meet him, while he is yet a great way off, he sends his messengers and asks for peace.

"Even so, every one of you must give up all that he has, if he would be my disciple."

Discussion Questions: *1. Who did Jesus say we should invite to dinner? 2. How much must you love Jesus to be his disciple?*

DAY 272

THE LOST SHEEP

Luke 15:1-10

WHILE Jesus was teaching, many of the publicans (those who collected the taxes from the people) came to hear him, and many others who were called "sinners" by the Pharisees and the scribes. The enemies of Jesus said, "This man likes to have sinners come to see him, and he eats with them."

Then Jesus told a parable called the Lost Sheep, to show why he was willing to talk with sinners.

"What man of you, who has a hundred sheep, if one of them is lost, does not leave his ninety and nine sheep in the field and go after the one that is lost until he finds it? And when he has found it, he lays it on his shoulders, glad to see his lost sheep again. And when he comes home, he calls together his friends and neighbors and says to them, 'Be glad with me; for I have found my sheep that was lost?'

"Even so," said Jesus, "there is joy in heaven over one sinner who has turned to God, more than over ninety and nine good men who do not need to turn from their sins."

THE PARABLE OF THE LOST SHEEP - LUKE 15:3-7

Then Jesus told the people the parable of the Lost Piece of Money.
"If any woman has ten pieces of silver and loses one piece, won't she not

light a lamp and sweep her house carefully until she finds it? And when she has found it, she calls together her friends and her neighbors, saying, 'Be glad with me, for I have found the piece of silver that I had lost.'

"Even so, there is joy among the angels of God over one sinner that turns from his sins."

Discussion Questions: *1. What did the Pharisees and scribes say about Jesus? 2. What parables did Jesus tell? What did they mean?*

DAY 273

THE LOST SON

Luke 15:11-32

THEN Jesus told another parable, the Parable of the Prodigal Son. A prodigal is one who spends everything he has, like the young man in this parable. Jesus said, "There was once a man who had two sons. The younger of his sons said to his father, 'Father, give me the share that will come to me, of what you own.'

"Then the father divided all he had between his two sons. Not many days after, the younger son took his share and went away into a far country, and there he wasted it all in wild and wicked living. And when he had spent it all, there arose a mighty famine of food in that country, and he began to be in want.

"And he went to work for one of the men in that land, and this man sent him into the fields to feed his hogs. The young man was so hungry that he would have been happy to eat the hogs' food. At last the young man began to think of his father's house, and he said to himself, 'How many hired servants of my father's have bread, while I am dying here with hunger! I will go to my father and will say to him, "Father, I have sinned against heaven and in your sight. I am no more worthy to be called your son. Let me be one of your hired servants."'

"And he rose up, to go back to his father's house. His father saw him coming, and ran, and fell on his neck, and kissed him.

"And the son said unto him, 'Father, I have sinned against heaven and in your sight. I am no more worthy to be called your son —'

"But before he could say any more, his father called to the servants, and said, 'Bring out quickly the best robe, and put it on him. Put a ring on his hand and shoes on his feet, and bring the fatted calf, and kill it, and let us eat and make merry, for my son was dead and is alive again. He was lost and is found.'

"Now his elder son was in the field. As he came near the house he heard music and dancing. And he called one of the servants, and asked what these things might be. And the servant said to him, 'Your brother has come. And your father has killed the fatted calf and is having a feast, because he is at home safe and sound.'

"But the elder brother was angry, and would not go in. His father came out and urged him, but he answered his father, 'I have served you for these many years, and I have never disobeyed your commands. And yet you never gave me even a kid, that I might make merry with my friends. But when your son has come who has wasted your living with wicked people, you killed for him the fatted calf!'

"And the father said to him, 'My son, you are always with me, and all I have is yours. But it was fitting that we should make merry and be glad, for your brother was dead, and is alive again. He was lost and is found.' "

By these parables Jesus showed that he came not to seek those who thought themselves so good they did not need him, but those who were sinful and needy.

Discussion Questions: 1. What parable did Jesus tell? 2. What did the younger son want the father to do? 3. What do you think he learned from what happened? 4. What was the elder brother like? 5. What was Jesus teaching in this lesson?

DAY 274

THE RICH MAN AND LAZARUS

Luke 16:19-31

 NOTHER parable that Jesus told was that of the Rich Man and Lazarus. He said:

"There was a rich man, dressed in garments of purple and fine linen, living in splendor. And at the gate leading to his house was a beggar named Lazarus, covered with sores and looking for his food in the crumbs that fell from the rich man's table. Even the dogs of the street came and licked his sores.

"After a time the beggar died, and his soul was carried by the angels into Abraham's bosom. The rich man also died, and his body was buried. And in the world of the dead, he lifted up his eyes, being in misery. Far away, he saw Abraham, and Lazarus resting in his bosom. And he cried out and said,

'Father Abraham, have mercy on me, and send Lazarus, that he may dip the tip of his finger in water and cool my tongue, for I am suffering in this flame!'

"But Abraham said, 'Son, remember that you had your good things in your lifetime, and that Lazarus had his evil things. But now he is comforted here and you are suffering. And besides all this, between us and you there is a great gulf fixed, so no one may cross over from us to you, and none can come from your place to us.'

"And he said, 'I pray, O father Abraham, if Lazarus cannot come to me, command that he be sent to my father's house, for I have five brothers. Let him speak to them, so they will not come to this place of torment.'

"But Abraham said, 'They have Moses and the prophets. Let them hear them!'

"And he said, 'O father Abraham, if one should go to them from the dead, they will turn to God.'

"And Abraham said, 'If they will not hear Moses and the prophets, they will not believe, even though one should rise from the dead!' "

And this was true, for just as the people would not listen to the words of Moses and the prophets about Christ, they would not even believe after Jesus himself arose from the dead.

_____

Discussion Questions: *1. What parable did Jesus teach? 2. How was Lazarus rich? How was the rich man poor? 3. What lesson was Jesus teaching in this parable?*

DAY 275

_____

THE UNJUST STEWARD

Luke 16:1-9; 18:2-7

JESUS told another parable, called the Unjust Steward.

"A certain rich man had a steward, a man who took the care of all his possessions. He heard that his steward was wasting his property, so he sent for him and said, 'What is this I hear about you? You shall soon give up your place and be my steward no longer.'

"Then the steward said to himself, 'In a few days I shall lose my place. What shall I do? I cannot work in the fields, and I am ashamed to go begging from door to door. But I have thought of a plan that will give me friends, so that when I am put out of my place, some people will take me into their houses because of what I have done for them.'

"And this was his plan. He sent for the men who were in debt to his master and said to the first one, 'How much do you owe to my master?'

"The man said, 'I owe him one thousand gallons of oil.'

"Then said the steward, 'You need only pay five hundred gallons.' Then to another he said, 'How much do you owe?'

"The man answered, 'I owe fifteen hundred bushels of wheat.' And the steward said to him, 'You need pay only twelve hundred bushels.'

"When his master heard of what his steward had done, he said, 'That is a sharp, shrewd man who takes care of himself.' "

And Jesus said, "Be as earnest and as thoughtful for the eternal life as men are for this present life."

Jesus did not approve the actions of this unjust steward, but he told his disciples to learn some good lessons from his wrong deeds.

Jesus spoke another parable to show that people should pray and not be discouraged. It was the parable of the Unjust Judge and the Widow. Jesus said:

"There was in a city a judge who did not fear God or seek to do right, nor did he care for man. And there was a poor widow in that city who had suffered wrong. She came to him over and over again, crying out, 'Do justice for me against my enemy who has done me wrong!'

"And for a time the judge, because he did not care for the right, would do nothing. But as the widow kept on crying, at last he said to himself, 'Even though I do not fear God or care for man, yet because this widow troubles me and will not be still, I will give her justice, or else she will wear me out by her continual crying.' "

And the Lord said, "Hear what this unjust judge says! And will not a just God do right for his own who cry to him by day and night, even though he may seem to wait long? I tell you that he will answer their prayer, and will answer it soon!"

Discussion Questions: *1. What parable did Jesus tell? 2. What did the master think of his steward? What did Jesus think of him? 3. What lesson was Jesus teaching in this parable? 4. What other parable did Jesus tell? What was the lesson he wanted people to learn?*

DAY 276

THE PHARISEE AND THE PUBLICAN

Luke 18:10-14

AND Jesus spoke another parable to some who thought they were righteous and holy. This was the parable of the Pharisee and the Publican.

"Two men went up into the Temple to pray, the one a Pharisee, the other a publican. The Pharisee stood and said, 'God, I thank you that I am not as other men are. I do not rob, I do not deal unjustly. I am free from wickedness. I am not even like this publican. I fast twice in each week. I give to God one-tenth of all I have.'

"But the publican standing afar off would not lift up so much as his eyes unto heaven, but beat his breast, saying, 'God be merciful to me, a sinner!'

"I say unto you," said Jesus, "this man went down to his house having his sins forgiven rather than the other. For everyone that exalts himself shall be brought low, and he that is humble shall be lifted up."

Discussion Questions: *1. Name the parable Jesus told. 2. What was the Pharisee like? What was the publican like? 3. Which one of the men pleased God?*

DAY 277

THE LITTLE CHILDREN

Luke 18:15-34

AT this time the mothers brought Jesus their little children, so he might lay his hands on them and bless them. The disciples were not pleased at this, and told them to take their children away. But Jesus called them to him and said, "Suffer the little children to come unto me, and forbid them not, for of such is the kingdom of God. Whoever shall not receive the kingdom of God as a little child, he shall not enter into it." Then he put his hands on them and blessed them.

A certain young man — a ruler — came running to Jesus and said, "Good Master, what shall I do that I may have everlasting life?"

"Why do you call me good?" said Jesus. "No one is good except one, and

JESUS BLESSED THE CHILDREN - MATTHEW 19:13

that is God. You know the commandments; keep them."

"What commandments?" asked the young man.

"Do not kill; do not commit adultery; do not steal; do not bear false witness; honor thy father and mother."

The young man said, "All these I have kept from my youth. What do I need more than these?"

"One thing more you need to do," said Jesus. "Go sell all that you have and give it to the poor, and you shall have treasure in heaven. Then come and follow me."

But when he heard this, he turned and went away very sad, for he was very rich. And when Jesus saw this, he said, "How hard it is for those that are rich to enter into the kingdom of God! It is easier for a camel to go through the eye of a needle than for a rich man to enter the kingdom of God."

At this the disciples were filled with wonder. They said, "If that be so, then who can be saved?"

And Jesus said, "The things that are impossible with men are possible with God."

Peter said, "Lord, we have left our homes and all we have, and have followed you."

And Jesus answered him, "No man who has left house, or wife, or brothers, or parents, or children, for the sake of the kingdom of God, shall not have given to him many more times in this life, and in the world to come, life everlasting."

Then Jesus again told his twelve disciples of what was going to happen in a few weeks. He said, "We are going up to Jerusalem, and there all the things written by the prophets about the Son of man shall come true. He shall be made a prisoner, and shall be mocked, and treated shamefully, and shall be spit upon, and beaten, and shall be killed. And the third day, he shall rise again."

But they could not understand these things, and they did not believe their Master was to die.

Discussion Questions: *1. Why did the disciples tell the mothers to take their children away? Did Jesus agree with them? 2. What did the young ruler want to know? 3. Why did Jesus want the man to sell all he owned? 4. How can anyone be saved? 5. What did Jesus say was going to happen to him? Did the disciples believe him?*

DAY 278

BARTIMAEUS

Luke 18:35-43

JESUS was passing through the land of Perea on his way to Jerusalem. His disciples were with him, and a great crowd of people, for again the feast of the Passover was near, and people from all parts of the land were going up to Jerusalem to take part in the feast. Although Jesus had said, over and over again, that he was to die in Jerusalem, many still believed that he would make himself king and would reign over all the land.

One day James and John, two of the disciples of Jesus who were brothers, came to Jesus with their mother. She knelt before Jesus, and her two sons knelt beside her. Jesus said to her, "What is it that you would ask of me?"

She said to him, "Lord, grant to me that my two sons may be allowed to sit beside your throne, one on the right hand, the other on your left, in your kingdom."

"You do not know what you are asking," answered Jesus. "Are you able to drink the cup that I am about to drink?" By *the cup*, he meant the suffering he was soon to endure, but this they did not understand, and they said to him, "We are able."

He said to them, "My cup you shall drink. But to sit on my right hand and on my left is not mine to give, but it shall be given to those for whom God has made it ready."

When the other disciples heard that James and John had tried to get the promise of the highest places in the Lord's kingdom, they were very angry with these two brothers. But Jesus called them to him and said, "You know that the rulers of nations lord it over them, and their great ones are those who bear rule. But not among you. Whoever among you would be great, let him serve the rest. The Son of man did not come to be served, but to serve others and to give up his life that he might save man."

Jesus with his disciples and a great crowd came to Jericho, which was at the foot of the mountains, near the head of the Dead Sea. Just outside the city, at the gate, a blind man was begging. His name was Bartimaeus. This man heard the noise of a crowd and asked what it meant.

JESUS HEALED BARTIMAEUS – MARK 10:52

They said to him, "Jesus of Nazareth is passing by."

As soon as he heard this, he began to cry out, "Jesus, son of David, have mercy on me!"

Many people told him not to make so much noise, but he just cried all the louder, "Jesus, son of David, have mercy on me!"

Jesus heard his cry, stopped, and said, "Call the man to me!"

Then they came to the blind man and said, "Be of good cheer. Get up. He calls you!"

The blind man sprang up from the ground, threw away his garment, and came to Jesus.

And Jesus said to him, "What do you wish me to do to you?"

"Lord, that I might have my sight given to me," answered blind Bartimaeus.

Jesus touched his eyes and said, "Go your way. Your faith has made you well."

Immediately sight came to his eyes, and he followed Jesus, while all the people who saw it gave thanks to God.

_____

Discussion Questions: *1. What did the people think would happen to Jesus in Jerusalem? 2. What did James's and John's mother want? What did Jesus tell them? 3. Why were the other disciples angry with the two disciples? 4. What did Jesus say to them all? 5. What happened with Jesus and the blind man?*

DAY 279

————

THE PARABLE OF THE POUNDS

Luke 19:1-28

THERE was another man in Jericho who had heard of Jesus and wanted to see him. This was a man named Zaccheus. He was a chief man among the publicans, the men who gathered the taxes from the people, and whom all the people hated greatly. Zaccheus was a rich man, for many of the publicans made a lot of money. Wishing to see Jesus, and being a small man, Zaccheus ran ahead of the crowd and climbed into a sycamore tree by the road, so he might see Jesus as he passed by.

When Jesus came to the tree, he stopped, looked up, and called Zaccheus by name, saying, "Zaccheus, make haste and come down, for today I must stop in your house."

At this Zaccheus was glad. He came down at once and took Jesus into his house. But many people were upset by this. They said, "He has gone in to lodge with a man who is a sinner!"

Because he was a publican, they counted him as a sinner. But Zaccheus stood before the Lord and said, "Lord, of my goods I give to the poor, and if I have wrongly taken anything from any man, I give him back four times as much."

And Jesus said, "Today salvation has come to this house, for this man is a son of Abraham. For the Son of man came to seek and save that which was lost."

Jesus was now getting close to Jerusalem, and all the people were expecting the kingdom of God to begin at once, with Jesus as its King. Because of this, Jesus told the people the Parable of the Pounds, saying, "A certain nobleman went into a far country, expecting there to be made a king, and then to return to his own land. Before going away, he called ten servants of his, and gave each one a pound of money, and said to them, 'Take care of this and trade with it until I come back.'

"But the people of his own land hated this nobleman, and sent messengers to the place where he had gone, to say, 'We are not willing that this man should be king over us.'

"But in the face of this message from the people, the nobleman received the crown and the kingdom, and then went back to his own land. When he had come home, he called his servants to whom he had given the pounds, so he might know how much each had gained by trading. The first servant came before him and said, 'Lord, your pound has made ten pounds more.'

"The king said to him, 'Well done, my good servant. Because you have been found faithful in a very little, you shall bear rule over ten cities.'

"And the second came, saying, 'Your pound, lord, has made five pounds.' And his lord said to him, 'You shall be over five cities.'

"And another came, saying, 'Lord, here is your pound, which I have kept wrapped up in a napkin. For I feared you, because you are a harsh master. You take up what you did not lay down, and you reap what you did not sow.' He said to the servant, 'Out of your own mouth I will judge you, you un-faithful servant. If you knew that I was a harsh master, taking up what I did not lay down and reaping what I did not sow, then why did you not put my money into the bank, so when I came, I should have had my own money and its gains?' And he said to those who were standing by, 'Take away from him the pound, and give it to him that has the ten pounds.'

"They said to him, 'Lord, he has ten pounds already!'

"But the king said, 'Unto everyone who cares for what he has, more shall be given. But the one who cares not for it, what he has shall be taken away from him.'

"And the king added, 'Those enemies who would not have me reign over them; bring them here, and slay them before me.' "

And after giving this parable, Jesus went ahead of his disciples up the mountains toward Jerusalem.

———————

Discussion Questions: *1. What kind of man was Zaccheus? 2. What did he do to see Jesus? 3. Why were the people angry when Jesus went to eat with Zaccheus? 4. What happened to Zaccheus? What did he promise Jesus he would do? 5. What parable did Jesus tell? What did it mean?*

DAY 280

MARY'S PERFUME

Matthew 26:6-16

FROM Jericho, Jesus and his disciples went up the mountains to Bethany, where his friends Martha and Mary lived and where he had raised Lazarus from the dead. Many people in Jerusalem heard that Jesus was there and went out of the city to see him, for Bethany was only two miles from Jerusalem. Some also came to see Lazarus, who Jesus had raised from the dead. The rulers of the Jews said to one another, "We must not only kill Jesus, but also Lazarus. Because of him, many of the people are following Jesus and believing in him."

The friends of Jesus in Bethany made a supper for Jesus at the home of a man named Simon. He was called Simon the Leper, and may have been the one Jesus cured of leprosy. Jesus and his disciples, with Lazarus, leaned on the couches around the table, and Martha was one of those who waited on them. While they were at the supper, Mary, the sister of Lazarus, came into the room carrying a sealed jar of very precious perfume. She opened the jar and poured some of the perfume on Jesus' head and feet, then wiped his feet with her long hair, filling the whole house with the fragrance of the perfume.

THE WOMAN WASHED THE FEET OF JESUS WITH HER TEARS - LUKE 7:37,38

But one of the disciples of Jesus, Judas Iscariot, was not pleased at this. He said, "Why was the perfume wasted? This might have been sold for more than forty-five dollars, and the money given to the poor!"

He didn't say this because he cared for the poor. Judas was the one who kept the money for Jesus and the twelve, and he was a thief, taking for his own use all the money he could steal.

But Jesus said, "Let her alone. Why do you find fault with the woman? She has done a good work for me. You always have the poor with you, and whenever you wish, you can give to them. But you will have me with you for only a little while. She has done what she could: She has come to perfume my body for its burial. Wherever the gospel shall be preached throughout the world, what this woman has done shall be told in memory of her." Perhaps Mary knew what others did not believe — that Jesus would die soon — and she showed her love for him and her sorrow at his coming death by this rich gift.

But Judas, the disciple who carried the money, was very angry at Jesus. He began looking for a chance to betray Jesus to his enemies. He went to the chief priest and said, "What will you give me if I put Jesus in your hands?"

They said, "We will give you thirty pieces of silver."

And for thirty pieces of silver, Judas promised to help them take Jesus prisoner.

———————

Discussion Questions: *1. Why did the rulers want to kill Jesus and Lazarus? 2. What did Mary do? 3. Why did that make Judas angry? What had he been doing? 4. What did Jesus say about Mary? 5. What did Judas do because he was angry with Jesus?*

DAY 281

———————

Palm Sunday

Matthew 21:1-11

N the morning after the supper at Bethany, Jesus called two of his disciples and said to them, "Go into the next village, and at a place where two roads cross, you will find an ass tied, and a colt with it. Bring them to me. And if anyone says to you, 'Why do you do this?' say 'The Lord has need of them,' and they will let them go."

They went to the place and found the ass and the colt, and were untying them when the owner said, "What are you doing, untying the ass?"

They said, as Jesus had told them, "The Lord has need of it!"

Then the owner gave them the ass and the colt for Jesus' use. They brought them to Jesus on the Mount of Olives, laid some of their own clothes on the colt for a cushion, and set Jesus on it. Then all the disciples and a great crowd threw their garments on the ground for Jesus to ride on. Others cut down branches from the trees and laid them on the ground.

As Jesus rode over the mountain toward Jerusalem, many walked before him, waving branches of palm trees. And they all cried together, "Hosanna to the Son of David! Blessed is he that cometh in the name of the Lord! Blessed be the kingdom of our father David, that cometh in the name of the Lord! Hosanna in the highest!"

They said these things because they believed Jesus was the Christ, the Anointed King, and they hoped he would set up his throne in Jerusalem. Some of the Pharisees in the crowd, who did not believe in Jesus, said to him, "Master, stop your disciples!"

But Jesus said, "I tell you that if these should be still, the very stones would cry out!" When he came into Jerusalem with all his followers, the city was filled with wonder. They said, "Who is this?"

The crowd answered, "This is Jesus, the prophet of Nazareth in Galilee!"

Jesus went into the Temple and looked around it, but he didn't stay, because it was getting late. He went back to Bethany and stayed the night with his friends.

These things took place on Sunday, the first day of the week, and that Sunday is called Palm Sunday, because of the palm branches the people carried before Jesus.

JESUS ENTERED JERUSALEM— JOHN 12:12-15

Discussion Questions: *1. What did Jesus tell the disciples to do? 2. What use did God have for the colt? 3. What did the people hope Jesus would do? How did they greet him?*

DAY 282

JESUS IN THE TEMPLE

Mark 11:12-17

ON Monday morning, Jesus rose very early in the morning and, without waiting to eat breakfast, led his disciples over the Mount of Olives toward Jerusalem. On the mountain, he saw at a distance a fig tree covered with leaves, and although it was early for figs to be ripe, he hoped he might find some figs to eat. According to Jewish law, anyone passing a tree could eat of its fruit, even though he was not the owner, but he could not take any away with him.

But when Jesus came near this tree, he saw there was no fruit on it, only leaves. Then a thought came to Jesus, and he spoke to the tree. "No fruit shall grow on you from now on." Then he walked on his way to Jerusalem.

You remember that when Jesus came to Jerusalem the first time after he began to preach, he found the courts of the Temple filled with people buying, selling, and changing money, and he drove them all out. But that had been three years before. Now when Jesus came to the Temple on the Monday morning before the Passover, he found all the traders there again, selling oxen, sheep, and doves for sacrifices and changing money at the tables.

Again Jesus rose up against these people who would make his Father's house into a place of profit. He drove them all out. He turned over the tables of the money-changers, scattering their money on the floor. He cleared away the seats of those selling doves. Whenever he saw anyone even carrying a jar, or a basket, or any load through the Temple, he stopped him and made him go back. He said to all the people, "It is written in the prophets, 'My house shall be called a house of prayer for all nations,' but you have made it a den of robbers!"

Discussion Questions: *1. What happened with Jesus and the fig tree? 2. What did Jesus see in the Temple? 3. What did Jesus do in the Temple? What did he say to the people?*

DAY 283

The Angry Temple Rulers

Matthew 21:14-17

THE Jews had made it a rule that no blind or lame man could go into the Temple, for they thought only those with perfect bodies should come before the Lord. But they forgot that God looks at hearts, not at bodies. And when Jesus found many blind and lame people at the doors of the Temple, he allowed them to come in and made them all well.

And the little children, who always loved Jesus, saw him in the Temple and cried out, as they heard others crying, "Hosanna to the Son of David!"

The chief priests and scribes were greatly displeased when they heard the voices of these children, and they said to Jesus, "Do you hear what these are saying?"

And Jesus said, "Yes. And have you never read what is written in the Psalms, 'Out of the mouths of babes and little ones, thou hast made thy praise perfect?' "

And all the common people came to hear Jesus as he taught in the Temple, and they listened to him gladly, for he gave them plain and simple teachings, with many parables. But the rulers and chief priests grew more and more angry as they saw the courts of the Temple filled with people eager to hear Jesus. They tried to find some way to lay hands on Jesus and kill him, but they dared not do it while the crowds were around him.

All that day, Jesus taught the people, and when night came, he went out of the city, over the Mount of Olives to Bethany, where he was safe among his friends.

Discussion Questions: *1. Why couldn't a blind or lame man go to the Temple? Was this what God had said? 2. What did the children say about Jesus? How did that make the Pharisees and scribes feel? 3. Who wanted to harm Jesus? What did they want to do?*

DAY 284

The Fig Tree

Mark 11:20-24

N the next morning, which was Tuesday of the week before the Passover, Jesus again went over the Mount of Olives with his

408

disciples. They passed the fig tree to which Jesus had spoken the day before. And now the disciples saw that the tree was withered and dried, with its leaves dry and rustling in the wind.

"Look, Master!" said Peter. "The fig tree to which you spoke yesterday is withered!"

And Jesus said to them all, "Have faith in God, for in truth I say to you, that if you have faith, you shall not only do this which has been done to the fig tree. If you say to this mountain, 'Be moved away and thrown into the sea!' it shall be done. And all things — whatever they may be — that you ask in prayer, if you have faith, shall be given to you." Again Jesus went into the Temple and taught the people.

Discussion Questions: *1. What had happened to the fig tree? Why? 2. What did Jesus promise the disciples?*

DAY 285

THE WEDDING FEAST
Matthew 22:1-14

HAT day Jesus told the people another parable, the Wedding Feast. He said:

"There was a certain king who made a great feast at the wedding of his son, and he sent out his servant to call those he had invited to the feast. But they would not come. Then he sent out other servants, saying, 'Tell those who were invited that my dinner is all ready. My oxen are killed, and the dishes are on the table. Say to them, "All things are ready. Come to the marriage feast!" '

"But the men who had been sent for would not come. One went to his farm, another to his shop, and some of them seized the servants he sent, beat them, and treated them roughly. Some of them were killed.

"This made the king very angry. He sent his armies and killed those murderers, burning their city. Then he said to his servants, 'The wedding feast is ready, but those that were invited were not worthy of such honor. Go out into the streets and call in everybody you can find — high and low, rich and poor, good and bad — and tell them they are welcome.'

"The servants went out and invited people of every kind and brought them to the feast, so all the places were filled. And to all who came they gave a wedding garment, so everyone would be dressed properly for the king.

"But when the king came in to meet his guests, he saw a man not wearing a wedding garment. He said to him, 'Friend, why have you come to the feast without a wedding garment?'

"The man said nothing. Then the king said to his officers, 'Bind him hand and foot and throw him out into the darkness, where there shall be weeping and gnashing of teeth. For in the kingdom of God many are called, but few are chosen.' "

Discussion Questions: *1. What parable did Jesus tell? 2. Who did the king ask to the feast? What did they do? 3. Who did the king ask next? What did they do? 4. What do you think this parable means?*

DAY 286

THE TREASURY

Matthew 22:15-22
Mark 12:41-44

THE enemies of Jesus thought they had found a way to get him into trouble with the people or the Romans, who were the rulers of the land. So they sent some men to him who acted as though they were honest and true, but really were trying to trick Jesus. These men came and said, "Master, we know you teach the truth and are not afraid of any man. Now tell what is right, and what we should do. Should the Jews pay taxes to the Roman Emperor Caesar, or not? Shall we pay or not pay?"

They waited for his answer. If he said, "It is right to pay the tax," then these men could tell the people, "Jesus is the friend of the Romans and the enemy of the Jews." Then the people would turn away from him. But if he said, "It is not right to pay the tax. Refuse to pay it," they could tell the Roman governor that Jesus would not obey the laws, and the governor might put him in prison or kill him. So whatever answer Jesus gave, they hoped he might make trouble for himself.

But Jesus knew their hate and the thoughts of their hearts, and he said, "Let me see a piece of the money given for the tax."

They brought him a silver piece, and he looked at it and said, "Whose head is this on the coin? Whose name is written over it?"

They answered him, "That is Caesar, the Roman emperor."

"Well, then," said Jesus, "give Caesar the things that are Caesar's, and give God the things that are God's!"

They wondered at his answer, for it was so wise that they could find nothing wrong about it. They tried him with other questions, but he answered them all and left his enemies with nothing to say. Then Jesus turned to his enemies and spoke his last words to them. He told them of their wickedness and warned them that they would bring the wrath of God upon themselves.

Jesus was in the part of the Temple called the treasury. Around the wall were boxes in which the people dropped their gifts when they came to worship. Some that were rich gave much money, but a poor widow came by and dropped in two little coins, the very smallest, the two together worth only a quarter of a cent. Jesus said, "I tell you that this poor widow has dropped into the treasury more than all the rest. For the others gave out of their plenty, but she, in her need, has given all she had."

And with these words Jesus got up and went out of the Temple for the last time. Never again was the voice of Jesus heard within those walls.

Discussion Questions: *1. How did the enemies of Jesus try to get him into trouble? 2. Did Jesus know what they were doing? How? 3. What answer did he give his enemies? What kind of answer was that? 4. What did Jesus say about the widow? Why did he say it?*

DAY 287

THE WOMEN AND THE OIL

Mark 13:1-37

AFTER Jesus had spoken his last words to the people and their rulers, he walked out of the Temple with his disciples. As they were passing through the great gates on the east of the Temple, the disciples said to Jesus, "Master, what a splendid building this is! Look at these great stones in the foundation!"

Jesus answered the disciples, "Do you see these great walls? The time is coming when these buildings shall be thrown down, when not one stone shall be left in its place. The very foundations of this house and this city shall be torn up!"

These words filled the followers of Jesus with the deepest sorrow, for they loved the Temple and the city of Jerusalem, as all Jews loved it. To them, its ruin would be the end of the world. Yet they believed the words of their Master, for they knew he was a prophet whose words were sure to come true.

He was more than a prophet; he was the Son of God. They walked with Jesus down into the valley of Kedron and up the slope of the Mount of Olives. On the top of the mountain they looked down on the Temple and the city, and some of the disciples said to Jesus, "Master, tell us. When will these dreadful things happen? Give us some sign, so we may know they are coming."

Then Jesus sat down with his disciples on the mountain and told them of many things that were to come to the city and the world. How wars would come, and earthquakes, and diseases would break out. How enemies would come and fight against Jerusalem, destroy it, and scatter its people. How trouble would come to all the earth. And he told them that he would come again as Lord of all, and all who believed in him should watch and be ready to meet him. Then he told the parable of the Ten Young Women.

"There were ten young women who were going out one night with their lamps to meet a wedding party. Five of these young women were wise, and five were foolish. Those that were foolish took their lighted lamps, but had no more oil than that in the lamps. But each of the wise young women carried a bottle of oil. It was night, and while they were waiting for the bridal party, they all fell asleep. At midnight they were all awaked by the sudden cry, 'The bridegroom is coming! Go out to meet him!'

"Then all the young women rose up and trimmed their lamps. The foolish ones said, 'Let us have some of your oil, for our lamps are going out.'

"But the other young women said, 'Perhaps there will not be enough for us and for you, too. Go to those who sell, and buy oil for yourselves.'

"The young women who had no oil went away, and while they were away, the bridal party came. Those who were ready went in with them to the feast, and then the door was shut. Afterward the other young women came knocking on the door and calling out, 'Lord, Lord, open to us!'

"But he said, 'I do not know you.'

"And he would not open the door. Watch, therefore, for you do not know the day or the hour when your Lord will come."

Discussion Questions: *1. What did Jesus say would happen to the Temple? 2. How did that make the disciples feel? Why? 3. What did the disciples want to know? 4. What parable did Jesus tell them? What did it mean?*

DAY 288

THE JUDGMENT TO COME

Matthew 25:31-46

JESUS also told his disciples another parable of what will happen at the end of the world. He said:

"When the Son of Man shall come in his glory, and all the angels of God shall come with him, then he shall sit on his glorious throne as King. And before him shall be brought all the people of the world. And he shall divide them, and separate them, just as a shepherd divides the sheep from the goats. He shall put his sheep on his right hand and the goats on his left. Then the King shall say to those on his right hand, 'Come, ye whom my Father has blessed. Come and take the kingdom God has made ready for you. For I was hungry, and you gave me food. I was thirsty, and you gave me drink. I was a stranger, and you took me into your home. I was naked, and you gave me clothes. I was sick, and you visited me. I was in prison, and you came to me.'

"Then all those on the right of the King will say, 'Lord, when did we see you hungry, and feed you? Or thirsty, and gave you a drink? And when did we see you a stranger and take you in? Or naked, and gave you clothes? And when did we see you sick, or in prison, and come to you?'

"And the King shall answer, and shall say to them, 'Inasmuch as you did it to one of these my brothers, even the very least of them, you did it to me.'

"Then the King shall turn to those on his left hand and say to them, 'Go away from me, you cursed ones, into the everlasting fire that has been made ready for the devil and his angels. For I was hungry, and you gave me no food. I was thirsty, and you gave me no drink. I was a stranger, and you did not open your doors to me. I was naked, and you gave me no clothes. I was sick, and in prison, and you did not visit me.'

"Then shall they answer him, 'Lord, when did we see you hungry, or thirsty, or a stranger, or naked, or sick, or in prison, and did not help you?'

"And the King shall say to them, 'Inasmuch as you did it not to one of these, the least of my brothers, you did it not to me.'

"And the wicked shall go away to be punished forever, but the righteous into everlasting life."

After these words, Jesus went with his disciples back to Bethany.

Discussion Questions: *1. What kind of parable did Jesus tell? 2. How would Jesus separate the people? 3. What does this parable tell you about doing good things for people? What can you do to help someone else?*

DAY 289

THE PASSOVER FEAST

Luke 22:7-20
John 13:1-16

O N one of the days in the week before the Passover, the disciples came to Jesus at Bethany and said, "Master, where shall we make ready the Passover for you to eat?"

Jesus called Peter and John, and said to them, "Go into the city, and a man carrying a pitcher of water will meet you. Follow him, and go into the house where he goes, and say to the head of the house, 'The Master says, "Where is my guest room? Where I can eat the Passover with my disciples?" '

"And he will show you a large upper room, furnished. Make it ready for us."

Peter and John went into Jerusalem and soon saw a man walking toward them carrying a pitcher of water. They followed him, went into the house where he took the pitcher, and said to the head of the house, "The Master says, 'Where is the guest room for me, where I may eat the Passover with my disciples?' "

The man led them upstairs and showed them a large upper room with a table and couches around it, all ready for guests. Then the disciples went out, brought a lamb, roasted it, and prepared the vegetables and the thin wafers of bread.

On Thursday afternoon, Jesus and his disciples walked out of Bethany together, over the Mount of Olives, and into the city. Only Jesus, who could read the thoughts of men, knew that Judas had made a promise to the chief priests to lead them and their servants to Jesus, when the time came to seize him. Judas was watching for the best time to do this.

They came into the house and went upstairs to the large room, where they found the supper all ready. The meal was spread on a table. Around the table were couches for the company, where each one lay down with his head toward the table, so he could help himself to the food, while his feet were at the foot of the couch, toward the wall of the room. Their feet were bare, for they had all taken off their sandals as they came in.

Jesus was leaning at the head of the table, and John, the disciple Jesus loved most, was lying next to him. While they were eating, Jesus took bread, and gave thanks. Then he broke it, and passed a piece to each one of the twelve, saying, "Take, and eat. This is my body, which is broken for you. Do this and remember me."

414

JESUS AND HIS DISCIPLES AT THE LAST SUPPER- LUKE 22:19

Afterward, he took the cup of wine and passed it to each one with the words, "This cup is my blood, shed for you, and for many, that their sins may be taken away. As often as you drink this, remember me."

While they were still leaning on the couches around the table, Jesus rose up, took off his outer robe, and then tied around his waist a long towel. He poured water into a basin, and while all the disciples were wondering, he carried the water to the feet of one of the disciples and began to wash them, just as though he were a servant. Then he washed the feet of another disciple, and then of still another. When he came to Simon Peter, Peter said to him, "Lord, are you going to wash my feet?"

Jesus said to him, "What I do, you cannot understand now, but you will understand it after a time."

"Lord, you will never wash my feet," said Peter.

"If I do not wash you," said Jesus, "then you are not mine."

Then Peter said, "O Lord, don't just wash my feet, but my hands and head, too!"

But Jesus said to him, "No, Peter. One who has already bathed only needs to wash his feet, and then he is clean. And you are clean, but not all of you."

For he knew that among those whose feet he was washing was one who would soon give him up to his enemies. After he had washed their feet, he put on his garments again, leaned on his couch, looked around, and said, "Do you know what I have done to you? You call me 'Master' and 'Lord,' and you

415

JESUS WASHES PETER'S FEET — JOHN 13:4-9

speak rightly, for I am. If I, your Lord and Master, have washed your feet, you ought to wash each other's feet. I have given you an example that you should do to each other as I have done to you."

By this Jesus meant that all who follow him should help and serve each other, instead of seeking great things for themselves.

Discussion Questions: *1. How would Peter and John know where to prepare the Passover? 2. What kind of food would they eat for the Passover? 3. What did Jesus do to the disciples? How did that make Peter feel? 4. What lesson was Jesus teaching his disciples?*

DAY 290

THE LAST SUPPER

John 13:20-17:26

WHILE Jesus was talking, he became very sad and sorrowful and said, "One of you that are eating with me shall betray me and give me up to those who will kill me."

All the disciples looked at one another wondering who was the one Jesus meant. They asked, "Am I the one, Lord?"

Jesus said, "It is one of you twelve men who are dipping your hands into the same dish and eating with me. The Son of man goes, as it is written of him, but woe to that man who betrays him and gives him up to die. It would have been good for that man if he had never been born."

While Jesus was speaking, Simon Peter made signs to John across the table, that he, leaning next to Jesus, should ask him who this traitor was. So John whispered to Jesus, as he was lying close to him, "Lord, who is it?"

Jesus answered softly, so no one else heard. "It is the one to whom I will give a piece of bread after I have dipped it in the dish."

Then Jesus dipped a piece of bread into the dish and gave it to Judas Iscariot, who was lying near him. And as he gave it, he said, "Do quickly what you are going to do."

No one except John knew what this meant. Not all heard what Jesus said to Judas, and those who heard thought that Jesus was telling him to do something belonging to the feast, or perhaps, since Judas carried the money, that he should make some gift to the poor. But Judas left at once, for he saw that his plan was known and must be carried out now or never. He knew that after the supper Jesus would go back to Bethany, so he went to the rulers, told them where they might watch for Jesus on his way back to Bethany, and went with a band of men to a place at the foot of the Mount of Olives, where he was sure Jesus would pass.

As soon as Judas had gone out, Jesus said to the eleven disciples, "Little children, I shall be with you only a little while. I am going away, and where I go, you cannot come now. But when I am gone away from you, remember this new commandment that I give you, that you love one another even as I have loved you."

Simon Peter said to Jesus, "Lord, where are you going?"

Jesus answered, "Where I go, you cannot follow me now, but you shall follow me afterward."

Peter said to him, "Lord, why can't I follow you now? I will lay down my life for your sake."

Jesus said, "Will you lay down your life for me? I tell you, Peter, that before the cock crows tomorrow morning, you will three times deny that you have ever known me!"

But Peter said, "Though I die, I will never deny you, Lord!"

And so said all the other disciples, but Jesus said to them, "Before morning comes, every one of you will leave me alone. Yet I will not be alone, for the Father will be with me."

Jesus saw that Peter and all his disciples were full of sorrow at his words, and he said, "Let not your hearts be troubled. Ye believe in God. Believe also in me. In my Father's house are many houses. If it were not so, I would have told you. I am going to make a place ready for you. And when it is ready, I will come again and take you to be with me."

Jesus talked with the disciples a long time, and prayed for them. About midnight, they left the room together and went to the Mount of Olives.

Discussion Questions: *1. Why did Jesus feel sad? 2. Who was going to betray Jesus? How did Jesus let him know he knew what he planned? 3. What did Jesus tell the rest of the disciples to do to one another? 4. What did Peter tell Jesus he would do for him? What did Jesus tell him would happen?*

DAY 291

THE CAPTURE

Matthew 26:36-57

AT the foot of the Mount of Olives, near the path to Bethany, there was an orchard of olive trees called the Garden of Gethsemane. The word *gethsemane* means "oil press." Jesus often went to this place with his disciples because of its quiet shade. At this garden he stopped, and outside he left eight of his disciples, saying to them, "Sit here, while I go inside and pray."

He took with him the three chosen ones — Peter, James, and John — and went into the orchard. Jesus knew that in a little while Judas would be there with a band of men to seize him. Within a few hours, he would be beaten, stripped, and led out to die. The thought of what he was to suffer filled his soul with grief. He said to Peter, James, and John, "My soul is filled with sorrow, a sorrow that almost kills me. Stay here and watch while I am praying."

He went a little further among the trees and flung himself down on the ground, crying out, "O, my Father, if it be possible, let this cup pass away from me. Nevertheless, not as I will, but as you will!" His suffering was so great that great drops of sweat, like blood, fell from his face to the gound. After praying for a time, he got up, went to his three disciples, and found them all asleep. He awaked them and said to Peter, "Couldn't you watch with me one hour? Watch and pray, that you may not go into temptation. The spirit indeed is willing, but the flesh is weak."

He left them, went a second time into the woods, fell on his knees, and prayed again. "O, my Father, if this cup cannot pass away, and I must drink it, then your will be done."

He came again to the three disciples and found them sleeping. But this time he did not wake them. He went back into the woods and prayed, using the same words, and an angel from heaven came to him, and gave him strength.

JESUS KNELT DOWN AND BEGAN TO PRAY - LUKE 22:41

He was now ready for the fate that was soon to come, and his heart was strong. Once more he went to the three disciples and said to them, "You may as well sleep now, and take your rest, for the hour is at hand. Already the Son of man is given by the traitor into the hands of sinners. But rise up, and let us be going. See, the traitor is here!"

The disciples awoke. They heard the noise of a crowd, saw the flashing of torches and the gleaming of swords and spears. In the throng they saw Judas standing, and they knew that he was the traitor Jesus had spoken of the night before. Judas came rushing forward and kissed Jesus, as though he were glad to see him. This was a signal he had given to the band, for the men of the guard did not know Jesus, and Judas had said to them, "The one I shall kiss is the man you are to take. Seize him and hold him fast."

Jesus said to Judas, "Judas, do you betray the Son of man with a kiss?"

Then he turned to the crowd, and said, "Whom do you seek?"

They answered, "Jesus of Nazareth."

Jesus said, "I am he."

When Jesus said this, a sudden fear came to his enemies. They drew back and fell to the ground.

After a moment, Jesus said again, "Whom do you seek?"

Again they answered, "Jesus of Nazareth."

And Jesus said, pointing to his disciples, "I told you that I am he. If you are seeking me, let these disciples go their way."

But as they came forward to seize Jesus, Peter drew his sword and struck at

JESUS IS BETRAYED BY JUDAS' KISS - MATTHEW 26:49

one of the men in front, cutting off his right ear.

Jesus said to Peter, "Put up the sword. Shouldn't I drink the cup my Father has given me? Don't you know that I could call on my Father and he would send me armies upon armies of angels?"

Then he spoke to the crowd. "Let me do this," and he touched the place where the ear had been cut off, and it came on again and was well. Jesus said to the rulers and leaders of the armed men, "Do you come out against me with swords and clubs as though I were a robber? I was with you every day in the Temple, and you did not lift your hands against me. But the words in the Scriptures must come to pass, and this is your hour."

When the disciples of Jesus saw that he would not allow them to fight for him, they did not know what to do. In their fear, they all ran away and left their Master alone with his enemies. These men took hold of Jesus, bound him, and led him away to the house of the high priest.

Discussion Questions: *1. Why did Jesus take the disciples to the Garden of Gethsemane? 2. Which disciples did Jesus take into the orchard with him? 3. What happened in the garden? 4. Who came to take Jesus away? 5. How did Peter try to help Jesus? What did Jesus do?*

DAY 292

PETER DENIES JESUS

Luke 22:54-62

A T that time, there were two high priests. One was Annas, who had been high priest until his office had been taken from him by the Romans and given to Caiaphas, his son-in-law. But Annas still had great power among the people, and they brought Jesus to Annas first.

Simon Peter and John, the disciple Jesus loved, followed the crowd that carried Jesus away, and they came to the door of the high priest's house. John knew the high priest and went in, but Peter stayed outside until John brought him in. He came in, but did not dare go into the room where Jesus stood before Annas. In the courtyard of the house, they had made a fire of charcoal, and Peter stood with those warming themselves at the fire.

Annas asked Jesus about his disciples and teaching. Jesus answered him, "What I have taught has been open in the synagogues and in the Temple. Why do you ask me? Ask those that heard me. They know what I said."

Then one of the officers struck Jesus on the mouth, saying to him, "Is this the way you answer the high priest?"

Jesus answered the officer calmly and quietly, "If I have said anything evil, tell what the evil is. But if I have spoken the truth, why do you strike me?"

While Annas and his men were showing their hate toward Jesus, who stood bound and alone among his enemies, Peter was still in the courtyard, warming himself at the fire. A maid in the house looked at Peter carefully and said to him, "You were one of those men with this Jesus of Nazareth!"

Peter was afraid to tell the truth, and he answered her, "Woman, I do not know the man, and I do not know what you are talking about."

To get away from her, he went out into the porch of the house. There another servant saw him and said, "This man was with Jesus!"

And Peter swore with an oath that he did not know Jesus at all. Soon a man came by. He looked at Peter, heard him speak, and said, "You are surely one of this man's disciples, for your speech shows that you came from Galilee."

Then Peter began to curse and swear, declaring that he did not know the man they were talking about.

Just at that moment the loud, shrill crowing of a cock startled Peter, and at the same time he saw Jesus, who was being dragged through the hall from Annas to Caiaphas, the other high priest. The Lord turned as he was passing and looked at Peter.

Peter remembered what Jesus had said the evening before: "Before the cock crows tomorrow morning, you will deny three times that you have ever known me."

Then Peter went out of the high priest's house, into the street, and he wept bitterly because he had denied his Lord.

PETER WENT OUT AND WEPT BITTERLY - LUKE 22:62

Discussion Questions: *1. Why were there two high priests? 2. Who did the crowd take Jesus to? What did he ask Jesus? 3. What did Jesus tell him? 4. What did Peter do?*

DAY 293

JESUS BEFORE CAIAPHAS

Luke 22:63-71

FROM the house of Annas, the enemies of Jesus led him to the house of Caiaphas, who the Romans had just made high priest. There all the rulers of the Jews were called together, and they tried to find men who would swear that they had heard Jesus say some wicked thing. This would give the rulers an excuse for putting Jesus to death. But they could find nothing. Some men swore one thing, and some swore another, but their words did not agree.

Finally the high priest stood up and said to Jesus, "Have you nothing to say? What is it that these men are speaking against you?"

JESUS STOOD BEFORE THE CHIEF PRIESTS - LUKE 22:66-71

But Jesus stood silent. Then the high priest spoke again. "Are you the Christ, the Son of God?"

Jesus said, "I am. And the time shall come when you will see the Son of man sitting on the throne of power and coming in the clouds of heaven!"

These words made the high priest very angry. He said to the rulers, "Do you hear these dreadful words? He says he is the Son of God. What do you think of words like these?"

They all said, "He deserves to be put to death!"

Then the servants of the high priest and the soldiers that held Jesus began to mock him. They spat on him, they covered his face, and struck him with their hands, and said, "If you are a prophet, tell us who is hitting you!"

The rulers of the Jews and the priests and the scribes voted that Jesus should be put to death. But the land of the Jews was ruled by the Romans, and no man could be put to death unless the Roman governor commanded it. The Roman governor at that time was a man named Pontius Pilate, and he was in the city. So all the rulers and a great crowd of people came to Pilate's castle, bringing with them Jesus, who was still tied up.

Discussion Questions: *1. What did the rulers want to do to Jesus? 2. What did the men say who swore against Jesus? 3. Why couldn't the Jews put Jesus to death?*

DAY 294

JUDAS'S DEATH
Matthew 27:3-8

UP to this time, Judas Iscariot; although he had betrayed Jesus, did not believe he would be put to death. Perhaps he thought Jesus would save himself from death, as he had saved others by a miracle. But when he saw Jesus bound and beaten, doing nothing to protect himself, and when he heard the rulers vote that Jesus should be put to death, Judas realized what he had done. He brought back the thirty pieces of silver that he had been given for betraying his Lord and said, "I have sinned in betraying one who has done no wrong!"

But they answered him, "What is that to us? You look after that!"

When Judas saw they would not take back the money and let Jesus go free, he carried the thirty pieces to the Temple and threw them down on the floor. Then he went away and hanged himself.

After that, the rulers didn't know what to do with the money. They said, "We cannot put it into the treasury of the Temple, because it is the price paid for a man's blood." After talking it over, they decided to use the money to buy a piece of ground called the potter's field. This was set apart as a place for burying strangers who died in the city and had no friends. But everyone in Jerusalem spoke of that place as the Field of Blood.

Discussion Questions: *1. Why didn't Judas believe Jesus would die? 2. What did Judas do when he found out Jesus would be put to death? 3. Why didn't the rulers want to put Judas's money into the Temple treasury? 4. Do you think the name they called the field was a good one? Why or why not?*

DAY 295

JESUS BEFORE PILATE
Luke 23:1-7

IT was very early in the morning when the rulers of the Jews brought Jesus to Pilate. They would not go into Pilate's hall because Pilate was not a Jew, so Pilate came out to them and asked, "What charge do you bring against this man?"

They answered, "If he were not an evil-doer, we would not have brought him to you."

Pilate did not wish to be troubled, and he said, "Take him away and judge him by your own law!"

The Jews said to Pilate, "We are not allowed to put any man to death, and we have brought him to you. We have found this man teaching evil, and telling men not to pay taxes to the Emperor Caesar, and saying that he himself is Christ, a king."

Then Pilate went into his courtroom and sent for Jesus. When he looked at Jesus, he said, "Are you the King of the Jews? Your own people have brought you to me. What have you done?"

Jesus said to him, "My kingdom is not of this world. If it were of this world, then those who serve me would fight to save me from my enemies. But now my kingdom is not here."

Pilate said, "Are you a king, then?"

Jesus answered him, "You have spoken it. I am a king. For this was I born, and for this I came into the world, that I might speak the truth of God to men."

"Truth," said Pilate. "What is truth?"

Then, without waiting for an answer, Pilate went out to the rulers and the crowd and said, "I find no evil in this man."

Pilate thought Jesus was a harmless man, perhaps whose mind was weak,

JESUS BEFORE PILATE - JOHN 19:4,5

and he could see no reason for the rulers and the people to be so bitter against him. But they cried out all the more, saying, "He stirs up the people everywhere, from Galilee to here."

When Pilate heard the word *Galilee*, he asked if this man had come from that land. They told him he had, and Pilate said, "Galilee and its people are under the rule of Herod. He is here in Jerusalem. I will send this man to him."

Discussion Questions: *1. Why did the Jews bring Jesus to Pilate? 2. What did Jesus tell Pilate? 3. What did Pilate think about Jesus? Why did he send Jesus to Herod?*

DAY 296

HEROD AND PILATE

Luke 23:8-24

SO, from Pilate's courtroom, Jesus was sent to Herod's palace. This was the Herod who had put John the Baptist in prison and had given his head to a dancing-girl. Herod was very glad to see Jesus, for he had heard many things about him, and he hoped to see him do some wonderful thing. But Jesus would not work wonders as a show to be looked at, and when Herod asked him many questions, Jesus would not speak a word. Herod would not judge Jesus, for he knew Jesus had done nothing wrong. He and his soldiers mocked Jesus, dressed him in a robe, as though he were a make-believe king, and sent him back to Pilate.

So Pilate, much against his will, was compelled to decide what to do with Jesus. Just as Jesus was standing before him, a message came to Pilate from his wife, saying, "Do nothing against that good man. Tonight I suffered many things in a dream on account of him."

Pilate said to the Jews, "You have brought this man to me as one who is leading the people to evil. I have seen no evil in him, nor has Herod. I will order that he be beaten with rods and set free. You know it is the custom to set a prisoner free at the time of the feast."

They always set some prisoner free as a sign of the joy at the feast. At that time there was in the prison a man named Barabbas, who was a robber and a murderer. Pilate said to the people, "Shall I set free Jesus, who is called the King of the Jews?"

But the rulers went among the people and urged them to ask for Barabbas to be set free, and the crowd cried out, "Not this man, but Barabbas!"

Then Pilate said, "What shall I do with Jesus?"

And they all cried out, "Crucify him! Let him die on the cross!"

Pilate wanted to spare the life of Jesus. To show how he felt, he sent for water and washed his hands in front of all the people, saying, "My hands are clean from the blood of this good man!"

They cried out, "Let his blood be on us and our children after us! Crucify him! Send him to the cross!"

To please the people, Pilate gave them what they asked. He set free Barabbas, though he was a robber and a murderer. But before sending Jesus to the cross, he tried once more to save his life. He had Jesus beaten, hoping this might satisfy the people. Since Jesus was spoken of as a king, the soldiers who beat Jesus made a crown of thorns and put it on his head, then put a purple robe on him. Bowing down before him, they called out, "Hail, King of the Jews!"

Then, hoping to awaken some pity for Jesus, Pilate brought him out to the people with the crown of thorns and the purple robe and said, "Look at this man!"

But again the cry arose, "Crucify him! Send him to the cross!"

At last, Pilate yielded to the voice of the people. He sat down on the judgment seat and commanded that Jesus, who he knew to be a good man who had done nothing evil, should be put to death on the cross.

Discussion Questions: *1. What had Herod done? 2. What did Jesus do when he was before Herod? Why didn't Herod judge Jesus? 3. Why did Pilate want to set Jesus free? Who did not want him to? 4. What did they insist that Pilate do to Jesus?*

DAY 297

THE CROSS

Luke 23:26-38
John 19:16-24

AND so Pontius Pilate, the Roman governor, gave orders that Jesus should die on the cross. The Roman soldiers took Jesus, beat him again, and then led him out of the city to the place of death. This was a place called Golgotha in the Jewish language, Calvary in that of the Romans. Both words meant the Skull Place.

With the soldiers went a great crowd of people, some of them enemies of

Jesus, glad to see him suffer. Others were friends of Jesus, the women who had helped him, now weeping as they saw him all covered with his blood and going out to die. But Jesus turned to them, and said, "Daughters of Jerusalem, do not weep for me, but weep for yourselves, and for your children. For the days are coming when they shall count those happy who have no little ones to be slain, when they shall wish the mountains might fall on them and the hills might cover them and hide them from their enemies!"

They had tried to make Jesus bear his own cross, but soon found he was too weak and could not carry it. They took a man named Simon and made him carry the cross to its place at Calvary.

It was a custom among the Jews to give to men about to die on the cross some medicine to deaden their feelings, so they would not suffer as much. They offered this to Jesus, but when he tasted it and found what it was, he would not take it. He knew that he would die, but he wanted his mind clear, even though his suffering would be greater.

At Calvary, they laid the cross down, stretched Jesus on it, and drove nails through his hands and feet to fasten him to the cross. Then they stood it upright with Jesus on it. While the soldiers were doing this dreadful work, Jesus prayed for them, saying, "Father, forgive them, for they know not what they are doing."

The soldiers also took the clothes that Jesus had worn, giving each one a garment. But when they came to his undergarment, they found it was woven, and had no seams, so they said, "Let us not tear it, but cast lots for it, to see who shall have it." So at the foot of the cross, the soldiers threw lots for the garment of Christ.

Two robbers who had been sentenced to die by the cross were led out to die at the same time with Jesus. One was placed on a cross at his right side, and the other at his left. Over the head of Jesus they placed, on Pilate's orders, a sign that said,

THIS IS JESUS OF NAZARETH,
THE KING OF THE JEWS.

This was written in three languages: Hebrew, which was the language of the Jews; Latin, the language of the Romans, and Greek. Many of the people read this writing, but the chief priests were not pleased with it. They urged Pilate to have it changed from "The King of the Jews" to "He said, I am King of the Jews."

But Pilate would not change it. He said, "What I have written, I have written."

Discussion Questions: *1. Who went to see Jesus suffer? 2. Who carried Jesus' cross for him? 3. Why didn't Jesus drink the medicine they tried to give him? 4. What did Pilate write about Jesus? Why didn't the chief priest like that?*

DAY 298

THE DEATH OF JESUS

Luke 23:35-47
John 19:25-30
Mark 15:27-39

AND the people who passed by on the road, as they looked at Jesus on the cross, mocked him. Some called out to him, "You that would destroy the Temple and build it in three days, save yourself. If you are the Son of God, come down from the cross!"

And the priests and scribes said, "He saved others, but he cannot save himself. Come down from the cross, and we will believe in you!"

One of the robbers who was on his own cross beside Jesus joined in the cry, and said, "If you are the Christ, save yourself and us!"

But the other robber said to him, "Have you no fear of God, to speak like

AT CALVARY JESUS WAS CRUCIFIED — JOHN 19:16-37

429

this while you are suffering the same fate with this man? We deserve to die, but this man has done nothing wrong." Then this man said to Jesus, "Lord, remember me when you come into your kingdom!"

And Jesus answered him as they were both hanging on their crosses, "Today you shall be with me in heaven."

Before the cross of Jesus stood his mother, filled with sorrow for her son. Beside her was one of his disciples, John, the disciple he loved best. Other women were there: his mother's sister; Mary, the wife of Cleopas; and a woman named Mary Magdalene, out of whom a year before Jesus had sent an evil spirit. Jesus wanted to put his mother into the care of John, so he said to her, as he looked from her to John, "Woman, see your son."

To John he said, "Son, see your mother."

That day John took Jesus' mother home to his own house and cared for her as his own mother.

At about noon, a sudden darkness came over the land and lasted for three hours. In the middle of the afternoon, when Jesus had been on the cross for six hours of terrible pain, he cried, "My Lord, my God, why have you forsaken me!"

After this he spoke again, saying, "I thirst!"

Someone dipped a sponge in a cup of vinegar, put it on a reed, and gave him a drink of it. Then Jesus spoke his last words on the cross: "It is finished! Father, into thy hands I give my spirit!"

And Jesus died. At that moment, the veil in the Temple was torn from top to bottom. The Roman officer who had charge of the soldiers around the cross saw what had taken place, and how Jesus died, and he said, "Truly this was a righteous man. He was the Son of God."

Discussion Questions: *1. Why did some people mock Jesus? 2. What did the second robber say about Jesus? Was he right? Why? 3. What happened when Jesus died? What did it mean?*

DAY 299

THE TOMB

Matthew 27:55-66

AFTER Jesus was dead, one of the soldiers, to be sure he was really dead, ran his spear into the side of his dead body. Out of the wound came both water and blood.

There were a few rulers of the Jews who were friends of Jesus, though they did not dare follow Jesus openly. One of these was Nicodemus, the ruler who came to see Jesus one night. Another was a rich man who came from the town of Arimathea and was named Joseph. Joseph of Arimathea went to Pilate and asked that the body of Jesus be given to him. Pilate wondered that he had died so soon, for often men lived on the cross for two or three days. But when he found that Jesus was really dead, he gave his body to Joseph.

Joseph and his friends took the body of Jesus down from the cross and wrapped it in fine linen. Nicodemus brought some precious spices, myrrh, and aloes, which they wrapped up with the body. Then they placed the body in Joseph's own new tomb, a cave dug out of the rock in a garden near the place of the cross. In front of the cave's opening, they rolled a great stone.

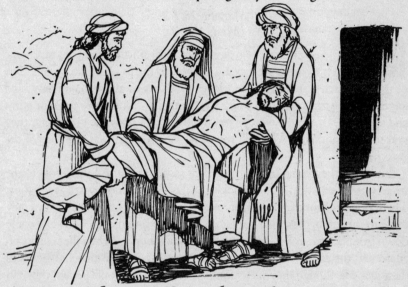

THE BODY OF JESUS WAS PUT IN JOSEPH'S TOMB - JOHN 19:38-42

Mary Magdalene, the other Mary, and some other women watched while they laid the body of Jesus in it. On the next morning, some of the rulers of the Jews came to Pilate, and said, "Sir, we remember that Jesus of Nazareth said, 'After three days I will rise again.' Give orders that the tomb be watched and made sure for three days, or else his disciples may steal his body and say, 'He is risen from the dead.' Even after his death he may do more harm than he did while he was alive."

Pilate said to them, "Set a watch, and make it as sure as you can." They placed a seal on the stone, so no one could break it, and they set a watch of soldiers at the door.

431

The body of Jesus lay in the tomb from the evening of Friday, the day he died on the cross, to the dawn of Sunday, the first day of the week.

Discussion Questions: *1. How did the Roman soldiers make sure Jesus was dead? 2. Who took Jesus' body? What did he do with him? 3. What were the rulers of the Jews afraid Jesus would do? What did Pilate order the soldiers to do?*

DAY 300

EASTER

Matthew 28:1-8
Mark 16:1-8

ON Sunday morning, two days after the death and burial of Jesus, some women went, as soon as it was light, to the tomb in the garden. One of these women was Mary Magdalene, another was also named Mary, and another was named Salome. They were bringing some more fragrant gums and spices to place in the wrappings on the body of Jesus. As they went, they said to one another, "Who will roll away the great stone at the door of the cave for us?"

But when they came to the cave, they saw that the seal was broken, the stone was rolled away, and the soldiers who had been on guard were gone. There stood the tomb of Jesus, all open! They did not know that before they came to the tomb, there had been an earthquake, and that an angel had come down from heaven, rolled away the stone, and sat on it. When the soldiers on guard saw the angel with his flashing face and dazzling garments, they fell to the ground as though they were dead. As soon as they could get up, they ran away in terror. So when the women came, there was no man in sight.

As soon as Mary Magdalene saw the tomb was open, without stopping to look into it, she ran quickly to tell the disciples. A moment after she had gone, the other women looked into the tomb and saw that the body of Jesus was not there. But they saw young men sitting at each end of the tomb, clothed in long white garments. Their faces shone like angels, and when the women saw them, they were filled with fear. One of the angels said to them, "Do not be afraid. You are looking for Jesus of Nazareth, who was crucified. He is not here. He is risen, as he said he would rise from the dead. Come, see the place where the Lord lay, and then go and tell his disciples, and tell Peter too, that Jesus will go before you into Galilee, and you shall see him there."

The women went away in mingled joy and fear. They ran in haste to bring this word of the angel to the disciples.

THE WOMEN FOUND THE ANGEL AT THE TOMB OF JESUS - MATTHEW 28:1-8

Discussion Questions: *1. What did the women find in the garden? 2. What had happened to the soldiers? 3. What did the women see? What did they tell the women?*

DAY 301

PETER, JOHN, AND MARY

John 20:1-17

BUT while these women were looking into the tomb and listening to the angel, Mary Magdalene was looking for the disciples, to tell them the tomb was open and the body of Jesus was not there, for she did not know he had risen. She found Peter and John, and said to them, "They have taken away the Lord out of the tomb, and we do not know where they have laid him!"

Peter and John rushed to the tomb. John outran Peter and arrived first, perhaps because he was the youngest. But when he saw the open door, the broken seal, and the stone lying at one side, he stood still for a moment. John

433

stooped and looked into the cave, and he could see the linen cloths that had been wrapped around the body of Jesus.

When Peter came up, he did not wait, but rushed into the tomb, followed by John.

Suddenly John thought, "Jesus has risen from the dead!" He had not seen the angel or heard his words. From that moment, John believed that Jesus was alive. Both Peter and John went away to think of the strange things they had seen, and very soon, Mary Magdalene came back to the tomb. No one was there, for both the women and the disciples had gone away. Mary Magdalene did not know that Jesus had risen, for she had not heard the angel's message.

She wept as she thought of her Lord, slain by wicked men and not even allowed to rest in his grave. Weeping, she stooped and looked into the tomb. There she saw two men in white garments sitting, one at the head, the other at the feet, where the body of Jesus had lain. They were the two angels the other women had seen, but Mary Magdalene did not know this. One of them said to her, "Woman, why do you weep?"

She answered, "Because they have taken away my Lord, and I do not know where they have laid him."

Something caused her to turn around, and she saw a man standing behind her. It was Jesus, but for a minute, she was kept from recognizing him. He said to her, "Woman, why do you weep?"

She supposed that he was the gardener, and said, hardly looking at him,

MARY MAGDALENE SAW THE RISEN LORD - JOHN 20:11-18

"Sir, if you have carried him out of this place, tell me where you have laid him, and I will take him away."

Then the stranger spoke her name, "Mary!" and she knew he was Jesus, no longer dead, but living. She turned around, fell down before him, and was about to seize his feet, as she said, "My Master!"

But Jesus said to her, "Do not take hold of me. I am not yet going away to my Father. But go to my brothers, and say to them, I go up to my Father, and to your Father, to my God, and your God!"

Discussion Questions: *1. What was Mary Magdelene doing while the other women were at the tomb? 2. Who followed her back to the tomb? 3. What did John think? 4. Who did Mary see after the disciples had left?*

DAY 302

The Travelers

Matthew 28:9, 10

Luke 24:13-32

MARY Magdalene told the disciples how she had seen the Lord, and how he had spoken these things to her. This was the first time that anyone saw Jesus after he rose from the dead.

You remember that the other women — another Mary, Salome, and the rest — had not seen the risen Christ, but they had seen an angel who told them he had risen and would meet his disciples in Galilee. They went into the city, and were looking for the disciples, when suddenly Jesus stood before them and said, "All hail!" That means, "Welcome to all of you!" They fell down before him and worshiped him. And Jesus said to them, as he had said to Mary Magdalene only a few moments before, "Do not be afraid. Find my brothers, and tell them to go into Galilee, and they shall see me there."

This was the second time Jesus showed himself on the day he rose.

On that same day, two of the followers of Jesus were walking out of Jerusalem to a village called Emmaus, about seven miles away. While they were talking over the strange happenings of the day, they saw a stranger walking beside them. It was Jesus, their risen Lord, but they were kept from knowing him. The stranger said to them, "What words are these that you are speaking with each other, which make you so sad?"

One of the two men, Cleopas, answered, "Are you a stranger in Jerusalem who has not heard what has taken place there in the last few days?"

The stranger said, "What things?"

JESUS SPEAKS WITH TWO MEN ON THE ROAD TO EMMAUS - LUKE 24:15

And they said, "The things about Jesus of Nazareth, who was a mighty prophet in his acts and his words before God and all the people. The chief priests and rulers caused him to be sentenced to death, and he died on the cross. But we hoped that he was the promised One, who was to save Israel. And now it is the third day since he was put to death. And today some women of our company who were at the tomb surprised us with the news that the tomb was empty. His body was not there, and they saw angels who said that Jesus was alive. Then some of us went to the tomb and found as the women had said. But they did not see him."

Then the stranger said to them, "O foolish men, the slow of heart to believe what the prophets have said! Wasn't it necessary for the Christ to suffer these things, and then to enter in his glory?"

Then he began with the books of Moses and went through the prophets, showing them the meaning of all that was said about Christ. As they went on, they came to the village where they were going, and he acted as though he would go beyond it. But they urged and persuaded him to stay with them, saying, "Abide with us, for it is now almost evening, and the day is at its close."

So he went in with them and sat down with them to a supper. As they were about to eat, he took the loaf of bread into his hands, blessed it, broke it, and gave it to them. And at that moment their eyes were opened, and they knew he was the Lord. Just then, he left their sight. They said to each other, "Wasn't our heart burning within us while he talked to us on the road and

436

opened the words of the Scriptures to us?"

This was the third time Jesus showed himself on that day.

_____

Discussion Questions: 1. Who saw Jesus on the day he arose? 2. How did he appear to Cleopas and his companion? 3. What did Jesus tell the two people on the road to Emmaus?

DAY 303

_____

EASTER EVENING

Luke 24:33-53

THESE two men hurried to Jerusalem that night, to tell what they had seen. They found ten of the disciples together, saying, "The Lord has risen and has been seen by Simon Peter."

We do not know what Jesus said to Peter, but this was the fourth time he was seen living on the day he rose.

The ten disciples and other followers of Jesus were together in a room that night, and the doors were shut. Suddenly Jesus himself was seen standing among them. He said, "Peace be unto you!"

SUDDENLY, JESUS STOOD IN THEIR MIDST — LUKE 24:36-48

Some of them were alarmed when they saw him, and thought he must be a spirit. But he said to them, "Why are you troubled? And why do fears come to you? Look at the wounds in my hands and my feet! Handle me, and see. A spirit does not have flesh and bones, as you see I have."

And he showed them his hands and his side. They could scarcely believe, for the joy of seeing him again. He said, "Have you anything to eat?"

They gave him a piece of broiled fish and honeycomb, and he ate before them. And he said, "This is what I told you while I was with you, that everything written of me in the law of Moses, in the prophets, and in the psalms, must come to pass. It was necessary that Christ should suffer, should rise from the dead, and that everywhere the gospel should be preached in his name. I will send the promise of my Father upon you. But stay in Jerusalem after I leave you, until power shall come upon you from on high."

Then, when the disciples saw that it was really the Lord, and he was alive from the dead, they were glad. And Jesus said to them again, "Peace be to you. As my Father has sent me, even so I send you. May the Spirit of God come upon you!"

And this was the fifth time that Jesus showed himself alive that day. This Sunday was the brightest day in all the world, because on it Jesus rose from the dead. _____

Discussion Questions: *1. Who did Jesus appear to the next time? 2. How did they feel? What did they think? 3. How did they know that he was really the Lord? How did they feel then? 4. Why was that Sunday the brightest in the world?*

DAY 304

———

THOMAS

John 21:24-29

WHEN Jesus showed himself to the disciples on the evening he rose from the dead, only ten of the disciples saw him, for Judas was no longer among them, and Thomas the Twin was absent. The other disciples said to Thomas, "We have seen the Lord!"

But Thomas said, "I will not believe he has risen unless I can see in his hands the marks of the nails on the cross. I must see them with my own eyes, and put my finger on them, and put my hand into the wound in his side, before I will believe."

A week passed, and on the next Sunday evening, the disciples were together again, and this time Thomas was with them. The doors were shut, but suddenly Jesus was standing in the middle of the room. He said, as before, "Peace be with you."

Then he turned to Thomas, and said to him, "Thomas, come here. Touch my hands with your finger, and put your hand into my side, and no longer refuse to believe that I am living, but have faith in me!"

And Thomas answered him, "My Lord and my God!"

Then Jesus said to him, "Because you have seen me, you have believed. Blessed are they that have not seen, and yet have believed."

Discussion Questions: *1. Who had not seen Jesus? 2. What did he say he wanted to do before he would believe? 3. Did that happen? What did Jesus say about it?*

DAY 305

PETER
John 21:1-17

YOU remember that the angels had told the women at the tomb of Jesus that his disciples should go into Galilee, and there they would see the risen Lord. They went to Galilee and waited for some days without seeing Jesus. Finally Peter said, "I am going fishing."

"We'll go with you," said James, John, Thomas, Nathanael, and two other disciples. They went out on the lake, worked all night, but found no fish. Just as the day was breaking, they saw someone standing on the beach. It was Jesus, but they did not know him. He called out to them, as one friend calls to another, "Boys, have you caught anything?"

They answered him, "No."

He said to them, "Cast the net on the right side of the ship, and you will find some fish."

The quick eyes of John, the beloved disciple, were the first to see who this stranger on the shore was. He said to Peter, "It is the Lord!"

When Peter heard this, he flung on his fisherman's coat, leaped into the water, and swam to the shore to meet his Lord. The other six disciples stayed in the boat and rowed to the shore, dragging the net full of fish. When they came to the land, they found a fire of charcoal burning, a fish broiling on it, and a loaf of bread beside it. They all knew now that it was the Lord Jesus, and he said to them, "Bring some of the fish you have caught."

Simon Peter waded out to where the net was lying, filled with fish, and drew it to the shore. Afterward they counted the fish that were in it and found 153 large fish, plus the small ones. Yet the net was not broken with all these fish in it. Jesus said to them, "Come and eat."

He took the bread and gave it to them, and gave them fish, and the seven disciples ate breakfast with their risen Lord. This was the third time that Jesus showed himself to his disciples in a group after rising from the tomb, and the seventh time altogether.

After the breakfast, Jesus turned to Simon Peter, the one who had denied he knew Jesus, and said to him, "Simon, son of Jonas, do you love me?"

Peter answered him, "Yes, Lord. You know I love you."

And Jesus said to him, "Feed my lambs."

Then, after a time, Jesus said again, "Simon, son of Jonas, do you love me?"

Peter answered him as before, "Yes Lord. You know I love you."

And Jesus said to him, "Tend my sheep."

The third time, Jesus said to him, "Simon, son of Jonas, do you love me?"

Peter was troubled to have this question asked again and again, and he answered, "Lord, you know all things. You know I love you."

Then Jesus said to him, "Feed my sheep." Then he added, "Follow me!"

So Peter, who had denied Christ three times, declared his love to Christ three times and was called to his place among the disciples.

Discussion Questions: *1. How had the disciples obeyed Jesus? 2. What did some of the disciples do while they waited for Jesus? 3. What did Peter do when he knew Jesus was there? What does that show you about Peter? 4. How did Jesus call Peter to him again?*

DAY 306

THE ASCENSION

Matthew 28:16-20

AFTER this, the followers of Jesus met on a mountain in Galilee, perhaps the same mountain where Jesus had given the Sermon on the Mount. More than 500 people were gathered there on the mountain, and Jesus appeared to them all, saying, "All power is given to me in heaven and earth. Go therefore, and preach my gospel to all the nations of the earth, baptizing them in the name of the Father, and of the Son, and of the Holy Spirit, teaching them to keep all the commands I have given you. I am with you always, even to the end of the world."

This was the eighth time Jesus was seen after he rose from the dead. The ninth was when he showed himself to James — not the apostle, but another James, who was called the Lord's brother and may have been a son of Joseph and Mary. We don't know what was said at this meeting, but from then on, James was a strong believer in Jesus.

Once more (the tenth time), the risen Saviour showed himself to all his eleven disciples. It may have been in Jerusalem, for he told them not to leave the city, but to wait until God sent them his Spirit, as he had promised. Jesus said to them, "When the Holy Spirit comes upon you, you shall have a new power, and you shall speak in my name in Jerusalem, and in Judea, and in Samaria, and in the farthest parts of the earth."

Jesus led his disciples out of the city and over the Mount of Olives, near the village of Bethany. He lifted up his hands to bless them, and as he did, he began to rise in the air, higher and higher, until a cloud covered him and the disciples saw him no more.

While they were looking up toward heaven, they found two angels with shining garments standing by them. These men said, "O you men of Galilee, why do you stand looking up into heaven? This Jesus, who has been taken up from you, shall come again from heaven to earth, as you have seen him go up from earth to heaven!"

Then the disciples were glad. They worshiped their risen Lord Jesus — now gone up to heaven — and went back to Jerusalem. There they were constantly in the Temple, praising and giving thanks to God.

Discussion Questions: *1. How many people met with Jesus on the mountain? 2. What did he tell them to do? 3. What did Jesus promise the disciples? How would that help them? 4. What does the word* ascension *mean? What happened at the Ascension?*

DAY 307

PENTECOST (PART 1)

Acts 1:12-2:13

AFTER the Lord Jesus had gone to heaven, the eleven disciples and a small group of those who believed in Christ were left alone on the earth. But they were not sad, as we would expect them to be. They were very happy, for their Lord had promised to send power from God to them. Every day they met together to praise God and pray in the large upper room where Jesus had eaten his last supper with them.

441

The eleven disciples chose a twelfth man to take the place of Judas the traitor. His name was Matthias. Also with them were Mary, the mother of Jesus; his brothers; the women who had been at the cross and the tomb; and a number of other men and women who believed in Jesus as the Christ. Altogether, there were 120 of them who believed in Jesus Christ.

Ten days after Jesus went to heaven came a day the Jews called Pentecost, which was celebrated fifty days after the Feast of the Passover. That day the believers of Christ were all together in the upper room praying, when suddenly a sound was heard — like the rushing of a mighty wind coming straight down from the sky. What looked like tongues of fire seemed to be over everyone's head. Then the Spirit of God came to them all, and they began to speak of Christ and his gospel with a power that none of them had ever known before.

WHAT LOOKED LIKE TONGUES OF FIRE RESTED ON EACH ONE OF THEM -ACTS 2:3

The noise of this strange wind was heard all over the city, and at once a great crowd of people gathered to learn what the sound meant. They saw all 120 of Jesus' followers singing, praising God, and telling of his wonderful works. And there was another marvelous thing. These people who had heard the noise and been drawn to the place were Jews from many lands, who had come up to Jerusalem to worship. Some were from lands far in the east, others from lands in the west, and others from islands. Every man heard these believers of Jesus speaking the language he understood! In every tongue of the earth, men were telling of God's wonderful work.

"What does all this mean?" asked some. Others said, "These people act as though they were drunk with wine!"

Discussion Questions: *1. Why weren't the people who believed in Jesus sad? How many of them were there? 2. What happened when the Spirit of God came to the people? What did it mean? 3. What could the people who believed in Jesus do then?*

DAY 308

PENTECOST (PART 2)

Acts 2:14-47

THEN Simon Peter stood up, with the other apostles around him. From that time, the twelve disciples were called *apostles*, which means "the men sent forth," because they were sent out to win the world to Christ. Peter spoke in a loud voice to all the people, saying, "You men of Judea, and all you that live in Jerusalem, listen to me. This you see is what the prophet said long ago should come to pass: That God would pour out his Spirit upon men. This is the great day of the Lord when everyone who shall call on the Lord shall be saved. Jesus of Nazareth, who worked wonders and signs among you, you put to death on the cross, by the hands of wicked men. But God has raised him up from death. We who have seen him living declare this to you, that he who you killed on the cross is now the Lord and the Christ."

Then many of the people began to see how wrong it had been to kill Jesus, who God had sent to them as his Son. They cried out to Peter and the other apostles, "Men and brethren, what shall we do?"

Peter told them, "Turn away from your sins, believe in Jesus, and be baptized in his name. Your sins shall be taken away, and you shall have this power of the Holy Spirit of God."

Then a great many people believed in Jesus Christ as their Saviour and were baptized by the apostles. And on that day, 3,000 joined the Church of Christ. They met with the believers daily in the upper room, worshiped in the Temple, and listened to the teaching of the apostles.

All the followers of Jesus were like one family of brothers and sisters. Those who had money gave it to help those who were in need, and some who had land and houses sold them and gave to those who were poor. All were happy, praising God, loving and loved by one another. And every day, more and more of those who were being saved were united in the Church.

Discussion Questions: *1. What does* apostles *mean? What were the apostles to do? 2. What did Peter tell the people? 3. How many people believed in Jesus that day?*

DAY 309

The Beautiful Gate (Part 1)

Acts 3:1-11

NE day Peter and John were on their way to the Temple for the afternoon hour of prayer, about three o'clock. They walked across the court of the Gentiles, a large, open square paved with marble. On its eastern side was a double row of pillars with a roof above them called Solomon's Porch. In front of this porch was the main entrance to the Temple, through a gate called the Beautiful Gate. At this gate outside the Temple, they saw a lame man sitting. He had never been able to walk. Since he was very poor, his friends carried him every day to this place, and there he sat, hoping some who went into the Temple might take pity on him and give him a little money.

Peter and John stopped in front of this man and Peter said, "Look at us!"

The lame man looked earnestly at the two apostles, thinking they were about to give him something.

PETER RAISED UP THE LAME MAN IN JESUS' NAME - ACTS 3:7

But Peter said, "Silver and gold have I none. But what I have, I will give you. In the name of Jesus Christ of Nazareth, walk!" Peter took hold of the lame man's right hand and lifted him up. At once the lame man felt new power enter his feet and ankles. He leaped up, stood on his feet, and began to walk. He walked up the steps with the two apostles and went into the Temple with them, walking, leaping, and praising God. The people who saw him leaping up and running knew him, for they had seen him every day begging at the Beautiful Gate. Everyone was filled with wonder at the change that had come over him.

After worshiping and praising God in the Temple, the man, staying next to Peter and John, went out with them through the Beautiful Gate into Solomon's Porch. And in a very few minutes a great crowd of people came to see the man who had been made well and the two men who had healed him.

Discussion Questions: 1. Why did the man sit at the gate of the Temple? 2. What couldn't Peter give the man? What could he give him? Which was better to have? 3. What did the man do next?

DAY 310

The Beautiful Gate (Part 2)

Acts 3:12-4:4

THEN Peter stood up before the throng of people and spoke to them. "You men of Israel," he said, "why do you look wondering on this man? Why do you fix your eyes on us, as though by our own power of goodness we made this man walk? The God of Abraham, Isaac, and Jacob has in this way shown the power and glory of his Son Jesus, who you gave up to his enemies and refused before Pontius Pilate, when Pilate was determined to set him free. But you refused the Holy One and the Righteous One, and chose the murderer Barabbas to be set free in his place. You killed the Prince of life, whom God raised from the dead. We who have seen him risen declare this is true. And the power of Jesus, through faith in his name, has made this man strong. Yes, it is faith in Christ that has given him this perfect soundness before you all. Now, my brothers, I am sure that you did not know it was the Son of God and your own Saviour you sent to the cross. Therefore turn to God in sorrow for this great sin. God will forgive you, and in his own time, he will send Jesus Christ again. God who has raised up his Son is ready to bless you and turn every one of you away from his sins."

While Peter was speaking, the priests, the captain of the Temple, and the rulers came up to them. They were angry when they heard Peter speak these words. They took Peter and John and locked them up for the night. But many of those who had heard Peter speaking believed in Jesus and sought the Lord, and the number of the followers of Christ rose from 3,000 to 5,000.

Discussion Questions: *1. What did Peter do before the throng of people?*
2. What did he tell them they had done? 3. Who had healed the lame man?
4. Why were the priests and the rulers of the Temple angry at what Peter said?
5. What did the people do when they heard Peter?

DAY 311

PETER AND JOHN

Acts 4:5-23

THE next day the Temple rulers met together. Annas and Caiaphas, the two high priests, were there, along with many of their friends. They brought Peter and John before the company. The lame man who had been healed was still by the side of the two apostles. The rulers asked them, "By what power or through whom have you done this?"

Peter spoke boldly to the priests and the rulers. He said, "You rulers of the people and elders, if you are asking us about the good deed done to this man who was so helpless — how he was made well — I will tell you it was by the name and power of Jesus of Nazareth, whom you put to death on the cross and God raised from the dead. Through him, this man stands here before you strong and well. And there is no salvation except through Jesus Christ, for there is no other person under heaven who can save us from our sins."

When these rulers saw how bold and strong were the words of Peter and John, they wondered, especially as they knew they were plain men, not educated and not used to speaking. They remembered seeing these men among the followers of Jesus, and they felt that in some way Jesus had given them this power. Since the man who had been healed was standing beside them, they could say nothing to deny that a wonderful work had been done.

The rulers sent Peter and John out of the room while they talked together. They said to one another, "What shall we do to these men? We cannot deny that a wonderful work has been done by them, for everyone knows it. But we must stop this from spreading any further among the people. Let us command them not to speak about Jesus, and let us tell them that if they do speak, we will punish them."

So they called the two apostles into the room again and said to them: "We forbid you to speak about Jesus and the power of his name to any man. If you do not stop talking about Jesus, we will take you, put you in prison, and have you beaten."

But Peter and John answered the rulers, "Whether it is right to obey you or obey God, you yourselves can judge. As for ourselves, we cannot keep silent. We must speak of what we have seen and heard."

The rulers were afraid to do any harm to Peter and John, because they knew the people praised God for the good work they had done and would be angry to have harm come to them. For fear of the people, they let them go. Peter and John went to their friends in the upper room and gave thanks to God for helping them speak his word without fear.

Discussion Questions: *1. What did Peter tell the Temple rulers? 2. Why were the rulers surprised? 3. What did the rulers tell Peter and John? How did the apostles answer? 4. Why were the rulers afraid to harm Peter and John?*

DAY 312

ANANIAS AND SAPPHIRA

Acts 4:32-5:11

IN those early days, the Church of Christ in Jerusalem was like a great family. Each person loved all the others. No one said anything he owned was his, but they shared everything. Those who owned land or houses sold them, brought the money, and laid it down at the feet of the apostles. This was not because a rule was made about it, but because each member loved the rest and wanted to help them. The money that was given this way was divided among those that were poor, so no one who believed in Christ was in need.

There was one man who gave away all he had to help the Church. His name was Joseph, but he was called Barnabas, which means "the one who encourages," because he was so helpful and cheering in his words. Barnabas sold his land and gave the money from it to the apostles so they could help the poor with it. Barnabas spent all his time, as well as his money, doing good.

But there was another man in the Church at Jerusalem whose spirit was not like Barnabas's. Ananias wanted to have the fame of giving everything while still keeping some. Ananias sold some land he owned and agreed with his wife, Sapphira, to give a part of the money to the apostles for the Church and to keep back a part for themselves. This they had a right to do. They could have kept it all. But they agreed to act as though they were giving *all* the money, and that was agreeing to tell a lie.

Ananias brought his money and laid it down before the apostles. But Peter understood what Ananias was doing and said to him, "Ananias, why has the evil spirit filled your heart to tell a lie by your act, in keeping back part of the money? Before it was sold, wasn't the land your own? And after it was sold, wasn't the money in your hand? You have tried to tell a lie, not to man, but to God, and God will judge you."

As Peter spoke these words, Ananias fell down before him, and in a moment was lying dead on the floor. The young men in the meeting took up his dead body, wrapped it with long rolls of cloth, carried it out, and buried it.

After three hours, Sapphira entered the room. She did not know her husband was dead, for no one had told her.

Peter said to her, "Tell me, did you sell the land for so much?" And he named the sum Ananias had placed before him.

Sapphira said, "Yes, that was the price of the land."

But Peter said to her, "Why did you two people agree to bring God's anger on yourselves? Those who have buried your husband are at the door, and they shall carry you out also!"

Sapphira fell down, struck dead by the power of God. The young men coming in found her dead, and they carried out her body and buried it beside her husband. A great fear came to all the Church and to everyone who heard how Ananias and Sapphira died. After that, no one dared to try and deceive the apostles in their gifts to the Lord's Church.

Discussion Questions: *1. What was the Church like? Why was it that way? 2. What did Barnabas do? Why? 3. What did Ananias do that was wrong? Why do you think he did it? 4. What happened to Ananias and Sapphira? Who caused this to happen? Why?*

DAY 313

The Apostles Freed

Acts 5:12-23

EVERY day the apostles went to the Temple, stood in Solomon's Porch, and preached to the people about Jesus and salvation through his name. They did many wonders healing the sick. Those that were sick were brought out into the street, lying on beds and couches, so that as the apostle Peter passed by, his shadow might fall on them. And from the villages around

Jerusalem they brought people that had diseases or were held by evil spirits, and by the power of God in the apostles, they were all made well.

All these wonderful works brought great crowds to hear the apostles when they spoke in Solomon's Porch. Many believed in Christ when they heard, and men and women were added to the Church in great numbers.

But all these things offended the high priest and the rulers, the ones who had led in sending Jesus Christ to the cross only a few months before. These rulers sent their officers, who seized all twelve apostles and put them into the city's prison. But at night, an angel of the Lord came, opened the doors of the prison, brought the apostles out, and said, "Go and stand in the Temple and speak to the people all the words of this life."

Very early the next morning, they went into the Temple and preached to the people. On that day the high priest and all the rulers met together and sent to the prison for the apostles.

But the officers who were sent did not find them in the prison. They came back to the rulers, and said, "The prison was shut and locked, and the keepers were standing at the doors, but when we opened the doors and went inside, we found none of the prisoners there!"

Discussion Questions: *1. What did the apostles do in Solomon's porch? 2. Who was offended by what the apostles did? Why? 3. What did they do to the apostles? 4. Who freed the apostles?*

DAY 314

THE APOSTLES BEFORE THE RULERS

Acts 5:24-42

WHEN the captain of the Temple and the rulers heard the apostles had escaped, they could not understand it. Then someone said, "The men you put in prison are standing in the Temple, teaching the people!"

The captain of the Temple went with his officers and captured the apostles, but without doing them any harm, for they were afraid the people would stone them if they were rough with these men, who all held in high honor. They brought them into the hall where the rulers were meeting, and the high priest said to them, "We told you not to speak in this name, or about that man. Now you have filled Jerusalem with your teaching, and you are trying to bring the blood of this man on us."

But Peter, speaking for all the apostles, replied, "We must obey God, not men. You put Jesus to death by hanging him on the cross. But the God of our fathers raised him from the dead, and lifted him up to be at his right hand as a Prince and a Saviour, to give forgiveness of sins. We declare these things, and God's Holy Spirit tells us they are true."

When the rulers heard these words, they were very angry, and thought about killing the apostles. But there was a very wise man named Gamaliel, a man honored by all the people. Gamaliel asked to have the apostles sent out of the hall while he spoke to the rulers. When the apostles were taken away, Gamaliel said, "You men of Israel, be careful what you do to these men. If what they say comes from themselves, it will soon pass away. But if it is of God, you cannot destroy it, and you may even find yourselves fighting against God. My advice to you is not to harm these men. Leave them alone."

The rulers agreed with these words. They sent for the apostles and had them beaten. Then they ordered them not to speak in the name of Jesus and let them go. The apostles went out of the meeting happy to be suffering for the name of Jesus. And they continued to preach Jesus as the Saviour and the Lord. _____

Discussion Questions: *1. Why were the rulers angry at the apostles? 2. What did Peter tell them? 3. What did the rulers want to do to the apostles? 4. What did Gamaliel tell them to do? Why?*

DAY 315
_____

STEPHEN (PART 1)

Acts 6:1-7:1

W E have read how the members of the Church in Jerusalem gave their money to help the poor. This giving led to trouble as the Church grew, for some of the widows who were poor were overlooked, and their friends complained to the apostles. The twelve apostles called the whole Church together, and said, "It isn't good that we must turn from preaching and teaching the word of God and sit at tables to give out money. Choose from yourselves seven good men, men who have the Spirit of God and are wise, and we will give this work to them so we can spend our time in prayer and preaching the gospel."

This plan pleased everyone in the Church. They chose seven men to take charge of the gifts and see that they were sent to those in need. The first man chosen was Stephen, a man full of faith and the Spirit of God. Also chosen were Philip and five other good men. These seven men were brought before the apostles, who laid their hands on their heads, setting them apart for their work of caring for the poor.

But Stephen did more than look after the needy ones. He began to preach the gospel of Christ with such power that everyone who heard him felt the truth. Stephen saw — before any other man in the Church — that the gospel of Christ was not only for Jews, but for all men. All men might be saved if they would believe in Jesus, and Stephen preached this with all his power.

Preaching that men who were not Jews might be saved by believing in Christ made many of the Jews very angry. They called all the people who were not Jews "Gentiles," and they looked on them with scorn, but they could not answer the words that Stephen spoke. They roused up the people and the rulers and set them against Stephen. At last they seized Stephen and brought him before the great council of the rulers. They said to the rulers, "This man is always speaking evil words against the Temple and against the law of Moses. We heard him say that Jesus of Nazareth shall destroy this place and shall change the laws that Moses gave to us!"

This was partly true and partly false, but no lie is so harmful as that which has a little truth in it. Then the high priest said to Stephen, "Are these things so?"

_____

Discussion Questions: *1. How did the giving in the Church lead to trouble? 2. How did the apostles solve the problem? 3. What kind of man was Stephen? 4. What did Stephen do? 5. Why did the Jews get angry at Stephen? What happened to him?*

DAY 316

_____

STEPHEN (PART 2)

Acts 7:2-8:4

WHEN Stephen stood up to answer the high priest, everyone looking at him saw that his face was shining like the face of an angel. Then Stephen began to speak of the great things God had done for his people of Israel in the past. How he had called Abraham, their father, to go into a new land. How he had given them great men like Joseph, Moses, and the prophets. He showed them how the Israelites had not been faithful to God, who had given them such blessings. Then Stephen said, "You are a people with hard hearts and stiff necks, who will not obey the words of God and his Spirit. As your fathers did, so you do also. Your fathers killed the prophets God sent to them, and you have slain Jesus, the Righteous One!"

As they heard these things, they became very angry at Stephen, like wild beasts.

But Stephen, full of the Holy Spirit, looked up toward heaven with his shining face. He saw the glory of God and Jesus standing on God's right hand, and he said, "I see the heavens opened and the Son of man standing on the right hand of God!"

STEPHEN PUT TO DEATH - ACTS 7:54-60

But they cried out angrily, rushed him, and dragged him outside the wall of the city. There they threw stones at him to kill him, while Stephen kneeled down among the falling stones and prayed, "Lord Jesus, receive my spirit! Lord, lay not this sin up against them!"

And when he had said this, he fell asleep in death, the first to die for the gospel of Christ.

Among those who stoned Stephen was a young man named Saul. He showed his fierce hatred for Stephen and the gospel Stephen preached by holding the garments the slayers of Stephen tossed off before they threw stones at him. Saul had heard Stephen speak, and he saw his glorious face, but he gave his help to those who killed him. After Stephen had been slain, Saul went out to seize those who believed in Christ. He dragged men and women out of their houses and put them in prison. He went into the synagogues, seized them as they were worshiping, stripped off their garments, and had them beaten.

By the hands of Saul and those who were with him, the Church of Christ, where so many had lived in love and peace, was broken up, and its members were scattered far and wide. The apostles stayed in the city, and no harm came to them, for they were kept hidden, but all the rest of the believers were driven away, and for a time, the Church of Christ seemed to have come to an end.

Discussion Questions: *1. How did Stephen answer the high priest? 2. How did that make the priests feel? 3. What did Stephen see when he looked up to heaven? What did that mean? 4. What happened to Stephen? Who was there when it happened?*

DAY 317

PHILIP

Acts 8:4-24

WE have seen how the first group of those who believed in Christ was broken up and its members driven away by the fury and rage of its enemy, Saul. But as those who were scattered went to other places, they told the people about Christ and his gospel. And very soon new groups of believers in Christ began to rise up all over the land. In place of one church in Jerusalem, there were many churches among the cities and villages of Judea. So Saul, for all his hate toward Christ, really helped in spreading the gospel of Christ.

Among those driven away by Saul was a man named Philip. He was not Philip the apostle, but another Philip, one of those chosen with Stephen to care for the poor. This Philip went down to the city of Samaria, near the middle of the land, and he began to tell the people there about Christ. These people were not Jews, but were of the race called Samaritans. The woman of Samaria who Jesus talked to at Jacob's well was one of these people.

The Lord gave Philip the power to work many wonders among these Samaritans. At Philip's word, evil spirits came out of men. Those who had the palsy were cured, and the lame were made to walk. The Samaritans saw these things done by Philip and believed he spoke the words of God to them. Very many of them became believers in Christ and were baptized, and there was great joy in that city.

At that time there was in Samaria a certain man named Simon, who had made the people believe he had great power and could do wonderful things by magic. But the works done by Philip through the power of Christ were so much greater and more wonderful than his own, that Simon listened to the teaching of Philip, claimed to believe in Jesus, and was baptized. But his heart had not been touched. He only thought that Philip's magic was better than his own, and he hoped to find out what it was, so he could use it.

The twelve apostles were still in Jerusalem. They did not leave the city when Saul broke up the church there. After a time, Saul ceased to be a trouble, and some of the believers began to go back to Jerusalem. A new church grew up in that city around the apostles, though it never became as large or as wholehearted as the church of the early days.

News came to the apostles of the great work being done by Philip in Samaria, and they sent Peter and John to visit the church in that place. Peter and John came to Samaria and were glad when they saw how many faithful believers were there. They prayed that the same power of the Holy Spirit that had come to the disciples in Jerusalem might come to those in Samaria, and the power of the Lord came when the apostles laid their hands on the heads of the believers.

When Simon saw that this strange power of God came with the laying on of the apostles' hands, he offered Peter and John money, saying to them, "Sell me this power, so I may give the Holy Spirit to those on whom I lay my hands."

But Peter said to him, "May your silver perish with you, if you think to buy the gift of God with money! You do not really belong to Christ, and your heart is not right with God. Turn away from this sin and pray God that he will forgive you. For I see that you are yet in your sins, sins that are as bitter as gall, and you are bound to evil!"

Simon could not understand this, but he said, "Pray for me to the Lord, that none of these evils you have named come to me!"

_____

Discussion Questions: *1. How did Saul help the church? Did he mean to? 2. Why did Philip go to Samaria? 3. What did Simon see about Philip that he wanted to have? 4. What did Peter tell him?*

DAY 318

_____

PHILIP'S TRAVELS

Acts 8:5-40

FTER this, Peter and John preached in many villages of the Samaritans, and then they went back to Jerusalem. Philip's work in

Samaria was now done. An angel of the Lord spoke to him, saying, "Rise up, and leave this city. Go toward the south, on the road that goes down from Jerusalem to Gaza."

This was a road through a desert region, without villages or people, but Philip obeyed the word of the Lord. He left Samaria and walked southward until he came to the road between Jerusalem and Gaza. While he was on this desert road, he saw a chariot drawing near, and in it was a black man reading from a roll. This man had come from the land of Ethiopia in Africa, far to the south of Egypt. He was a nobleman of very high rank, the treasurer of the queen in that land. Although he was not a Jew, he had taken a journey of more than 1,000 miles to Jerusalem, riding in his chariot all the way, so he might worship God in his Temple. He was now going back to his own land, and in his hands was the roll of the prophet Isaiah, from which he was reading aloud.

As the chariot of this black man came in sight, the Spirit of the Lord said to Philip, "Go near, and stand close to the chariot." Philip ran toward the chariot and spoke to the man, saying, "Do you understand what you are reading?"

The nobleman answered him, "How can I understand it, unless someone tells me what it means? Can you show me? If you can, come up into the chariot and sit with me."

Philip climbed up and sat in the chariot. The man was reading the fifty-third chapter of Isaiah, the words that the prophet spoke of Jesus many hundreds of years before he came to earth. Philip began with those words and told the Ethiopian nobleman all about Christ. The man believed, and took into his heart the word of the Lord. As they went on the way, they came to some water, and the nobleman said, "See, here is water! Why can't I be baptized?"

Philip said to him, "If you believe with all your heart, you may be baptized."

He answered, "I believe that Jesus Christ is the Son of God."

The nobleman ordered the chariot stopped, and they went down into the water together, and Philip baptized him a follower of Christ. And when they came up out of the water, the Spirit of the Lord took Philip away, so the nobleman saw him no more, but he went home happy in the Lord.

Philip went next to a city near the shore, and preached there. From there he went northward through the cities by the Great Sea, preaching in them all, until he came to Caesarea, where he stayed for many years.

Discussion Questions: *1. Why did Philip travel south? Who did he meet on the way? 2. What was the man reading? What did he ask Philip to do? 3. Why did they stop traveling? What did Philip do for the man?*

DAY 319

God Comes to Saul

Acts 9:1-9

SAUL, the young man who had taken part in the death of Stephen and scattered the believers in Christ, was still the bitter enemy of the gospel. He heard that some of those who had run away from Jerusalem had gone to Damascus, a city outside the Jewish land far in the north, and they were still at work teaching Christ. Saul made up his mind to destroy this new church in Damascus, as he thought he had destroyed the church in Jerusalem. So he went to the high priest, and said, "Let me have a letter to the chief of the Jews in Damascus. I have heard there are some followers of Jesus of Nazareth in that city. I will go with some men, take these people, bind them, and bring them in chains to Jerusalem."

The high priest gave Saul the letters he asked for, and Saul found a band of men to go with him to Damascus. It was a journey of about ten days, riding on horses or mules. While Saul was on his way to Damascus, he had tried to think about Christ and his gospel. He saw again in his mind Stephen's shining face and heard his words. He thought of the sweet, patient way the followers of Jesus had met suffering at his hand. Deep in Saul's heart, there rose a feeling

A Light From Heaven Flashed Around Saul - Acts 9:3

he could not put down that said the gospel of Christ was true and it was wicked for him to fight it. Yet he went on, firm in his purpose to destroy the Church of Christ.

At last he came near Damascus. Suddenly, at full noon, a light flashed from heaven, brighter than the sun. For the time, the light blinded Saul. It came so suddenly that it struck him down, and he fell on the ground. In the midst of the light, Saul saw One he had never seen before. A strange voice came to him, saying, "Saul, Saul, why are you fighting against me?" Saul answered, "Who are you, Lord?"

Then the answer came, "I am Jesus, who you are trying to destroy!"

Trembling with surprise and alarm, Saul said, "Lord, what will you have me do?"

The Lord said to Saul, "Rise up and go into the city. You will be told what you must do."

Those who were with Saul wondered, for they had seen a light and heard a sound, but they had seen no face and heard no words. The vision of Christ had come to Saul alone. They picked him up from the ground and found he had been blinded by the brightness of the light. They led him by the hand into the city and took him to the house of a man named Judas. There Saul stayed for three days, suffering in body and mind. He could see nothing, and he didn't eat or drink. But in the darkness, he was praying to God and Christ with all his heart. _____

Discussion Questions: *1. Why did Saul want to go to Damascus? 2. What did Saul ask the high priest for? 3. What happened when Saul came close to Damascus?*

DAY 320

ANANIAS

Acts 9:10-21

IN the city of Damascus was a follower of Christ named Ananias, a good man, held in respect by all who knew him. God spoke to him, calling him by name, "Ananias."

Ananias answered, "Here I am, Lord."

The Lord said to Ananias, "Rise, and go into the street named Straight, and find the house of Judas. In that house, ask for a man named Saul from Tarsus. This man Saul is praying, and in a vision he has seen a man named Ananias coming into his room and laying his hands on him, to give him his sight."

This command from the Lord was a surprise to Ananias. He answered the Lord, "Lord, I have heard from many people about this man Saul. He has done great evil to all your people in Jerusalem, and he has an order from the high priest to bind and carry away all who call on your name! Shall I go and visit a man like him?"

But the Lord said to Ananias, "Go. I have chosen this man to bear my name before the people of all nations, kings, and the children of Israel. I will show him how many things he must suffer for my sake."

Then Ananias went as the Lord had told him. He found the house and came to Saul. He laid his hands on the head of Saul and said, "Brother Saul, the Lord Jesus, who met you on the way as you were coming, has sent me, that you may have your sight and the Holy Spirit may come to you. Now, wait no longer, but rise up and be baptized, and call on the name of Jesus, who will wash away your sins."

Then there fell from the eyes of Saul what seemed like scales, and at once his sight came to him. Saul was baptized, food was given to him, and he became strong in body and soul. Saul had gone out to bind the disciples of Christ in Damascus, but now he came among them, as a brother. He went into the synagogues where the Jews worshiped in Damascus and began to preach Jesus to them, declaring that Jesus is the Christ and the Son of God. And all that heard him were amazed, and they said to one another, "Isn't this the same man who persecuted us in Jerusalem? And didn't he come to this place intending to bind the believers in Jesus, and bring them before the chief priests?"

Discussion Questions: 1. What did God ask Ananias to do? 2. Why was Ananias surprised at God's command? Did he do it anyway? 3. What did God want Saul to do? Did Saul obey him?

DAY 321

SAUL IN JERUSALEM

Acts 9:22-28

SAUL grew stronger and stronger in his spirit and his words. None of the Jews in Damascus could answer him, as he showed that Jesus is the Anointed One, the Christ. But he did not stay long in Damascus. After a time he left the city and went away to a quiet place in the desert of Arabia, where he stayed for a year or longer, thinking about the gospel and learning from the Lord.

Then Saul returned to Damascus and preached Christ and salvation not only for Jews, but for Gentiles, all people besides the Jews. This made the Jews in Damascus very angry. They formed a plan to kill Saul, and they watched the gates day and night, hoping to seize him as he went out. But Saul's friends — the disciples of Jesus — brought him to a house on the wall and let him down in a basket to the ground, so he escaped from his enemies and got away safely.

Saul now journeyed back to Jerusalem. He had left it three years before as a bitter enemy of Christ. He came to it as a follower of Christ. But when Saul wanted to join the believers in Jerusalem, they were all afraid of him. They could not believe that one they had known as the fierce destroyer of the Church was now a friend to Jesus. But Barnabas, the man who had given all his land to the church, believed Saul when he heard his story. He brought him to Peter, told him how he had seen the Lord on the road and how boldly he had preached in Damascus in the name of Jesus.

Then Peter took Saul's hand and received him as a disciple of Christ. For a few weeks Saul stayed in Jerusalem and preached in the synagogues of the Jews, as Stephen had preached before, that Jesus is the Saviour not only of Jews, but also of Gentiles.

———————

Discussion Questions: *1. Why did Saul go to Arabia? 2. What did Saul do when he came back to Damascus? How did that make the Jews feel? 3. Why didn't the followers of Christ want to trust Saul when he returned to Jerusalem? Who helped Saul?*

DAY 322

———

SAUL GOES HOME

Acts 9:29-31

WHEN Saul preached that Gentiles might be saved by Jesus Christ, it made the Jews angry, just as it had made Saul angry to hear Stephen preach this same gospel. They would not listen to Saul, and they wanted to kill him, as they had killed Stephen. One day Saul was praying in the Temple. The Lord came to him once again, and Saul saw Jesus and heard his voice saying, "Make haste, and go quickly out of Jerusalem, for the people here will not believe your words about me."

Then Saul said to the Lord, "Lord, they know that I put into prison and

459

beat in the synagogues those who believed in you. And when your servant Stephen was slain, I was standing by and was keeping the garments of those who stoned him."

And the Lord said to Saul, "Go from this place. I will send you far away to preach to the Gentiles."

Then Saul knew that his work was not to preach the gospel to the Jews, but to the Gentiles, the people of other nations. The disciples in Jerusalem helped him get away from his enemies in the city and led him down to a place called Caesarea, on the seashore. There Saul found a ship sailing to Tarsus, a city in Asia Minor. Tarsus was Saul's birthplace and his early home. He went back to Tarsus and stayed for a few years, safe from the Jews. He was a tentmaker, and he worked at his trade while preaching the gospel in Tarsus.

Now that Saul the enemy had become Saul the friend, all the churches in Judea, Samaria, and Galilee had rest and peace. The followers of Christ could preach without fear, and the number of those who believed grew rapidly, for the Lord was with them.

All through the land — from Galilee down to the desert on the south — there were meetings of those who believed in Jesus as the Saviour, and the apostles Peter and John went to teach them the way of life.

Discussion Questions: *1. Why were the Jews angry when Saul preached that the Gentiles could be saved? 2. Where did God send Saul next? What did he do there? 3. What happened after Saul stopped being the church's enemy?*

DAY 323

TABITHA

Acts 9:32-43

SINCE the church was now planted in many cities throughout the land of the Jews, Peter, who was a leader among the apostles, went from place to place visiting the believers in Christ and preaching the gospel. Once he went down to the plain beside the Great Sea and came to a city named Lydda. There Peter found a man named Aeneas who had the palsy and could not walk. He had been lying on his bed for eight years. Peter said to him, "Aeneas, Jesus Christ makes you well. Rise up, and roll up your bed."

At once Aeneas arose and was well. He took up the roll of matting on which he had been lying so long and put it away. All the people in Lydda and

Sharon heard of this great work, and many turned to the Lord.

A very good woman who everyone loved was living in Joppa, near Lydda. She was called the gazelle, which is the name of a beautiful animal like a deer. Her name in Hebrew was Tabitha, but in Greek it was Dorcas, which means gazelle. Tabitha (or Dorcas) was a believer in Christ, and like her Lord, she loved the poor and helped them by her work and her gifts.

While Peter was at Lydda, Dorcas was taken ill and died. They laid her body in an upper room and sent two men to Lydda for Peter, begging him to come without delay. Peter went to Joppa at once. When he came to the house where the body of Dorcas was lying, he found the room filled with widows and poor women who were weeping and showing the garments Dorcas had made for them.

Peter sent them all out of the room. When he was alone with the body of Dorcas, he knelt down and prayed. Then he turned to the body and said, "Tabitha, arise!"

She opened her eyes, and when she saw Peter, she sat up. Peter took her by the hand and lifted her up. Then he called into the room the widows and the believers in Christ, and showed Dorcas to them, alive and well. The news of this wonderful work amazed all the city of Joppa and led many to believe in Christ. Peter stayed many days in Joppa, at the house of a man named Simon, who was a tanner, and lived near the sea.

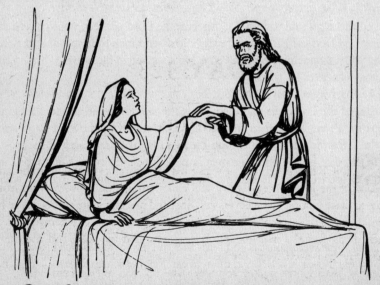

PETER RESTORED DORCAS TO LIFE - ACTS 9:40-41

DAY 324

PETER'S VISION (PART 1)

Acts 10:1-13

AT that time an officer of the Roman army was at Caesarea, about thirty miles north of Joppa, beside the Great Sea. His name was Cornelius, and he was the commander of a company of 100 soldiers. We would call such an officer a captain but in the Roman army he was called a centurion. Cornelius was a Gentile, but he did not worship idols, as most of the Gentiles did. He always prayed to the God of Israel, feared God, gave to the poor, and taught his family to worship the Lord.

One day, in the afternoon, Cornelius was praying in his house when an angel came to him and called him by name. "Cornelius!" Cornelius looked at this strange shining being and was filled with fear, but he said, "What is it, Lord?"

And the angel said to him, "Cornelius, the Lord has seen your gifts to the people and has heard all your prayers. Now send men to Joppa, and let them bring you a man named Simon Peter. He is staying in the house of Simon the tanner, who lives by the sea."

The angel went away, and Cornelius called two servants and a soldier who worshiped the Lord. He told them what the angel had said and sent them to Joppa for Peter. These men traveled all night, following the road southward by the Great Sea, and about noon the next day they approached Joppa.

On that day, just before these men came to Joppa, Peter went up to the roof of the house to pray. He became very hungry and wanted food, but while they were making dinner, he fell into a strange sleep, and a vision came to him. In his vision he saw what seemed to be a great sheet let down by its four corners from above. In it he saw all kinds of beasts, birds, and creeping things. Some of these were animals and birds that the Jews were allowed to eat. But many were those the law forbid them to eat. Peter saw many beasts, birds, and creeping things that he believed were unclean. As he looked, he heard a voice saying to him, "Rise, Peter. Kill and eat."

DAY 325

PETER'S VISION (PART 2)

Acts 10:14-23

ETER had always been very strict in keeping the Jewish rules about food, and he answered, "No, Lord. I have never eaten anything common or unclean."

Then he heard the voice saying to him, "What God has made clean, don't you make common or unclean."

Three times Peter heard these words spoken, and then the great sheet with all the living creatures in it was lifted up to heaven and passed out of his sight.

Peter knew at once that the vision and the words he had heard must have great meaning, but he could not see what the meaning was. While he was thinking of the vision and wondering at it, the Spirit of the Lord spoke to him, saying, "Peter, three men are looking for you. Go down to the door and meet them, and go with them, without doubting, for I have sent them."

Just at that moment the three men from Caesarea knocked at the door and asked for Simon Peter. Peter met them, and said to them, "I am here, the man you are looking for. Why have you come to me?"

And they said, "Cornelius, a centurion at Caesarea — a good man, one that fears God and is well spoken of by all the Jews — was yesterday commanded by a holy angel to send for you and to listen to words from you."

Then Peter called the men into the house, heard all their story, and kept them there that night.

Discussion Questions: *1. Why didn't Peter want to eat the unclean food? 2. What did God tell him? 3. What happened while Peter was thinking about the vision?*

DAY 326

THE GENTILES

Acts 10:23-11:18

THE next morning, Peter went with the men. Some of the believers from the church of Joppa went with them. On the next day they came to Caesarea and entered the house of Cornelius. There they found Cornelius waiting for them, and with him a number of his family and friends. As Peter came into the room, Cornelius fell down at his feet and was about to worship him, but Peter raised him up, saying, "Stand up. I am a man, not God."

When Peter looked around, he saw many people had met together, and they were all Gentiles, not Jews. Peter said, "You know it is against the law of the Jews for a Jew to come into the house with one of another nation or to meet with him. But God has showed me that I should not call any man common or unclean. For this reason I came at once when I was sent for. Now I ask why you have sent for me."

Cornelius said, "Four days ago I was praying, at three o'clock in the afternoon, when a man stood by me, clad in shining garments and said to me, 'Cornelius, your prayer is heard, and your good deeds are known to God. Send now to Joppa, and send for Simon, who is called Peter.' I sent at once for you, and you have done well to come so soon. Now we are all here before God to hear whatever God has given to you to say to us."

Peter opened his mouth and began to speak, for he saw now what the vision meant. He said, "I see now that God cares for all men alike, not for the people of one nation only. In every nation, those who fear God and do right please him." Then Peter began to tell the story of Jesus: how he lived, how he did good works, how he died, how he rose again, and how in Jesus Christ everyone who believes may have his sins forgiven.

While Peter was speaking, the Holy Spirit fell on everyone in the room. And the Jews who were with Peter were amazed as they saw the Spirit of God given to Gentiles.

Then Peter said, "Can any man forbid that these should be baptized with water, upon whom the Spirit has come, as he came upon us?" At Peter's command, these Gentile believers with Cornelius were baptized as members of Christ's Church. Peter stayed with them a few days, living with Cornelius and eating at his table, though he was a Gentile, something which Peter would never before have thought to do. Soon the news went through all the churches in Judea that Gentiles had heard the word and been baptized. At first the Jewish believers could not believe this should be allowed. But when Peter told them all the story of Cornelius and the angel, of his own vision of the great sheet full of animals, and of the Spirit coming upon the Gentiles, then they all praised God and said, "So to the Gentiles, as well as to the Jews, God has given to turn from their sins and to be saved in Jesus Christ, and to have everlasting life."

_____

Discussion Questions: *1. Who did Cornelius think Peter was when he first saw him? 2. Why didn't Peter want to go into Cornelius's house? 3. How did Peter learn what the vision meant? 4. What happened that day at the centurion's house? 5. What did the Jews say at first when they heard Peter's news? What did they do in the end?*

DAY 327

_____

PETER IMPRISONED (PART 1)

Acts 12:1-9

YOU remember that in the years while Jesus was teaching, Jerusalem and part of the land near it was ruled by a Roman governor named Pilate. He was the ruler who sent Jesus Christ to the cross. After some years, the emperor at Rome gave all the country of the Jews to a man named Herod Agrippa, making him King of Judea. He was the nephew of the Herod who killed John the Baptist and the grandson of the Herod who killed all the little children of Bethlehem. Herod Agrippa was the King of Judea when Peter saw the vision on the housetop and preached to the Gentiles.

Herod wanted to please the Jews in Jerusalem, so he captured one of the apostles: James, the brother of John, one of the three disciples who had been nearest to Jesus. He had his guards kill James with the sword, just as John the Baptist had been killed. When he saw how much this act pleased the chief priests and rulers, he captured Simon Peter and put him in prison, intending to put him to death during Passover.

Peter was kept in the prison with sixteen soldiers guarding him, four at a time. All the Church prayed very earnestly for him. On the night before the day Peter was to die, he was sleeping in the prison, tied with two chains, while guards watched the door. Suddenly a bright light shone in Peter's cell, and an angel of the Lord stood by him. The angel struck him on the side to wake him up. "Rise up quickly."

As Peter stood up, his chains fell from his hands. The angel said to him, "Get dressed."

Peter did as he was told, scarcely aware of what he was doing.

Then the angel said, "Wrap your cloak around you, and follow me." Peter followed the angel, thinking he was dreaming.

THE ANGEL LED PETER TO SAFETY - ACTS 12:5-10

Discussion Questions: *1. Why did Herod kill James? Who else did he want to kill? 2. How did Peter get out of prison?*

DAY 328

PETER IMPRISONED (PART 2)

Acts 12:10-23

PETER and the angel passed the first guard, then the second. No one tried to stop them. Then they came to the great iron gate on the outside of the prison, and this opened as if unseen hands were turning it. They went out of the prison into the city, and passed through one street. Then the angel left Peter as suddenly as he had come to him. By this time, Peter was fully awake, and he said, "Now I am sure the Lord has sent his angel and has set me free from the power of King Herod."

Peter thought about what he should do and where he should go. He turned toward the house of a woman named Mary, who was a relative of Barnabas and had a son named John Mark, who many years afterward wrote the gospel according to Mark. Many people were at Mary's house praying for Peter.

Peter came to the house, knocked on the outside door, and called to those inside. A young woman named Rhoda came to the door. She listened and recognized the voice of Peter. She was so glad that she did not think to open the door, but ran into the house and told them all that Peter was standing at the door. They said to her, "You're crazy!" But she said she was sure Peter was there, for she knew his voice. They said, "It must be an angel who has taken Peter's form!"

But Peter kept on knocking. When they finally opened the door and saw him, they were filled with wonder. He beckoned to them to listen and told them how the Lord had brought him out of the prison. Then he said to them, "Tell these things to James and the other apostles."

Then Peter went away to a place where Herod and his men could not find him.

Morning came, and there was a great stir among the soldiers. Herod looked for Peter, but could not find him. In his anger, he ordered that the guards in the prison be put to death. Not long after this, Herod died so suddenly that many believed his death came from the wrath of God. So Herod perished, but Peter lived many years, working for Christ.

The James Peter meant when he said, "Tell these things to James," was not James the apostle, the brother of John. That James had been put to death by Herod. He spoke of another James, a son of Joseph and Mary, a younger brother of Jesus, one who was always called the Lord's brother. This James was a very holy man, and a leader of the church in Jerusalem, where he lived for many years. Some time after this, James wrote the book of the New Testament called the epistle of James.

Discussion Questions: *1. Where did Peter go after he left the prison? 2. What did Rhoda do when she saw Peter? 3. What did Peter tell the followers of Christ? 4. Which James was Peter talking about? What did this James write?*

DAY 329

ANTIOCH

Acts 11:19-26

WE have seen how, after the death of Stephen, those who were driven out of Jerusalem went everywhere telling of Jesus. Some of these men traveled as far as Antioch in Syria. This was a great city far in the north, 250 miles from Jerusalem. At first they spoke only to Jews, preaching the word of Christ. But soon many Gentiles heard about the gospel and wished to have it preached to them. So these men began preaching to the Gentiles, telling them about Jesus Christ and how to be saved.

The Lord was with the gospel, and in a very little time, many Jews and Gentiles believed in Christ. In Antioch, Jews and Gentiles worshiped together and forgot that they had ever been apart. The church in Jerusalem heard that Gentiles in Antioch were coming to Christ. As all the followers of Christ in Jerusalem were Jews, they were not sure that Jews and Gentiles should worship together as one people. It was decided that some wise man should go from Jerusalem to Antioch and see this new church of Jews and Gentiles. For this errand, they chose Barnabas, the good man who had given his land to help the poor and who had brought Saul to the church when the disciples were afraid of him.

So Barnabas took the long journey from Jerusalem to Antioch. When he saw these new disciples so strong in their love for Christ, so united in their spirit, and so earnest in the gospel, he was glad, and he spoke to them all, telling them to stand fast in the Lord.

The church at Antioch was growing so fast that it needed men as leaders and teachers. Barnabas thought of Saul, who had once been an enemy but was now a follower of Christ. Saul was in Tarsus, so Barnabas went to find him. He brought Saul to Antioch, and they both stayed there for a year, preaching to the people and teaching those who believed in Christ. It was at Antioch that the disciples were first called *Christians*.

Discussion Questions: *1. Who did the followers of Jesus tell about him at first? Who else listened to their preaching? 2. What was the Church at Antioch like? 3. Why did the believers in Jerusalem send Barnabas to Antioch? 4. Who did Barnabas bring to Antioch? 5. What were the disciples at Antioch called?*

DAY 330

BARNABAS AND SAUL

Acts 11:27-30; 12:24–13:12

A T one time some men came from Jerusalem to Antioch, to whom God had shown things that would happen. These men were prophets, speaking from God. One of them, a man named Agabus, said that a great famine was soon to come to all the lands. This came in the days when Claudius was emperor at Rome. Over all the land, food was very scarce, and many suffered from hunger. When the followers of Christ in Antioch heard that their brethren of Jerusalem and Judea were in need, they gave money to help them and sent Barnabas and Saul with it. Barnabas and Saul carried the gifts of the church to Jerusalem and stayed there for a time. When they went back to Antioch, they took along John Mark.

Some time after they returned to Antioch, the Lord called Barnabas and Saul to go out and preach the good news of Christ to the people in other lands. At one time, when the members of the church were praying together, the Spirit of the Lord spoke to them, saying, "Set Barnabas and Saul apart for a special work to which I have called them."

Then the leaders of the church at Antioch prayed and laid their hands on the heads of Barnabas and Saul. Barnabas and Saul went out, taking John Mark, the young man from Jerusalem, as their helper. They went down to the shore of the Great Sea at Selucia, took a ship, and sailed to the island of Cyprus. On that island they visited all the cities and preached Christ in all the synagogues of the Jews.

At a place called Paphos they met the Roman ruler of the island, a man named Sergius Paulus. He was a good man, and sent for Barnabas and Saul, that he might learn about Christ. But with the ruler was a Jew named Elymas, who claimed to be a prophet and opposed Barnabas and Saul in their teaching, trying to persuade the ruler not to hear the gospel.

Saul, full of the Holy Spirit, fixed his eyes on Elymas the false prophet and said to him, "You man full of wickedness, you child of the evil one, you enemy of the right, won't you stop opposing the word of the Lord? The hand of the Lord is on you, and you will be blind for a time, not able to see the sun!"

At once, darkness fell on Elymas, and he groped about, feeling for someone to lead him by the hand. When the ruler saw the power of the Lord, he was filled with wonder and believed the gospel of Christ.

From this time on, Saul was called Paul. He was no longer Saul, but Paul the apostle, having all the power that belonged to Peter, John, and the other apostles.

_____

Discussion Questions: *1. Who was Agabus? What did he say? Did it happen? 2. Why did the Church at Jerusalem send Barnabas and Saul to Antioch again? Who did they take with them? 3. What did God call Barnabas and Saul to do? 4. Why did Sergius Paulus send for Barnabas and Saul? 5. What did Elymas do? What happened to him? Why was Saul's name changed?*

DAY 331
___

ANTIOCH, ICONIUM, AND LYSTRA
Acts 13:13-14:11

FROM the island of Cyprus, Paul, Barnabas, and John Mark sailed to a place called Perga. Here John Mark left them and went back to his home in Jerusalem. Paul and Barnabas went into Asia Minor and came to a city called Antioch. This was not Antioch in Syria, from which they had come, but another Antioch in a region called Pisidia. There they went into the synagogue and Paul preached to both Jews and Gentiles. Not many of the Jews believed Paul's words, but a great number of the Gentiles became followers of Christ. This made the Jews very angry and they drove Paul and Barnabas away.

They went to Iconium, another city, and preached the gospel with such power that many Jews and Gentiles believed in Christ. But the Jews who would not believe stirred up the city against Paul and Barnabas. They gathered a crowd of people, intending to seize the apostles and kill them. But Paul and Barnabas heard of the plan and quietly left the city.

Next the two of them went to the city of Lystra, in the land of Lycaonia, and preached the gospel. There were few Jews in that city, and they preached to people who were worshipers of idols. Among those who heard Paul speak at Lystra was a lame man who had never been able to walk. Paul fixed his eyes on this man and saw that he had faith to be made strong. He said to him with a loud voice, "Stand up on your feet!"

At these words, the man leaped up and walked. When the people saw how the lame man had been healed, they were filled with wonder and said, "The gods from heaven have come down to us in the form of men!"

Discussion Questions: *1. What did Barnabas and Paul do in Antioch in Pisidia? 2. Why did this make the Jews angry? 3. What happened at Iconium? What did the apostles do? 4. What happened at Lystra? What did the people who lived there do?*

DAY 332

LYSTRA'S SACRIFICE

Acts 14:12-28

THE people of Lystra thought that Barnabas was Jupiter, who they worshiped as the greatest of the gods. Because Paul was the chief speaker, they thought he was Mercury, the messenger of the gods. In front of their city was a temple to Jupiter. The priest of the temple brought oxen and garlands of flowers, and was about to offer a sacrifice to Barnabas and Paul as gods.

It was some time before the two apostles understood what the people were doing. But when they saw that they were about to offer sacrifice to them, Paul and Barnabas rushed out among the people and cried out, "Men, why do you do such things as these? We are not gods, but men like yourselves. We bring you word that you should turn from these idols, which are nothing, to the living God who made the heaven, and the earth, and the sea, and all things. It is God who has done good to you and given you from heaven rains and fruitful seasons, filling you with food and gladness."

Even with words like these, they could scarcely keep the people from offering sacrifices to them. But after a time some Jews came from Iconium. These Jews stirred up the people against Paul, so that instead of worshiping him, they stoned him and dragged out of their city what they thought was his dead body. Then they left him, and as the believers gathered around weeping, Paul got up alive and went back to the city. The next day, he journeyed with Barnabas to Derbe. There they preached the gospel and led many as disciples to Christ. After this they went again to the cities where they had preached, to Lystra in Lycaonia, Iconium and Antioch in Pisidia, and to Perga in Pamphylia, and visited the churches they had founded. They encouraged the believers, telling them to continue in the faith, and saying to them that those who would enter the kindgom of God must expect to meet with trouble, and God would give them a full reward.

Discussion Questions: *1. What did the apostles do when they found out what* *the people thought? 2. What did the Jews from Iconium do at Lystra? 3. What happened to Paul? What did he and Barnabas do next? 4. Why do you think the apostles returned to the cities they had already visited?*

DAY 333

THE DECISION ABOUT THE GENTILES

Acts 15:1-41

AFTER Paul and Barnabas brought Antioch the news that the Gentiles had turned to the Lord, a great question arose in the Church. Some of the strict Jews said, "All these Gentile believers must become Jews and keep the Jewish laws about food, feasts, washings, and offerings."

Others said that the laws were made for Jews only, and that Gentiles who believed in Christ were not called to live as Jews. After many words on both sides, Paul and Barnabas, with other believers, went up to Jerusalem to lay this matter before the apostles and the elders of the Church. They listened to Paul's story of God's great work among the Gentiles, talked about it, and sought God in prayer. At last the apostles, elders, and the whole Church in Jerusalem sent a message to the Gentiles who believed, telling them that Jews and Gentiles were alike before God, that both were saved by believing in Christ, and that Gentiles who believed were not called to keep the laws given to the Jews.

The apostles Paul, Barnabas, Judas, and Silas were sent to bring this news to the Church at Antioch. They went and read the letter, which brought great joy to the Gentile believers. Now the Gentiles who believed in Christ were able to serve the Lord without obeying all the rules the Jews themselves found very hard to keep.

After a time Paul said to Barnabas, "Let us go out again and visit the brethren in the cities where we preached the gospel, and see how they are doing."

Barnabas was willing to go and wanted to take along John Mark as their helper. But Paul did not think it was a good idea to take with them the young man who went home in the middle of their journey and left them to visit strange lands alone. Barnabas was determined to take Mark, and Paul refused to have him go, so at last Paul and Barnabas separated. Barnabas took Mark and went to the island of Cyprus. Paul chose as his helper Silas, who had come from Jerusalem to Antioch, and Paul and Silas went through the lands in Asia

Minor that Paul had visited on his earlier journey. Everywhere they sought out the churches that had been planted by Paul and Barnabas, encouraging the disciples to be faithful in the Lord.

Discussion Questions: *1. What question arose in the Church? 2. Who had to decide what was right? What did they decide? 3. How did their decision make the Gentiles feel? 4. Why didn't Paul want to take John Mark on their next journey? What happened?*

DAY 334

THE MACEDONIAN CALL

Acts 16:1-15

WHEN Paul came to Derbe and Lystra, he found a young man named Timothy, whose mother was of the Jewish race and a believer in Christ. Timothy had known the word of God from his childhood. He had given his heart to Christ, and all the believers in Christ at Lystra and Iconium knew him and spoke well of him. Paul asked Timothy to leave his home and go out with him as his helper. Timothy went and stayed with Paul from then on.

Paul, Silas, and Timothy went through many lands in Asia Minor, preaching the gospel and planting the Church. The Spirit of the Lord would not let them go some places that were not ready for the gospel, and they came down to Troas, which was on the sea opposite the land of Macedonia in Europe.

While they were at Troas, a vision came to Paul in the night. He saw a man of Macedonia standing before him and pleading with him, "Come over to Macedonia and help us."

When Paul told this vision to his friends, they all knew this was a call from the Lord to carry the Gospel of Christ to Macedonia. As soon as they could find a vessel sailing across the sea, they went on board. With them went a doctor named Luke, who joined Paul. Luke stayed with Paul for many years, and Paul called him the beloved physician. Afterward, Luke wrote two books of the Bible, the gospel according to Luke and the Acts of the Apostles.

Paul and his three friends set sail from Troas. On the third day, they came to the city of Philippi, in Macedonia, where they stayed for a few days. There was no synagogue in that city, and scarcely any Jews. On the Sabbath, Paul and his company went out of the city gate to the riverside, where was a place of prayer. There they sat down and talked with a few women who had met together to pray. One of these was a woman named Lydia, who had come from Thyatira in Asia Minor and was a seller of purple dyes. She was seeking after God, and the Lord opened her heart to hear the words of Paul and believe in Christ. She was baptized, the first one brought to the Lord in Europe, and all in her house were baptized also. Lydia said to Paul and his friends, "If you count me as one who is faithful to the Lord, come into my house, and stay there."

She urged them so strongly that they all went to Lydia's house and made it their home while they were in the city.

Discussion Questions: *1. Who was Timothy? Silas? 2. What was the vision that Paul saw? 3. Who was Luke? What did he write? 4. Where did Paul preach in Troas? How was that different from where he usually preached? 5. Who believed in Paul's message?*

DAY 335

PAUL IN PRISON (PART 1)

Acts 16:16-28

ONE day while they were going to the place of prayer, a young woman who had an evil spirit met them. She was a slave, and through the spirit in her, her owners pretended to tell what was to happen. Through her, they made a lot of money. As soon as she saw Paul and his friends, she cried out, "These men are servants of the Most High God, who tell you the way to be saved."

She did this day after day, following Paul and his companions. Paul was upset to see her held by the power of the evil spirit, and he spoke to the spirit, "I command you in the name of Jesus Christ to come out of her!"

That very hour, the spirit left the girl. But with the evil spirit gone from her, there was no profit to her masters. They were very angry, and took hold of Paul and Silas, dragging them before the rulers of the city and saying, "These men, who are Jews, are making great trouble in our city, and are teaching the people to do what is against the law for Romans."

They stirred up the crowd and made them very angry at them. To please the throng, the rulers took their garments from Paul and Silas and commanded that they be beaten with rods. When they had received many cruel blows, they were thrown into the prison, and the jailer was ordered to watch them carefully. He took them into the dungeon in the very middle of the prison and made their feet fast in the stocks.

About midnight, Paul and Silas were praying and singing hymns of praise to God, and the other prisoners were listening to them. Suddenly there was a great earthquake. The foundations of the prison were shaken, every door was opened, and all the chains on the prisoners were loosed. Everyone could have gone free, if fear had not held them in their places. The jailer of the prison woke up and saw the prison doors wide open. By the law of the Romans, a man in charge of a prisoner must take his place if his prisoner escaped, and the jailer, thinking the men in the prison had gotten away, drew out his sword and was going to kill himself, when Paul called out, "Do yourself no harm, for we are all here."

Discussion Questions: *1. What did the young woman with the evil spirit say about Paul and his friends? Why did her masters become angry at Paul? 2. What did they do to Paul and Silas? 3. What happened to the two men in prison?*

DAY 336

PAUL IN PRISON (PART 2)

Acts 16:29-40

THEN the jailer called for lights and sprang into the room where Paul and Silas were. Trembling with fear, he fell down at their feet and cried out, "O, sirs, what must I do to be saved?"

They said, "Believe on the Lord Jesus Christ, and you shall be saved, and those in your house with you."

That night in the prison, they spoke the word of the Lord to the jailer and all that were with him. The jailer washed their wounds, and he and all his family were baptized. Afterward, he brought them from the prison into his own house, and set food before them. The jailer and his household were all happy in the Lord, believing in Christ.

The rulers of the city knew they had done an unjust act by beating Paul and Silas and throwing them in prison. But they did not know that Paul and Silas, though Jews, were also free citizens of Rome. It was unlawful to beat a citizen or put him in prison without a fair trial. In the morning the rulers sent their officers to the jailer, saying, "Let those men go." The jailer told their words to Paul and said, "The rulers have told me to let you go. Come out of the prison and go in peace."

THE JAILER BEFORE PAUL AND SILAS - ACTS 16:29

But Paul said, "We are free citizens of Rome, and without a trial they have beaten us and thrown us into prison. Now they want to throw us out secretly? No. Let those rulers come and bring us out!"

The officers told these words to the rulers, and when they learned that these men were Roman citizens, they were frightened, for their own lives were in danger for having beaten them. They came to Paul and Silas and begged them to go away from the prison and the city. Then Paul and Silas walked out of the prison and went to the house of Lydia. They met the brethren who believed in Jesus and spoke to them words of comfort and of help, then they left the city.

Discussion Questions: *1. What did the jailer ask Paul and Silas? 2. How did the rulers let Paul and Silas go? 3. Why did Paul want the rulers to bring them out of the jail? Why were the rulers afraid?*

DAY 337

THESSALONICA

Acts 17:1-12

ROM Philippi, Paul and Silas went to Thessalonica, which was the largest city in Macedonia. There they found many Jews and a

476

synagogue where the Jews worshiped. For three weeks Paul spoke at the meetings in the synagogue and showed the meaning of the Old Testament writings about the Saviour. "This Jesus, whom I preach to you, is the Christ, the Son of God, and the King of Israel."

Some of the Jews believed Paul's teachings, and many Greeks in the city became followers of Christ. Among them were some of the leading women of the city, so a large church of believers arose in Thessalonica.

But the Jews who would not believe in Jesus were very angry when they saw so many seeking the Lord. They stirred up a crowd of the lowest people in the city, raised a riot, and led a noisy throng to the house of a man named Jason, where they thought Paul and Silas were staying. The crowd broke into the house and looked for Paul and Silas, but could not find them. Then they seized Jason and some other friends of the apostles and dragged them before the rulers of the city.

"These men, who have turned the whole world upside down, have come to this city, and Jason has taken them into his house. They are acting contrary to the laws of Caesar, for they say there is another king, a man whose name is Jesus."

The rulers of the city were greatly troubled when they saw these riotous people and heard their words. They knew that Jason and his friends had done nothing against the law of the land, but to quiet the crowd, they made the believers promise to obey the laws, then they let them go free. The brethren of the church sent Paul and Silas away to the city of Berea, which was not far from Thessalonica. There again they found a synagogue and, as in other places, Paul went into its meetings and preached Jesus — not only to the Jews, but also to the Gentiles, many of whom worshiped with the Jews.

Discussion Questions: 1. Who in Thessalonica believed in Jesus? Who did not believe? 2. Why did the Jews become angry? What did they do? 3. Who did they drag before the rulers of the city? 4. What happened to Paul and Silas?

DAY 338

BEREA AND ATHENS

Acts 17:13-21

 HE people of Berea were of a nobler spirit than the Jews of Thessalonica, for they did not refuse to hear Paul's teachings. They listened with open minds, and every day they studied the Old Testament writings, to see whether the words spoken by Paul were true. Many of them became believers in Jesus. Not only the Jews, but the Gentiles also, for those who study the Bible will always find Christ in its pages. But the news went to Thessalonica that the word of Christ was being taught in Berea. The Jews of Thessalonica sent some men to Berea who stirred up the people against Paul and Silas. To avoid a riot like that in Thessalonica, the brethren in Berea took Paul away from the city, but Silas and Timothy stayed for a time.

The men who went with Paul led him down to the sea and went with him to Athens. There they left Paul, taking back with them Paul's message to Silas and Timothy to hasten to him as quickly as they could come. While Paul was waiting for his friends in Athens, his spirit was stirred as he saw the city full of idols. It was said that there were more idols in Athens than there were citizens. Paul talked with the Jews in the synagogue, and in the public square of the city with the people he met. All the people of Athens — and those visiting that city — spent most of their time telling or hearing whatever was new. There were many men who were thought very wise and were teachers of what they called wisdom. Some of these men met Paul, and when they heard him, they said scornfully, "What does this babbler say?"

Because he preached to them of Jesus, and of his rising from the dead, some said, "This man seems to be talking about some strange gods!"

There was a hill in Athens called Mars' Hill, where court was held on seats of stone. They brought Paul to this place and asked him, "May we know about this new teaching you are giving? You bring to our ears some strange things, and we wish to know what these things mean."

Discussion Questions: 1. What kind of people lived in Berea? What did they do? 2. What did the Jews from Thessalonica do? 3. What were the people of Athens like? Why did they listen to Paul?

DAY 339

PAUL ON MARS' HILL

Acts 17:22-34

PAUL stood in the middle of Mars' Hill, with people all around him, and said, "Men of Athens, I see that you are very fond of worship. For as I passed by, I saw an altar on which was written these words: 'TO THE UNKNOWN GOD.' That God, whom you know not and seek to worship, is the

God that I make known to you. The God who made the world and all things in it is Lord of heaven and earth, and does not dwell in temples made by the hands of men. Nor is he served by men's hands, as though he needed anything. For God gives all men life, and breath, and all things. And he has made of one blood all the peoples who live on the earth, that all men should seek God, and should feel after him, and should find him, for he is not far away from any of us. For in him we live, and move, and have our being. Even as some of your own poets have said, 'For we also are the children of God.' Since we are God's children, we should not think that God is like gold, or silver, or stone, made by the hands of men. God calls on men to turn from their sins. He tells us he has fixed a day when he will judge the world through Jesus Christ, whom he has chosen and has raised from the dead."

PAUL PREACHING IN ATHENS - ACTS 17:16-34

When they heard Paul speak of the dead being raised, some laughed in scorn, but others said, "We will hear you again about this." After a time Paul went away from Athens. Very few people joined Paul and believed in Jesus. Among these few was a man named Dionysius, one of the court that met on Mars' Hill, and a woman named Damaris. A few others joined with them, but there were not many followers of Christ in Athens.

Discussion Questions: *1. What did Paul do in Athens? What did he tell the people there? 2. What did most of the people think of Paul's message?*

DAY 340

CORINTH

Acts 18:1-6

PAUL went from Athens to Corinth, another city in Greece. He was alone, because Silas and Timothy had not yet come from Thessalonica. But in Corinth, Paul met people who soon became his friends. They were a man named Aquila and his wife, Priscilla, who had come from Rome to Corinth. Every Jew in those times was taught some trade, and Paul's trade was weaving a rough cloth used for making tents. It happened that Aquila and Priscilla were also tentmakers, so Paul went to live in their house and they worked together at making tents.

On the Sabbath, Paul went into the synagogue to preach the gospel and talk about Christ with the Jews and the Greeks who worshiped God in the synagogue. Some believed Paul's words and some refused to believe.

Eventually, Silas and Timothy came from Thessalonica to meet Paul. They brought him word of the church at Thessalonica and some questions that were troubling the believers there. To answer these questions, Paul wrote two letters you can read in the New Testament: the first epistle to the Thessalonians, and the second epistle to the Thessalonians. These two letters are the earliest of Paul's writings that have been kept. We don't know if Paul wrote any earlier letters to churches, but if he did, the letters have been lost.

Now that Silas and Timothy, as well as Aquila and Priscilla, were with Paul, he began to preach even more earnestly than before, telling the Jews that Jesus was the Christ. When he found that the Jews would not listen, but spoke against him and Christ, Paul shook out his garment, as though he were shaking dust from it, and said to the Jews, "Your blood shall be on your own heads, not on me. I am free from sin, for I have given you the gospel, and you will not hear it. From this time I will stop talking to you and go to the Gentiles."

Discussion Questions: *1. Who did Paul meet in Corinth? 2. What did Paul write? Why? 3. What did Paul tell the Jews in Corinth?*

DAY 341

PAUL'S JOURNEY CONTINUES

Acts 18:7-22

PAUL found a house near the synagogue in Corinth, and in that house he preached the gospel to all who came, both Jews and Gentiles. Many who heard believed in Christ, and were baptized. Among them was a Jew named Crispus, who had been the chief ruler of the synagogue. But most of those who joined the Church of Christ in Corinth were not Jews, but Gentiles, men and women who turned to God from idols. One night the Lord came to Paul in a vision and said to him, "Paul, do not be afraid. Speak, and do not hold your peace. I am with you, and no one shall do you harm, for I have many people in this city."

Paul stayed in Corinth a year and six months, teaching the word of God. After a while, the Jews seized him and brought him into the court before the Roman governor of Greece, a ruler whose name was Gallio. They said to the governor, "This man is persuading people to worship God in a way forbidden by the law."

Paul was just opening his mouth to speak in answer to this charge when Gallio, the governor, spoke to the Jews, "O you Jews, if this were a matter of wrongdoing or wickedness, I would listen to you. But if these are questions about words, and names, and your law, look after it yourselves, for I will not be a judge of such things." And Gallio drove all the Jews out of his court. Then some of the Greeks seized Sosthenes, who was the chief ruler of the synagogue, and beat him before the judge's seat in the courtroom. But Gallio did not care for any of these things; he thought it was a quarrel over small matters.

After staying many days, Paul took leave of the brethren in the church at Corinth and sailed to Ephesus, which was a great city in Asia Minor. With Paul were his friends Aquila and Priscilla. At Ephesus, Paul went into the synagogue of the Jews and talked with them about the gospel and about Christ. He could stay for only a little while, although they asked him to remain longer. But he said, "I must go away now. But if it be the will of God, I will come again to you."

And he set sail for Ephesus, leaving Aquila and Priscilla there until he returned. Paul sailed over the Great Sea to Caesarea, in the land of Judea. From there he went to Jerusalem and visited the mother church. Then he journeyed back to Antioch.

And this was the end of Paul's second journey among the Gentiles preaching the gospel.

_____

Discussion Questions: *1. What did God tell Paul in Corinth? How long did he stay there? 2. Why did the Jews seize Paul? What did they do? 3. Why didn't Gallio even listen to the Jews' complaint? 4. Who went with Paul to Ephesus? What did they do when Paul left?*

DAY 342

_____

EPHESUS

Acts 18:23-19:12

THE apostle Paul did not stay long at Antioch, but soon started out for another journey among the churches and into new fields. He went through Syria, the country around Antioch, and then to the region near Tarsus, which had been his home, preaching Christ. He crossed over the mountains and entered into the heart of Asia Minor, coming to the land of Galatia. The people in this land were a warmhearted race, eager to see and hear new things. They listened to Paul with great joy, and believed his teachings. Paul wrote afterward that they received him as an angel of God, as though he were Jesus Christ himself, and they were ready to pluck out their own eyes and give them to him, so eager were they to have the gospel.

But soon after Paul went away some Jewish teachers came, saying to these new believers, "You must all become Jews and obey the whole Jewish law, with all its rules about things to be eaten, fasts, and feast days, or you cannot be saved."

The people in Galatia quickly turned away from Paul's words to follow these new teachers, for they were fond of change, and were not firm in their minds. There was danger that all Paul's work among them would be undone. But as soon as news came to Paul of their sudden turning from the truth of the gospel, he wrote them a letter, the epistle to the Galatians. In this letter he called them back to Christ and showed them that they were free, not slaves to the old law, and urged them to stand fast in the freedom Christ had given them.

Paul went through Phrygia, and from there returned to Ephesus, which he had visited before. This time he stayed in Ephesus more than two years, preaching the gospel of Christ. At first he spoke in the synagogue, telling the

Jews that Jesus was the Anointed Christ, the King of Israel, and proving it from the prophets of the Old Testament. But when the Jews would no longer listen to him, Paul left the synagogue and spoke every day in a schoolroom that was opened to him. His work became so well-known that almost all the people in Ephesus, and many in the lands around the city, heard the word of the Lord.

God gave Paul great powers of healing. They carried to the sick the cloths with which Paul had wiped the sweat from his face, and the aprons he had worn while he was at work making tents, and the diseases left the sick, and evil spirits went out of men. These wonderful works drew great crowds to hear Paul, and led many more to believe his words.

Discussion Questions: *1. What were the people of Galatia like? 2. What did the Jewish teachers tell the people of Galatia? Why did the people listen to this false teaching? 3. What did Paul write to the Galatians? What did he say? 4. When Paul rturned to Ephesus, how long did he stay? What happened there?*

DAY 343

The Pretenders

Acts 19:13-23

THERE were some Jews in Ephesus who wandered from place to place pretending to drive evil spirits out of men. These men saw how great Paul's power was when he spoke in Jesus' name, and they also began to speak in Jesus' name, saying to the evil spirits in men, "I command you to come out in the name of Jesus, whom Paul preaches."

The evil spirit in one man answered two of these pretenders: "Jesus I know, and Paul I know, but who are you?" And the man with the evil spirit leaped on them, threw them down, tore off their clothing, and beat them, so they ran out of the house naked and covered with wounds. Everybody in the city, both Jews and Greeks, heard of this, and all knew that even the evil spirits feared the name of Jesus as spoken by Paul. Many of those who had dealt with evil spirits came and confessed their deeds and turned to the Lord. And some who had books claiming to tell how to talk with spirits brought them and burned them as bad books, although the books had cost a great sum of money. So the word of the Lord grew in Ephesus, a great number believed in Christ, and a large church arose.

Paul now began to feel that his work in Ephesus was nearly finished. He thought he would go visit the churches in Philippi, Thessalonica, and Berea, in the land of Macedonia, and then the church at Corinth in Greece, and then go back to Jerusalem.

"And after I have been there," said Paul, "then I must also see Rome."

To prepare for his visit to Macedonia, Paul sent Timothy and another friend named Erastus ahead, while he stayed in Ephesus a little longer. But soon after this a great stir arose in that city over Paul and his preaching.

Discussion Questions: *1. Why did the Jews try to use Jesus' name to drive out evil spirits? What did one spirit say to them? 2. What did those who had dealt with evil spirits do? 3. Where did Paul want to go?*

DAY 344

THE CRAFTSMEN (PART 1)

Acts 19:24-31

THE city of Ephesus had an idol temple, one of the greatest and richest in all the world. Around the temple stood 120 great columns of white marble, each column the gift of a king. And in it was an image of the goddess Diana that the people believed had fallen from the sky. People came from many lands to worship the image of Diana, and many took home little images like it, made of gold or silver. The making and selling of these little images gave work to many who worked in gold and silver, and brought them great riches.

One of these workers in silver, a man named Demetrius, called together his fellow workmen and said to them, "You know, my friends, that by this trade we earn our living and win riches. And you can all see and hear that this man Paul has persuaded and turned away many people, not only in this city, but also throughout all these lands, by telling all men that there are no gods made by hands. There is danger that our trade will come to an end, and danger that the temple of the great goddess Diana may become unimportant. It may even be that the goddess all Asia and the world worships shall fall down from her greatness." When the workmen heard this, they became very angry and set up a great cry, shouting out, "Great is Diana of the Ephesians! Great is Diana of the Ephesians!"

Soon the whole city was in an uproar. People were running through the streets shouting, and a great multitude was drawn together, most of them not knowing what had caused the crowd. In the side of the hill near the city was a great open place with stone seats around it on three sides. It was used for public meetings and was called the theatre. Into this place all the people rushed, until it was thronged. Demetrius and his fellow workers led the shouting. "Great is Diana of the Ephesians!"

They seized two of Paul's friends, Gaius and Aristarchus, and dragged them with them into the theatre. Paul wanted to go in and try to speak to the people, but the disciples of Christ would not let him go. Some of the chief men of the land, who were Paul's friends, sent word to him, urging him not to venture into the theatre.

_____

Discussion Questions: *1. Who was Demetrius? Why was he angry with Paul? 2. Why did the people of his city follow Demetrius? 3. Why did Paul want to talk to the people? Why wouldn't his friends let him?*

DAY 345

THE CRAFTSMEN (PART 2)
Acts 19:32-20:1

THE noise, the shouting, and the confusion kept up for two hours. When the crowd began to grow tired and were ready to listen, the clerk of the city came forward, quieted the people, and said, "You men of Ephesus, what is the need of all this riot? Is there anyone who does not know that this city guards the temple of the great goddess Diana, and of the image that fell down from the heavens? Since these things cannot be denied, you should be quiet, and do nothing rash or foolish. You have brought here these men, who are not robbers of temples, nor have they spoken evil against our goddess. If Demetrius and the men of his trade have a charge to bring against any men, the courts are open, and there are judges to hear their case. But if there is any other business, it must be done in a regular meeting of the people. For we are in danger from this riot, and may be brought to account for it, since there is no cause for it and no reason we can give for this gathering."

After the city clerk had quieted the people with these words, he sent them away. When the riot was over and all was peaceful again, Paul met the disciples of Christ and spoke to them once more. He had been in Ephesus for three years preaching. While there he had written, besides the epistle to the Galatians, that to the Romans and two letters to the Corinthians, the believers at Corinth, in Greece. He now sailed away from Ephesus to Macedonia, where he had preached the gospel before on his second journey.

_____

Discussion Questions: *1. Who talked to the people of the city? What did he say? 2. How long had Paul been in Ephesus? What had he done while he was there? 3. Where did Paul go next?*

DAY 346

GIFTS FOR JERUSALEM

Acts 20:2-12

AFTER his three years at Ephesus in Asia Minor, Paul sailed to Macedonia. There he visited again the churches in Philippi, Thessalonica, and Berea. Then he went southward into Greece and saw the church at Corinth, to which he had written two long letters. While Paul was visiting these churches, he told them of the believers among the Jews in Jerusalem and Judea. Many of these were very poor, and since they had become disciples of Christ, the other Jews would not help them. Therefore Paul asked the Gentile churches everywhere to send gifts to these poor people. He said in his letter, "These people have sent the word of Christ to you. Now send them your gifts to show that you love them, and to show that you thank God for the gift of his Son who saves you from your sins."

From each of the churches men were chosen to go with Paul and carry these gifts to Jerusalem. From Berea, the place where so many had studied the Scriptures, went a man named Sopater. From Thessalonica went Aristarchus and Secundus. From Derbe in Asia Minor, Gaius and Timothy were sent, and from the other churches in Asia Minor, Tychicus and Trophimus. All these went on ahead and waited for Paul at Troas, on the shore of the Aegean Sea. Paul's friend Luke the doctor joined him at Philippi, and they sailed together to Troas. There the other disciples met them, and they stayed for a week.

On the evening of the first day of the week, a farewell meeting was held at Troas for Paul and his party, who were to start on their journey to Jerusalem. The meeting was in a large upper room on the third story of a house, and it was filled with people who had come to hear Paul. While Paul was speaking, a young man named Eutychus, who was sitting in a window, dropped asleep and fell out the window to the ground, two stories below. He was taken up dead, but Paul went down, fell on him, and placed his arms around him, saying, "Do not weep for him, for his life is still in him."

Then Paul went up again, broke bread with the believers, and held the Lord's Supper. Then he talked for a long time, until the break of day. And they brought in the young man living, at which they were very happy.

Discussion Questions: *1. What did Paul tell the churches in Macedonia about? 2. What did Paul tell them to do? 3. What happened to Eutychus? What did Paul do?*

DAY 347

Paul's Farewell

Acts 20:13-38

ALL the rest of the party going to Jerusalem, except Paul, went on board the ship at Troas. But as the ship was to stop on the way at a place called Assos, Paul chose to go to that place on foot. At Assos, they took Paul on board and sailed among the islands of the Aegean Sea, then stopped at Miletus, which was not far from Ephesus. Paul did not wish to go to Ephesus, but he sent to the elders of the church, asking them to come and meet him at Miletus. They came, and Paul said to them, "You know from the first day that I set foot in this part of Asia, how I was with you all the time, serving the Lord with a lowly mind, and with tears, and with many troubles that came on me from the plots of the Jews. You know, too, how faithfully I spoke to you, teaching you in public and from house to house to repent of your sins and believe in our Lord Jesus Christ.

"And now, bound in my spirit, I am going to Jerusalem, not knowing what will come to me there, except that the Holy Spirit tells me that chains and troubles will meet me. But I do not hold my life of any account, as dear to me, so I may run out my race in Christ, and may do the work given me by the Lord Jesus: to preach the good news of God's grace. And now I know that you, among whom I went preaching the kingdom, shall see my face no more.

"Take care of yourselves and all the flock the Holy Spirit has placed in your care, as shepherds to feed the church the Lord Jesus bought with his own blood. I know that after I go away, enemies, like savage wolves, shall come among you, not sparing the flock, and also among yourselves men shall rise up, speaking false things and leading away disciples after them. Therefore watch, and remember that for three years I did not cease warning you, night and day, with tears.

"And now I leave you with God, and with the word of his grace, which is able to build you up and to make you fit to dwell among his holy ones. I have not sought gold, silver, or fine clothing. Your yourselves know that these hands of mine have worked for my own living and to help those who were with me. I have tried to show you by my own life how you should help those who are weak. Remember the words of the Lord Jesus, 'It is more blessed to give than to receive.' "

When Paul had said this, he knelt down and prayed with them all. And they all wept, and hugged Paul, and kissed him, because they would not see him again. They went with him to the ship and watched him sail away from them.

_____

Discussion Questions: *1. What did Paul remind the leaders of the churches at Miletus and Ephesus about? 2. What did Paul know would happen to him in Jerusalem? 3. What did Paul warn the leaders about? 4. How did the leaders feel when Paul left? Why?*

DAY 348

_____

AGABUS'S PROPHECY

Acts 21:1-15

PAUL and his group sailed toward the land of Judea and went ashore at Tyre. There they found disciples and stayed with them a week. Some of these spoke to Paul in the Spirit of God and told him not to go into Jerusalem. But Paul had made up his mind, and when he found a ship going from Tyre to Judea, all the disciples, with their wives and children, went with him out of the city. They all knelt down together on the beach and prayed before they parted from one another. Paul's party left the ship at a place called Ptolemais, from which they walked down the shore to Caesarea. This was the place where, years before, Peter had given the gospel to the Roman centurion Cornelius. There Paul found Philip, the man who had preached to the Samaritans and the nobleman from Ethiopia. In those old days, Paul had been Philip's enemy and had driven him out of Jerusalem. Now they met as friends, and Paul stayed as a guest at Philip's house.

While they were at Caesarea, an old man named Agabus came down from Jerusalem. He was a prophet, to whom God had shown some things that would happen. This man came to Paul, took off Paul's girdle, and with it bound his own feet and hands, then said, "Thus saith the Spirit of God, 'So shall the Jews at Jerusalem bind the man that owns this girdle, and shall give him into the hands of the Gentiles.' "

When they heard this, all Paul's friends, Philip, and the disciples of Caesarea pleaded with Paul and begged him not to go up to Jerusalem. But Paul answered, "What are you doing, weeping and breaking my heart? I am ready not only to be bound, but also to die at Jerusalem for the name of the Lord Jesus!"

When they saw that Paul would not change his mind, they stopped trying to persuade him, saying, "The will of the Lord be done."

After some days in Caesarea, Paul and his friends, with some of the believers from Caesarea, went up the mountains to Jerusalem. This was the last time Paul would be in the city of his people.

Discussion Questions: *1. Why didn't some of the disciples at Tyre want Paul to go to Jerusalem? Did Paul do what they wanted? 2. What did Agabus tell Paul? 3. Why was Paul willing to go to Jerusalem?*

DAY 349

PAUL'S ARREST

Acts 21:17-39

WHEN Paul and his friends came to Jerusalem, they met with the church in that city and gave the money that had been gathered by the Gentiles to help the Jewish believers in Christ who were poor. The apostle James, the Lord's brother, who was the head of the church in Jerusalem, gave Paul and his friends a glad welcome and praised God for the good work they did among the Gentiles.

About a week after Paul came to Jerusalem, he was worshiping in the Temple when some Jews from the lands around Ephesus saw him. They at once stirred up a crowd and took hold of Paul, crying out, "Men of Israel, help! This is the man who teaches all men everywhere against our people, and against our law, and against this Temple. Besides, he has brought Gentiles into the Temple, and has made the holy house unclean!"

They had seen Paul walking in the city with one of his friends from Ephesus who was not a Jew, and they started the false report that Paul had taken him into the Temple. When the Jews set up this cry against Paul, all the city was stirred up, and a great crowd gathered around Paul. They dragged Paul out of the Temple into the outer court, and were about to kill him in their rage.

But in the castle on the north of the Temple was a Roman guard of soldiers, 1,000 men under the command of an officer. Word came to this officer that all Jerusalem was in a riot and a wild mob had seized the Temple. He called out his soldiers and their captains, and rushed quickly into the Temple, into the midst of the crowd beating and trampling Paul. The chief captain took Paul from their hands, and, thinking he must have done something very wicked to start such a riot, ordered him to be fastened with two chains.

Then he asked who Paul was and what he had done. Everyone answered at once, some shouting one thing and some another. Since the chief captain could understand nothing in the confusion, he commanded the soldiers to take Paul into the castle. The crowd made a rush to seize Paul and take him away from the soldiers, but they carried him through the throng and up the stone steps that led into the castle, while the angry Jews cried, "Away with him! Kill him!"

Just as they reached the platform at the door of the castle, Paul very quietly spoke to the chief captain in his own language, which was Greek. He said, "May I say something to you?"

The officer was surprised, and he answered Paul, "Do you know Greek? Aren't you that man from Egypt who rose up against the rulers and let out into the wilderness four thousand murderers?"

But Paul said, "I am a Jew, of Tarsus in Cilicia. I belong to no small city. I beg you, give me permission to speak to the people."

Discussion Questions: *1. How did the apostle James greet the people from the churches and Paul? 2. What happened when Paul went to the Temple? 3. Why did the chief captain put Paul in chains? 4. What did Paul ask the captain to do?*

DAY 350

Paul's Speech in the Temple
Acts 21:40-22:29

HE chief captain thought that if Paul spoke to the people, he might learn something about him, so he gave him permission. Then Paul, standing on the stairs, beckoned to the crowd, to show that he wanted to speak. Soon everybody became quiet, for all wanted to hear, and Paul began to speak to the people. But he did not speak in Greek, as he had spoken to the chief captain. He spoke in the Hebrew tongue, their own language, which they loved to hear. And when they heard him speak in Hebrew they were more ready to listen to him. And this was what Paul said:

"Brethren and fathers, hear the words I speak to you. I am a Jew, born in

Tarsus of Cilicia, but brought up in this city at the feet of the wise teacher Gamaliel and taught in a strict way the law of our fathers. I was earnest for God, as all of you are this day. And I was a bitter enemy of the way of Christ, binding and putting in prison both men and women who believed in Jesus. The high priest himself knows this, and all the council of the elders, for they gave me letters to our people in Damascus. And I went on a journey to that place to bring in chains those who followed Jesus, to punish them.

"And it came to pass as I made my journey and drew near Damascus, suddenly there shone from heaven a great light round about me. I fell to the ground and heard a voice saying to me, 'Saul, Saul, why are you fighting against me and doing me harm?' And I answered, 'Who are you, Lord?' And he said to me, 'I am Jesus of Nazareth, whom you are trying to destroy!'

"Those who were with me saw the light, but they did not hear the voice that spoke to me. And I said, 'What shall I do, Lord?' And the Lord said to me, 'Rise up, and go into Damascus, and it shall be told you what things are given to you to do.'

"When I stood up, I could not see, from the glory of that light, and I was led by the hands of those who were with me into Damascus. And a man named Ananias, a man who worshiped God and kept the law, of whom all the Jews in the city spoke well, came to me, and standing by me, said, 'Brother Saul, receive your sight.'

"And in that very hour I looked up and saw him. And he said to me, 'The God of our fathers has chosen you to know his will, and to see the Holy One, and to hear his voice. For you shall speak in his name to all men, telling them what you have seen and heard.'

"And afterward, when I came back to Jerusalem and was praying in the Temple, I saw the Lord again, and he spoke to me, 'Go forth, and I will send you to the Gentiles.' "

The Jews listened to Paul quietly until he spoke that word *Gentiles*. They began to cry out, "Away with such a fellow from the earth! It is not fit that he should live!"

As they tossed off their garments and threw dust into the air in their rage, the chief captain ordered that Paul be taken into the castle and beaten with rods until he told what dreadful thing he had done to arouse such anger. For the chief captain, not knowing the Jews' language, had not understood what Paul had said.

They took Paul into the castle, and were tying him up when Paul said to the centurion who stood by, "Have you any right to beat a Roman citizen who has not been tried before a judge?"

When the centurion heard this, he hurried to the chief captain and said to

THE CHIEF CAPTAIN COMMANDED PAUL TO BE BROUGHT TO THE CASTLE - ACTS 22:24

him, "Take care what you do to that man. He is a Roman citizen!"

Then the chief captain came and said to Paul, "Tell me, are you a Roman citizen?"

And Paul answered, "Yes, I am."

The chief captain said, "I bought this right to be a citizen with a great sum of money."

And Paul said to him, "But I am a freeborn citizen."

When those who were about to beat Paul knew that he was a Roman citizen, they left in haste. The chief captain was afraid because he had bound Paul, for no one could place a chain on a Roman citizen until he had been tried before a Roman judge.

They took Paul into the castle, but were careful not to do him any harm.

Discussion Questions: *1. Why did the captain let Paul speak to the people? 2. What did Paul tell them about? 3. What did the Jews do when Paul used the word* **Gentiles**? *4. What did the captain want to do to Paul? Why did he stop?*

DAY 351

PAUL IN FRONT OF THE COUNCIL

Acts 22:30-23:11

AFTER Paul had been rescued from the Jewish mob, he was taken into the castle on the north of the Temple for safekeeping. The chief captain wanted to know why the Jews were so bitter against Paul. To learn this, he commanded the chief priests and rulers to meet, brought Paul down from the castle, and set him before them. Paul looked seriously at the council and said to them, "Brethren, I have lived with a right feeling toward God all my life until this day."

The high priest, whose name was Ananias, was sitting in the council, clad in the white garments worn by all priests. He was so enraged at these words that he said to those standing near Paul, "Strike him on the mouth!"

Paul, angry at such unjust words, said, "God shall strike you, O whited wall! Do you sit to judge me by the law and yet command me to be struck against the law?"

Those standing by said to Paul, "Do you speak such words against the high priest of God?"

"I did not know," answered Paul, "that he was high priest. It is written in the law not to speak evil of a ruler of your people."

Paul saw that there were two parties in the council, and by a few wise words he made some of the rulers friendly to him. They stood up and said, "We find no evil in this man. Perhaps a spirit has spoken to him, or an angel."

This made the rulers on the other side all the more furious, and such a quarrel arose between them that the chief captain feared Paul would be torn in pieces. He sent down soldiers to take him by force from the council and bring him into the castle.

On the night after this, while Paul was in his room in the castle, the Lord stood by him and said, "Be of good cheer, Paul. As you have spoken for me at Jerusalem, so shall you speak for me at Rome."

Discussion Questions: *1. How did the captain try to find out why the Jews were so bitter against Paul? 2. What did the high priest command those standing near him to do to Paul? Was he right? 3. What did Paul do? Why did he say he was sorry? 4. What happened between the Jews? 5. What did God promise Paul?*

DAY 352

THE PLOT AGAINST PAUL

Acts 23:12-30

EARLY the next morning, more than forty Jews made a plan to kill Paul, swearing that they would not eat or drink until they had slain him. These men came to the chief priests and said, "We have bound ourselves under a great oath that we will taste nothing until we have killed Paul. Ask the chief captain to bring Paul down again to meet the council, so they may hear him and try his case. While he is on his way to the council, we will rush in and kill him."

Now Paul had a sister living in Jerusalem, and her son heard of this plot, came to the castle, and told it to Paul. Then Paul called one of the officers and said to him, "Take this young man to the chief captain, for he has something to tell him."

So the officer brought the young man to the chief captain and said to him, "Paul called me to him and asked me to bring this young man to you, for he has something to say to you."

The chief captain took the young man aside and asked him, "What is it that you have to say to me?"

And he said, "The Jews have agreed to ask you to bring Paul before the council again. But do not let him go, for there are more than forty men watching for him who have sworn they will neither eat nor drink until they have killed Paul."

The chief captain listened carefully and then sent the young man away after saying to him, "Do not tell anyone that you have spoken of these things to me." After the young man had gone, the chief captain called two centurions and said to them, "Make ready two hundred soldiers to go as far as Caesarea, and seventy men on horseback, and two hundred men with spears, at nine o'clock at night." He also told them to have ready horses for Paul, so he might send him safe to Felix, the governor of the land, at Caesarea. Then he wrote a letter for Felix.

"Claudius Lysias sends greeting to the most noble governor Felix. This man was seized by the Jews, and would have been killed by them, but I came upon him with the soldiers and took him from their hands, having learned that he was a citizen of Rome. And to find out the reasons they were so strongly against him, I brought him down to their council. I found that the charges against him were about questions of their law, but nothing deserving death or bonds. When I heard that there was a plot to kill the man, I sent him at once to you and told his enemies to go before you with their charges."

Discussion Questions: *1. What did forty Jews plan to do to Paul? 2. How did Paul find out about the plot? 3. How did the captain save Paul's life?*

DAY 353

FELIX AND PAUL
Acts 23:31-24:27

IN the night, almost 500 men were sent as a guard for Paul. He was brought out of the castle and taken that night as far as to Antripatris, about forty miles. The next day, the soldiers left him, thinking him out of danger, and returned to Jerusalem, while the horsemen rode on with him to Caesarea, where the governor Felix lived. The officer in charge gave the letter to the governor. He read the letter and then asked Paul from what land he had come. Paul told him that he belonged to the land of Cilicia in Asia Minor. And Felix said, "I will hear your case when those who bring charges against you have come."

He sent Paul to be kept in a castle that had once belonged to Herod. After five days, the high priest Ananias and some others came to Caesarea, bringing with them a lawyer named Tertullus.

When Paul was brought before them in the presence of Felix Tertullus made a speech charging him with riot, lawbreaking, and many evil deeds. They also said he was "a ringleader in the party of the Nazarenes," which was the name they gave to the Church of Christ. The Jews all joined in the charge, saying all these things were true.

After they had spoken, the governor motioned with his hand toward Paul, showing that he might speak, and Paul began, "I know you have been for many years a judge over this people, and for that reason I speak to you willingly. For you may know that it is only twelve days since I went up to worship at Jerusalem. I was not quarreling with anyone in the Temple, or stirring up a crowd in the Temple, the synagogues, or the city. Nor can they prove the things they have said against me.

"But I do admit to this, that I do serve the God of our fathers, believing all things in the law and the prophets, and having a hope in God that the dead shall be raised up. And I have always tried to keep my heart free from wrong toward God and toward men.

"Now, after many years, I came to bring gifts to my people and offerings for the altar. And with these they found me in the Temple, but not with a crowd, or with a riot. But there were certain Jews from Asia Minor who ought to have been there, if they have anything against me."

Felix knew something about the Church of Christ, and he said, "When Lysias, the chief captain, comes down, I will settle this case." And he ordered Paul to be kept under guard, but said his friends could come to see him. After a few days Felix and his wife, Drusilla (who was a Jewess) sent for Paul, and heard the gospel of Christ. As Paul preached to him of right living, of ruling one's self, and of the judgment of God, Felix was alarmed, and said, "Go away for now. When a fit time comes and I am ready to listen, I will send for you."

Felix was not a just judge, for he hoped Paul might give him money to be set free. With this in mind, he sent for Paul, and talked with him many times. Two whole years passed, and Paul was still in prison in Caesarea. At the end of that time, Felix was called back to Rome, and a man named Porcius Festus was sent as governor in his place. Felix wanted to please the Jews, and he left Paul a prisoner.

Discussion Questions: *1. What did Felix say to Paul? 2. Who came to Felix's court to bring charges against Paul? What did they say Paul had done? 3. Who did Paul preach to? 4. What kind of judge was Felix? What did he want Paul to do? 5. What did Felix do to please the Jews?*

DAY 354

Paul Before Festus

Acts 25:1-12

WHEN Festus came to rule the land of Judea in place of Felix, who had kept Paul in prison so long, he went up to Jerusalem to visit that city. The chief priests and leaders spoke to him against Paul, asking that he be sent to Jerusalem to be tried. It was their plan to kill Paul on the way. But Festus told them that Paul would be kept at Caesarea and he would soon go there himself.

"Let some of your leaders go down with me," said Festus, "and bring your charges against him, if you have any."

When Festus came down to Caesarea, he called them all together, sat on the judge's seat, and commanded Paul to be brought. The Jews accused Paul of many things, but they could not prove any of them. Paul said, "I have done no wrong against the laws of the Jews, the Temple, or the rule of Caesar the emperor."

Festus wanted to please the Jews, but he did not know of their plan to kill Paul. He said, "Are you willing to go up to Jerusalem and be tried on these charges before me?"

But Paul said, "I am standing before the Roman court, where I should be judged. I have done no wrong to the Jews, as you know very well, and no man will give me to them. I ask for a trial before Caesar, the emperor at Rome."

It was the law throughout the Roman lands that any citizen of Rome (as Paul was) could ask to be tried at Rome before Caesar, the emperor. When Festus heard Paul's words, he said, "Do you ask to be tried before Caesar? Then to Caesar you shall go."

Discussion Questions: *1. What did the chief priests and leaders want Festus to do with Paul? Why? 2. What did Paul ask Festus to do? Why?*

DAY 355

FESTUS AND AGRIPPA

Acts 25:13-22

O Paul was taken back to the prison at Caesarea, to be sent to Rome when it was time. A few days after this, a Jewish ruler named Agrippa and his sister, Bernice, came to visit Festus. King Agrippa ruled over part of the land to the east of the river Jordan. While Agrippa and Bernice were at Caesarea, Festus said to them, "There is a certain man left by Felix who the chief priests and elders of the Jews asked me to have killed or turned over to them. I told them that the Romans never judge against any man until he stands face-to-face before his enemies and can answer their charges. When they came down and the man was brought before them, their charges were not the wicked acts I expected to hear. They had some questions about their ways of worship and somebody named Jesus, who was dead, but who Paul said was alive. Since I did not understand these questions, I asked Paul if he would go to Jerusalem to be tried. But Paul asked for a trial before Caesar, and I am keeping him to be sent to the emperor at Rome."

"I would like," said Agrippa, "to hear this man myself."

"Tomorrow," said Festus, "you will hear him."

Discussion Questions: *1. What had the Jews asked Festus to do to Paul? 2. Why had Festus been surprised at the charges against Paul? 3. Who did Festus tell about the case? What did he say?*

DAY 356

Paul Before Agrippa

Acts 25:23-26:32

THE next day Agrippa, Bernice, Festus, the chief men of the city, and the officers of the army came to the hall of judgment. Paul was brought before them chained to a Roman soldier. After a few words by Festus, Agrippa said to Paul, "You may now speak for yourself."

Paul told Agrippa, "I'm happy, King Agrippa, to answer before you all the charges against me by the Jews, because I am sure you know all the Jewish ways and questions about the law.

"My way of life is known by the Jews, for I have lived among them. If they told the truth, they would say I kept the laws of our people most carefully. And now I stand here to be judged because of the promise God made to our fathers. The Jews charge me with doing evil because I believe that Jesus Christ rose from the dead to be the King of Israel. Why is it hard to believe that God raises the dead to life?

"Once I really thought I should do things against the name of Jesus of Nazareth. I shut up many good men and women in prisons, and when they were put to death, I testified against them. I caused them to be beaten, and I tried to make them curse the name of Jesus. Being exceedingly angry with them, I even looked for them in faraway cities.

"As I journeyed to Damascus with letters from the chief priests, I saw a light from heaven, brighter than the sun, shining around me. As we all fell down on the ground, I heard a voice saying to me, 'Saul, Saul, why are you fighting against me?'

"And I said, 'Who are you, Lord?'

"And the Lord said, 'I am Jesus, who you are trying to destroy. But rise up, and stand, for I have shown myself to you to make you my servant and my messenger. I will keep you safe from the Jewish people and from the Gentiles, to whom I send you.'

"King Agrippa, I did not disobey the voice from heaven. First at Damascus, then at Jerusalem and throughout all the land of Judea, and also among the Gentiles, I have spoken, telling men to turn from sin to God and to show deeds of right doing. This is why the Jews seized me in the Temple and tried to kill me. Having gained help from God, I say only what is given in the law of Moses and in the prophets: That the Christ must suffer and die and, by rising from the dead, give light to our people and the Gentiles."

PAUL BEFORE FESTUS AND AGRIPPA - ACTS 25:24

While Paul was speaking, Festus said in a loud voice, "Paul, you are mad! Your great learning has turned you to madness!" Festus, being a Roman, knew nothing of Jesus or the truths that Paul spoke.

But Paul said to him, "I am not mad, most noble Festus. I speak only sober, truthful words. The king knows of these things, and I speak freely to him. None of these things are hidden from him, for these things are not done in secret. King Agrippa, do you believe the prophets? I know that you do believe."

Agrippa said to Paul, "A little more, and you will persuade me to become a Christian!"

Paul said, "I wish that not only you, but all that hear me this day, might become as I am, except for these chains!"

After these words King Agrippa, Bernice, Festus, and those who were there went away by themselves and said to one another, "This man has done nothing deserving death or prison." And Agrippa said to Festus, "He could have been set free if he had not asked to be tried before Caesar."

Discussion Questions: *1. Why was Paul happy to tell Agrippa about his case? 2. What did Paul start doing as he talked to the king? Did Paul always do this when he spoke to important people? Why? 3. Why did Festus think Paul was mad? 4. Why couldn't these rulers set Paul free?*

DAY 357

PAUL'S TRIP TO ROME (PART 1)

Acts 27:1-13

WHEN Paul chose to be tried before Caesar — which was his right as a Roman — it became necessary to send him from Caesarea to Rome, where Caesar lived. There were no ships sailing at regular times from city to city, so people who needed to travel waited until they could find ships going to their destination. Paul and some other prisoners were given to a Roman centurion named Julius for the trip to Rome. Julius found a ship sailing from Caesarea to Asia Minor, which would take them part of the way to Rome. He took Paul and the other prisoners on board this ship. With Paul went his friends, Luke the doctor and Aristarchus from Thessalonica. Perhaps Timothy was also with them, but we are not certain of this.

They set sail from Caesarea after Paul had been in prison more than two years, following the coast northward to Sidon. There they stopped for a day. Julius the centurion was very kind to Paul and let him go ashore to see his friends living there. From Sidon they turned to the northwest and sailed past the island of Cyprus, and then westward by the shore of Asia Minor. At a city called Myra they left the ship and went on board another ship, which was sailing from Alexandria to Italy with a load of wheat from the fields of Egypt.

Soon a heavy wind began to blow against the ship, and it sailed very slowly for many days. At last they came to the large island of Crete and followed its southern shore until they found a harbor, where they stayed for a few days. But this harbor was not a good one, and they decided to leave it and sail to another.

Paul said to them, "Sirs, I see that this voyage will be with great loss and great danger to the lives of us all." He urged them to stay where they were. But the owner of the ship and its captain thought they could travel safely, and Julius the centurion listened to them rather than to Paul. When a gentle south wind began to blow, they set sail once more, closely following the shore of Crete.

Discussion Questions: *1. Why did Paul have to wait to go to Rome? 2. Name some of the people who might have gone to Rome with Paul. 3. How long had Paul been in prison? 4. What did Paul say to the centurion? Did the centurion listen?*

DAY 358

PAUL'S TRIP TO ROME (PART 2)

Acts 27:14-32

BUT soon the wind grew into a great storm, and the ship was driven off course. Behind the ship was a little boat, and they drew this up on board. As the ship creaked and seemed in danger of breaking up, they tied ropes around it to hold it together.

The storm grew and drove the ship away from the island, into the open sea. To make the vessel lighter, they threw overboard part of the load. The next day they cast away all the loose ropes and everything on the ship that could be spared.

THE SHIP WAS DRIVEN BY THE STORM INTO THE OPEN SEA - ACTS 27:15

Day after day went on with no sight of the sun, and night after night with no sight of the stars. The great waves rolled over the ship and beat on it until those on board thought they would die. In their fear, for days the men and prisoners had eaten nothing. In the midst of the storm, Paul stood up and said, "Sirs, you should have listened to me and not have set sail from Crete, for then we might have been saved much harm and loss. But even as it is, be of good cheer. For though the ship will be lost, all of us on board shall be saved. This night there stood by me an angel of the Lord, and the angel said to me,

501

'Fear not, Paul. You shall stand before Caesar, and God has given you all those who are sailing with you.'

"Now, friends, be of good cheer. I believe God, and it will be as the angel said to me. But we must land on some island."

When the storm had lasted fourteen days, at night the sailors thought they were coming near land. They dropped down the line and found that the water was twenty fathoms deep. In a while, they let down the line again and found the water only fifteen fathoms deep. They were sure land was near, but they were afraid the ship might be driven on the rocks, so they threw out four anchors to hold the ship and waited for day to come.

The sailors let down the little boat, saying they would throw out some more anchors, but really intending to row away and leave the ship to be destroyed. But Paul saw their purpose and said to the centurion, "Unless these sailors stay in the ship, none of us will be saved."

Then the soldiers cut the ropes of the little boat and let it fall, so the sailors could not get away.

Discussion Questions: *1. What happened to the ship? 2. How did Paul know what would happen to the ship? 3. What else did Paul warn the centurion of?*

DAY 359

SHIPWRECK

Acts 27:33-28:1

AS dawn neared, Paul urged them all to take some food. He said, "This is the fourteenth day you have gone without any food. Now I beg you to eat, for you need it to save your lives. You will all be saved. Not a hair shall fall from the head of one of you."

He took some bread and gave thanks to God before them all, then broke it and began to eat. This encouraged all the others, and they all ate. In total, there were 276 people on the ship — sailors, soldiers, prisoners, and others. After they had eaten, they threw out what was left of the wheat, so the ship was lighter and could go nearer the shore.

As soon as day dawned, they could see land, but they did not know what land it was. They saw a bay with a beach, into which they thought they might run the ship. So they cut loose the anchors, hoisted up the foresail, and made for the shore. The ship ran aground with the front end stuck in the sand, but the rear part began to break up from the beating of the waves.

Now came another danger — just as they were beginning to hope for their lives. By Roman law, a soldier in charge of a prisoner must take his place if he escaped. These soldiers feared their prisoners might swim ashore and get free, so they asked the centurion to let them kill all the prisoners while they were still on board the ship. But Julius the centurion liked Paul and kept them from killing the prisoners. He commanded those who could swim to jump overboard and swim to shore. Then the rest went ashore, some on planks and some on broken pieces of the ship. All made it to the shore safely.

They found they were on the island of Melita, which is in the Great Sea, south of the larger island of Sicily.

Discussion Questions: *1. What did Paul do before he broke the bread? Why? 2. Why were the soldiers in danger? What did they want Julius to do? Would he? 3. Where did the people land?*

DAY 360

MELITA

Acts 28:2-10

THE people who lived on the island of Melita were very kind to the strangers who had been thrown onto their shore. It was cold and rainy, and the men from the ship were soaked by the waves. But the people made a fire, brought them all around it, and gave them good care. Very soon they found that many of the men were prisoners under guard.

Paul gathered a bundle of sticks and placed them on the fire, when suddenly a poisonous snake came from the pile, driven out by the heat, and seized Paul's hand. When the people saw the snake hanging from his hand, they said to one another, "This man must be a murderer. He has saved his life from the sea, but the gods will not let him live because of his wickedness."

But Paul shook the snake off into the fire without harm. They watched to see his arm swell with poison and see him fall down dead. But when they watched him for a long time and saw no evil come to him, they changed their minds and said he was a god, and were ready to worship him.

Near the place where the ship was wrecked were lands and buildings belonging to the ruler of the island, whose name was Publius. He took Paul and his friends into his house and treated them very kindly. The father of Publius was very ill with a fever and a disease called dysentery, from which people often died. But Paul went into his room and prayed by his side. Then he laid his hands on him, and the sick man became well. As soon as the people of the island heard of this, many others troubled with diseases were brought to Paul, and all were cured. The people of Melita gave great honor to Paul and those with him. When they sailed away, they provided everything the ship would need, at no cost.

Discussion Questions: *1. How did the people of Melita act toward the shipwrecked people? 2. What happened to Paul? What did people think he was? 3. What did the people think when Paula healed Publius's father?*

DAY 361

PAUL IN ROME
Acts 28:11-28

THE centurion found a ship from Alexandria on its way to Italy, which had been waiting out the winter on the island. The name of this ship was *The Twin Brothers*. After three months on the island, the centurion sent on board this ship his soldiers and prisoners, with Paul's friends, and they sailed away from Melita. After stopping at a few places on their voyage, they left the ship at Putcoli, in the south of Italy, and from there traveled to Rome. The church at Rome heard he was coming, and some of the brethren went out to meet him a few miles from the city. When Paul saw them and saw they were glad to see him, even though he was in chains, he thanked God and took heart once more. He had long wanted to go to Rome, and now he came into the city at last — but as a prisoner chained to a Roman soldier.

When they came to Rome, the good centurion Julius gave his prisoners to the captain of the guard in the city. Because of his kind words, Paul was allowed to go to a house by himself, although he always had a soldier at his side. After three days in Rome, Paul asked the chief Jews of the city to meet in his house, because he could not go to the synagogue to meet with them. When they came, he said to them, "Brethren, though I have done no harm to our people or against our law, I was made a prisoner in Jerusalem and given into the hands of the Romans. When the Romans had given me a trial, they found no cause for putting me to death, and wished to set me free. But the Jews spoke against me, and I had to ask for a trial before Caesar, though I have no charge to bring against my own people. I have asked to see you and speak with you because for the hope of Israel I am bound with this chain."

They said to Paul, "No letters have come to us from Judea, nor have any of

PAUL PREACHED AT ROME – ACTS 28:20

the brethren brought us any evil report of you. But we would like to hear about these people who follow Jesus of Nazareth. Everyone is talking against them."

So Paul named a day, and they came in great number to Paul's room. He talked with them, explaining the teaching of the Old Testament about Christ, from morning until evening. Some believed the words of Paul, and others refused to believe. When they would not agree, Paul said to them as they were leaving, "Truly indeed did the Holy Spirit say of this people, in the words of Isaiah the prophet, 'Hearing ye shall hear, and shall not understand, and seeing ye shall see, and yet not see. For this people's heart is become hard, and their ears are dull, and their eyes they have shut; for they are not willing to see, nor to hear, nor to understand, nor to turn from their sins to God.' But know this, that the salvation of Christ is sent to the Gentiles. They will listen to it, even though you do not."

Discussion Questions: *1. What happened when the church at Rome heard Paul was coming? 2. Why was Paul allowed to go to a house instead of prison? 3. Why did Paul want to talk to the chief Jews? What did he do when he talked to them?*

DAY 362

PAUL'S LAST YEARS

Acts 28:29-31

PAUL lived for two years in the house he rented in Rome. Every day a soldier was brought from the camp, and Paul was chained to him all day. The next day, another soldier came. To each one, Paul spoke the gospel, until after a time many of the soldiers in the camp were believers in Christ. When these soldiers were sent away, they often carried the gospel with them to other lands. So Paul, though a prisoner, was still doing good and working for Christ.

Then, too, some of Paul's friends were with him in Rome. Timothy, whom Paul loved to call his son in the gospel, and Luke the doctor were there, perhaps in the same house. Aristarchus of Thessalonica, who had been with him in the ship and the storm, was still with Paul. Mark, the young man who years before went with Paul and Barnabas on their first journey from Antioch, visited Paul in Rome.

At one time, when Paul had been a prisoner nearly two years, a friend came to see him from Philippi in Macedonia. His name was Epaphroditus, and he brought Paul a loving message from that church and gifts to help Paul in his need. In return, Paul wrote the church at Philippi a letter, the epistle to the Philippians, full of tender, gentle words. It was taken to the church by Epaphroditus and Timothy.

In Rome, a man named Onesimus met Paul. He was a runaway slave who belonged to a friend of Paul named Philemon, who lived at Colosse. Paul led Onesimus to Christ, and then, although he would have liked to keep him with himself, he sent him back to Philemon, his master. But he asked Philemon not to treat him as a slave, but as a brother in Christ. This he wrote in a letter called the epistle to Philemon. Onesimus also delivered a letter to the church at Colosse, the epistle to the Colossians. And about the same time Paul wrote one of the greatest and most wonderful of all his letters, the epistle to the Ephesians, which he sent to the church in Ephesus.

It is thought — though it is not certain — that Paul was set free from prison after two years. He lived a free man, preaching in many lands for a few years. Then it is believed that he was again made a prisoner and taken to Rome, where Emperor Nero had him put to death. Among his last words were, "I have fought a good fight. I have run my race. I have kept the faith. And now there is waiting for me the crown which the Lord himself shall give me."

DAY 363

JOHN ON PATMOS

Revelation 1:9-4:1

YOU remember the apostle John, the disciple Jesus loved. When John was an old man, he was made a prisoner by a cruel emperor of Rome and kept on a little island called the isle of Patmos, which is in the Aegean Sea not far from Ephesus. While John was shut up on this island, the Lord Jesus Christ came to him and showed him some things that were going to happen.

It was on the Lord's Day, the first day of the week, when suddenly John heard behind him a loud voice, as loud as the sound of a trumpet. He turned to see where the voice came from and saw seven golden candlesticks and Jesus Christ. Christ was far more glorious than he had been while living as a man on the earth. He was dressed in a long white garment, with a girdle of gold over

JOHN WRITING WHILE ON THE ISLAND OF PATMOS - REVELATION 1:9-11

his chest. His hair and face were shining white as snow. His eyes flashed like fire. His feet were like polished brass, glowing like a furnace, and his voice sounded like the rushing of a mighty waterfall. In his right hand he held seven stars.

When John saw his Lord in all this splendor, he fell at his feet in great terror. Then he felt the right hand of Christ on him and heard his voice saying, "Fear not. I am the first and the last, and the Living One. I was dead, and now I am alive for evermore. Write the things you have seen, and other things I will show you, and send them to the seven churches in Asia. The seven stars you see in my hand are the ministers of the seven churches, and the seven candlesticks standing around me are the seven churches."

Then the Lord gave John the words of a letter that he commanded John to write to the seven churches. Each church received a different letter praising it for some things, and rebuking it for others. When these words had been given to the churches, John saw a door opened in heaven. He heard a voice like the sound of a trumpet saying to him, "Come up, and I will show you things that shall come to pass."

———————

Discussion Questions *1. What happened to John while he was on the isle of Patmos? 2. Name some of the things John saw. 3. Who was John to write to?*

DAY 364
———————

JOHN IN HEAVEN
Revelation 4:2-5:14; 7:9-17

JOHN was taken up to heaven two times. The first time John saw a rainbow-colored throne of God and around the throne sat twenty-four white-clad elders of the Church. Beside the throne were four strange creatures, each having six wings, who were saying, "Holy, holy, holy is the Lord God, the Almighty, which was, and which is, and which is to come." At this the elders would fall down and worship God.

In the right hand of the One on the throne John saw a scroll written on both sides and sealed with seven seals. "Who is worthy to open the book and to loose its seals?" called out a mighty angel. Because no one in all of heaven or earth or under the earth was able to open the scroll, John began to cry. "Weep not," said one of the elders. "The Lion of the tribe of Judah, he who

came from David, has won the right to open the book and its seven seals."
At that the Lamb of God, Jesus Christ, came and took the book and all around
the throne fell down and worshiped the Lamb.

When John next saw the throne of God he witnessed so many people—
all dressed in white, holding palm branches—he could not count them. As
John did not know who they were, one elder explained. "These are they who
have come up out of great trouble and sorrow, and have washed their robes,
and made them white in the blood of the Lamb. For that cause they are before
the throne of God and serve Him day and night. The Lamb who is in the
midst of the throne shall lead them as a shepherd, and shall guide them unto
the fountains of waters of life. And God shall wipe away every tear from their
eyes."

After this, John heard a great voice from the throne, "Behold, the tabernacle of God is with men. And God shall dwell among men, and they shall
be his people, and he shall be their God. He that was sitting on the throne
then said: "Behold, I make all things new. I will give to him who is thirsty
of the fountain of the water of life freely."

Discussion Questions: *1. Who could open the scroll and loose the seven
seals? 2. Why is Jesus called the Lamb of God? 3. Who were the crowds of people
who stood around the throne? 4. What was God's final promise to John?*

DAY 365

THE NEW JERUSALEM
Revelation 21:1-22:21

THEN John seemed to be standing on a high mountain. He saw a
glorious city—the new Jerusalem—coming down out of heaven from
God, having the glory of God. Over the city was a rich light, like that which
glows in some precious stone, clear as crystal. Around the city was a lofty
wall, and on each side of the wall were three gates, for the city was foursquare,
having twelve gates in all. Beside each gate stood an angel, and on the gates
were written the names of the twelve tribes of Israel. And the wall had twelve
foundations, and on them were written the names of the twelve apostles of
the Lord. The wall was like jasper, and the city was built of pure gold, but
a gold that seemed clear as glass. The twelve gates were twelve pearls; each
one of the gates was one great pearl. And the street of the city was pure gold,
as clear as glass.

John could see no Temple in the city, and it needs none, for the Lord God and Jesus Christ are its Temple. And the city has no need of the sun or moon to shine on it, for the glory of God gives it light, and the Lamb of God is as a lamp in it. And the gates of the city shall not be shut by day, for there shall be no night there.

And the nations of men shall walk in the light of this city, and the kings of the earth bring their glory into it. And all the honor and glory of the nations shall be brought into it. And into it shall never come anything that is evil or unclean, or anyone who does what God hates, or anyone who makes a lie. But they come into it whose names are written in the Lord's book.

And John saw a river of water of life, clear as crystal, coming from the throne of God and of the Lamb and flowing through the street of the city. On each side of the river grew the tree of life, bearing its fruit every month, twelve times a year. The leaves of the tree were to heal all people of their diseases. And in the city, the Lord God and the Lamb shall reign as kings.

When John had seen and heard all these things, he fell down to worship the angel who had showed them to him. But the angel said to him, "Do not worship me, for I am a fellow servant with you, and with your brethren the prophets, and with those who keep the word of the book. Worship God."

And the angel said to John, "Do not seal up the words you have heard and seen, but tell them to all men. And the Spirit and the bride, the Church of Christ, say 'Come.' And let him that hears say 'Come.' And let him that is thirsty come. And whoever will, let him take the water of life freely."

Discussion Questions *1. What did John see? What did it look like? 2. Why was there no Temple? 3. Why were the gates open?*